D0597497

A CALL *to the* SEA

A CALL *to the* SEA

CAPTAIN CHARLES STEWART
of the USS CONSTITUTION

CLAUDE G. BERUBE *and* JOHN A. RODGAARD

Potomac Books, Inc.
Washington, D.C.

Library of Congress Cataloging-in-Publication Data
Berube, Claude G., 1966–
    A call to the sea : Capt. Charles Stewart of the USS Constitution / Claude G. Berube and John A. Rodgaard.—1st ed.
        p.   cm.
    Includes bibliographical references and index.
    ISBN 1-57488-518-9 (acid-free paper)
    1. Stewart, Charles, 1778–1869.   2. Ship captains—United
States—Biography.   3. United States. Navy—Biography.   4. Constitution
(Frigate)   5. United States—History—War of 1812—Naval operations.   6. United
States—History, Naval—19th century.   I. Rodgaard, John A., 1948–   II. Title.

    E353.1.S8B47   2005
    973.5'25'092—dc22
                                                                            2005001242

Printed in Canada on acid-free paper that meets the American
National Standards Institute Z39-48 Standard.

Potomac Books, Inc.
22841 Quicksilver Drive
Dulles, Virginia 20166

First Edition

10   9   8   7   6   5   4   3   2   1

For our parents, members of the "greatest generation," and their service in World War II:

- Cpl. Gerard R. Berube, U.S. Third Army, Fourth Infantry Division, 1944–45
- Tech Sgt. Arnold Rodgaard, U.S. Army Medical Corps, 5th Evacuation Hospital, 1942–45
- Pvt. Helena (McCowen) Rodgaard, Royal Artillery, British Army, 1942–46

I really don't know why it is that all of us are so committed to the sea, except I think it is because in addition to the fact that the sea changes and the light changes, and ships change, it is because we all came from the sea. And it is an interesting biological fact that all of us have, in our veins the exact same percentage of salt in our blood that exists in the ocean, and, therefore, we have salt in our blood, in our sweat, in our tears. We are tied to the ocean. And when we go back to the sea, whether it is to sail or to watch it we are going back from whence we came.

President John F. Kennedy
Newport, Rhode Island
14 September 1962

CONTENTS

Contents

ILLUSTRATIONS

PREFACE

Who was Charles Stewart? It has been nearly a century and a half since his death yet no biography has emerged. What title would suit the extensive career of one who witnessed and participated in so much of early American history? We first considered "Constitution" as a title for this book.

Why "Constitution"? People who see a book so titled in a bookshop might well ask the same question. They may be puzzled by the book's placement in the shop's biography section because the title "Constitution" doesn't match the definition of the word that initially comes to mind. But we considered "Constitution" because Como. Charles Stewart embodied each of the word's definitions throughout his devoted career to the U.S. Navy and to his country.

Those in the medical and psychological healthcare professions may assume the word "constitution" describes Charles Stewart's physical and emotional health. Those in the healing arts may wonder how these interrelated aspects of well-being contributed to the sailor's long and vigorous life.

Few sailors in U.S. history served with the U.S. Navy as long as Stewart. In 1798, at age nineteen, he was commissioned a lieutenant aboard the frigate USS *United States*. Eight years later he was promoted to captain. He continued to serve throughout most of the nineteenth century, surrendering his final command of the Philadelphia Navy Yard in 1860, and in 1861 Stewart offered to serve yet again when the Union was threatened by secession.

Webster's Encyclopedic Unabridged Dictionary of the English Language offers several definitions of "constitution": "the way in which a thing is composed or made up," "the state of formation," and "any established arrangement or custom." These definitions could apply to any person's life: the people, places, and events that influence the makeup of an individual. "Constitution" is, therefore, an apt title for a biography that identifies those particulars, those pieces of the puzzle.

Implied synonyms for "constitution" include resolve, dependability, and commitment—all characteristics of Charles Stewart, who devoted himself to the sea and the growth of American naval power.

The U.S. Navy recognizes the hallowed *Constitution* as its most revered ship, the oldest commissioned U.S. warship, and the oldest warship afloat in the world. (Lord Nelson's dry-docked HMS *Victory* is the oldest commissioned warship in the world.) Setting the standard for the U.S. Navy, it is the USS *Constitution* that never failed; she defeated each of her opponents in battle and earned the nickname "Old Ironsides." Today, the USS *Constitution* continues her dutiful watch from her station in Boston harbor. She is the grand representative of U.S. naval and maritime tradition.

No captain of the *Constitution* commanded her for a longer period in war, nor through more naval engagements, than Charles Stewart. Ironically, during his lifetime Stewart, and his estate, came to be known by the *Constitution*'s moniker—"Old Ironsides." The captain's ability to survive controversy and surmount disappointment and setbacks mirrored the *Constitution*'s ability to repel enemy shots off her hull.

Stewart went to sea at age thirteen from Philadelphia's port and entered the new Navy at nineteen.

Jurists may well have read the proposed title for this book and immediately thought in terms of the legal document, the cornerstone of the U.S. legal system, which has been amended twenty-seven times and continues to invoke vigorous and complex interpretations in America's courts, legislative bodies, and media.

It can be argued that during the Age of Sail Stewart served on more courts of inquiry and courts-martial than almost anyone else. These numerous naval legal proceedings included some very fundamental cases—Como. James Barron's court of inquiry, the USS *Somers* mutiny court of inquiry, and the court-martial of Capt. Thomas ap Catesby Jones—which involved interpretations of naval jurisprudence and corresponding civil law. In addition to being a naval jurist, Stewart on at least two significant occasions demonstrated an accurate understanding of the intent of the U.S. Constitution and the ramifications of its interpretation. As commander of the frigate USS *Essex*, Captain Stewart pointed out to his superior officer, Como. John Rodgers, that military action required congressional approval. This act brought the young commander to the attention of President Thomas Jefferson.

The second instance in which Stewart correctly interpreted the law was when, during a cruise on Pacific Station in the early 1820s, he pointed out to the revolutionary government of Peru in a detailed letter that their maritime blockade was unlawful under international law. Chief Justice John Marshall considered Stewart's letter on the law of neutrality one of the finest interpretations he had read.

The U.S. Constitution, which the Founding Fathers designed to be amended as the republic evolved overtime, sets forth basic principles. Stewart, too, had fundamental beliefs, but he was not so much a Luddite that he did not recognize the necessity to affect change. This was evident when he assumed command of the Philadelphia Navy Yard. He supervised the construction and fitting out of the U.S. Navy's largest sailing warship, the 120-gun USS *Pennsylvania,* while simultaneously overseeing the construction of a new steam Navy. Stewart's role in the debate over the creation of a naval academy offers another example of his appreciation of change. He initially opposed the Naval Academy, preferring instead that young naval officers get "on-the-job training" at sea, like that which he and every other captain in the Age of Sail experienced. However, upon further reflection and full consideration of the arguments, Stewart reversed his position and became an advocate for the institution, which still stands on the banks of the Severn River. In fact, three of Stewart's junior officers served as commandants at the Naval Academy.

Historians may associate the word "constitution" with the emergence of a new government forged from the fires of the American Revolution, tempered by the Articles of Confederation, and honed during the "Miracle at Philadelphia."

Charles Stewart was born in Philadelphia during the American Revolution and was raised during his city's service as the new country's capital. Living in the largest English-speaking population outside of London and the biggest city in the thirteen colonies, Stewart's earliest impressions were formed at the end of the American Revolution and during the birth of America's international shipping trade, which Philadelphia led for the next several decades.

Perhaps each of these interpretations of the word "constitution" captures the essence of Charles Stewart, but it is more likely that all of them together capture the essence of the man. No one in U.S. naval history better exemplifies the word, the document, the intent, the ship, or the characteristics of "constitution" than Como. Charles Stewart, U.S. Navy. And it is the "constitution" of this forgotten sailor that this book will explore.

This biography could not have been published with only the author's, or, in this case, authors', labor. First and foremost, we thank Mr. Rick Russell of Potomac Books who supported the project. But, it could not have begun without Maine genealogist Danny Smith who asked the simple question: "Can you tell me a little about Capt. Charles Stewart?" This tome is his answer.

Our team of readers provided exceptional guidance: Dr. Michael Crawford, head of the Early History Branch of the Naval Historical Center; Cdr.

Ty Martin, U.S. Navy (Ret.), author of many works related to the USS *Constitution* and a former commander of America's "most remarkable ship"; Cdr. Mark Perry, U.S. Naval Reserve; and Mr. Leonard Guttridge, author of the seminal work *The Commodores*. We are most appreciative for their time and effort in reviewing our work.

There were numerous repositories, museums, and individuals essential to our research. We thank the following individuals: Sarah Watkins and Kate Lennon of the USS *Constitution* Museum and Library; Regina Reay of the Bordentown Public Library; Megan Fraser of the Independence Seaport Museum; Dr. David Rolfe and Sarah Friedman of the Historical Society of Pennsylvania; Dr. Milton Gustafson and the staff of the National Archives and Records Administration; Milton Hathaway, the librarian of Episcopal Academy who provided a perspective on private religious schools of the 1780s in Philadelphia; Earl Wood, an informative guide at Woodlands Cemetery; Milton Botwinick and Suzanne Nurnberg, who provided research assistance; Al Lejambre of Bordentown, who kindly offered his time and recollections; Dr. William E. Howard III, a descendant of Charles Stewart McCauley (Charles Stewart's nephew), whose extensive knowledge of his family tree gave us valuable insights. Laura Haines Belman and Capt. Macauley Howard, U.S. Navy (Ret.), both descendants of McCauley, kindly provided photos.

And we would be remiss if we did not acknowledge the work of Dr. Judy Pearson, who provided invaluable editing assistance and whose ear found harmonic convergence between two disparate voices.

We would also like to thank many individuals who have played an unknowing role in this project. These include our teachers who brought history into our lives and gave us an appreciation for the past. Claude thanks Gerry St. Pierre, Joe Moore, Vincent Capowski, LaVerne Kuhnke, and Ray Robinson. John thanks Professor Louis Tuckerman, Dr. Eleanor Johnson, and Dr. Gerald McKnight.

We would also like to thank those individuals—the sailors—who helped us to understand the past and present Navy. For Claude: Capts. Ted Kosmela, Kevin Latham, Larry Staudmeister, and Bob Denbigh; Cdrs. Daryl Hancock, Keith Kirk, and Mark Perry; Lt. Cdrs. Kim Himmer and Jeff Freeland; CWO Joe Suldo; and the old tars MCs Dick Curtis and Mark Eller, and POs Don Connelly and Don Gibbons. For John: uncles and sailors George Barnaby and George McCowen, who left their hometown, King's Lynn, Norfolk, England, at an early age to set sail upon England's *Glory*.

Finally, and most importantly, we would like to thank our wives, Katy and Judy, for their love and support during this work.

CHAPTER ONE

Stewart's Call to the Sea

In the spring of 1895 a sailor named Joshua Slocum began a historic journey, spending the next three years doing what no one else had done—sailing alone around the world. The voyage was challenging enough without modern tools of electronic navigation and radar. The thirty-seven-foot yawl, *Spray*, successfully completed her journey and reminded many of Philadelphia's indomitable maritime spirit. The *Spray* had been constructed there in 1789, more than one hundred years before Slocum's adventure.

When the *Spray* was built, Philadelphia was well established as the center of shipbuilding and shipbuilding dynasties of colonial America. Such shipbuilding families as the Penroses and the Whartons were known for many years for the quality of their ships and craft. In 1700 the Penroses established the Penrose Shipyard. Together with their more famous cousins, the Humphreys, they laid the groundwork for building the first American naval shore establishment.[1]

Between 1727 and 1766, over seven hundred ships were built in Philadelphia, with another forty-five built between 1769 and 1772. By some estimates nearly nine hundred ships in total were built in Philadelphia prior to the Revolutionary War. Between 1781 and 1787, as the new nation struggled in the aftermath of the war under the government outlined in the Articles of Confederation, some 160 were constructed, including 56 "sizable deep-sea square-riggers." In 1783 alone, forty vessels of various types and tonnage were built: thirteen ships and barks totaling 2,943 tons, fifteen brigs totaling 1,243 tons, four schooners totaling 91 tons, and eight sloops totaling 200 tons. In addition to these, the *Alliance* (700 tons), the *Thomson* (300 tons), and the *Pigou* (300 tons) were completed.[2] These ships helped Philadelphia's trade exceed all of New England's combined as well as New York's.

Along with Boston, New York, and Baltimore, Philadelphia was a shipping nexus in the New World, sought out by generations of seafarers. The city was a center of trade and financial houses, with financiers like Robert Morris, who funded the Revolution and helped to create a nation. It was the home of one of the age's greatest minds, Benjamin Franklin, and the birthplace of America's Constitution. Philadelphia also produced the majority of ship captains in the nascent country's first four wars on the sea.

With 44,000 citizens, postrevolutionary Philadelphia was the greatest English-speaking city outside of London, England. In 1790, when it became the new country's temporary capital, the city was bigger than the other three most-urbanized areas in the former colonies: New York had 33,000 residents, and Boston and Baltimore had 18,000 and 13,500 residents respectively. Philadelphia continued to be America's largest city through 1800. Her residents were largely freemen, as the Commonwealth of Pennsylvania passed a law in 1780 providing for the gradual abolition of slavery.

Charles Stewart Sr. and Sarah Harding Ford Stewart were part of the Scotch-Irish wave of immigrants to the New World in the decades before the American Revolution. Charles Stewart Sr. was the son of Robert Stewart, a descendant of an officer in the army of the Prince of Orange. Charles himself joined the British army and made his way to the New World, although it is

Young Charles Stewart's Philadelphia was the second-largest English-speaking city (after London) and was a bustling seaport. (Bowles & Carver after George Heap; courtesy of the Independence Seaport Museum)

unknown if he arrived in the colonies as a soldier. In Philadelphia Charles Sr. became a ship's captain and the co-owner of a merchant business that traded in rare linens and silks from the Far East. Sarah was the niece of a lord mayor of London and reputedly came from a wealthy family in Northern Ireland.

Six days after Pennsylvania ratified the Articles of Confederation, Charles and Sarah welcomed their eighth and last child, Charles Jr., on 28 July 1778, in Philadelphia's Southwark section. By his own admission, young Charley was a plucky, rude, erratic little fellow who obtained some of his education from the streets of Philadelphia. His oldest sister, Sarah, married into the McCauley family, who also produced a long line of U.S. Navy sailors.

In November 1780 Charles Sr. died, leaving Sarah to provide for her four surviving children. Hagiographic articles about Stewart depict young Charles as born to poor immigrants and raised illiterate until he went to sea, but neither was the case. According to probate records, Charles's father left some £5,000 to his wife and to his business partner.

The widowed Sarah subsequently met and married a Captain Britton who has been referred to in some biographical sketches as a friend of George Washington's, a member of the Continental Congress, and the head of Washington's personal guard during his stay in Philadelphia. Two sources suggest that Britton was a member of Congress, although neither specifies if he served in one of the Continental Congresses or the post-1789 Congress. The comprehensive "Biographical Directory of the United States Congress: 1774–1989" lists no Britton or variations of the name.

Britton is also elusive in other records. There is, for example, no Britton or variations in the "Writings of George Washington" except for a Major Britton who could not correspond to Stewart's stepfather. Three other sources, the Daughters of the American Revolution list, Francis Heitman's "Historical Register of Officers of the Continental Army during the War of Revolution" and Carlos E. Godfrey's "The Commander-in-Chief's Guard" likewise fail to support the claims of earlier historians.

While at first these assertions regarding Britton may appear unfounded, they could be slight exaggerations or, more likely, misunderstandings. For example, Britton, who was a local Philadelphia merchant and ship owner, may have served in a legislative body of the Commonwealth of Pennsylvania and as an officer in the local militia, rather than serving in the Continental Congress or Army. As an officer in the local militia, Britton would have met General Washington at some point, e.g., when Washington and the Continental Army entered then-garrisoned Philadelphia in July 1778 (coincidentally, the same month and year of Charles Stewart Jr.'s birth). Regardless of whether he moved within General Washington's circles, Britton was not without responsibility and influence in the city.

In the summer of 1787 Philadelphia was the site of the Constitutional Convention, an event that was not lost on nine-year-old Stewart, particularly as the city welcomed such luminaries as George Washington, George Mason, James Madison, and Philadelphia's own Robert Morris, a major financier of the American Revolution.

When he was twelve, Stewart accompanied his stepfather into the town's center and was introduced to President Washington. It is said that America's first president paid the young Charles Stewart considerable attention, something that would place him in high esteem among his boyhood friends. As Stewart later recollected, none of the boys of Philadelphia would dare to knock the chip off his shoulder after that. Stewart's introduction to America's first president, like the eagle that fell into Claudius's lap portending that he would become the emperor of Rome, foreshadowed the sailor's familiarity and influence with succeeding presidents, from Jefferson through Lincoln, as well as his own brief presidential bid and his encounters with kings, emperors, and military leaders.

Young Charley attended Dr. Abercrombie's Academy in Philadelphia. Known later as the Episcopal Academy, it was attended by the elite sons of the city.[3] Little other than the name of the school is known, except that it was one of several Episcopal academies located in the city before the turn of the eighteenth century. One such Episcopal academy was founded in 1785 by Reverend William White to educate the sons of Philadelphia's Episcopalian community. Courses included Greek, Latin, mathematics, and business—all practical courses for young boys who would become the city's merchants, traders, and ship owners, if not ship captains. At the academy, Charley met three other youths whose futures figured prominently in his life and in the U.S. Navy and diplomatic service.

The first and most famous friend was Stephen Decatur Jr., the son of an American Revolution ship captain, Stephen Decatur Sr. The elder Decatur was a sailing master on board a ship owned by the Philadelphia merchant firm of Stewart and Nesbitt.

A second friend, Richard Somers, less than two months Stewart's junior, was born in Great Egg Harbor, New Jersey, but during the American Revolution his family lived in Philadelphia. His father served as a militia colonel and judge. As he grew, Somers was described as having "middle stature—rather below than above it."[4] Somers's father died in 1794 and so, like his friend

Charles, young Richard lost his father at a very early age. Also like Charles, Richard Somers entered into the shipping trade when he came of age. However, Somers's voyages were restricted to the coastal routes between New York and Philadelphia.

Stewart's third friend was Richard Rush. Born on 29 August 1780, Rush was the second son of a prominent Philadelphia physician, Benjamin Rush, and his wife, Julia Stockton Rush. Benjamin Rush served as a member of the Continental Congress, signed the Declaration of Independence, and was surgeon general of the Revolutionary Army. After preparing at Dr. Abercrombie's Academy, Richard entered Princeton at fourteen and graduated in 1797 at seventeen, the youngest of a class of thirty-three.

In scenes that would replay themselves in their naval careers, the young Stewart, Decatur, and Somers often crossed the street from the academy, located on Fourth Street, to settle their arguments with fisticuffs. Stewart remembered that Decatur "would sooner lose his dinner than miss an opportunity of avenging the wrongs of some small boy who had been imposed

A boyhood friend of Stewart's, Richard Rush was a career diplomat. Stewart later transported his friend on board the *Franklin* to his assignment as ambassador to the Court of St. James. (Thomas Waterman Wood; courtesy of the National Portrait Gallery)

upon by a superior in size. Steve was the universal champion of the small boy."⁵ Fortunately they did not yet have the pistols they used later in formal duels.⁶ But if one feature of Philadelphia life influenced Stewart, Decatur, and Somers more than any other, it was the call to the sea.

On any given day, except in winter when the river froze, Charles and the other boys witnessed the maritime life of Philadelphia.⁷ They walked through the shipyards and along the busy wharfs of the port daily. They watched the hustle and bustle of the arrivals and departures of countless ships and craft. In 1805 alone 547 vessels arrived in Philadelphia from foreign ports while 617 ships departed. An additional 2,400 coastal vessels passed through the port during that year. Maritime trade was the lifeblood of the boys' city and permeated every sector of their lives. They absorbed all of this, including the intricate actions of men working sailing vessels within the confines of the Delaware River. They themselves may have "mucked about" on the river in small boats. Just as important, their collective imaginations likely were captured by many a sailor's story of voyages beyond the shores of the Delaware.

Many a Philadelphian merchant ship captain served during the Revolution, and later the new Navy recruited them again from the merchant ship community. Such early naval heroes and sons of Philadelphia as John Barry and Thomas Truxtun served as merchant captains before commanding their own naval frigates. Stewart's and Decatur's fathers would have known these famous men. It was John Barry's influence that helped Stewart obtain a commission in the new Navy.

The boys experienced the day-to-day business of Philadelphia's merchant class. "Philadelphia's merchants, as a group, traded through the North Atlantic, but few individual merchants traded in more than one or two markets."⁸ The shipping industry had three major trade routes. The first extended along the U.S. East Coast to the West Indies, plying cod from Massachusetts, tobacco from Maryland, and naval stores from North Carolina. The second major route was a direct line from Philadelphia to the wine islands, like Madeira, of Spain and Portugal. The third formed a three-legged route between Philadelphia, England, and the West Indies along which merchants traded rice, indigo, sugar, and rum.⁹ Stewart, Decatur, and Somers likely knew about these valuable trading routes, and they probably heard many a disgruntled story of how badly the former mother country was treating its former colonial, now "Yankee," traders.

Although the United States maintained many of its trading partners, England took a heavy hand with its wayward child. "The loss of British citizenship denied American vessels open entry into the British West Indies and the home islands."[10] The inexpensive American grain and timber supplied to the islands were now barred. This was not well-received by the British West Indian communities. The British navigation laws had them depending on British Canada, but the Canadian colonies were not capable of replacing the former American colonies as trading partners. As a result, an illegal trade between the merchants of Philadelphia and their former trading partners in the Caribbean was born. But when such young zealous Royal Navy officers as Capt. Horatio Nelson began enforcing the laws, the more cautious Philadelphia merchants and shipmasters sought other opportunities.

However, the 1780s witnessed the birth of a new trade route that, at that time, was spectacular because of its length and the exotic goods it returned to the new country, especially to Philadelphia. On 22 February 1784 the ship *Empress of China* sailed from New York to become the first American-built trader to reach Canton, China. It returned to Philadelphia on 15 May 1785 with not only remarkable goods but also an incredible 25 percent profit. Shortly after the *Empress*'s successful journey, another Philadelphia ship, built by the Humphreys and owned and captained by Thomas Truxtun, sailed for the Orient on 30 December 1785. The *Canton*'s departure drew such fanfare that Charles Stewart and his friends could not have missed it.

The *Canton* made several trips to China. Her account books show that she carried cotton fabric muslin, bales of chintz (a printed cotton fabric), yards of hum hums, bandano hanks (kerchiefs), pieces of sannas from Patna, India, and pieces of taffeta silk.[11] In addition to Truxtun's *Canton*, a ship that figured into one of Charles Stewart's cruises forty years later, other Philadelphia ships plied their trade in the Orient, including later Navy Capt. John Barry's *Asia* and William Rush's *Ganges*. In 1785 the Revolutionary War frigate *Alliance* was purchased by the residents of Philadelphia and converted to a merchant ship for use on the China trade route.

In addition to the maritime character of his city, the legacies of Stewart's father, a shipmaster and merchant, and his stepfather, a ship owner and merchant, influenced young Charles. Charles was destined to be called to the sea. Philadelphia and the sea were integral parts of his entire life. He returned to the city throughout his merchant and naval careers. He knew its ships and their designers. He watched their construction frame by frame, plank by plank. The shipyards assembled the very ships whose decks he walked during his long naval service; in fact, most of the ships he commanded were Philadelphia-built.

At age twelve, Charles Stewart sailed as a cabin boy aboard the Indiaman

7

Loraine under the command of a Captain Church. The *Loraine* was co-owned by the firm of Britton and Massey and provided a good opportunity for Britton's stepson to learn the sea and merchant trade.

On board the *Loraine* Stewart learned what it meant to be a sailor. There was little opportunity on the small trader for personal time. In addition to maneuvering the ship by its sails, constant maintenance, such as repairing rigging and sails and ensuring the water-tight integrity of the vessel's hull, was required. One young sailor once commented that "in no state prison are the convicts more regularly set to work, and more closely watched."[12] Shipboard life formed a series of contradictions where "the beautiful is linked with the revolting, the sublime with the commonplace and the solemn with the ludicrous."

Charles was not an illiterate cabin boy like many others who were shipped by their large families to sea to find a functional place in society and trade. His education at Dr. Abercrombie's school provided him with the basic skills to learn the Philadelphia maritime trade. His keen observation made him an outstanding sailor and drove him to pursue a naval officer's career.

Of the three major Philadelphia trade routes, Stewart spent most of his time plying the West Indies route. Charles was not unlike other boys who had mischievous or even dangerous moments. His daredevil nature was perhaps most apparent during his adventure on Santo Domingo, an island split

The earliest known image of Charles Stewart, who was twenty-four at the time. (Charles Balthazar Julian Febret de Saint-Memin; courtesy of the National Portrait Gallery)

into two European colonies by a mountain range, with Haiti on the western half, controlled by France, and the eastern half governed by the Spanish, which became known as the Dominican Republic. It was 1793, Charles was fifteen years old, and Haitian slaves were revolting against their French rulers. The slaves' leader, Toussaint L'Ouverture, was born in 1743 into slavery but was educated in French, Latin, and mathematics. Still fresh in the memories of the colonists and slaves in Haiti was the 1789 French Revolution, the storming of the Bastille, and the executions of nobles, who had previously been considered untouchable. In 1791 L'Ouverture raised an army with Jacques Dessalines as his deputy. Despite significant French reinforcements, L'Ouverture's army proved victorious, due in no small measure to Spanish arms suppliers. L'Ouverture consequently ended slavery in Haiti in 1793.

The *Loraine* pulled into a port on the Haitian side of the island of Santo Domingo, and as it sat in port, one of the rebellion's leaders pulled alongside the Indiaman in a rowboat with several of his men.

The young, blond-haired Stewart watched closely as the slave leader, Henri Christophe, approached his ship. Christophe was a Grenada-born slave who was later freed and who fought in the French army in Savannah, Georgia, during the latter part of the American Revolution. Christophe subsequently and quickly rose through the ranks of the Haitian rebels to become one of Toussaint L'Ouverture's generals. As Stewart recounted, Christophe "was attired in the elegant uniform of a French officer, which illy accorded with his ungainly carriage, and bare black feet. Two of the teeth of his lower jaw protruded like the tusks of an animal and added to the incongruous and grotesque effect."[13] The sight of the Haitian general amused Charles. Christophe, seeking to board the *Loraine*, demanded that the crew provide him with a ladder or other means to climb on board. Instead of acceding to Christophe's order, Charles took a rope, shook it in the man's face, and burst out laughing.

Charles knew immediately that this was grievous error in judgment, and he ran toward the *Loraine*'s main cabin. Instinctively, he realized that if he holed up in the cabin he would be caught and killed, so he then rushed toward the cook's area, where the wood was kept, slipped through a trapdoor, and secured the cover so that only he could open it.

A few minutes later he heard Christophe and his men running around the small vessel in search of the teenager. Stewart's instinct was not wrong; Christophe demanded the boy's life. With few firearms on board, Captain Church could do little to prevent Christophe from carrying out his threat. At first the captain tried to convince the Haitian thug that the boy had jumped overboard and swum to another nearby vessel. Then he pretended to help in the search. Christophe thoroughly searched the *Loraine* until he and his men found the trapdoor.

> The moment the sailors found that this had been fastened from beneath, they knew that Charley must have here made his hiding place, and they swore still more stoutly that he had swam to the French vessel. They exerted themselves, however, in fruitless mock efforts to lift the door; but Christophe, not satisfied, thrust his sword down on every side, the blade just escaping young Stewart, who cuddled himself up into small space in the centre.[14]

Christophe eventually gave up and seemed, if not satisfied, then at least temporarily appeased when Captain Church provided him with expensive stockings and a good pair of shoes. While Charley stayed in the hold, his shipmates treated Christophe to their alcohol, more alcohol, and yet more, until the Haitian could be safely escorted off the boat.

Some days later, with the *Loraine* still in port trying to find buyers for her cargo, Stewart went ashore with Captain Church's permission. Charley decided that since Christophe had seen only the color of his hair, he would wear a different-colored wig and a hat.

No sooner had Stewart begun his tour of the streets than he saw Christophe strutting down the road in full military uniform and heavily armed. With a "presence of mind and coolness in the face of danger" that would characterize him throughout his combat service in the Navy, Stewart simply whistled and kept walking, even brushing against Christophe's uniform. As soon as he was able, Stewart darted through the streets to the mountains until dark when he returned to the ship.

Christophe later became the army chief under Dessalines, and in 1806 he participated in a successful plot to overthrow Dessalines. He was elected president of Haiti from 1806 to 1811 when he declared himself King Henri I. He built a spacious sixteen-acre fortress, La Ferriere (the ruins of which still can be seen) in north Haiti. Ironically, before being sold to a French sugar plantation in Haiti, Christophe himself had been a cabin boy aboard a ship.

Perhaps his experience in Haiti transformed Charley from the mischievous Philadelphia boy to a man of the sea and of trade. Some sources say that within only four years of his brush with Christophe, Charles had command of his own ship—a merchantman that traveled to the Far East. Stewart matured at sea, and the experience would serve him and the country well.

CHAPTER TWO

From Commissioning
to Captaincy

On 30 April 1798 Congress created the Navy Department. The Honorable Benjamin Stoddert was appointed the new department's first secretary, entering his office in June after President Adams's first choice had declined the opportunity. Prior to this congressional legislation, Charles Stewart had decided to leave the merchant trading world on the high seas to seek a commission in the new Navy. In fact, his commissioning, on 9 March 1798, predated the creation of the modern U.S. Navy. The nineteen-year-old Lt. Charles Stewart was one of those merchants and seamen whose experience immediately ranked them in the middle grade of the new naval officer corps.

Stewart's appointment occurred during a period when growing hostility with France moved Congress to fund in 1797 the completion and manning of three new frigates. However, it was the Congressional Act of 1794 authorizing the Navy's officer corps that had been the instrument that selected the young Stewart and his peers.

Prior to the passing of the act by Congress in 1797, the War Department received approximately 350 applications for commissions. Of those 350, only 59 were selected for all grades, ranging from midshipman to captain. Charles was one of them. To be commissioned a lieutenant at his age says a great deal about his experience and the level of his maturity gained through seven years of being at sea.[1]

Beside the fact that Stewart had already spent a third of his life at sea,

11

what really made him stand out among so many candidates? After all, many of his contemporaries also possessed "at sea" credentials. In his book, *A Gentlemanly and Honorable Profession*, Christopher McKee wrote extensively about the factors that shaped the U.S. Navy's early officer corps. McKee looks at the analysis of Navy Secretary William Jones, who tried to determine what factors contributed to the highly effective and successful 1798 officer corps. Jones was the first person to "attempt a systematic analysis of the reasons why this officer corps had developed into a successful, professional body."[2] He was the Navy secretary during the War of 1812, and his interaction with Stewart and the surviving "Class of '98" was likely considerable.

McKee explains that Jones's criteria for analysis were rudimentary and straightforward. First, Jones considered whether an officer at the time of his appointment was a "mature man," that is, someone who had considerable experience at sea prior to his commissioning. The second criterion that Jones considered important was whether an officer had served in the Navy, but when furloughed, went to sea in the merchant service. The third element in Jones's thinking was whether an officer had sailed beyond the Cape of Good Hope or Cape Horn. And the final criterion was whether a serving officer had won great victories during the War of 1812. Beside each category that an officer achieved, Jones placed a symbol.

By Jones's own analyses, Charles Stewart did not stand out prior to the War of 1812. Neither did Stewart's boyhood friend, Stephen Decatur. In fact, Decatur received the same marks in Jones's analysis as Stewart. This puzzled the former Navy secretary, who certainly asked the question, "Why didn't Charles Stewart or Stephen Decatur stand out?" To settle it, one has to look at the criteria Jones established, which did not take into account Stewart's seven years of experience prior to his commissioning, the years likely responsible for the young Charles Stewart's receiving a commission.

During those seven years prior to his commission, Stewart sailed the world's oceans and gained experience ranging from work as a ship's "boy" to commanding a merchant ship. Jones did not recognize Stewart's adolescent experience. If he had, Stewart would have had two additional marks and would have led the entire list of officers. With his victories during the War of 1812 in addition, Stewart would have stood out from his contemporaries, including Stephen Decatur.

Other factors probably come into play to rank the young Charles Stewart favorably with his contemporaries. First, Charles Stewart was from Philadelphia. His business and the ships he sailed called Philadelphia their homeport.

He was well known within the Philadelphia merchant and sailing classes by prominent sailing professionals like Como. John Barry, the father of the U.S. Navy. Stewart's stepfather was similarly prominent in the community. Stewart's Irish ancestry also gained him favor; like John Barry, Charles was of Irish extraction. Finally, Charles had his own personal drive to be successful.

Shortly after his commissioning, the young Charles Stewart was appointed fourth lieutenant on the Joshua Humphrey–designed and Philadelphia-built forty-four-gun frigate, the USS *United States*. Stewart's first man-of-war, under the command of Capt. John Barry, was quayside and fitting out in his hometown. Captain Barry was one of those, like President John Adams, who provided War Secretary James McHenry with their advice on who should be selected in the Class of '98.

Once on board, Charles Stewart found himself sharing a wardroom with a controversial man in U.S. naval history, Lt. James Barron. As first lieutenant, Barron was second in command to Barry, but in a testament to Stewart's character, Barry "liked much better the young man who reported for duty as the fourth lieutenant."[3]

In the midshipman berth on *United States* were two future standouts of the young navy: Charles's friends Mid. Stephen Decatur and Mid. Richard Somers. With the three childhood friends together again, one could imagine that all three thought that the USS *United States* was an extension of their childhood days at Dr. Abercrombie's Episcopal Academy in Philadelphia.[4]

Under Barry's watchful eye, the four junior officers worked the *United States* through the rest of her fitting out work. When the frigate was ready for sea, Captain Barry set sail for the West Indies.

The imperative directing the *United States* to the West Indies was concurrent with the ongoing war between England and Napoleon's France. This was the last in a series of global wars that had raged between the two empires throughout the eighteenth century. These wars were an overarching influence affecting the young American Republic and the naval career of Charles Stewart.

With the outbreak of war between France and the European alliance in 1796, both British and French warships began interfering with American trade, as the enterprising "Yankee Traders" conducted commerce with both countries and their colonial possessions. Shortly before Stewart's commission, the French had stepped up their seizures of American merchant ships. Revolutionary France saw the 1794 commercial agreement between Britain and the United States as violating Royalist France's 1778 treaty with the

American colonies' Continental Congress. In April 1798 President John Adams addressed Congress and informed them of France's attempt to extort a large sum from the United States for the restoration of diplomatic relations and the cessation of American merchant ship seizures by French warships and privateers. The president labeled France's extortion attempt the "XYZ Affair" and considered it an affront to the honor of the new republic. That month the equally outraged "Congress authorized the President to acquire, arm, and man no more than twelve vessels, of up to twenty-two guns each."[5]

With congressional authority and presidential directive in hand, Navy Secretary Benjamin Stoddert charted his campaign against aggressive French naval activity in the Caribbean. The Navy secretary realized the best way to arrest the situation was not only to convoy American merchant ships but also to go on the offensive. Thus began America's Quasi-War with France, and so too began Stewart's first war cruise on board Barry's *United States*.

While operating in the Caribbean, an incident occurred that demonstrated the personality differences between Stewart and his two old friends, Decatur and Somers. Stephen Decatur did nothing to dispel the image of his younger, pugnacious self from Philadelphia after his commission. Shortly after the *United States* arrived in Newcastle, he engaged in a duel with the first mate of an Indiaman. According to one account, Decatur intentionally shot the mate in the hip. Richard Somers served as Decatur's second in the duel while Charles Stewart stood on the gangway.[6]

Decatur's duel appears to be the most memorable event of Stewart's first war cruise. Compared to the record of her near sister ship, the frigate USS *Constellation*, the *United States*'s record during this period of the Quasi-War was unremarkable.[7] Under the command of Como. Thomas Truxtun, *Constellation* handily defeated the French frigate *l'Insurgente* in February 1799. One year later, on 1 February 1800, Truxtun's *Constellation* fought the more powerful frigate *la Vengeance* to a draw. Although the *United States* did not win comparable glory, Stewart's performance while on board was recognized, and upon his frigate's return, he received orders to assume command of his first man-of-war.

On 16 July 1800, twelve days before his twenty-second birthday, Stewart took command of the twelve-gun schooner USS *Experiment*. While no record of the *Experiment*'s design exists, she was probably a sister ship of the first USS *Enterprise*, for which a design record remains.[8] Both schooners were authorized by Congress in 1798. *Experiment* was built at Baltimore, and

The night before his fateful trip on the *Intrepid*, Richard Somers broke his ring into three parts and gave one to each of his boyhood friends, Stephen Decatur and Charles Stewart. (Unattributed; courtesy of the Atlantic County Historical Society)

Stewart assumed command from Lt. Cdr. William Maley, who successfully maneuvered and fought *Experiment* in a fight against French privateers and Haitian pirates earlier that year.[9] One can imagine the ship's lines in the most recent adaptation of the famed Baltimore clipper, *The Pride of Baltimore II*. *Experiment* measured just short of eighty-five feet in length overall, with a twenty-two-foot molded beam and a nine-and-a-half-foot depth of hold.[10]

Charles Stewart's junior officers were David Porter, *Experiment*'s first lieutenant, and Mids. James Caldwell and John Trippe. Stewart and Porter formed a life-long friendship.[11] Stewart also formed a close bond as mentor and friend to Caldwell and Trippe. Caldwell served as first lieutenant aboard Stewart's next command, the USS *Syren*, during the Barbary Wars, while Trippe commanded *Syren*'s sister, the USS *Vixen*, in the same campaign. Together, the four sailed their schooner to rejoin the expanding number of American warships operating in the Caribbean and around the West Indies.

On 26 July Stewart received orders from Secretary Stoddert to take the *Experiment* to sea. Stoddert's orders concluded by saying, "Nothing is so imperious to the reputation of the Navy service—nothing so injurious to the character of the officers, as delay, in Port. I pray you let nothing retard your sailing two days after the receipt of this letter." Charles Stewart was directed to proceed to Bermuda and stay in the vicinity of the island for ten days. After ten days he was to proceed south to St. Kitts and to place himself and

During Stewart's first command, his *Experiment* quickly dispatched three enemy ships—the *Deux Amis*, the *Diane*, and the *Louisa Bridges*. (Unattributed)

the *Experiment* under the command of Capt. Stephen Decatur Sr.[12] Two days later, on his twenty-second birthday, Charles Stewart took his first command to sea. The cruise to Bermuda and the short operational time patrolling near the island were uneventful. However, on the way to the Caribbean, *Experiment* fell in with an eight-gun French privateer *les Deux Amis*. Stewart maneuvered his agile craft so superbly that he took the ship after slight resistance, not more than ten minutes after the first shots were fired. He quickly directed Lieutenant Porter to lead four men in boarding the ship and claiming it as a prize—his first.

At this time, the United States and Great Britain were fighting France, and their two navies cooperated to some degree. Both navies shared recognition signals that were supposed to prevent accidental combat between their warships, and also allowed their respective merchantmen to join the other nation's convoys. Additionally, the British sold naval stores and munitions to the American government.[13] Shortly after *Experiment's* victory over *les Deux Amis*, Stewart put this cooperation to the test, setting a precedent for both navies.

While the *Experiment* was taking on freshwater in Prince Rupert's Bay on the island of Dominica, two twenty-gun British sloops-of-war (one of which was the *Siam)* arrived in the bay. An American named Amos Seeley had been pressed into the Royal Navy on *Siam*. He managed to smuggle a letter to Stewart asking him to obtain his release. Stewart wrote to the British captain demanding the release of the American, and then followed up his letter with a visit to the captain on his ship. Stewart argued diplomatically, with such logic, persuasiveness, and skill that the Englishman reluctantly freed Amos Seeley to Stewart.

With the successful release of Seaman Seeley, Stewart completed his freshwater replenishment and returned to his assigned operating area. Shortly after his departure, *Experiment* was cruising to windward of the island of St. Bartholomew when two sails approached the small American schooner. What followed on that day, 13 September, demonstrated Charles Stewart's highly developed sailing and tactical skills, as well as his sense of justice. Seeing that the two oncoming ships were flying British colors, he ordered the raising of American colors and the appropriate recognition signal for that day. The two ships, one an eighteen-gun brig and the other a fourteen-gun schooner, did not respond. The *Experiment* had to act quickly. Realizing the ships were not British, Stewart turned his schooner about and pressed on more sail. The vessels began to pursue *Experiment*, but realizing the American ship could out-sail them, they soon abandoned the chase. The two ships ran up the French flag and fired a gun apiece of defiance to windward. Stewart immediately tacked ship and worked to windward, and gaining the gauge on them, became the pursuer. About eight o'clock in the evening the *Experiment* ranged up on the larboard quarter of the sternmost Frenchman and poured a broadside into her. Despite his long career, including dozens of military engagements, Stewart received his only wound during this early exchange. During the broadsides, a pigeon nestled on Stewart's left shoulder. "The next instant a bullet struck its foot at the junction of the toes and penetrated his shoulder. That wound was trifling itself, but the surgeon stated that the pigeon was the means of saving him from a shattered shoulder."[14] Within a few minutes the schooner struck and surrendered to the *Experiment*. She proved to be the French schooner *Diane*. Stewart quickly sent a prize crew aboard.

The *Diane* was found to be carrying sugar, coffee, and cotton bales, which, with the ship, would bring a respectable sum in prize money. In addition to the material goods, the *Experiment*'s party found on board a crew of sixty-five men, a French Army lieutenant, a detachment of thirty invalid soldiers, and French Gen. Andre Rigaud. Haiti was still in the throes of gaining its independence from France, and Rigaud had fought to suppress the revolt. When Haitian slaves, led by Toussaint L'Ouverture and Gen. Jean-Jacques Dessalines, defeated and captured Rigaud and his soldiers, Napoleon personally intervened to free his general by offering L'Ouverture and Dessalines the rank of general in the French Army in return for Rigaud's release. Consequently, Rigaud and his soldiers were returning to France on board the *Diane* when it was intercepted by *Experiment*.

During his time on the island before his capture, Rigaud became the leader of the mulatto population and led them against L'Ouverture. He also attacked Americans and their commercial interests in the area. Apparently Rigaud's actions were well known to the young captain of the *Experiment*, for Stewart quickly recognized the man and the importance of his capture. In his after-action report to Secretary Stoddert, dated 3 October, Stewart wrote, "This is the man, sir, that has wrested millions from my countrymen. The depredations, the piracies, plunder and murders he has committed are too well known."[15]

With the capture of the *Diane* complete, Stewart started off after the brig, but the Frenchman was able to sail beyond his reach. Stewart gave up the chase and took his captives to St. Christopher. After disposing General Rigaud and the other prisoners with Commodore Truxtun at St. Christopher,

Lieutenant Stewart returned to sea to carry out his orders to protect American commerce and engage the enemy when they appeared.

For Stewart and the *Experiment*, the rest of September and the entire month of October passed without further contact with the enemy. But, around midnight on 16 November, *Experiment* fell in with an armed vessel. When Stewart's repeated efforts to hail the stranger and determine her identity failed, the lieutenant ordered a shot put into her. A full broadside from the stranger immediately returned *Experiment*'s single shot, and a running fight between the two commenced. Adm. David Dixon Porter later wrote this from his father's account of the action:

> The *Experiment* now opened fire with all her guns, and began to close with the stranger, intending to carry the latter by boarding.
>
> It was blowing quite fresh at the time, and the *Experiment* being very light, owing to a short supply of provisions in the hold, laid over so much on her side as to be unable to depress her guns sufficiently to strike the supposed enemy's hull; and all her shot was expended among the rigging. But this difficulty was soon remedied, and the resources of the trained seamen made manifest; planks were cut and placed under the trucks, which expedient made it possible to depress the *Experiment*'s guns sufficiently, and the fire told with so much effect that in a few minutes the stranger struck her colors.[16]

The action lasted for almost forty minutes. At that point, the strange sail surrendered. Stewart quickly sent a prize crew led by Lieutenant Porter. As the prize crew approached the strange vessel, Porter was hailed and warned off or be fired at. "The boat was then moved out of the line of fire and the *Experiment* was about to recommence the action, when the stranger hailed again to say that he submitted. This vessel proved to be a privateer out of Bermuda, *Louisa Bridges*, with an armament of 8 guns, and a crew of forty men: she was much cut up, and had four feet of water in her hold."[17]

Upon seeing that she was British, Stewart immediately ordered his crew to assist the stricken ship. Stewart, Porter, and *Experiment* lay by the damaged *Louisa Bridges* through the night and all the next day assisting in the repair of the British privateer and attending to her dead and wounded. Stewart, Porter, and the crew also effected repairs on *Experiment*'s rigging and buried their sole casualty. At the end of the day the two ships parted company, Stewart and *Experiment* continuing on their mission. The British privateer returned to Bermuda, for her captain and many of her crew were in no shape to continue their letter of marque.

19

Admiral Porter summed up his father's recollection of the action when he wrote,

> this action showed the superiority of the *Experiment*'s fire; and it will be observed that in all the fights in which this vessel was engaged the battle was finished in a short time. The vessels captured by the schooner were not, it is true, ships of war, except in the case of the *Diane*, which was a superior vessel to the *Experiment* in guns and men, if we include the thirty soldiers on board and when we consider the rapid manner in which that contest was brought to a close, we cannot but admire the precision of the *Experiment*'s fire. Up to this time, the *Experiment* had given an excellent account of herself, and the reputation of her commander and first lieutenant stood high a compliment not to be despised when so many gallant fellows were vying in a noble zeal for their country's service.[18]

This unfortunate encounter marked the last major action for Charles Stewart and *Experiment* during the Quasi-War. By midyear in 1800, the infant U.S. Navy's aggressiveness and the Royal Navy's remorselessness combined to create a more conciliatory France. The U.S. and British navies' semi-cooperative effort produced a marked reduction in the activity of the French privateers and warships against American and British trading interests in the Caribbean. In mid-December 1800 news reached Washington that peace with France had been obtained. Concurrently Napoleon had also obtained a treaty with Britain. The Convention of Mortefontaine, signed on 30 September 1800, ended the Quasi-War, but for Britain and the United States, peace was fleeting. Britain faced Napoleon again in Europe in 1801, and for America, the threat emanating from the North African shores loomed large.

Charles Stewart and his *Experiment* were ordered home. On their way back, they came across a vessel that had wrecked on a reef off Saons Island and was breaking up under pounding waves. Stewart and his crew moved quickly to rescue sixty-seven souls, sixty of them women and children. With the survivors safely aboard *Experiment,* Stewart and his crew carried them home to Santo Domingo. The Spanish governor, Don Joaquin Garcia, whose family was among those rescued by *Experiment,* wrote a warm letter of thanks to President Jefferson.[19]

> The great humanity (the offspring of a magnanimous breast) of a military officer of the United States deserves the greatest applause and consideration from me and my whole nation. This officer is Charles Stewart, Esq., Captain of the

armed schooner *Experiment*, who, whilst the accidents of the sea threatened to overwhelm him, observed that near the Island of Saons, a schooner, with a multitude of women and children, cried out for help to save themselves from becoming the unhappy victims of the tempest, or of the want of nautical skill in Captain Christian Graneman, a Dane, who in the hardness of his heart, strove to save his person and effects, by going on shore and leaving so many human creatures exposed to the turbulence of the waves.

Governor Garcia concluded his letter by reiterating that Captain Stewart "deserves the greatest applause and consideration from me and my whole nation."[20]

With the end of the war, the Congress of 1801 mandated that President Thomas Jefferson reduce the size of the Navy. Ships, officers, and ships' companies were laid up or disbanded. Thirteen warships were retained, of which six would remain in active service and seven were kept laid up in reserve. The officer corps was reduced to 9 captains, 36 lieutenants, and 150 midshipmen.[21] Lieutenant Stewart was one of the thirty-six lieutenants who retained their commissions in active service. Shortly upon his return with *Experiment*, he was ordered to the thirty-eight-gun frigate USS *Chesapeake*.

Upon leaving his first command Stewart must have had mixed emotions, but he also had a longer perspective at hand than many of his contemporaries. After all, he had left a profitable merchant sailor career for service in his country's new Navy. Stewart had acquitted himself well. In two and a half years, he had risen from fourth lieutenant to commander of his own man-of-war. And although he felt the exhilaration for his first command that all naval officers share, he may also have felt a sense of disappointment when he did not acquire another command immediately. A quiet sense of duty carried him through until his next assignment. Had he been there when Stewart relinquished command, Commodore Barry would probably have recognized the young man's dissatisfaction. In a letter to Navy Secretary Stoddert, Barry wrote, "I am perfectly satisfied with your appointment of Lt. Stewart. I hope he will be more active when he commands than when he is commanded."[22] Stewart was ultimately rewarded for his performance during the Quasi-War by being retained on the active service list.

Having the broad perspective of his experiences in the just-concluded war, Charles Stewart, more than many Americans, realized how vulnerable American commerce was to the interests of Georgian Britain and Napoleonic France. But before tackling the problem of vulnerability, he and the young U.S. Navy first dealt with another threat that had harried European seaborne commerce for centuries and American enterprise since independence: the Barbary States of North Africa.

Charles Stewart was aboard the *Chesapeake* in the summer of 1801 when word came that the bashaw of Tripoli, the North African ruler most aggressive against American commercial interests, had declared war on the United States. Foreseeing the need to protect American merchantmen, the new president, Thomas Jefferson, ordered a "squadron of observation" to make ready for a deployment to the Mediterranean.[23] He did this shortly after assuming the presidency on 4 March 1801.

Thomas Jefferson was all too aware of seizures of American merchantmen and their crews by the Barbary States, and especially by the bashaw of Tripoli. As early as 1784, in a letter to James Monroe, Jefferson complained about the U.S. policy of paying tribute to the Barbary States. He wrote, "Would it not be better to offer them an equal treaty? If they refuse, why not go to war with them? . . . We ought to begin a naval power, if we mean to carry on our own commerce."[24] Jefferson's and Adams's opinions of the Barbary States, and of Tripoli in particular, had hardened during their interactions with the ambassador from Tripoli in Paris. The Americans had asked the ambassador to justify the outrageous savagery his city-state inflicted upon defenseless American ships. Jefferson wrote, "The Ambassador answered us that it was founded on the Laws of the Prophet, that it was written in their Koran, that all nations who should not have acknowledged their authority were sinners, that it was their right and duty to make war upon them wherever they could be found, and to make slaves of all they could take as Prisoners."[25]

Jefferson asked John Adams for his opinion about whether the United States should organize "an international task force comprised of all European nations whose shipping was being victimized."[26] The ever-practical Adams wrote "that Jefferson's solution, while bold and wholly honorable in its own terms, was an idea whose time had not come."[27] Adams continued by saying the Congress would never consider such an aggressive option and that without a naval force, paying tribute was a better option than allowing the outrages to continue. "We ought not to fight them at all unless we determine to fight them forever."[28]

In mid-May 1801 Jefferson dispatched a squadron under Como. Richard Dale. The squadron consisted of Dale's flagship, the forty-four-gun frigate *President*, the thirty-eight-gun frigate *Philadelphia*, and the thirty-two-gun frigate *Essex*. Charles Stewart and *Chesapeake* were not selected; Stewart had to wait his turn.

He sailed with *Chesapeake* through 1801 and into 1802, before his chance finally came. He was selected to become the first lieutenant to Capt. Alexander Murray of the thirty-eight-gun frigate *Constellation*. Murray, a Marylander, had mastered a merchantman at age eighteen. During the American Revolution, he served in the famous Maryland Regiment of the Continental Line and fought at the Battles of Long Island and White Plains. Murray later commanded a Maryland privateer, and in 1781 he was commissioned a lieutenant in the Continental Navy. By the time Charles Stewart reported on board, the forty-seven-year-old Murray was one of the most senior in age and rank of the captains in the Navy. Although the age difference was certainly great between the young Stewart and his captain, it was not so great between Stewart and the junior officers on board. The young Stewart had much to learn.

On 12 January 1802 Navy Secretary Smith issued orders to form a second squadron to be fitted out and sent to the Mediterranean. The squadron was originally to be commanded by Como. Thomas Truxtun, but Truxton threatened to resign when he learned he would have to command not only the squadron, but also his own flagship, the *Chesapeake*. President Jefferson took the commodore at his word and Secretary Smith dismissed him. Como. Edward Preble was also considered, but he was ill at the time so command ultimately was given to Como. Richard Valentine Morris. Morris's appointment was unexpected, for he was not one of the more experienced naval commanders. He had been to sea as a young man, but had been appointed a captain only during the Adams administration in 1798.

The ships selected for the squadron were the frigates *Chesapeake, Constellation*, the thirty-six-gun *New York*, the twenty-eight-gun *John Adams*, and the twelve-gun schooner *Enterprise*. However, these ships were in different states of readiness, and as such, they did not depart as a squadron. Instead, each ship departed when it was ready. The consequence of this decision was felt later during the campaign. *Constellation* and her new first lieutenant departed for the Mediterranean in March.[29]

On 7 May the *Constellation* reached Gibraltar and found the USS *Philadelphia* and USS *Essex* waiting. Charles Stewart met up with his old boyhood friend Stephen Decatur Jr., who was the first lieutenant of the *Essex*. Although no record has been found of their meeting, the two friends likely caught up with old times and marveled at their respective fortunes as officers.

In Gibraltar, Stewart also experienced his most intensive professional and social interaction with the Royal Navy to date, an interaction typical of the first decade of the U.S. Navy. In *A Gentlemanly and Honorable Profession*, McKee notes, "For a decade the officers of the U.S. Navy interacted, profes-

One of Stewart's oldest friends, Stephen Decatur served with Stewart on the *United States*, and later they served together under Commodore Preble. (H. Peterson after Gilbert Stuart; courtesy of the Naval Historical Center)

sionally and socially, with their peers from the British service. Given such continuous contact it would have been impossible for the younger American force to avoid absorbing the British naval mentality unconsciously."[30]

Commodore Murray received permission to anchor in Gibraltar and was shown great civility and attention by no less a personage than V. Adm. Lord Keith.[31] "Murray and his officers were the guests of Lord Keith at dinner the day after their arrival, and the Vice Admiral gave assurance of his desire to help the American expedition."[32] This generosity was extended even further when Commodore Morris and his weathered, battered flagship *Chesapeake* arrived in Gibraltar on 31 May.[33] Keith graciously offered them the use of the dockyard to effect repairs to the *Chesapeake*. Numerous Royal Navy officers visited her and the other American frigates and smaller warships, developing an appreciation for the soundness of U.S. ships and men.

Shortly after Commodore Morris's arrival in Gibraltar, the *Constellation* was ordered to sail for Tripoli and establish a blockade of the port. Arriving off the shores of Tripoli in early June, the *Constellation*'s senior officers un-expectedly found the U.S. twenty-eight-gun frigate *Boston*, under the command of Capt. Daniel McNeill, blockading the port. A Swedish frigate was blockading the port with *Boston*, as Sweden was also at war with the bashaw of Tripoli. *Boston*'s commanding officer had taken his commission and orders beyond what was considered prudent.

Earlier that year, McNeill had been directed to take *Boston* to sea and convey Mr. Robert Livingston to France where he would take the office of U.S. minister to France. Upon completion of the Livingston mission, McNeill's orders stipulated that he take his ship to join the squadron in Gibraltar. He arrived in Gibraltar before *Constellation* and the flagship, and seeing that his squadron had not yet arrived, McNeill sailed his frigate to Tripoli. Prior to *Constellation*'s arrival, McNeill and *Boston* had taken four Tunisian coastal craft. McNeill handled the *Boston* more like a privateer than a U.S. Navy warship. As one author described McNeill's actions, "He commanded loosely. He left some of his officers and men behind at ports and picked up and carried off others, notably three French officers, whom he should have left at Toulon. He was indifferent to quarantine regulations."[34] McNeill's conduct was so appalling to Commodore Dale, Commodore Morris's predecessor, that he wrote a letter of protest to the Navy secretary. President Jefferson had personally relieved McNeill of command, though that word was long in coming. From McNeill, Lieutenant Stewart learned firsthand what not to do as a senior naval officer. More lessons in wartime senior naval leadership were on the horizon.

For most of June *Constellation* maintained a blockade of Tripoli with the Swedish squadron that proved relatively effective, save for an incident that left the captain of the Philadelphia-based merchant brig *Franklin* flabbergasted. Capt. Andrew Morris and his brig had been captured by a Tripolitan corsair, and as the galley-rigged corsair approached the American and Swedish men-of-war, the Tripolitan captain rendered a salute to the infidels and then proceeded into Tripoli Harbor. Neither frigate offered to challenge this obvious blockade-runner. Captain Morris later wrote an account to U.S. Counsel Cathcart in Leghorn, Italy, which was relayed to the State Department and then to President Jefferson. It was becoming increasingly evident to those back in Washington that this latest naval expedition was not faring well.

When the Swedish ships had to depart Tripolitan waters to provision, *Constellation* remained to blockade the port alone. Como. Richard Morris had yet to send the rest of the squadron forward from Gibraltar. *Constellation*'s attempts to blockade the port without the squadron were not very effective, and during the month of June five oar-powered galleys managed to give the blockade the slip. Keeping inshore, these agile craft could hug the coast and row into the wind. To pursue, *Constellation* had to tack frequently, allowing the galleys to outstrip the frigate. Unable to enter the shallows, Captain Murray was forced to break off pursuit, not wanting to leave Tripoli uncovered, allowing more pirates to escape. This was certainly a frustrating time for all on board *Constellation*. With the young first officer fresh from a small hardy ship which had acquitted itself well in the Caribbean, Stewart's frustration level would have been higher than most.

But *Constellation* continued her blockade with and without a Swedish presence. Sweden signed a treaty with Tripoli and later withdrew its ships. According to James Fenimore Cooper's history of the U.S. Navy, *Constellation,* operating in loose company with a Swedish frigate, confronted several smaller craft hugging the shore, hoping to make their way into Tripoli. Captain Murray ordered all possible sail to be sent aloft on *Constellation*.

As first officer, Stewart quickly responded to his captain's orders and the frigate was in full chase of the smaller craft. It soon became apparent there were now seventeen craft, divided into two roughly equal divisions. The leading division of seven boats managed to evade the American frigate by rowing across her bows. But, under Murray's and Stewart's watchful eyes, the *Constellation* was able to bring the second and numerically larger division under fire. One of the craft was able to slip past the American frigate while the remaining nine were cut off from the port. Both sides commenced an exchange of cannon and small arms fire, with the corsairs receiving considerable damage. Trying to disengage, they rowed toward the shore in an attempt to beach themselves between the numerous rocky outcroppings. Murray and Stewart took their larger and more powerful vessel inshore and then thought to launch *Constellation*'s small boats with an assault force to capture the beached corsairs. Before they deployed the frigate's small boats, a large formation of Tripolitan cavalry appeared on the sandhills overlooking the shoreline. Thinking it better to stand offshore, Murray directed *Constellation*'s gunners to fire at the cavalry as well. The cavalry and small craft suffered considerably, while the *Constellation* suffered only minor damage to her rigging. Cooper continued by saying, "this little affair was the first that occurred off the port of Tripoli, in this war; and it had the effect of rendering the enemy very cautious in his movements."[35]

Finally Commodore Morris and the American squadron departed Gibraltar on 17 August leading a convoy eastward to Leghorn. *Constellation* never met the squadron off Tripoli. For the next two months Commodore Morris took his squadron on what seemed to many a grand tour of every port between Gibraltar and Leghorn. Murray and his first lieutenant did not meet their commodore until they took their frigate off blockading duties to effect repairs. *Constellation* was waiting at Leghorn when the American convoy and the naval squadron finally pulled in on 12 October. Assessing *Constellation*'s condition, Commodore Morris decided to send her home. Murray, Stewart, and the crew took *Constellation* back across the Mediterranean and the Atlantic. Upon her return, the frigate was ordered to the Washington Navy Yard, and under the watchful eye of her first officer, she began an extensive refit.

Meanwhile, the Jefferson administration and Congress realized the conflict was far from over, and that "getting at" the Tripolitan corsairs required smaller ships. In Washington with their frigate, Murray and Stewart most likely provided excellent testimony as to the requirements of the nation and its Navy to effectively counter the Barbary threat. On 28 February 1803 Congress passed another naval construction act calling for the construction and/or purchase of four sixteen-gun vessels and ten gunboats. Two of the four vessels were brigs named *Argus* and *Syren*. Navy Secretary Robert Smith selected Charles Stewart to command the latter, while Stephen Decatur commanded the former.[36]

In March, with *Constellation* still in the yards, Stewart was granted a furlough. He returned to Philadelphia to spend time with his mother and family. While at home, he received orders to report as the construction superintendent and commanding officer of the *Syren*. On 3 May 1803 he assumed command of his brig; his primary responsibility was to supervise her construction and fitting out. Lt. James Caldwell joined him as first officer. The men rapidly developed a professional and warm personal relationship that would serve them well on their return to the shores of Tripoli.

Syren was under construction at Benjamin Hutton's Shipyard in Philadelphia, not far from Stewart's old neighborhood.[37] According to historian Howard Chapelle, "Hutton was a brilliant naval architect, a splendid draftsman and a practical shipwright. . . . He was the equal of Fox and Humphreys as a designer."[38] As *Syren*'s captain, Charles Stewart worked with Hutton on the details of her construction. On 6 August 1803 at 4:30 P.M., the U.S. brig *Syren* was launched, and by 5 P.M. she was hauled up to Wilcox's wharf to begin her fitting out.[39] As a brig, the *Syren* possessed solid lines, and she carried her sixteen twenty-four-pound carronades and two long twelve-pound guns well. However, according to Stephen Decatur, his *Argus* easily outsailed *Syren* on two trial runs. Most likely Decatur would have lost no time boasting to his old friend whose ship was the better. *Argus* did seem better at handling, and "in a heavy blow held her own considerably better than the other vessel."[40] *Argus* "would be roughed up . . . [while] the same conditions threw *Syren* on her beam ends."[41] *Syren*'s flaws put Stewart's considerable ship-handling and leadership skills to the test on more than one occasion during the next two years.

As with *Argus*, *Syren* had two masts, brig-rigged, and measured ninety-three feet, three and a half inches between perpendiculars (one foot less than *Argus*), with a twenty-seven-foot molded beam. Compared to *Argus*, *Syren* had a blunter hull, with less tumblehome, and fewer sheer lines fore and aft. Despite the marked differences between the two brigs, the *Syren* was a good craft, and in many ways she reflected her commander's personality—not flashy but reliable and staunch.

Syren was launched into the Delaware River on 6 August 1803, and exactly three weeks later Charles Stewart got her under way. In the absence of a formal commissioning ceremony, such as occurs now, this latter date is considered the equivalent moment when the ship becomes a serving member of the Navy. Stewart had overseen every detail of *Syren*'s construction and now he took her and her crew to the Mediterranean to join a third American squadron and Como. Edward Preble, a squadron commander who relied on the lieutenant and tested him beyond what he had experienced before.

CHAPTER THREE

Master Commandant

The first batch of captains commissioned in the new U.S. Navy in 1794 were accorded seniority based upon their experience in the Revolution. As the first ships neared completion in 1798, the needed lieutenants were commissioned in much the same way. Thus, both Edward Preble and Charles Stewart were commissioned lieutenants, but Preble was the more senior because he had served in the Massachusetts Navy during the Revolution in addition to having subsequent merchant experience. When Preble was appointed, he was intended to be the first lieutenant in the *Constitution*. However, he was outside the country on a merchant voyage at the time orders were issued and another lieutenant replaced him. When he finally became available, near the close of 1798, he was, instead, selected to command the USS *Pickering*, a fourteen-gun brig-of-war. Preble and the *Pickering* served under Barry when the future commodore and Barry's young fourth lieutenant cruised the Caribbean.[1] So when Stewart and *Syren* reported to Commodore Preble in 1803, the men were not strangers. Preble's selection as the new commodore was a wise choice, for he knew his orders, and he would carry them out aggressively against those who threatened American interests.

As with the previous two, Preble's squadron arrived piecemeal. Again, as each ship was ready, she went to sea to rendezvous at Gibraltar. The first, the twelve-gun schooner *Nautilus*, commanded by Charles Stewart's boyhood friend Lt. Richard Somers, arrived on 27 July. The thirty-eight-gun frigate *Philadelphia*, commanded by Capt. William Bainbridge, arrived on 24 August. The twelve-gun *Vixen*, commanded by Lt. John Smith, arrived on 12

September. The flagship carrying Preble, the forty-four-gun frigate *Constitution*, arrived on 14 September. The thirty-six-gun frigate *New York*, commanded by Capt. John Rodgers, and the twenty-eight-gun frigate *John Adams*, commanded by Capt. Hugh G. Campbell, had preceded her by one day, while Charles Stewart brought *Syren* into Gibraltar on 1 October. Stephen Decatur joined his friends when he arrived with his brig, the sixteen-gun *Argus*, in Gibraltar on 1 November. Upon his arrival, Preble directed Decatur to relinquish command of *Argus* to Lt. Isaac Hull, who was senior, and then assume command of the schooner USS *Enterprise* on 6 November. Decatur was fortunate because *Enterprise* was as splendid a hull as the *Argus*.

The naval force Preble had at his command was the most formidable squadron to leave American shores up to that time. As of May 1803, the bashaw of Tripoli had a maritime force consisting of one polacre (his largest and best unit), three xebecs, two brigs, five galliots, and nine gunboats. The gunboats, of which type more were built, were used for harbor defense; the other units raided afar against hapless merchantmen.

Although the respective naval forces appeared relatively equal, there was a difference between the U.S. and Tripolitan officer corps. Again, many of the American officers were from the Class of '98, and Charles Stewart was one of the most experienced. Stewart joined a group of officers of whom Commodore Preble said in a letter to the Navy secretary, "I have . . . many remarkable fine young men whose conduct promise great things for their country."[2] None of the commanding officers of the ships in the squadron were over thirty years of age. One historian wrote that "from a group in which individualism was so pronounced among Preble's boys, it is almost impossible to select one as either completely representative or outstandingly in character . . . but if it has to be made, the choice must undoubtedly fall on Charles Stewart."[3]

On 1 October *Syren* met *Constitution*, *John Adams*, and *Nautilus* off Gibraltar. Commodore Preble informed Stewart and the other commanders of his intention to deal with Morocco first. While the rest of the squadron set sail for Tangier and a confrontation with the Moroccan emperor, Stewart and *Syren* were directed to provide escort for a convoy of American merchant ships. On 9 October *Syren* rendezvoused with the squadron off Tangier, where he found only the frigates *New York* and *John Adams* and the schooner *Enterprise* lying in the bay. Stewart had just missed Preble's show of force and his subsequent diplomacy, which culminated in reestablishing the peace between Morocco and the United States. Preble's efforts reaffirmed the foundation for peaceful relations that have lasted for two hundred years.

On 11 October a fresh gale blew into Tangier Bay. Stewart watched the weather deteriorate and saw the senior officer afloat in the frigate *New York* getting under way and standing out toward the *Syren*. The wind increased; the weather thickened. By 1:45 P.M. the *New York* signaled, stating she wanted to speak with Stewart. Stewart directed Lieutenant Caldwell to have *Syren* heave to with the brig's head in a suitable position to receive *New York*'s hail. As *Syren* was lying to, Stewart expected *New York* to heave to herself at some small distance to windward of his ship, but the frigate continued her run toward the brig. According to one of Stewart's midshipmen, F. Cornelius DeKraft, "the dangerous situation in which we were plac'd required an immediate maneuver."[4] The *New York* tried to maneuver ahead of the *Syren*, then turned to heave to into the wind. However, the speed of her coming to brought the frigate's sails flat to the mast, and with the seas running very heavy, forced her starboard side against the brig's port bow. In this critical moment the *Syren* seemed doomed, but Stewart acted quickly and ordered the brig's helm put up and shiver the after sails. This well-timed maneuver saved *Syren*, but she lost her jib boom, spritsail yard, portside cathead, and bow anchor. The *New York* sustained greater damage, especially to her rigging, but she was able to send one of her boats to the *Syren* with a packet for Stewart to pass on to an American-bound convoy.[5] Stewart, Caldwell, and the Syrens rode out the rest of the gale, and with the onset of a better sea state, they quickly effected repairs to their damaged brig from the spares found on board.

With peace secured between Morocco and the United States, Preble was ready to sail eastward toward Tripoli. However, he did not wait for the conclusion of peace with Morocco to send Tripoli a message of American resolve. Preble had dispatched the USS *Philadelphia* and USS *Vixen* to Tripoli on 16 September. His orders to Captain Bainbridge and Lieutenant Smith stated that they were to "annoy the enemy with all the means in your power."[6]

While Preble negotiated with the emperor of Morocco, and Stewart convoyed American merchantmen, Bainbridge's small command arrived off Tripoli on 7 October and immediately commenced a blockade. What followed three weeks later said much for Bainbridge's lack of tactical judgment and provided Charles Stewart and his contemporaries with several examples of what not to do when conducting a blockade.

Into his second week of the blockade, Bainbridge heard that two of the bashaw's corsairs were at sea. He decided to split his small force, a tactical pair that Preble had smartly formed so that the large frigate, *Philadelphia*, could enjoy the company of the smaller and shallower draft vessel, *Vixen*. Bainbridge ordered the *Vixen* to a position over three hundred miles westward of his frigate (off Cape Bon, Tunisia) to attempt an intercept of Tripoli-bound shipping. This left the *Philadelphia* alone to maintain the blockade in shallow and poorly charted waters. On 31 October *Philadelphia* ran hard aground off the city. That night she was captured with Bainbridge, David Porter, and the entire crew as prisoners. Two days later the *Philadelphia*'s crew was astonished to see their frigate refloated, brought into the harbor, and anchored under the guns of the city's fortifications.

Prior to this incident, Preble had begun planning his squadron's move to Syracuse, on the east coast of Sicily. Adm. Horatio Nelson's blockade of the French Fleet in Toulon had stripped every supply from the Rock, and it had become necessary for Preble to find another port with the necessary logistics support. In any case, Syracuse offered a closer deepwater port to stage his blockading force against Tripoli. From Syracuse, Preble calculated that he could expand his force with the purchase of bomb ketches and shallow-draft gunboats from the king of the Two Sicilies, who had suffered for many years from the outrages of the Barbary States.

Preble hoped that acquiring bomb ketches would greatly augment the combat power of his squadron, because bomb ketches could lob shells into the city and the smaller gunboats could more easily work inshore against Tripoli's shallow draft corsairs. On 9 November Preble sent Stewart's friend Stephen Decatur and his new command, the USS *Enterprise*, eastward to escort a provision ship to Syracuse and establish a logistics base for the squadron. When the lieutenant finished that duty, Preble directed Decatur to join *Philadelphia* and *Vixen* on blockade duty. On 12 November Preble issued a proclamation stating that he had implemented "a blockade of Tripoli and notified the leading European powers through the American consuls in London, Madrid, and Paris."[7] Preble and the squadron had not yet heard of *Philadelphia*'s disaster.

Meanwhile, Stewart and *Syren* continued to operate through the western Mediterranean. On 10 November two strange ships flying French colors approached *Syren*. Although the United States was at peace with France, this was a tense moment for Stewart. In the fading sunlight as the two frigates approached *Syren*, they lowered their French colors and raised the white ensigns of the Royal Navy. They turned out to be HMS *Narcissus* and HMS *Sea Horse*, two frigates that were part of Admiral Nelson's squadron blockading the French Fleet at Toulon. The frigates signaled the smaller American vessel to verify her nationality, and with all being satisfied of their respective nationalities, they swapped information regarding their respective blockades.

Stewart and *Syren* continued to operate in the western Mediterranean through the rest of November, and rapidly changing weather conditions all but ended the American blockade of Tripoli and tested Stewart's highly developed ship-handling skills. Just past midnight on 29 November *Syren* weathered a severe gale. While under close reefed topsails, a reefed foresail, and main and fore topmast mainstay sails, "a very heavy sea struck us, at the same time another tremendous one struck us and laid us on our beam ends, but by the management of an able Captain, we righted in about 15 minutes by tacking all sail except the for top mast stay sail and shifted her helm hard a weather, which paid her off before the gale."[8] It must have been a cold, exhausting, wet night for all hands with only partial relief coming with daylight. Stewart and his crew were happy to meet up with Lt. Isaac Hull's *Argus* the next day. Together, they cruised south, and, on orders from Commodore Preble, Stewart took his brig to Algiers, arriving on 20 December. Upon his arrival, the American consul informed Stewart of the *Philadelphia*'s capture. (Preble had been informed of the capture on 24 November, when the *Constitution* met the frigate HMS *Amazon* off southern Sardinia.) Losing no time, Lieutenant Stewart shifted into his dress uniform and left his brig to personally present to the dey of Algiers gifts that would augment the recently concluded peace. After a brief stay in Algiers, Stewart set sail for Syracuse, Sicily, and Preble's squadron. Arriving in Syracuse on 29 December, Stewart and his crew saw the new year in with the rest of the squadron as it anchored in Augusta Bay. Preparations for the coming offensive against the bashaw of Tripoli and dealing with the *Philadelphia* problem occupied all in the squadron. As one of the squadron's senior officers, Stewart knew the coming year would be one to test him further.

The capture of *Philadelphia* and its crew greatly complicated Preble's plans. He said as much to Navy Secretary Smith in his year-end roundup report, dated 10 December, which detailed the squadron's operations. Preble had thought that with *Philadelphia*'s help he would have had a peace treaty with the bashaw before the spring of 1804 turned to summer. Now that would not be the case. He further wrote in his report that *Philadelphia* would never be used by Tripoli for "I shall hazard much to destroy her."[9] Preble also sketched out his plan to execute a surprise attack on *Philadelphia* to retake the frigate, then burn her under the guns of the city's fortifications.

Despite the loss of *Philadelphia*, Preble maintained very active operations. He kept his brigs and schooners busy during the winter of 1803, cruising along the Tripolitan coastline. *Syren* spent many a cold stormy day patrolling the coastline with *Argus, Vixen, Nautilus,* and *Enterprise.* Stewart was the officer in tactical command of the five ships. In fact, as senior officer present, Stewart found himself commanding most of the squadron's warships in Preble's absence. As then–second in command in the Mediterranean, Stewart led the inshore operations against Tripoli, while Commodore Preble continued his preparations for the overall offensive against the bashaw.[10]

By the end of January 1803 Preble was prepared to act on the first unanticipated prerequisite to taking on the bashaw: destroying the *Philadelphia.* Decatur had recommended that the recent addition to the American squadron, a Tripolitan ketch named *Mastico*—captured by Decatur just before Christmas and renamed the *Intrepid*—was an ideal platform for a raiding party to enter the harbor and, from her decks, board the stranded frigate. Preble also thought that Decatur was the ideal person to lead the boarding party.

> About this time, Lieutenant Commandant Stewart . . . who had just arrived from below, offered to cut out the *Philadelphia* with his own brig; but Commodore Preble was pledged to Mr. Decatur, who, at first had proposed to run in with the *Enterprise* and carry the ship. The more experienced Preble rejected the propositions of both these ardent young men, substituting a plan of his own.[11]

On 31 January Preble directed both Stewart and Decatur to the flagship and issued detailed orders for the *Syren* and *Intrepid* to get under way the next day. Preble realized how well these two lifelong friends complemented one another and how well they would work together to execute his wishes.

> Decatur was to take seventy-five officers and men . . . seventy volunteers from his own ship *Enterprise,* and five midshipmen from the *Constitution.* Decatur was to proceed to Tripoli in company with Stewart who received separate orders for his role in the adventure. Decatur was directed to enter the harbor at night, board the frigate, burn her, and retire with the *Intrepid* if possible, unless she might be converted into a fire ship to destroy other vessels in the harbor. In that case the men were to retreat in their small boats or those of the *Syren,* which was to be the covering ship for the operation.[12]

Additionally, Preble directed Stewart to alter the appearance of *Syren* in such a way as to make the Tripoli defenders think she was a merchantman.

Syren would follow *Intrepid* and stand in as close to her as possible to provide support to the assault, effect the assault party's withdrawal, and destroy as many of the small Tripolitan cruisers as possible.

With orders in hand, Stewart returned to *Syren*. Midshipman DeKraft remembered, "At 9 all hands were mustered when the intention of the expedition was made known to the crew, with which they were pleas'd to express their satisfaction by 3 hearty cheers."[13] Stewart and Decatur prepared their respective vessels for the operation and "that evening the ketch sailed, under the convoy of the *Syren*, Lieutenant Commandant Stewart, who was properly the senior officer of the expedition, though, owing to the peculiar nature of the service, Mr. Decatur was permitted to conduct the more active part of the duty, at his own discretion."[14] The tiny assault force left that evening with those seventy-five men on board the crowded little *Intrepid*. Adding to the discomfort were the meat rations brought on board, which were rotten; the only food that Decatur and his men had to eat was crackers, water, and whatever Stewart was able to provide. Despite the hardship, all felt confident that a few days of discomfort would be worth it if they succeeded in their mission.

The weather held fair while Stewart's crew altered their ship and Decatur's volunteers prepared for the upcoming action. During the transit to Tripoli, the old friends found time to be together on board *Syren*, where Decatur spent his evenings. During the late afternoon hours of 7 February, Stewart and Decatur found themselves off of Tripoli. The lateen-rigged *Intrepid* preceded the disguised *Syren* toward the harbor, and, with the onset of darkness, Stewart directed his first lieutenant, James Caldwell, to make anchor and swing the ship's boats out, and to ready them for the upcoming action.

However, as darkness came over them, the weather turned foul. From *Syren* Stewart could see the *Intrepid*'s light bouncing about as the winter storm whipped up the waves and tossed the small ketch about with increasing violence. Decatur was reluctant to quit his action, but, through a combination of small boat reconnaissance, which he directed toward the harbor's entrance, and the advice of an experienced pilot who accompanied the expedition, he was convinced to give up an opportunity to enter the harbor for the moment. The report back from the small boat reconnaissance proved the pilot's worst fears. The seas were breaking over the entrance to the harbor, and if the ketch did not alter course, it would very shortly face the dangers of a lee shore. It was just too dangerous to proceed farther, and, with the prospects of disaster looming, Decatur reluctantly turned his craft seaward.

35

So quickly had the gale strengthened that Stewart was unable to communicate with Decatur and determine his intentions. The only thing he saw of his friend was the lantern suspended from the *Intrepid*'s mast. Stewart could see it was moving seaward and fading from his view. Realizing the mission was off for the night, Stewart ordered his ship to weigh anchor and proceed out to sea with Decatur's *Intrepid*. However, Stewart, Caldwell, and the *Syren* had their own difficulties. In the face of increasing seas and blowing wind, it seemed that it took forever to remove what equipment there was from the boats and to hoist the boats back on board *Syren*. As conditions degraded, *Syren* found herself rolling dangerously. She was still at anchor and the gale made it increasingly difficult to raise it. While Caldwell was busy supervising the recovery of the boats, Stewart personally lent a hand to heave the anchor in, and he was with his men on the ship's capstan when the capstan ran away from them. All attending the capstan, including the *Syren*'s captain, were injured when the bars were thrown from the spinning capstan head. Although hurt, Stewart continued in command and directed his crew in one last-ditch attempt to retrieve the anchor. Daylight would soon be upon them, and with it, detection by the Tripolitans. Stewart ordered the cable cut and *Syren* sailed seaward to find and eventually rendezvous with Decatur's tiny *Intrepid*.

For the next six days the gale continued. Stewart's *Syren* doggedly stayed with the *Intrepid* throughout the storm. With conditions so bad, Stewart could only watch as Decatur's ketch was thrown about by the sea and wind. Charles could see Stephen on the small quarterdeck struggling to keep his craft afloat, while he struggled to counter *Syren*'s tendencies to turn on her beam ends. Watching *Intrepid*'s condition, he feared that the ketch might founder at any moment. On the fifth day of the storm, the wind shifted, driving both vessels up into the Gulf of Sidra and far to the southeast of Tripoli, a situation that presented additional dangers for the ships. With the wind blowing west to east, a lee shore was now before them. Both Stewart and Decatur realized their vessels were in danger of being blown aground and smashed by a combination of wave, wind, and rock. On 15 February the weather moderated, and the wind shifted again. Thankfully, neither officer had to face the prospects of running aground.

As the storm abated, Stewart's assault force came about and beat westward toward Tripoli. On the afternoon of 16 February the tiny assault force came abreast and seaward of the city. Seeing the tops of the minarets of the city on the horizon, Stewart, fearing their presence was now compromised, directed that eight of his crew join Decatur to compensate for the possible increase in reinforcements brought on board the *Philadelphia*. Stewart's timely decision paid unexpected dividends.

The transfer of the reinforcements was completed before nightfall, and, with nightfall upon them, the two vessels sailed toward the city. Being a faster craft, *Intrepid* was ahead of *Syren* when the wind began to die. Outpacing Stewart, Decatur was unwilling to wait for his friend's heavier ship. Decatur pressed in alone on to the attack in increasing darkness. Despite the fading wind, Stewart was able to bring *Syren* in closer, and just after 8 P.M. he was close enough to *Intrepid* to see her moving into the harbor. With *Syren* approximately three miles off of the port, Stewart directed Caldwell to heave to and put out the ship's boats. When the boats were in the water, Caldwell and thirty crewmembers from the *Syren* cast off and rowed after the *Intrepid*. As Caldwell dropped into the boat, Stewart directed his first lieutenant to find Decatur and place himself under his command for the assault. With Caldwell's departure, Stewart ordered the ship to resume her heading, and he followed his first officer toward the harbor. Unfortunately, the wind had died out completely, so Stewart ordered his crew to row their brig as close as possible in pursuit of Decatur and Caldwell. He knew that his own advance toward the city could raise suspicions, and he proceeded with all due deliberativeness. At this point, Stewart was taking soundings of the bottom, and as *Syren* reached a point offshore with the water depth marking eight fathoms, he ordered the anchor dropped and the ship cleared for action.[15] To avoid arousing the Tripolitan defenses, the Syrens moved deliberately and quietly to their quarters and prepared for immediate action should Decatur's force be discovered prematurely. With the lights of the city before them and a rising crescent moon above, *Syren* and Stewart had to stand idly by and anxiously wait for events to unfold.

Decatur's luck held. *Intrepid* slowly moved through the harbor, and around 9:30 P.M. he had her alongside the *Philadelphia*. Not until the last moment did some of *Philadelphia*'s Tripolitan crew recognize the situation and shout "Americanos!" The surprise approach was successful. Decatur and his men scrambled up the frigate's sides and onto her main deck. Wielding axes, knifes, pikes, swords, and tomahawks, Decatur's men cut down those defenders who stood their ground. Those who survived did so by jumping overboard. The entire action took about ten minutes, but the clash of steel and the screaming voices of the Tripolitan crew reached the shore and brought to life the city's defenses. Stewart could see movement through the city, and he could hear the increasing noise of battle, but he could not determine the fate of his friend and his assault force. Nor did he know at the time that Decatur was executing his orders exactly as Preble had prescribed.

With the ship taken, Decatur ordered all the combustible materials stored on the *Intrepid* to be brought across to the frigate and placed strategically within her. As his men hurried with their bundles, those who had their cache first were now setting them alight. To the surprise of the Americans, the ship began to burn, and it burned quickly. Many of Decatur's men were still below decks stowing their combustibles when the fire raced through the ship. Fortunately, all below managed to light their bundles and scramble back on deck before being trapped in the flames.

From his vantage point offshore, Stewart and his crew observed the firing of the American frigate, then saw a rocket climbing skyward from the *Philadelphia*, signaling that the frigate was recaptured. Seeing this, Stewart raced below to fetch his own rocket and return on deck to fire it off as an acknowledgement to Decatur.[16] He was gone from his quarterdeck for just an instant, but when he returned, Midshipman DeKraft observed, "the frigate *Philadelphia* . . . burst into a flame fore and aft, and the castle and batteries then commenced the fire on the *Intrepid*, all around the frigate in every direction."[17] Stewart and his crew could see the fire shining through the frigate's gun ports, and within a few more minutes the flames caught the ship's tar-coated standing rigging and raced upward through the ship's running rigging, masts, and yards. The *Intrepid* was now bathed in the glow of the burning frigate, making the ship a highly visible target for the city's guns. Fortunately for all on board the *Intrepid*, the defenders either had poor aim or suffered from only minimal training. Without the slightest wind and with shells from the city's guns sending splashes skyward about the tiny ketch, Decatur ordered his men to row *Intrepid* clear of the burning frigate. Just past midnight on 17 February, with the *Philadelphia* burning on the near horizon, Stewart saw *Intrepid* and *Syren*'s boats under Caldwell's command pulling for his ship. All on board *Syren* were elated, and cheering broke out along the brig's main deck as Decatur and his men rowed closer to the brig.

Shortly after this, *Intrepid* came alongside *Syren*. Decatur quickly scampered aboard Stewart's command, and to his officer in charge he conveyed the success of an action that left only one American, Reuben James, slightly wounded. From *Syren*'s quarterdeck, both men watched the *Philadelphia* burn. Congratulations were offered to those who risked so much. All on board the *Syren* who witnessed the frigate's death throes regretted her loss. At the height of the fire, the frigates anchor cable burned through, casting the ship adrift toward the city's castle. Before reaching the fortification, the

American frigate "blew up, rocking the city with a fearful concussion."[18] As *Syren* departed, with the *Intrepid* in tow, the frigate's fire glowed in the distance as *Syren* sailed farther out to sea. On 19 February they arrived at Syracuse to a highly satisfied Preble, who offered them heartfelt congratulations. The Sicilians also gave the tiny force resounding acclaim; they had been at war with Tripoli for years, and this raid was sweet satisfaction.

An apocryphal tale by Stephen Decatur's first biographer, which has since become part of the legend, has it that when Lord Nelson, who was then blockading the French at Toulon, heard of the exploit, he commented that it was "the most bold and daring act of the age." No record of it exists. When the news finally reached the United States, it brought tremendous exultation, in contrast to the American people's initial reaction to news of the *Philadelphia*'s capture.

Success has many fathers, and soon after the mission some men in the squadron questioned whether Decatur originated the idea to destroy the *Philadelphia*. The debate continued throughout Decatur's career and well after his death. It was exaggerated months later when news reached the squadron that Preble's recommendation to promote Decatur to captain immediately was granted by President Jefferson. To many in the service, promoting twenty-five-year-old Decatur to captain, the highest rank in the Navy at that time, was too much of an acknowledgment. By all accounts, Stewart stood by his friend, insisting that destroying *Philadelphia* was Decatur's idea first. "Where another might have been jealous, having coveted the assignment, Stewart was unrestrained in his commendation of Decatur."[19] Stewart's defense of his friend continued even after Decatur's death at the hand of Como. James Barron in 1820. Stewart later wrote, "The recollections of the difficulties and dangers he had to encounter in that expedition, of which I was an eye witness, excites more and more my admiration of his gallantry and enterprise, and although the result shed a lustre throughout Europe, over the American character, and excited an unparalleled emulation in the squadron, in our country alone is where it has never been duly estimated, or properly understood."[20]

Stephen Decatur's leapfrog promotion meant Charles Stewart was no longer the second-most senior officer of the Mediterranean Squadron. However, because news traveled slowly in those days, Stewart remained as Preble's second until official word arrived of Decatur's promotion. There was still a great deal that Preble planned for the upcoming spring and summer that he depended on his "most faithful and competent subordinate" to execute.[21]

Charles Stewart's primary responsibility in Commodore Preble's absence before the shores of Tripoli was to command the blockading force. With Preble and *Constitution* away at different ports around the Mediterranean in search of bomb vessels, small gunboats, crews, and diplomatic support for the recovery of the *Philadelphia*'s crew and the winning of the peace, Stewart commanded the blockade. While conducting the blockade with the USS *Nautilus*, which his friend Richard Somers commanded, lookouts on board *Syren* spotted a strange sail to seaward. It was 18 March, just a little over a month since *Philadelphia* was destroyed, and this strange sail was attempting to run past the two American ships as it made its way toward Tripoli. Stewart quickly took up the pursuit, and *Syren* cut the brig off from its destination. After a very brief action, Stewart captured what was the Tripolitan brig *Transfer*, the second ship captured by Stewart that month and an invaluable prize. The bashaw had bought *Transfer*, a former British privateer, in Malta, and used her as a blockade-runner. Stewart's prize crew returned the privateer, condemned with her cargo as a prize, to Malta. Once the prize was cleared and awarded to Stewart and the crew, the *Transfer* was then rearmed to carry sixteen six-pound guns and was rechristened as the USS *Scourge*, under the command of Lt. John Dent. As the winter of 1804 turned to spring, not only the *Scourge* and *Vixen* augmented Stewart's flotilla, but Isaac Hull's *Argus* was also directed by Preble to join Stewart. *Argus* arrived from her duties in the western Mediterranean in April, giving Stewart command of the first blockading force ever assembled by the fledgling U.S. Navy.

With each passing day, Stewart made that blockade more effective. On 22 March Stewart and the Syrens captured a prize trying to run the blockade. After a short action, the *Madonna de Catapoliagne* and her Russian captain sailed to Malta as an American prize. By the end of March, Stewart had already taken three vessels, and the other squadron members were experiencing similar success. The mission changed, however, when Commodore Preble and his flagship *Constitution* arrived on the scene on 26 March.

Upon *Constitution*'s arrival, Stewart was ordered to report on board to meet with the commodore. Preble informed his young second in command of his decision to try to obtain the release of *Philadelphia*'s crew. For months they had been languishing as pawns of the bashaw's strategy of maintaining hostages as bargaining chips. Captain Bainbridge had been corresponding with Commodore Preble, and with each successive letter, it became apparent that Bainbridge and his crew were reaching the limits of their endurance. Considerable diplomatic negotiations were conducted by several European governments, including Napoleon Bonaparte's foreign ministry, on behalf of the Americans. However, Preble held little confidence in Napoleon's or any other country's efforts. He intended to make one more direct contact with the bashaw.

His meeting with Preble over, Stewart returned to *Syren* and, together with other members of the blockading force, followed *Constitution* toward the harbor. The impressive collection of warships must have been imposing to those watching from ashore in the morning light. In fact, the Tripolitan commander of the defending gunboats was so convinced of an impending attack that he rushed his vessels to block the entrance. As the flagship approached to within four miles of the port, Commodore Preble ordered a single gun to be fired to leeward and hoisted a large white flag atop of *Constitution*'s foremast. Over the next few days, messages were sent back and forth, with the French consul to Tripoli acting as the intermediary. These negotiations bore no fruit and Preble finally broke them off. On 28 March he left Stewart's blockade and sailed for Naples to complete his preparations to bring the necessary firepower to force the bashaw to come to terms.

Again, Stewart reinstituted the blockade, though his management of the blockading force was tested by his ship's growing need for critical repairs and by the crews' need to be relieved. But despite these increasingly debilitating circumstances, Stewart was still able to maintain an effective blockade. He shuttled his vessels between blockade duty and port calls to obtain repairs at Messina or Syracuse. The enlistments of many of the men in the squadron had expired months previously, and they asked for relief. The sailors felt, and Commodore Preble and Stewart agreed, that they had served with distinction and selflessness, but their morale was certainly becoming more of a problem than the material condition of squadron. Preble informed the sailors that they would be sent home as soon as new crews were brought out on the frigate USS *John Adams*, and because of Preble and Stewart's personal leadership, morale remained stable. The arrival of the first gunboats and bomb ketches from the king of the Two Sicilies also helped matters—a true offensive was now possible.

What was so striking about the relationship between officers and enlisted was that all of the sailors were volunteers. They entered the service for a specified duration, terms of enlistment different than those of their British cousins in the Royal Navy.

As the reinforced squadron took shape in Naples, Stewart continued the blockade, and with improving weather, he waged a more aggressive operation. On 28 April Stewart brought Lieutenants Hull and Smith aboard *Syren* to discuss his plans for working more closely inshore. With Caldwell present, he laid out his thoughts for harassing the bashaw's defenses and spoke at length about how his operational plan presented an excellent opportunity for the squadron to sharpen its bombardment skills against land defenses. The next day saw excellent weather and Charles led his flotilla, *Syren*, *Argus*, and *Vixen*, inshore toward a small fort located west of Tripoli. Under light breezes the three Americans aligned themselves against the fort and a small beachside gun battery located with it. At 3:30 P.M. the flotilla commenced a "brisk fire" on the fort and the gun battery, and it continued "to sport 'till ½ past 6."[22] The fortifications returned fire, but their shots ranged consistently high and over the ships, causing very little damage to the American's rigging and no casualties among the crews. At 7 P.M., with the sun setting, the battered fort lowered its colors, and Stewart signaled ceasefire. Satisfied with a good day's work, he signaled the flotilla to withdraw, and they smartly wore away together, standing off the fort as darkness fell.

Stewart's day was not quite over. At the clearing of the evening meal, he ordered *Syren*'s cutter to be fitted out. At 10:30 P.M. he left Caldwell in charge and took the cutter and its crew inshore to take soundings of the waters just west of Tripoli. This type of operation was necessary and routine because the American charts were so unreliable. Taking soundings at night also hid the American squadron's intentions. Just before sunrise, Stewart and the boat crew returned to *Syren* tired but successful.

By the second week in May, Stewart's blockading flotilla was reinforced with the arrival of Lt. John Dent's newly acquired USS *Scourge* and Stephen Decatur's USS *Enterprise*. *Scourge* had just been refitted and commissioned into the fleet, and *Enterprise* had just completed her long-delayed overhaul. On 12 May Stewart's commanders came on board *Syren* to discuss his plan of action. Again, the operation would be another demonstration against the bashaw's defenses. They would attack positions west of the city. In addition, they would bombard defenses in the city itself. Stewart hoped this operation would draw the bashaw's gunboats out, so that he might engage them. The commanders stayed with Stewart throughout the afternoon, Decatur being the last one to return to his command.

May 13 dawned as another pleasant Mediterranean day. Under light breezes, the flotilla formed a line of battle and stood in for the fort and the town. *Syren* split from the flotilla and concentrated on the fort, while Decatur took the rest of the ships to engage the town. The action commenced just before noon, with both sides exchanging heavy fire. Around 1 P.M. the bashaw's gunboats stood out of the harbor to attack the flotilla. While concentrating on the fort, Stewart could see Decatur and the rest of the flotilla taking on the gunboats. The battle continued throughout the afternoon, and, with the silencing of the fort's guns, Stewart brought *Syren* about and bore down on the brisk sea battle. Seeing this, the badly shot-up gunboats withdrew into the harbor. Stewart ordered his flotilla to ceasefire and wear away from the city. At 7 P.M., Stewart arrived on board Decatur's *Enterprise* to discuss the outcome of the day's warm work, their biggest action to date.

Charles discussed with Stephen his intentions to follow up this action the next day, by striking the enemy east of the city. Leaving Decatur to maintain the blockade, Stewart took *Syren* and *Vixen* twenty miles down the coast and east of Tripoli. On the afternoon of 14 May he led an amphibious raid. The force Stewart commanded consisted of each ship's barge with its well-armed crew and a section of Marines. Leaving Caldwell in command of *Syren*, Stewart ordered the barges to pull closer toward the shore. Reaching the beach, the raiding party was greeted with sporadic musket fire. The Marines in both barges returned fire, clearing the beach of the skirmishers. The sailors continued rowing the barges toward the beach, and once onshore, Stewart, the Marines, and the sailors quickly leapt from their boats and rapidly crossed over the beach toward a nearby village. As they pressed on, resistance increased. Seeing that his men were vastly outnumbered, Stewart ordered them back to the barges. Under the cover of the approaching nightfall, the raiding party shoved off and returned safely to their ships. This short excursion marked one of the first times that U.S. sailors and Marines conducted amphibious operations under fire outside the Western Hemisphere; Porter had done so the previous summer. Stewart's flotilla returned to the routine of close blockade, interrupted by the occasional exchange of gunfire with the forts and replenishment forays back to Malta and Syracuse.

This routine continued through 7 July, when through the morning fog a large galley was spotted by the flotilla. She approached from the west and hugged the shoreline. As with others who tried earlier, this galley had every intention of running past the blockade and entering the city. Stewart gave chase and ordered *Vixen* to follow. Despite every effort on Stewart's part to intercept this blockade-runner, the galley beached herself before either *Syren* or *Vixen* could close to capture her. Seizing the chance to run inshore with his ship's boats to destroy the beached craft, he ordered Caldwell to launch the *Syren*'s barge and make for the galley before its crew could unload all of her cargo. The raiding party of Marines and sailors, supported by the barge's twelve-pound carronade and the boat's heavy swivel gun, approached the beached galley. Success seemed certain until both raiding craft ran aground on an uncharted reef. Stewart looked on in horror as his raiding force, hung up on the reef, began to take heavy musket fire from enemy forces, who suddenly appeared from beyond the dunes. Unable to dislodge themselves, Caldwell and his men exchanged fire with their heavy guns while the Marines replied with well-aimed musketry. *Vixen* had already placed her boats and raiding party into the water, and Stewart directed them to assist Caldwell. He then brought *Syren* and *Vixen* as close as he dared to the beached craft. The action was joined by large number of Tripolitan cavalry. Caldwell managed to get both boats off the reef and back off from the heaviest musket fire. From a new vantage point, he resumed the firing of his heavy guns into the galley. *Syren* approached the massed defenders close enough to pour a broadside of grapeshot into their ranks. They scattered and allowed the outnumbered raiding party to break off cleanly. The galley was shot through and rendered unseaworthy; the casualties among the defenders were assessed as being very heavy. However, this was the most expensive action for the Americans in the campaign to date, and for Stewart personally. The several killed and wounded Americans, most from the marine contingent, were from *Syren*. Although the Americans cut the enemy to ribbons, for Charles Stewart, James Caldwell, and the crew, it was a somber evening meal that night.

This action was the last of its kind before the main event, for on 27 July Commodore Preble returned with the main force, which consisted of his flagship *Constitution*, Decatur's *Enterprise*, Somers's *Nautilus*, two Neapolitan bomb ketches, six gunboats, and a force of just over one thousand men. On 1 August Preble signaled for all of his commanders to report on board the flagship. Here he gave details of his attack plan. Preble knew that he could not take the city with the force at his disposal, but he thought he now possessed sufficient force in the guise of his bomb ketches, gunboats, and his own squadron to force the bashaw to release the *Philadelphia*'s crew and agree to a peace on acceptable American terms. The object was to get close enough inshore for the bomb ketches to lob their shells into the city and for the gunboats to pour their shot into the outer defenses and the array of gunboats. *Constitution*'s heavy gun battery would, at the same time, hammer the seaward fortifications. Stewart would take the brigs and schooners inshore to support Decatur and Somers, who in turn would lead separate gunboat divisions, consisting of three gunboats apiece, against the defending craft arrayed across the harbor entrance and the immediate land-based fortifications. Final preparation, reconnaissance, and surveillance of the Tripolitan defenses was completed on 2 August. The surveillance of the defenses left no doubt in the mind of the Americans how formidable the Tripolitans arrayed against them were.

Tripoli's fortifications mounted over 150 pieces of heavy artillery. That equaled Preble's entire force in number and weight of shot. But, it was with the bashaw's fleet that the numerical advantage swung in the favor of the defender. The protecting fleet was drawn across the harbor entrances and in between the rocks that formed a protective crescent boundary to the harbor. It consisted of gunboats, now nineteen in number and possessing heavier guns and crewed by more men than those of their American counterparts. Two galleys and two schooners, possessing eight guns apiece, together with a ten-gun brig, rounded out the bashaw's fleet. Preble was outnumbered, but he believed his force was superior in ability, discipline, and skill.

On 3 August Preble's force moved forward under easy canvas. By noon the American squadron's position lay between two to three miles from the fortifications. Preble could see movement among the protective screen of gunboats. Several were advancing to meet the oncoming Americans. Preble correctly guessed they would try to foil the American attempt to use the bomb ketches and *Constitution*'s heavy-gun battery against the city. He signaled Stewart, Decatur, and Somers to engage them. After dropping the towlines to the gunboats, Stewart moved in first with his flotilla of brigs and schooners, followed by Decatur's and Somers's gunboats. The American gunboats were extremely difficult to handle and their progress toward the shore was agonizingly slow. By the time the action commenced, Stewart's flotilla had sailed ahead and formed a rough line of battle. With the bomb ketches, the *Constitution*, Stewart's flotilla, and the gunboats in position, Preble raised the signal for general action. The mortars from the bomb ketches opened fire first, and when the first of their shells landed in the city, the defenders commenced a tremendous return cannonade. The remaining American vessels soon opened fire with everything they could bring to bear.

The bashaw's gunboats that rushed forward against the Americans consisted of two divisions with nine gunboats apiece. Stewart maneuvered his flotilla to engage the more easterly division and the city's defenses, while he watched Decatur's and Somers's gunboat divisions of three boats each move toward the same defenders. Through the billowing smoke, Stewart saw his friends weather a withering barrage. He continued to support them, but as Decatur and Somers closed with the enemy, Stewart and the flotilla had to shift their fire lest they hit their comrades. Stewart could offer little aid at this time, so he directed the flotilla's guns against the city's fortifications in hopes of reducing their fire upon his friends. Decatur and Somers were now on their own and the subsequent action was costly but victorious. Of the three gunboats captured that day, Decatur claimed two. At the height of the action, his younger brother, Lt. James Decatur, who commanded one of the American gunboats and was Richard Somers's first lieutenant on board *Nautilus*, fell. Surprisingly, only one other sailor was killed with thirteen Marines and sailors wounded. Although it was a personal loss for Decatur and his friends, 3 August 1803 was recognized by the U.S. Navy as the Battle of the Gunboats—a day of unparalleled tactical success for the young Navy.

For the remainder of the afternoon, all American ships and craft were hotly engaged against the enemy in cannonade and hand-to-hand fighting. Around 4 P.M., the wind began to shift and Preble ordered the gunboats and bomb ketches to retire and rejoin the heavier ships. At the same time he ordered Stewart to stand in closer to support the withdrawal. As Preble brought *Constitution* in closer to support both maneuvers, Stewart smartly maneuvered the brigs and schooners close to cover the retiring gunboats and their prizes. The final action by the heavier American ships added considerably to the distress of the bashaw's forces, as three more gunboats were sunk in the harbor and many of the larger vessels heavily damaged.

The American squadron hauled off and anchored about ten miles from Tripoli to repair its damage, fit out its prizes as American craft, tend to the wounded, and bury its dead. Stewart, Somers, and Decatur were together at this time, with Stephen and Richard describing to their friend Charles what had transpired and how Stephen's brother died. They had little time to lament, for Commodore Preble wanted to press his advantage with another attack.

Repairs to the fleet and the refurbishment of the captured gunboats were required prior to the second attack. Preble selected Charles Stewart's highly capable first officer, James Caldwell, to refurbish and command one of the captured gunboats. As the gunboat was tied alongside the *Syren*, Stewart provided every support to Caldwell and those crew who were selected to be the crew of the little gunboat. On the morning of 7 August, as the crew of the gunboat and Caldwell climbed down to the tiny gunboat's deck, Stewart wished them good luck in the fight to come, for they could expect the action to be hot.

The second action demonstrated Stewart's operational and tactical skill and also tested his ability to overcome personal loss. "The plan for the second attack owes much to Preble's junior officers, especially Charles Stewart. Stewart argued against another frontal assault and proposed instead to bombard the town from a small bay just to the west."[23] Taking Stewart's recommendations, Preble directed the two bomb ketches to take up a bombardment position in the small bay Stewart had suggested and commence lobbing their mortar shells into the city. Building on Stewart's persuasive argument, Preble directed the lieutenant to take *Syren* and *Vixen*, together with the two gunboat divisions under Decatur and Somers, and closely engage the fort located on the northwest perimeter of the city. Lying just east of the bomb ketches' position, the fort named the French Castle or Battery Français would be singled out for reduction. Preble would take the remaining members of the squadron and position them farther eastward, and if the opportunity presented itself, he would intercept those enemy craft that might sortie to intercept the gunboats.

Stewart, Decatur, and Somers put the Battery Français out of action, while Preble kept the bashaw's fleet at bay. Unfortunately, Caldwell's gunboat was struck by a hot shot, exploding its store of gunpowder. The explosion cut the boat in two, killing Caldwell together with one of his midshipman, Mr. Dorsey, and ten other crew members. Six others were wounded then, and on 12 August Seaman Francis Rogers became the eleventh fatality when he died from his wounds.[24] When the boat was hit, it was approximately two hundred yards away from Stewart and the *Syren*. Stewart immediately ordered his ship's boats to attempt a rescue of the survivors. As the gunboat sank, there was a momentary lull in American fire. But as Stewart commented after the battle, "it was redoubled on the enemy, so that it seemed to say for four hours we revenge our brave companions."[25] With this loss, Stewart and his crew had now suffered the highest casualties of the entire squadron. This was Charles's first loss of a close friend, as it was for many of his crew. Caldwell's death weighed heavily on him, but he had no time to mourn.

As the battle raged, a strange sail appeared to seaward. It turned out to be the twenty-eight-gun frigate USS *John Adams*, under the command of M. Cdr. Isaac Chauncey. At the end of the day's action, the squadron withdrew to lick its wounds, assess the day's work, and rendezvous with the newly arrived frigate. The frigate's arrival presented a mixed blessing to Preble and his squadron. The *John Adams* had her long guns and carriages stowed below as ballast so that the upper decks could be used for the transport of provisions and stores. Once these were transferred, the guns could be broken out and remounted. The limewater brought by the frigate certainly helped all those who had begun to suffer from scurvy, but the *John Adams*'s arrival was still a major disappointment to all concerned because Master Commandant Chauncey also brought news that was troubling. First, he informed Preble that President Jefferson had directed the Navy secretary to dispatch additional ships, including the frigates *President, Congress, Constel-*

lation, and *Essex*, and that they were expected shortly. Chauncey also informed Preble that Como. Samuel Barron, who was senior to Preble, commanded this squadron. He further stated that Barron carried orders that would relieve Preble, news that shocked all in the squadron. The squadron felt Preble was performing superbly and Barron's orders were seen as a slap in the face. On a happier note, Chauncey conveyed the list of promotions recommended by the president and confirmed by the Senate: Stephen Decatur received his captaincy and became second-most senior officer under Preble. Charles Stewart, Isaac Hull, John Smith, and Richard Somers were promoted to the reestablished rank of master commandant. Charles was now the third-most senior officer in the squadron (his date of rank being 19 May 1804), while Stephen Decatur would have overall command of the frontline forces in the next series of actions.[26]

Expecting the arrival of the additional forces, Preble held off the next attack. Unknown to all, Barron was taking his time to arrive. In his defense, the incoming ships had run into bad weather. However, after a fortnight of waiting, Preble felt that he could not wait any longer for Barron. He initiated a second daylight attack and then followed up with the first night attack against the city and its defenses. During the remaining dog days of August, "he was determined that as long as he had command the Bashaw would have no rest until he displayed a white flag over his castle."[27] Preble's next move certainly made the bashaw reconsider, and it had a profound effect on Stewart, Somers, and Decatur.

Preble had wreaked havoc on the city throughout August, but he felt that he needed to do more to bring the bashaw to terms. For some time he had considered sending a fireship, an "infernal," into the harbor.[28] This could tip the balance, forcing the bashaw to treat. Master Commandant Somers was the first one to express the desire to fit out such an instrument and to sail it into the center of Tripoli's harbor. The instrument would be the plucky little USS *Intrepid*, and between the series of actions that took place during that hot August, Somers and another volunteer, Lt. Henry Wadsworth, supervised the conversion of the tiny ketch.

By the first week of September *Intrepid* was converted into a massive floating bomb. Somers and Wadsworth supervised the loading of one hundred barrels of black gunpowder and 150 charged shells into a specially rebuilt hold that was located forward of the mainmast. Farther aft, a large quantity of combustible materials were placed. To add to the destructive power of the infernal, countless pieces of metal shrapnel were scattered throughout the vessel. Although the odds were stacked against them, Somers, Wadsworth, and Lt. Joseph Israel, with four volunteer seamen from the *Nautilus* and six from the *Constitution*, did not see sailing the vessel as a suicide mission. They selected the two fastest boats from the squadron to be their escape craft, once they had successfully entered the harbor and set the fifteen-minute fuse. With everything ready, the only task left to do was wait for the right moment to execute this extremely dangerous action.

The opportunity came with the first dark night of the new month. On 4 September Somers and his volunteers said their tentative good-byes. Charles Stewart and Stephen Decatur joined Somers to offer their personal encouragement. What followed next was documented in a brief Somers biography:

> He carried out his share of the preparations with a grave and calm demeanour. To his friends, Decatur and Charles Stewart, he talked as one would, to cherished companions on whom he might be looking for the last time. When the hour came for them to separate he took from his finger a ring, broke it in three pieces, and, keeping one for himself, gave one of the remaining parts to Decatur, the other to Stewart.[29]

This act seemed typical for the friends. If their roles had been reversed, Stewart and Decatur would have offered some comparable gesture to honor the lifelong bond between them. As Charles and Stephen each accepted his piece of their friend's ring, a sense of finality must certainly have been their collective mood—maybe this would be the last time all of them would be together. Charles and Stephen spoke their final words of encouragement and offered their wishes of good luck to Richard Somers and his volunteers. Then the three friends repaired to their respective commands.

Around 8 P.M., under a gentle warm breeze and in the gathering darkness of a moonless night, the *Intrepid*, escorted by Somers's own *Nautilus*, together with *Vixen* and *Argus*, proceeded slowly under light canvas toward the harbor. They accompanied the "infernal" as close as they dared without raising suspicion, with the *Nautilus* staying close to Somers the longest. Both Stewart and Decatur watched their friend's progress as long as possible even though "the sea was covered with a dense haze, though the stars were visible, and the last may be said to have been seen of the *Intrepid*, was the shadowy forms of her canvass, as she steered slowly, but steadily, into the obscurity, where the eyes of the many anxious spectators fancied they could still trace her dim outline."[30] What happened next remains shrouded in uncertainty today.

The *Intrepid* was met by enemy gunfire as it entered the channel between the natural rock breakwaters of the harbor. At 9:45 P.M. "the harbor . . . the town, the desert, and the sea were lighted by a great blinding flash, followed by the roar and concussion of a fearful explosion."[31] The squadron could see the *Intrepid's* mainmast and suspended sail fly straight up into the air and above the fireball. Then, as suddenly as the flash and attendant secondary explosions from the stored shells occurred, there was darkness and silence. At "¹/₂ past 11 the Commodore [made] signal for Capt Somers, which was not answer'd, backed the mainsail." Midnight passed; the commodore still made signals, without being answered. The first light of morning saw the *Argus* and *Vixen* standing offshore. The commodore was "informed by the *Argus* that nothing had been heard or seen of Capt Somers and the ketch's crew, after she had been blown up."[32] A heavy sense of gloom and loss settled among all in the squadron. Decatur, who had lost his brother the previous month, now lost a best friend. And Charles Stewart lost a friend who was like a brother.

Shortly after the disaster, the saddened Stewart was ordered to take his *Syren* out of the blockade and return to Syracuse. He and the other commanders of those departing brigs and schooners towed their allotment of gunboats back to Sicily. Commodore Preble had decided the season was too advanced to risk the small craft to the fickle autumn weather of the Mediterranean. While Stewart sailed *Syren* and her gunboats back to Syracuse, Preble stayed behind with *Constitution*, *Argus*, and *Vixen*. A few days later Commodore Barron arrived, and on 10 September the *Constitution's* quarterdeck witnessed a change of command that left many in Preble's old squadron puzzled.

Much was said about Preble's departure. A document drafted by all of his officers deeply regretted his relief from command, and all signed it with deep sadness. Stewart was the second signature on the document, below Stephen Decatur. Sir Alexander Ball, the governor of Malta and a friend of Lord Nelson, wrote to his friend Edward Preble, "I beg to repeat my congratulations on the service you have rendered your country, and the hair-breadth escapes you have had in setting a distinguished example. Their bravery and enterprise are worthy a great and rising nation. If I were to offer my opinion, it would be that you have done well not to purchase a peace with the enemy. A few brave men have, indeed, been sacrificed, but they could not have fallen in a better cause, and I even conceive it advisable to risk more lives rather than to submit to terms which might encourage the Barbary States to add fresh demands and insults."[33]

When Preble returned to the United States, talk circulated around Washington that the commodore would be offered the position of Navy secretary from a very apologetic President Jefferson. When Stewart heard this speculation from his far-off station in the Mediterranean, he said that it would "give more real pleasure to his boys of the infant squadron."[34] But Preble was not given the office. Instead, he was directed to supervise the construction of "Jefferson's gunboats," an assignment that came, possibly for presidential expediency, after Preble's tireless lobbying to ensure smaller craft would be included in the fledgling Navy's inventory. Preble believed American-built craft would serve better in the faraway waters of the Mediterranean than captured craft. For Jefferson, the decision to build a gunboat flotilla would play better to the ever-increasing number of congressman and senators from western states, who would not allocate funding for an ocean-going navy. The argument for a balanced fleet (that is, one comprised of small and large men-of-war) continues to the present day. Regardless, the gunboats authorized by Congress in succeeding appropriations in the years before the War of 1812 played a significant role in Stewart's future naval service. Unfortunately, Preble very shortly succumbed to tuberculosis, which he had contracted prior to his command of the Mediterranean Squadron and with which he had struggled during his entire time before the shores of Tripoli.

Stewart was now only one of several commanding officers serving with the most powerful squadron the U.S. Navy had ever put to sea. He and his *Syren* did their part to maintain a vigorous blockade, but the seaborne offensive action against Tripoli ceased during Barron's short tenure as commodore. When Barron fell ill, the second-most senior captain in the squadron, Capt. John Rodgers, relieved him. Twenty-seven-year-old Stewart continued to command *Syren* through all of 1804 and most of 1805, while Decatur commanded the *Constitution* for a scant seven days and, later, the *Congress* in the same squadron. Decatur received multiple assignments because he was a junior captain; he found himself being bounced about as more senior captains joined the squadron. For Stewart, maintaining his command brought continuity and its own rewards.

Barron dispatched *Syren* to sail westward to monitor the activities of Morocco and Algiers, as well as to escort American merchantmen. Stewart spent much of his time during the first six months of 1805 in the western Mediterranean, moving routinely in and out of Gibraltar. Using Gibraltar as his base of operations, Stewart conducted reconnaissance against the Moroccans and submitted his intelligence findings to Commodore Barron and, later, to Commodore Rodgers. Using a relay ship sailing between Gibraltar and the Mediterranean Squadron, Stewart provided considerable intelligence and routinely expressed his desire to reengage in more active pursuits. In one such correspondence, dated 1 April 1805, Stewart conveyed to his commodore:

> I had the honor to acknowledge the receipt of your favour of the 6th March on the 1st Inst since when nothing of importance has transpired in this Quarter. I was at Tangier a few days past, but Mr. Simpson remains of the opinion that this Station ought not be left without one or more Vessels of War of the United States, altho' no appearance of hostility on the part of the Emperor has manifested itself. The Emperor's Frigate and Brig still remain at Lisbon and have made no movement whatever; the other vessels of the Emperor are hard up in the different ports. I cannot but lament the inactive situation a continuance on this Station places us in while there remains anything to be done off Tripoli; however I trust we shall yet receive your orders in time to join the Squadron for effective service against the Enemy. Yesterday arrived, the Ship *Ceres* from Baltimore with Provisions and stores for the Squadron and as another will shortly follow her I have advised her being forwarded to Malta without delay. Accounts from Algiers state that the Dey has been assaulted in his Palace and received fourteen different wounds with fragnards of which he is since dead. Admiral Nelson left this a few days past in pursuit of the Toulon fleet, which passaged the Straight about a month since and was joined off Cadiz by several sail of the line, 6 of which were Spanish, bound for America. All the papers I possess are enclosed but no doubt you will receive them much later information from the Packages, which this ship brings. PS, Arrived here this morning three sail of the line and a number of transports with 6000 troops onboard, said departing for Italy.[35]

A few days later, he assessed that the ship's main battery was experiencing problems and that he did not consider the ship in a situation to engage with an enemy. Although Stewart never mentioned what challenged the main battery, five weeks later it must have been remedied because he advised Commodore Rodgers that he hoped for orders to engage the enemy soon.

Stewart's letter to the commodore shows that the master commandant and his crew were well aware of another drama that was playing itself out, first in the Mediterranean, then across the Atlantic, and back again to a point just off a Spanish cape named Trafalgar. The Battle of Trafalgar, the greatest naval battle in the Age of Sail, was fought on 21 October 1805, and the news of the battle reached Stewart after he had joined Como. John Rodgers and had taken command of the thirty-two-gun frigate USS *Essex*. Stewart commanded this beautiful frigate for only a few months, but David Porter commanded her to lasting fame in the history of the U.S. Navy during the War of 1812.

It must not have been easy for the master commandant to leave *Syren*. When he was relieved in September, the brig, the crew, and Stewart had been together for over two years. He had brought the ship to life, forged her crew into a highly skilled team, and from her quarterdeck he directed most of the squadron in the commodore's absence. They had performed brilliantly together, and their service off the shores of Tripoli formed the foundation for the many accomplishments for which others in the squadron have been recognized in the U.S. Navy and the Marine Corps annals.

With Commodore Rodgers's decision to shift the offensive part of the war against the bashaw to a landward assault, Stewart and the *Essex* continued the blockade of Tripoli. The land offensive against Tripoli, conducted by Consular William Eaton, a handful of Marines, and a few hundred Arab mercenaries, resulted in a peace of sorts with the bashaw of Tripoli. U.S. Consul Tobias Lear had negotiated terms with the bashaw, to include a ransom of $60,000 for the release of Bainbridge and the crew of the *Philadelphia*. This decision met with criticism not only from politicians in Washington but also from the military officers leading forces in the Mediterranean. Shortly after they returned to the United States in late 1805, Stewart, Decatur, and Eaton themselves "spoke without much reserve in condemnation of the treaty concluded by Consul Lear . . . by which the latter stipulated to pay $60,000 to the Bashaw for the Ransom of Cap. Bainbridge & crew."[36]

Once peace had been made with Tripoli, the U.S. Navy set to work on another Barbary State. Tunis had followed Tripoli's lead by seizing American merchantmen. Rodgers ordered his squadron to proceed to the city, with the intent of bringing the dey of Tunis to terms one way or another. The beleaguered American consul in Tunis must have been inspired on that first day of August 1805, when from over the horizon appeared sail after sail—frigates, brigs, schooners, and gunboats all moving together in formation, under easy canvas and flying the Stars and Stripes at their mizzens. The events that unfolded next proved to be nearly disastrous, and were it not for Stewart's intercession, Commodore Rodgers might have acted beyond his authority and set back the Navy's hard-won reputation in the eyes of its country's citizenry.

> Stewart sailed with the squadron for the purpose of checking in that regency [Tunis] a rising disposition to commence depravations on our commerce. The

feeling there became so hostile that Mr. George Davis, our consul, deemed it prudent to seek refuge on board the fleet. In this critical state of affairs our consul-general, Colonel Lear, advised that the Commodore ask the advice of his principal officers. A council was convened on board the flagship, the situation of affairs was explained, and the opinion of the officers demanded whether hostilities ought not to be immediately commenced. Captain Stewart gave it as his opinion, that there was no power under the Constitution which authorized hostilities and wars on others, but that which was lodged exclusively with Congress; that the President could not exercise this power without the action and authority of Congress, much less the Commander of an American squadron; that due respect for the laws of nations forbade aggression, and only justified self-defence by vigilance and convoy for the protection of our citizens, their property and commerce; but where hostile attempts were made on either, he would be justified in seizing all persons engaged in them, but no further would his country sanction his acts. This sound reasoning and discretion prevailed, and amicable relations were soon restored; our consul returning to his post, and the Dey of Tunis sent a special minister to the United States. When President Jefferson received from our consul general a copy of that opinion as delivered in the council, he expressed to his cabinet the high satisfaction he felt at having an officer in the squadron who comprehended the international law, the constitution of his country and the policy of his government.[37]

Master Commandant Stewart's time in the Mediterranean was now coming to an end. With a peace of sorts established between the United States and the Barbary States, the American squadron was now being withdrawn. Stewart was relieved as commander of the *Essex* in November 1805 and returned to Philadelphia and his family that same year. Upon his return, he asked for and received permission to take leave prior to his next assignment. The chain of command, including President Jefferson, recognized the service of this veteran of the Quasi and Barbary Wars. Even though the fleet was drawn down and altered in its composition, President Jefferson recognized the importance of maintaining an experienced officer corps for the Navy. In a speech before Congress on 3 December 1805, he said, "I think it would be useful encouragement as well as a just reward to make an opening for some present promotion by enlarging our peace establishment of captains and lieutenants."[38] Master Commandant Stewart was one of the few mid-grade officers to benefit from this decision; on 22 April 1806 he was promoted to captain. At twenty-seven the newly promoted Captain Stewart was selected by the Navy secretary to be one of the senior officers responsible for the construction of President Jefferson's gunboats.

Without orders between 1807 and the outbreak of the War of 1812, Stewart returned to the merchant trade; he and fellow captain Isaac Hull were engaged in at least one joint commercial venture. (John Trumbull; courtesy of the Greenbrier)

In his history of the U.S. Navy, James Fenimore Cooper capsulated the criticism leveled on Mr. Jefferson's gunboat navy: "There can be no question, that in certain circumstances, vessels of this sort may be particularly useful; but these circumstances are of rare occurrence, as they are almost always connected with attacks on towns and harbours." He continued by writing that with a two-thousand-mile coastline, a navy comprised of gunboats, even if it were a practical method, would require such a large federal outlay that the country could provide a fleet of larger, more mobile ships that was capable of offensive and defensive operations instead.[39] Other criticism was less diplomatic; historian Charles Oscar Paullin considered the gunboat navy "a blunder and a misdirection of the national resources."[40] Despite the controversy, which continues to this day, Stewart and other officers shared Commodore Preble's beliefs that such craft were needed. The young captain emphasized the need to maintain a balanced fleet. This was evident in his correspondence to Navy Secretary Paul Hamilton, dated 12 November 1806, when he urged Hamilton "to push for a mixed force of both large and small vessels."[41] Stewart's tactical appreciation of the relationship between large and small vessels was demonstrated to great effect seven years later during the War of 1812.

Between 1803 and 1807 Congress authorized the construction of 272 gunboats of varying designs, built in all of the major U.S. ports.[42] The largest of these craft measured only seventy-five feet in length and carried two great guns (eighteen pounders or heavier). One hundred and seventy six of the authorized ships were actually built. Captain Stewart left Philadelphia for New York to supervise the construction of his allotted number.[43]

Stewart actually took over the supervision of the construction of gunboats number forty-six through fifty-seven from Como. Isaac Chauncey, who in June 1806 had received a furlough from active duty. "The . . . boats were already under progress when Stewart arrived in August."[44] A number of New York shipbuilders had received contracts to build the gunboats. Stewart reviewed Chauncey's design with each of the young shipbuilders. Adam and Noah Brown were responsible for gunboats number forty-six through forty-nine; Henry Eckford and Lester Beebe, for gunboats number fifty through fifty-three; and Christian Bergh, for gunboats number fifty-four through fifty-seven.[45] With his recent Mediterranean experience in mind, Stewart saw that Chauncey's design for the gunboat masts were not in proportion to the boats' hulls, and he directed that they be shortened.[46] The captain decided to alter Chauncey's design on the first eight boats. Stewart wrote of his changes: "As these boats carry their guns amidships, I cannot perceive the advantage of making the fore mast forward in the manner exhibited by the draughts but would recommend placing it more upright and giving the boats a jib, which will be very useful to them in turning to windward."[47]

With Stewart's change in the design for the first eight boats, the remaining four, built by Bergh, were altered into schooners. They were designed for sailing rather than rowing. Each of the Bergh gunboats measured approximately forty-seven feet, four inches on the keel, with an eighteen-foot molded beam, and they were five feet, six inches in the hold. Their armament consisted of either a twenty-four- or a thirty-two-pound long gun located amidships, which could pivot to port or starboard. Two twelve-pound carronades were also fitted on either side in the traditional manner. Each boat was rigged as a two-mast schooner without jibs.[48] Although they upheld President Jefferson's idea of small craft providing harbor defense, Charles Stewart had something else in mind.

Stewart was satisfied with the gunboats, which were launched in November 1806. "They set handsomely on the water and should they be required on foreign service, they appear to me better calculated to pass over the ocean than the boats built formerly, indeed there are few times occur at sea, when I should not feel myself as safe in one of them as any of our small Cruisers."[49]

With this assignment completed, Charles Stewart received his own furlough to pursue his private commercial interests.

In the years preceding the War of 1812, the government encouraged Stewart and many other officers to engage in commercial enterprises. With Stewart's background as a merchant and his recently gained knowledge of the Mediterranean, he lost no time reestablishing his business. However, world events, and President Jefferson and Congress's response to these events, soon affected Stewart's pursuit of commercial success.

Although Charles Stewart had returned to a country increasingly oriented toward the West and the recently explored lands traversed by Lewis and Clark, the era of American self-sufficiency had yet to be realized. America still depended on Europe for most of its manufactured products, while the United States provided Europe and the West Indies with raw materials, particularly foodstuffs, and a few finished products. Under ordinary circumstances, Stewart stood to gain considerably as a merchant-sailor, and it appears that he was able to make a good living in the years preceding the second war with Britain. However, the global war between Britain and France, the same one embodied by the battle fleets Stewart saw exiting the Mediterranean and sailing toward their destiny off Trafalgar, made it increasingly difficult for him and the United States to pursue their commercial interests overseas.

Upon Lord Nelson's victory at Trafalgar, the Royal Navy was able to concentrate its fleet on tightening Britain's blockade of French commerce. With Napoleon's conquest of Europe, Britain's major weapon became the blockade aimed at bottling up the remnants of the French fleet and disrupting French overseas trade. In 1807 Napoleon countered the blockade by establishing the Continental System that was devised to stop all British imports into European ports. Britain countered this paper blockade with a series of Orders in Council that forbade trade to ports possessed by France and her allies. Neither side cared for the rights of neutrals, and the plight of American shipping and commerce was now in a very sorry state. Both the British and the French sent out privateers and warships to the American side of the Atlantic to capture any American merchant ships they could run down. The Royal Navy also impressed those sailors from their American prizes whom it considered British subjects. The need for men to man Britain's "Wooden Walls" was insatiable and eventually involved a confrontation with a warship of the U.S. Navy and a member of the Class of '98.

In 1807, while Charles Stewart worked on his gunboats, his former first lieutenant on board John Barry's *Constellation*, Como. James Barron, became the new commodore for the Mediterranean Squadron. His flagship, the frigate *Chesapeake*, under the command of M. Cdr. Charles Gordon, prepared for the years that it would be away on its appointed station. But neither Gordon nor his commodore expected that they would have to engage in battle so close to home.

The *Chesapeake* departed Norfolk on the morning of 22 June 1807. It was preceded that very same morning by one of the British ships anchored off Lynnhaven, Virginia—HMS *Leopard* of fifty guns. The squadron at Lynnhaven was anchored in American territorial waters, where it was positioned to intercept any of the four French frigates that had taken refuge farther up the Chesapeake Bay at Annapolis, Maryland. What transpired later that day outraged American public opinion and forced President Jefferson to enact a draconian measure tantamount to a self-inflicted wound: an embargo of American trade to Britain. The *Chesapeake* incident also represented a major grievance that the young republic factored into its decision to declare war against Great Britain in 1812. For Capt. Charles Stewart and others in service at that time, the misfortune of Commodore Barron and Master Commandant Gordon stood as a lesson that one's ship must not only to be ready for sea, but it must be prepared to fight once it cast off its mooring lines.

Sailing off the Virginia capes, the *Chesapeake* was intercepted by the *Leopard*. The British demanded that *Chesapeake* hand over three "British subjects" who had deserted from the frigate thirty-eight-gun HMS *Melampus*. Barron replied that he had no such deserters. *Leopard* then fired into the unprepared *Chesapeake*, forcing Barron to surrender and give up the men that *Leopard* said were deserters. Subsequently, Barron and Gordon received courts-martial. "The first was distinctly acquitted of cowardice, but was found guilty of neglecting, on the probability of an engagement, to clear his ship for action. The sentence was a suspension from pay and rank for five years."[50] Serving on Barron's court-martial board were Stephen Decatur and Charles Stewart.

Gordon was privately reprimanded, but subsequently he suffered debilitating wounds from a duel that was the result of the *Chesapeake-Leopard* affair. His wounds left him unable to continue his service. For Charles Stewart and his contemporaries, the incident left an indelible mark, to be expunged from their collective being through their conduct in the second war for American independence—the War of 1812.

CHAPTER FOUR

An Abbreviated Cruise:
Stewart and the Constellation

After supervising the construction of the New York gunboats, Stewart was on furlough, and like many officers without orders, he pursued the merchant trade with which he was already familiar. In one instance, for example, he pursued joint interests with a fellow naval officer, Isaac Hull.[1] Between 1807 and 1812 Stewart's acumen for business allowed him to amass a small fortune, certainly enough to buy an estate in Bordentown, New Jersey, and secure a reputation as a wealthy man for the next six decades. His travels took him to the Adriatic, the East Indies, and the Mediterranean. During one of his mercantile ventures he repeated an episode he'd had as commander of the *Experiment* when, as a private citizen and businessman in the Adriatic, he managed to release several fellow Americans who had been impressed by British warships.[2]

Although peace of sorts with the Barbary States of North Africa caused a lull in U.S. naval activity, international events quickly required that the Navy and its experienced officers answer a new call.

The wartime rights of combatants and neutral countries pushed Great Britain, embroiled in a global war with Napoleon's France, and the United States, neutral since the Barbary Wars, in diametrically opposed and irreconcilable positions. Two interrelated areas of contention existed: (1) Britain aggressively attempted to prevent "contraband" goods from entering French ports, crippling American trade; and (2) British sailors continued to impress American seamen into the Royal Navy.

Britain held that "every nation has a right to enforce the services of her subjects wherever they may be found."[3] For years Britain, hard-pressed to find men for its massive and far-flung fleet, resorted to the press gang. The Royal Navy aggressively stopped the neutral shipping of other countries in the pursuit of "British" seamen who dodged their obligations as British subjects. Such was the state of affairs within the Royal Navy that many a ship's captain, finding himself short of crewmen, would stop a merchant ship and take the seamen he needed, regardless of nationality.

As a successful sailing merchant, Stewart was all too familiar with this British practice. His feelings matched those expressed in a letter that he received from his schoolboy friend Richard Rush: "Mr. Monroe says, without disguise, that a war with England is inevitable. I think we shall never cease to be colonial until it takes place."[4] Stewart shared his friend's assessment. In fact, the two men had much in common throughout their lives—both were fervent patriots. Rush finished his letter to his friend by saying, "Have you ever reflected that as soon as we come to blows, we shall be the first genuine democracy engaged in a war since the ancients?"

When America declared war in 1812, Captain Stewart left Philadelphia and his business interests, traveling to Washington to lobby for a command. As a senior captain with an excellent record, he knew he stood a good chance of returning to active service and taking command of one of the precious gems of the fleet—a big frigate. Before he assumed command of the USS *Constellation*, Stewart commanded the USS *Argus* between June and July 1812. He took both ships to sea and patrolled off the Atlantic coast, before the British blockade began to take effect.

Prior to the heady days of summer, Stewart finished some personal business. He gave a gift to his mother, a portrait of himself by one of America's great early portrait artists, Thomas Sully. Sully began the work on 10 June 1811 and finished on 13 April 1812. Art historians have recognized that during this period in American art history, "American connoisseurs judged portraits by the romantic, even theatrical, standards set by Thomas Sully. Gifted with the ability to make the difficult look easy, Sully dashed off both flattering likenesses and scenes from history with equal facility. During his eighty-nine-year life, he documented his incredible productivity in an account book that lists 2,631 paintings, of which 2,017 were portraits. According to Sully's Register, the artist's second full-length, life-size portrait was Captain Stewart."[5]

During the spring of 1812 President Madison and his cabinet were faced

Although he became a strong supporter of a naval academy, Stewart had earlier said, "The best school for the instruction of youth in the profession is the deck of a ship." (Thomas Sully; courtesy of the National Portrait Gallery)

with the overwhelming power of the Royal Navy, among other concerns. The Royal Navy numbered over one thousand sails, and its talent after nearly a full century of war made any one of its ships a formidable foe. Every English-man, and his American cousins, recognized the Royal Navy's brilliant success over such a long period of time. The potential for continued success was intimidating to those uninitiated in the history of naval warfare, especially the members of the Madison administration.

Arrayed against "England's Glory" was a fledgling U.S. Navy of only six-teen ships and the dozens of gunboats whose construction Stewart had helped to oversee.[6] All too aware of this mismatch, Madison and his cabinet ordered the tiny American fleet to make for New York, where it would be used to defend the city and port.

Shortly after his arrival in Washington, Captain Stewart, with Como. Wil-liam Bainbridge, was shown the orders effecting the president's decision to bottle up the fleet. Immediately, both men requested a meeting with Navy Secretary Paul Hamilton to lay out their argument for sending the fleet to sea, as opposed to letting it rot in the waters of U.S. harbors. With experi-ence-laden reasoning, they argued that American ships and sailors were as good as, if not better than their English counterparts. They argued that an offensive strategy would frustrate British designs, disrupt Britain's com-merce, and force its fleet to spread its resources across a broader expanse of water than just the American coast. Stewart and Bainbridge successfully won over the secretary, who in turn arranged for them to meet with the president. "Mr. Madison listened to the representations of the two captains, with attention, and observed that the experience of the Revolution confirmed their opinions."[7] Madison convened his cabinet, but the members adhered to their original recommendation. Hearing this, Stewart and Bainbridge sent a strongly worded message to President Madison, urging him to send the fleet to sea. This letter convinced the president to reject his cabinet's advice and to direct Hamilton to send the Navy to seek out the enemy, adding that he, Madison, would take sole responsibility for the decision.

On the next day, 22 June 1812, Secretary Hamilton ordered Stewart to take command of the brig USS *Argus*. The order followed President Madison's decision and reflected the spirit of Stewart's impassioned letter. "You will proceed immediately to New York and take command of the *Argus*, with her you will then proceed to sea and scour the West Indies and Gulf Stream—Consider yourself as possessing every belligerent right of attack, capture and defence of and against any of the public or private ships of the Kingdom of Great Britain, Ireland and other dependencies."[8]

Accompanying the order was a personal letter from the secretary. This

At the outbreak of the War of 1812, President Madison's cabinet, which included Navy Secretary Paul Hamilton (above), recommended that all U.S. Navy ships be sent to New York Harbor for safety. Stewart and Bainbridge convinced President Madison that the U.S. Navy should be sent to sea to challenge the might of the Royal Navy. (G.B. Matthews; courtesy of the Naval Historical Center)

letter gives a clear indication as to who really was instrumental in changing the president's mind and establishing the credentials of the U.S. Navy. "You know not how you have risen in my mind by the magnanimous conduct you exhibited yesterday. May God Almighty bless you and crown you with success and honor."[9] Stewart was on the cusp of great accomplishments, but his greatest service to his country and its Navy was performed during those first few days in June 1812.

After only a few months, which included a short war cruise off the American East Coast as the captain of the *Argus*, Stewart received new orders from Secretary Hamilton. Upon his return from searching the waters between Bermuda and the Atlantic seaboard for English commerce, Stewart was ordered to take command of the frigate USS *Constellation*, which was fitting out at the Washington Navy Yard.

Stewart was not the secretary's first choice, for at the time, the ship was under the command of Como. William Bainbridge. Bainbridge had lobbied the secretary to give him orders to the *Constitution* as her new commander. The secretary acquiesced to Bainbridge's request, but only after *Constitution*'s current commander, Capt. Isaac Hull, had taken the frigate to sea on his own volition, sailing from Boston on 2 August. This left Bainbridge in command of *Constellation* and in a sullen state. When Stewart returned to Washington to assume command, he found his frigate had not progressed very far in her refit, thanks in part to Bainbridge's poor morale.[10] There were certainly other factors that contributed to the frigate's slow preparation for a war cruise.

Constellation's refit at the Washington Navy Yard had commenced in March 1812, months before the war declaration. Capt. Thomas Tingey was the Navy yard's commandant and his inspection of the frigate in March found the ship in a very bad condition. He quickly realized that the funding Congress had allocated for the frigate's refit would not cover her repairs. Compounding the lack of funding was a general lack of artisans, materials, and ships' equipment.[11] Everything was in short supply. In addition, Captain Tingey had been operating without a naval constructor for three years; his relationships with several constructors had been difficult. So with the lack of resources and personnel, Stewart's future command was brought back into fighting condition in a painfully slow fashion.[12]

Although faced with a considerable amount of work to get his command ready for sea, Stewart felt a strong sense of accomplishment, joy, and pride in being captain of such a ship. However, his feelings were likely tempered by his strong sense of accountability and responsibility in assuming command of "the favourite of the fleet."[13] After all, Preble had called him his most staunch and dependable officer, raising expectations for Stewart's performance in the new war.

When Stewart stepped aboard *Constellation*, a ship he knew well, he not only had the immediate duty to continue the preparations for getting his ship to sea, but he had the never-ending challenges of acquiring enough quality seamen to man his frigate and enough quality officers to lead them. Stewart and the Navy had a difficult time competing against America's private navies to recruit able seamen. The lure of the privateer was difficult to counter, but because of his excellent reputation and previous exploits, Stewart was able to recruit a number of qualified seamen.

For junior officers, Stewart had to select promising midshipmen from an overstocked midshipman's berth. The *Constellation* had a very large excess of midshipmen, and Charles had to decide which of the thirty assigned to the frigate would remain. Mid. Josiah Tattnall was one of those asked to leave, and he thought Stewart's criteria unfair. "When the *Constellation* was ready for sea, it was found necessary to detach a number of the Midshipmen. . . . The selection of such as were to remain was left to the Captain, Stewart. . . . To my chagrin I was one of those detached."[14] Tattnall had thought that being the longest-serving midshipman on board the ship, he would be selected before all the other midshipmen. Instead, Stewart picked the most experienced, though he made sure that those not selected found a good berth, and he provided for the young Tattnall such a berth aboard a smaller man-of-war. However, what occurred next said a great deal about both men.

Having family influence with Navy Secretary Paul Hamilton, Tattnall immediately obtained a meeting with the secretary, during which he lobbied for his return to the "favourite of the fleet." His efforts proved successful, for Secretary Hamilton wrote him a new set of orders for the *Constellation*. With orders in hand, the brash young Tattnall returned to the ship. When Tattnall reported on board and made his way to the ship's great cabin, Captain Stewart, sitting behind his desk, looked up to find his former midshipman, whom he had just successfully transferred to a good ship, with orders from the secretary, directing the captain to take this officer on board. According to Tattnall, Captain Stewart read the orders and was very cool. He dismissed the young officer. Tattnall, misjudging the demeanor of his captain and believing he'd been rejected by Stewart returned to his boarding house room in dismay. After three days the frigate's boatswain arrived at the boarding house, informing Midshipman Tattnall that the captain wished to speak with him. Feeling a sense of dread, the young Tattnall returned on board. Again,

Josiah Tattnall was one of Stewart's midshipmen on the *Constellation* during the defense of Norfolk in 1813. During the Civil War, Tattnall commanded the CSS *Virginia*. (Unattributed; courtesy of the Naval Historical Center)

finding himself in the ship's great cabin, he was shocked to hear Stewart asking why he had not moved himself on board three days before. Thus began young Tattnall's relationship with Stewart, which continued for decades, until the commencement of the American Civil War. Their relationship played a significant role in the *Constellation*'s fate during the following months.

Stewart placed the *Constellation* into commission on 10 October, but the ship did not get under way from her wharf-side berth on the Anacostia River until 6 November. "Captain Tingey's logistical problems at the yard caused by shortages of materials, equipment, and ordinance delayed the completion of Constellation."[15] Another twenty-eight days passed before the frigate finally took on her great guns and provisions for sea. "On the morning of November 6, with eight launches towing her, assisted by gunboats and laborers from the yard, the frigate was hauled off downriver. At a position below Greenleaf Point on the Potomac River, she stuck fast on a mud bar and moored. Gunboats delivered anchors, guns, and provisions, which the ship's booms hoisted aboard where she lay down-stream."[16] Because of the shortage in naval stores, the provisioning of the frigate continued for the next twenty days. When completed, Stewart formally presented the fleet's favorite to President and Mrs. Madison, Secretary Hamilton, and members of Congress at a grand party set on board the frigate on 26 November.

65

On 8 December Stewart received additional and unexpected praise for his decisive action that persuaded President Madison and his cabinet to send the fleet to sea. He and his officers were honored guests at a ball given by the city of Washington. As a surprise to all in attendance, Midshipman Hamilton, the son of the secretary, entered the hall carrying the flag of HMS *Macedonian* and dispatches from Capt. Stephen Decatur stating that he had captured the British frigate. The flag was unrolled at the feet of President Madison and First Lady Dolly Madison. With a touch of drama, Midshipman Hamilton then read the dispatch detailing the battle to all those assembled. A joyous celebration followed, with the cheering reaching its highest level after Secretary Hamilton stated to the president and the revelers that "it is to Captains Bainbridge and Stewart you owe your naval victories."[17]

At least one contemporary historian has criticized Stewart for his apparent preoccupation with lobbying the Madison administration and Congress, instead of tending to his duties as the *Constellation*'s commanding officer. In his book *USS* Constellation: *From Frigate to Sloop of War*, Geoffrey Footner implies that had Stewart dedicated his energies to getting the *Constellation* to sea earlier, the fate that awaited the frigate could have been avoided.[18] In addition to the factors previously covered that directly delayed the frigate's fitting out, Stewart had to divide his attention between his duties as the frigate's commanding officer and his duties as one of the Navy's most senior and capable uniformed officers. He found himself walking through the Capitol's corridors, lobbying on behalf of his service and the war effort.[19] By the end of the year Stewart received personal gratification for his tireless efforts.

Navy Secretary Paul Hamilton relied on Stewart's wisdom, experience, and knowledge of ships. Hamilton's official line of questions included those about the relative efficiency of ships-of-the-line versus frigates and those of frigates versus sloops. In the case of the former, Stewart suggested the relative force of a ship-of-the-line (seventy-four guns) was one to three (based on three fifty-gun frigates), and one to two in terms of the latter, an estimate he was to prove in battle little more than two years later. Stewart's detailed argument supporting his answer was likely one of the reasons Hamilton and the department later pursued the construction of ships-of-the-line, particularly because Stewart noted that they were the best for defense of coasts and the protection of commerce; after all it could not be supposed that a foreign power would only send frigates and smaller cruisers to U.S. coasts.

The lobbying duties he assumed were certainly unofficial. But being a senior officer present, he felt compelled to continue his lobbying efforts at several governmental levels.

At the executive level, the president did not have a clear mandate for prosecuting the war that he asked Congress to declare. In fact, during the summer and autumn months of 1812, Madison could not forge ahead with the naval strategy that Stewart and other senior naval officers championed because he did not have the votes in Congress, where many members were preoccupied with the idea of invading Canada. Stewart was active in the halls of Congress lobbying on behalf of the Navy, and after the congressional elections in November, Madison was granted the necessary authority. Also, the execution of the Navy's part of the war strategy was burdened by the Navy secretary's alcoholism. Paul Hamilton's disease increasingly made him ineffective as secretary and forced him to resign before the end of the year. Stewart was certainly not blind to Hamilton's troubles. Although funding was available to get the present fleet to sea, the impaired Navy secretary could not convince Congress to provide the financial backing for a balanced fleet. This is likely why the *Constellation*'s captain became so involved in the overarching issues facing the fleet, to include showcasing American naval power by holding a gala party for the political elite of the day on a modern frigate. The Navy further benefited when Midshipman Hamilton arrived at the 8 December gala with the colors of HMS *Macedonian*, which were laid at the feet of the president. Finally, Stewart and his brother officers, Captains Hull and Morris, lingered in Washington long enough to ensure the passing of legislation on 23 December that authorized the expansion of the Navy.

With the passing of this legislation, Stewart took *Constellation* down the Potomac. Heavy icing on the river had made it increasingly dangerous for Stewart to keep his frigate near Washington. Although far from being completely satisfied with the quality of the yard work, he had every hope of clearing the Chesapeake before the British blockade sealed the estuary shut.[20] No news had reached Stewart that the British ships of Admiral Warren's consolidated Caribbean and North American stations were operating in the Chesapeake.[21] In fact, no British warships were covering the Chesapeake Bay at this time, as the Royal Navy was having considerable difficulty establishing the blockade.[22]

Stewart sailed *Constellation* down the Potomac with orders from the newly appointed Navy secretary, William Jones, to take his frigate to Annapolis, Maryland, to check the quality of the gunpowder that was taken on board during the Washington yard period.[23] For Stewart, this order offered an opportunity to rectify some of the repair deficiencies that were not taken care of during the yard period. Stewart stayed in weather-exposed Annapolis Roads until 23 January 1813, when severe icing conditions forced him to sail farther south. He left with orders in hand from the secretary to continue the testing of the frigate's gunpowder, and proceed to Norfolk, Virginia, to receive additional communication from the Navy Department. The consequences of these delays ruined Stewart's and the *Constellation*'s chances for a successful breakout into the Atlantic.

The *Constellation* arrived off Hampton Roads late on 2 February and anchored for the night. Stewart planned to sail into Norfolk with the new day and tide. However, just after sunrise, a harbor pilot informed Stewart and the Constellations that a British squadron was spotted entering the bay.[24] Stewart ordered *Constellation* to weigh anchor and set her course toward Cape Henry to determine the force aligned against him.[25] Seeing that he could not escape, Stewart came about and proceeded to Norfolk. He realized that his frigate could not break out into the Atlantic against clearly superior forces. For the moment, they were trapped.

Time, tide, and wind were not on his side. Stewart had to act fast because he felt the British squadron under Admiral Warren would surely try to take advantage of its numbers, the changing tide, and the wind to attack his ship. With the tide ebbing, Stewart ordered his crew to sail toward Norfolk, and then to kedge her farther up into the roads until she was grounded on the tidal flats. He did this to prevent the larger British ships from following, gambling that the British lacked the detailed knowledge of Hampton Roads and that they would not risk grounding as well. The seeming "luck of the *Constellation*" contributed to its successful evasion. The British commander might not have recognized the frigate because winter lighting conditions prevented her identification. Also, with the American frigate blocked, there was little reason to leave their effective blockading position and risk letting other American warships, privateers, and merchantmen breakout into the open sea. The frigate could be dealt with later, and after all, Admiral Warren was under considerable pressure by the Admiralty to show results, which meant maintaining a blockade of the Chesapeake was his highest priority.[26]

With the flood tide, *Constellation* floated free. Before the British could mount an attack, Stewart brought his frigate up to Norfolk and anchored her between the city's two seaward-facing forts late on 4 February. Over the next few months Stewart struggled to establish cooperative interaction between land and naval forces for mutual defense.

The shock of seeing the British squadron certainly took its toll on Stewart's morale and on his crew. Shortly after his arrival in Norfolk, Stewart wrote a situation report for Secretary Jones in which he expressed his doubt as to what should be done next.[27] Stewart and his officers then conferred with Norfolk's defenders to determine a course of action. Together with Capt. John Cassin, the superintendent of Gosport Navy Yard, and local army and state militia officers, they established a defensive plan. All parties agreed that additional defensive positions should be constructed, especially on Craney Island. As a result of the decision to defend Norfolk, its environs, and the *Constellation*, Stewart sailed the *Constellation* back down the Elizabeth River to anchor her near Craney Island so that the ship could cover the construction of fortifications on the island.[28] To everyone's surprise, the British squadron did not attempt to close on the lone American frigate. However, to Stewart's disappointment and increasing frustration, construction of the island's defensive positions proceeded slowly. With March rapidly giving way to better spring weather, Stewart knew time was running out before the British would conduct an all-out assault.

Stewart placed his ship at a narrow point in the channel, running very close to the east end of Craney Island near where a battery of guns would be positioned. To the east of *Constellation*'s anchored position was a relatively large expanse of shallow water, followed by the low shoreline and entrance to Tanner's Creek.[29] One wonders if Como. Josiah Tattnall, who commanded the ironclad CSS *Virginia* fifty years later, thought of his early days on board the *Constellation*, when he ran his ironclad aground near the very same place that Captain Stewart positioned his frigate to meet the British.[30]

With the *Constellation* anchored in the middle of the channel, an array of Jefferson gunboats, seven on either side of the frigate, also moored. Stewart directed that a circle of booms be constructed and secured around each gunboat nest. He then dispersed his officers and men to man the gunboats. The resulting hedgehog defense secured the *Constellation*'s flanks. This tactic spread shipmates across the multiple hulls blocking the channel, for Stewart realized that if attacked, the ship stood a better chance if defended by fellow shipmates, acting as one.

Stewart then turned his attention to making his frigate into a floating fortress. Again, he had to act quickly because he was not sure of the British squadron's intentions. He secured *Constellation*'s main gun deck and sealed her individual gun ports. He then ensured that nothing on the ship's hull or in her rigging could assist a British boarding party's ability to climb on board. He had the ship's running rigging and upper yards removed, and also removed the stern ladders and boarding cleats. Stewart directed that boarding nets made of twenty-one thread ratlines be woven and then boiled in watered-down pitch so that they would be impervious to cutting. Adding to the nets' strength, nail rods and chain were strung between the horizontal rungs of each net. He then directed the nets to be triced up out board of the ship and suspended by the fore, main, and mizzen yards of the ship, and from her bowsprit, spiritsail yard, and forestay. Before these nets were rigged, heavy kentledge was added at the out board edge of each net. Once hoisted into position, the deployed nets had sufficient weight that, in the event of a boarding party coming close aboard, the cutting of the supporting tricing lines would cause the heavy nets to crash on the assailants' heads, trapping them and crushing their boats.

Stewart reinforced his ship's defense by positioning the foc'sle and quarterdeck carronades so that they could sweep as close aboard the ship as possible. Each carronade was loaded to the muzzle with musketballs and depressed as far as each one would bear. Coupled with these steps to harden his ship against assault, he lightened her of all unnecessary weight. This raised the *Constellation* and exposed the downward curve of her hull, thus adding to the frustration of a boarding party trying to find handholds along the ship.[31] "It was the opinion of the best judges, that defended as she would certainly have been, under the officers who were with her, she could not have been carried without a loss of several hundred men to the enemy."[32]

These preparations were completed by spring. Incredible as it seemed, the British squadron did nothing to interfere with the construction of these defenses. Three assaults were attempted, and the *Constellation*'s crew discovered each one before they could be executed. Finally, with the land defenses strengthened and block ships in position to be sunk across the channel, Stewart moved his frigate up toward Norfolk proper. It is ironic that his action before Norfolk in no small part secured the port from the British. Its capture would have caused the American effort in the Chesapeake considerable distress. In addition, the loss of Norfolk would have given the British a base of operations and would have deprived the United States of the Gosport Navy Yard. Comparing Stewart's defense of Norfolk with his subsequent achievements on board *Constitution*, his imaginative and inspired actions to secure *Constellation* and merge her into Norfolk's overall defense stand out in their consequences.

In a final act of defiance and justice, Stewart wrote to Admiral of the Blue Sir John Warren, who commanded the British force, to denounce the detention by Commodore Beresford of two American sailors returning from Jamaica on parole as prisoners of war (they had been on board the *Vixen*). "This violation of the rights of prisoners on parole," he wrote, "is so contrary to the usage of civilized nations, that I trust your Excellency will give instructions upon that head as will prevent a similar violation in future."[33] Stewart also noted that four British subjects would be selected and held, subject to the same treatment as the American sailors, in U.S. response to the British act.

Captain Cockburn of the HMS *Marlborough*, responding on behalf of Admiral Warren, denied any knowledge of the detention and suggested an inquiry would have been made had it not been for Stewart's threat. The matter was later resolved, but yet again, Stewart made demands on behalf of American sailors in the face of overwhelming odds.

CHAPTER FIVE

USS Constitution

In May Charles Stewart left the USS *Constellation*, which was still besieged in Norfolk, upon orders to take command of the USS *Constitution,* which was then fitting out at the Boston Navy Yard. His arrival was noted by the yard's commandant, Como. William Bainbridge, in his letter to the Navy secretary dated 22 June 1813, which simply stated that "Captain Charles Stewart arrived this date," and that "the ship is ready to heave out for recoppering." On the twenty-fourth, Stewart relieved Commodore Bainbridge as the ship's commanding officer. He worked through the rest of the year preparing the ship for sea.

His preparations were thorough and again innovative. An example of this can be seen in his correspondence to the Navy secretary, dated 5 December 1813:

> I have constructed a portable sheet iron furnace for heating red hot shot of the following dimensions which would answer as well for land service as sea service. . . . The construction of the pipe is such as it gives it a great draught. From its dimensions you can readily conceive it occupies little room, and is calculated to set to the back of our Galley where it interferes with nothing—My purpose is only to use it against the enemy's ships of such force as would render our safety precarious, (if we cannot otherwise escape) by bringing them under our stern battery and firing red hot shot in their hull. They are not very expensive and all our frigates having them, the use of which might facilitate their escape from a superior force by the confusion they would be thrown into,

if not the destruction of an enemy that is not disposed to contend with us on fair and equal terms.

The importance of Stewart's invention lay not in that it represented something new, for red-hot shot had been used in the past, but that he considered it a tool of last resort, a tool to be used to preserve one of the nation's preciously few frigates. This attitude was not only a reflection of his own integrity; it can also be seen in the series of orders he received from the Navy secretary.[1]

Stewart also modified how the ship's beef provision was stowed. Traditionally, meats were stowed individually in barrels of salt. Instead, he had built two large stowage tanks with the beef and salt packed inside.[2]

With summer coming to an end, Stewart received orders from Navy Secretary William Jones specifically detailing what was expected from the ship. These orders reflected the changing fortunes of the United States at sea during this pivotal year of the war, and in no uncertain terms they restricted Stewart's choices in sending his ship to sea. The final directive, dated 19 September, shows the mind of the secretary and President Madison:

> The United States Frigate *Constitution* . . . must ere this be nearly ready for sea, and as it is desirable to take the first fair opportunity, after the Equinox to push into the open Ocean. . . . As the enemy appears to be correctly apprised of our intended operations, he will doubtless ascertain the precise period of your intended departure and probably blockade or station a competent force near you. It will be prudent therefore to put to sea only under circumstances of the most favorable nature. . . . Should any attempt be made to allure you by a challenge to single combat, I am directed by the President to prohibit strictly the acceptance either directly or indirectly.

The recent loss of the USS *Chesapeake* to HMS *Shannon* was certainly on the president's mind, and it was certainly on Stewart's mind also, because he had been one of Capt. James Lawrence's pallbearers, when the *Chesapeake*'s captain was returned from Halifax, Nova Scotia, for burial. Secretary Jones's orders continued:

> When you shall meet upon equal terms without premeditation with your crew practiced and disciplined, his confidence in your skill and gallantry is entire, and no apprehensions are entertained for the honor for the flag, and the safety of the precious ship entrusted to your care.[3]

These orders reflect the United States' concerns with how the war was faring. Two distinct military campaigns had been waged during 1813. The first was a serious challenge to America. The Royal Navy swept up the Chesapeake Bay. Through successive littoral operations, to include the continued blockade of Norfolk, which still harbored *Constellation,* the Royal Navy cleared the great bay of opposition, ending waterborne commerce, disrupting fishing, and harrassing the countryside. In marked contrast to this humiliating campaign against the heart of the new republic, the culmination of the second campaign proved an extremely positive event for the country and the small U.S. Navy. The northern campaign against British Canada ended with Como. Oliver Hazard Perry's great victory on Lake Erie.

The consequences of both campaigns delayed Stewart's cruise. A tighter blockade by the Royal Navy against the U.S. coastline prevented America's merchant houses, ranging from Savannah, Georgia, up the coast to the city of Portland (then still a port of Massachusetts) from moving their goods to markets overseas. The blockade of Boston forced Stewart to wait for winter to attempt a breakout.

The needs of the Lake Erie campaign resulted in serious competition for the few able seamen and stores at the disposal of the fledgling Navy and *Constitution.* Volunteers were nearly impossible to find. "Lake service was an anathema to deep-water sailors."[4] Commodore Bainbridge, now commandant of the Boston Navy Yard, had ordered successive drafts of men during the spring and summer from the ships and craft present, including Stewart's command. They traveled cross-country to join Commodore Chauncey's and, later, Commodore Perry's Lakes Squadron. The self-inflicted wound to Boston's defense added to Stewart's concerns, but proved decisive in the outcome of America's fortunes upon the Great Lakes.

Stewart's life was not just a series of professional duties. After all, this extremely eligible thirty-three-year-old had social responsibilities too. As a senior naval officer and a prosperous merchant, Stewart was in the midst of Boston high society. Stewart realized that he could find someone suitable to marry in this town.

During the fitting out of the *Constellation*, Stewart had met Miss Virginia Mayo, eleven years his junior. She later became the wife of Gen. Winfield Scott, a contemporary of his, and the future commanding general of the U.S. Army. Stewart had sought her hand, but the lady saw him as only one of many suitors.

Boston was not Washington, however, and years before, a fortune-teller had told Charles that he would marry "the belle of Boston." Little did he know the truth of the seer's prediction, for in the summer of 1813 he met Miss Delia Tudor, and they were married in November the same year. Just before the *Constitution*'s departure, Stewart's bride asked him to bring back a British frigate. Stewart responded that he would bring her two.

Finally the day of departure had arrived. After a considerable effort to get the *Constitution* ready for sea, Stewart had an opportunity to execute his orders. A winter gale had blown the blockading British ships from the outer reaches of Boston Harbor, allowing Stewart to sortie. He had to act quickly because he had no idea how far the British ships lay off the harbor, or how long it would take them to regain their station off the port. The *Constitution*'s log briefly and with typical naval understatement read, "31 Dec 1813: 3 pm Sailed from Boston."

From Boston, Stewart steered the *Constitution* south-southeast heading toward the northern coast of South America. On this course, Stewart intended to continue south until the ship picked up the westerly trade winds and then to skirt westward along the Venezuelan coast. Following the directive set by the Navy secretary, the *Constitution* would then enter the Caribbean between Windward Islands and the Venezuelan coast.

The first two weeks of the cruise saw the loss of one of the ship's crew, who fell overboard and drowned on 4 January 1814. On 8 January the *Constitution* experienced "rolling heavy seas" common to the North Atlantic in the dead of winter. This entry to the log, with other entries about how wet the ship was in rolling seas, made it clear to Stewart that the *Constitution* possessed deficiencies in addition to the well-documented strengths that made her and her sisters the most capable of frigates. Howard Chapelle's *The History of the American Sailing Navy* highlights the problems the heavy frigates possessed, among them, their tendency to be very wet in moderate rolling seas. Years later, in a letter dated 30 November 1842, to the then-Navy secretary, Capt. Foxhall A. Parker reported upon his return from a twenty-one-day cruise "that shortly after getting underway, [the crew] discovered several leaks which rendered the wardroom, steerage and berth deck very uncomfortable, driving the officers from their rooms and wetting the men's clothing. Had the weather been cold, the crew would have been rendered helpless."

A copy of the letter was also sent to Commodore Stewart, who by that time was the commander of the U.S. Navy's Home Squadron. This report would have certainly reminded the older Stewart of his own experience of cruising on board the *Constitution*.

On the morning of 14 January Stewart gave chase to his first two un-known sails. The first turned out to be the American schooner *Regulator*. By 11 A.M. he gave chase to the second. Pressing on all canvas, only darkness and the springing of both fore-topmast studding sail booms prevented the *Constitution* from catching the unknown ship.

The next day brought successive disappointments. They began early, around 7 A.M., when the *Constitution*'s lookouts spotted another sail and Stewart ordered his crew to the chase. Unfortunately, the ship turned out to be the twenty-gun Portuguese sloop-of-war *Adriana*. That afternoon, Stew-art lost another man, Quarter Gunner Thomas Courtney, who died of ty-phus. That evening, the ship's chaplain conducted the burial service. By this time in the cruise, the ship's log exhibited a developing theme of bad luck that certainly wore on the crew's morale.

Through the remainder of January, Stewart continued to steer *Constitu-tion* farther south toward the westerly trades. The log entries were very brief, recording only his ship's position, and the deaths and injuries of four more of his crew. One, BM Richard Ormerod, was wounded during the exercis-ing of the great guns when his pistol accidentally discharged while it was tucked into his belt. The log simply recorded the event as a "pistol going off at half cock in his belt wounded him severely in the thigh." Nothing else was mentioned of the incident. The remaining log entries for the month also recorded that the *Constitution* had chased three more sails. All eluded Stewart's efforts to catch them. Stewart's log also provides another glimpse into the *Constitution*'s sailing manner. On 26 January he wrote, "the ship rolling deep but easy and taking in a good deal of water at her gun deck ports."

The first day of February 1814 found Stewart steering the *Constitution* on a westerly heading. Picking up the westerly blowing trade winds, she sailed along the South American coast and due east of Georgetown, Guyana. At 2 P.M. lookouts reported a sail. Stewart must have sensed that warmer weather and a new month would change his ship's luck. The chase did not last long. With the coast in sight, the unknown ship had run herself inshore. Fearing his deep draft frigate would run aground, Stewart quickly wore away to seaward. Two days later, while the *Constitution* was just north of George-town, Guyana, positioned to intercept shipping entering or leaving the port, he gave chase to another unknown sail. In the early morning of 3 February the *Constitution* began to chase the eighteen-gun brig-of-war HMS *Mos-quito*. The chase lasted until 4:30 P.M., when the *Mosquito* appeared to deliberately run herself aground. This action prevented Stewart's ship from closing as the shallows again proved too dangerous to risk. The frustration for all on board the *Constitution* was certainly building by now. Another five days passed before they saw another sail and a fresh opportunity for a change of luck.

The *Constitution* was steering due north from Georgetown and east of the Lesser Antilles. On the afternoon of 8 February, lookouts spotted what was thought to be a British packet. The *Constitution* was able to gain ground very rapidly on this type of ship, but nightfall ended the chase. Later, Stewart found out that this packet was actually a British man-of-war. The eighteen-gun brig-of-war HMS *Columbine* had escaped. This was dutifully noted in the log, and Stewart intuitively added that she would likely alert Admiral Durham's squadron, which Stewart believed was operating windward of Barbados. Although not stated in his log, Stewart realized he had to do something to change the ship's luck, or the morale of the ship would suffer even more. On 11 February, in a deliberate effort to change his fortunes, Stewart ordered the ship to heave to and instructed the crew to change the frigate's paint scheme. He had the white stripe that marked the main gun deck along her hull painted yellow to give the *Constitution*, at a distance, the appearance of a British man-of-war. Stewart's order was a calculated effort at deception that the captain hoped would allow the *Constitution* to get closer to an unknown sail, before the ship would attempt to flee from his grasp, and it apparently helped, for on the evening of 13 February, Stewart and the *Constitution*'s luck changed.

At 11 P.M. the *Constitution* took up the chase of two sails. The pursuit continued past midnight on 14 February, when the British merchant, the *Lovely Ann,* was "prized." She carried lumber, fish, and flour. At 8:45 A.M. Stewart was able to sail his frigate close enough to fire a shot through the sails of the second craft, the eighteen-gun schooner HMS *Picton*. She hove to and surrendered without a fight. Taking the crew from the *Picton*, Stewart ordered the transfer of its crew to the *Lovely Ann*, and he directed Mid. Pardon Mawney Whipple to take the prize to Barbados. There, Whipple released *Picton*'s crew to be paroled under a flag of truce. Then Midshipman Whipple presented the British merchant for assessment by a prize agent. With the midshipman, his prize crew, and the captured seaman aboard the *Lovely Ann*, Stewart ordered HMS *Picton* burned.

Stewart and the officers and men of the *Constitution* may have thought their luck continued to improve, because two days after their double success, Stewart turned *Constitution* westward toward Tobago and, in the morning light of 17 February, he was again in pursuit of another sail. This time he took the schooner *Phoenix* as a prize. She carried lumber and official dispatches. After the captured crew was taken on board the *Constitution*, the schooner was scuttled.

Later that day Stewart sighted Grenada. He had hoped the waters off this island would bring additional success, but he departed empty-handed. However, on 18 February Stewart wrote in *Constitution*'s log that one shot from *Constitution*'s bow chaser forced the British brig *Catherine* to stop. The ship was scuttled after a thorough search was made for dispatches and worthwhile cargo.

While continuing northwestward and then up along the east side of the West Indies, *Constitution* passed St. Croix and Puerto Rico without any additional captures. At this time, Stewart transferred the crews of the *Phoenix* and the *Catherine* to a Swedish merchantman that was heading for the West Indies.

The twenty-third of February proved to be a busy but, again, frustrating day. At 10 A.M. Stewart was in pursuit of what appeared to be another merchantman. Both ships passed through the Mona Passage, with *Constitution* slowly gaining on the fleeing vessel. By 4 P.M. Stewart saw that she was a frigate. Suddenly, the winds died away for this unknown frigate, and *Constitution* rapidly closed the range. Stewart counted fourteen gun ports at the gun-deck level and thought that she could be the USS *President*. In the fading light, Stewart ordered a day signal to be sent to the unknown ship. The frigate returned the signal by hoisting British colors and firing a gun to windward. Stewart quickly responded by steering his frigate toward the British frigate's port quarter. Once gaining this advantage, he apparently intended to veer off the British frigate's quarter and level a measured broadside into the ship. He ordered *Constitution*'s foresail set for light wind and sent down her royals. Afterward, Stewart noted in the log that at this moment, both ships simultaneously cleared for action. The frustration of frustrations came for Stewart and his men when *Constitution* too became becalmed in the twilight. Now the British frigate, which Stewart identified as the thirty-six-gun HMS *Pique*, got the breeze and made sail. By 7:15 P.M. *Pique* was nearly out of sight. Stewart found the wind and continued his pursuit into the light of the next morning. But, HMS *Pique* gave him the slip. The rest of February offered no additional sightings.

In the first two weeks of March *Constitution* sailed slowly northwestward. Stewart intended to brush the Bahamas, hoping to catch additional prizes. He continued northwestward until *Constitution* lay off of Charleston, South Carolina, on 13 March. His sightings were few and neutral. During this time,

Stewart logged three additional deaths from *Constitution*'s crew. After lingering off the Carolina coast for a brief period, Stewart continued on orders and headed eastward into the Atlantic.

After passing due east and south of Bermuda for ten days, *Constitution* found no sail to pursue. He must have expected that this particular heading might promise some reward, because *Constitution*'s course was astride the primary sailing route for British shipping coming from the West Indies past Bermuda. Having Bermuda to his northwest and failing to make any sighting, Stewart steered northward. This change of course laid *Constitution* astride of the shipping lanes connecting Bermuda with Britain. Three days later a serious deficiency to the ship's integrity as a fighting sail was unexpectedly discovered.

On 26 March Stewart entered in his log that a serious crack, which extended from the neck of the mast all the way down to the fife rail, was observed in *Constitution*'s mainmast. For all on board, this was a major surprise because Stewart and the crew had gone over the frigate's fitting out with a fine-tooth comb. The crack must have been a product of a deficiency in the inner workings of the lower mast, which comprised more than two-dozen pieces, arranged about a central spindle and united by mast hoops. The next day Stewart again noted in the ship's log, "the mainmast was still very much bent although the stops were slack." He further noted on that day that *Constitution* ran into a heavy squall. With a defective mast, this abrupt change in the weather must have caused some anxious moments for Stewart and the crew.

Having to continue eastward toward a heavily defended eastern Atlantic with an obviously defective mast, and presented with the increasing probability that the frigate's next sail would not be one to pursue, but one of pursued, Stewart made the weighty decision to return to Boston.

Heading due north, *Constitution* found herself off of Cape Cod and over the George's Bank on a foggy April Fools' Day 1814. In deciding a course for *Constitution*, Stewart now had to consider the very real likelihood the next sail or two to appear would be British men-of-war. Stewart knew the coast was still in a wintry grip and that a close blockade by the Royal Navy would be difficult to maintain before Boston Harbor. He also knew that if the Royal Navy was blockading the coast, it was doing so with mostly its smaller vessels (brigs, frigates, and possibly smaller craft). *Constitution* could handle these, even with a defective mainmast. Stewart recognized his chances of returning to Boston to effect repairs were good. He also figured that if he could effect a quick repair, he had a good chance of returning to sea, because he also recognized that many of the British first-rate ships would still be off the French coast.

On 3 April *Constitution* was heading for Portsmouth, but at sunrise the wind shifted and Stewart steered toward Boston. By 8 A.M. the wind had almost completely died out. Shortly after the changing the watch, the lookouts sighted two sails standing toward the ship. There was no doubt as to their nationality. They were the two thirty-eight-gun frigates, HMS *Tenedos* and HMS *Junon*. Still becalmed, Stewart knew he was in a tight spot, and he ordered the setting of skysails and royal studding sails. No one on board knew the channel between Baker's Island and the Misery, which could have run the *Constitution* directly into Salem. Because no one had such knowledge and Stewart did not have a pilot, the *Constitution* was now the pursued. *Tenedos* and *Junon* closed the range rapidly to only three and a half miles astern. Soon, the still-becalmed *Constitution* would be in range of their pursuers' bow chasers, and disaster would come with a lucky shot to the rigging. At 10 A.M. Stewart's luck began to change when *Constitution* finally caught a breeze, but without a pilot he had to hold to his course, even with the risk of being cut off.

The British ships had the wind and were coming up fast, so Stewart began lightening his ship by throwing overboard the most replaceable items—the fresh water, spare spars, and some salted beef. This was accomplished in quick order, and just after Stewart ordered the ship's spirits to be thrown over the side, he noticed the British were no longer gaining. In fact, *Constitution* was opening the range on its two pursuers. Around noon, *Constitution* turned around Halfway Rock and bore for Marblehead. A life-long Salem resident, Nathanial Silsbee, who was eight years old at the time, recounted in the *Salem Register* on 28 July 1879 what followed next.

On hearing the news that the British had chased an American frigate into the bay, Nathaniel and his father hopped into their horse-drawn chaise and drove up Essex Street to see what was happening. On their way up the hill they met the chairman of Salem's Selectmen, who told them that "the frigate *Constitution* has been chased into Marblehead—we mean to defend her and we want all the men and all the guns you can send us."[5] The chairman asked young Silsbee's father to carry the message to the authorities. Mr. Silsbee immediately turned his chaise around and headed for General Hovey's residence. Hovey ordered the great guns to be hauled out of the gun house where they were stored and brought forward through the town as quickly as horse teams and men could be organized.

Meanwhile, the citizens of Marblehead were gathering toward the town's fort. They were worried, seeing three frigates bearing down upon the town. According to Silsbee's account, the *Constitution*'s ensign could not be seen, and the townspeople believed they "could be all enemies."[6] In an extremely tense moment, the frigate came abreast of the fort that protected the town, and the guns in the fort were brought to bear against the intruder, whose ensign was still hidden from view. Realizing the town couldn't identify his vessel, Stewart ordered a seaman aloft, "lay out on the mizzen peak, and clear the stars and stripes from the sail." Once the ensign was seen unfurled, "a shout, which rang through all the ships, went up from the shore, and the *Constitution* was safe."[7] The rejoicing was especially enthusiastic because the townspeople knew that many of the ship's company came from nearby Marblehead. *Constitution* remained for some days in Salem Harbor, and "a public ball was given to Captain Stewart and his officers in Franklin Hall."[8]

When the conditions were right, Stewart slipped out of Salem Harbor and returned to Boston. Thus the abbreviated and frustrating cruise came to an end. Within a few days of his arrival in Boston, Stewart's disappointment and frustration were replaced with consternation and no slight feeling of embarrassment, when he received notification to appear before a court of inquiry, which required him to answer for his early return from his cruise.

Captain Stewart received an unexpected response from the Navy secretary to his 4 April report spelling out the events of the cruise and the reasons for his return. In accordance with procedure, he forwarded the report via the senior officer in the area, Commodore Bainbridge. Bainbridge, who harbored no love for Stewart (or any of the surviving officers who "starred" in the Barbary War while he languished as a prisoner of war), saw an opportunity for a little maliciousness and recommended a court of inquiry to Secretary Jones. Jones's letter dated 19 April 1814 found Stewart's report inadequate and two days later another letter ordered a court of inquiry with Bainbridge as president. Stewart was primarily charged with aborting his six-month cruise without sufficient cause, i.e., because of poor judgment. There was also the matter of the unauthorized beef tanks.

When the court convened on 2 May, it had only one other member besides the commodore: newly promoted Capt. Oliver Hazard Perry, ordered to Boston from his new duty station at Newport, Rhode Island. Stewart opened his defense by establishing that scurvy had been breaking out in the crew, that some provisions had proved to be in inadequate supply and the crew had refused to submit to reduced rations, that water was becoming a problem, that some sails were not in as good a condition as had been thought, and of course, that the mainmast was threatening to give way. He capped his defense presentation by pointing out that, early return notwithstanding, his recently completed cruise was the longest any unit of the Navy had endured between port calls during the war.

As Stewart was recounting the problems he had encountered with matters relating to the outfitting of the ship for war service, Bainbridge seems to have become concerned that some of the criticisms reflected on his performance as commander of the outfitting yard and that he could be caught in fallout. At that point, his focus zeroed in on the beef-tanks matter. (Captain Perry had little to say during the course of proceedings and had no effect on the direction they took.) After puffing the matter up to his satisfaction and getting testimony—his own—on the record that had he known about the tanks he would have forbidden their installation, the commodore recessed the court and prepared a report for the secretary. Its opinion was predictably political:

> The reasons assigned by Captain Stewart in his narrative and statements before the Court do not appear to this Court to comprise sufficient cause for his return . . . yet the Court believes that Captain Stewart considered them reasons sufficient to justify his return; and if he has erred it is in the opinion of this Court that it was an error in judgment.

There would be no court-martial, and nothing so egregious had been said that Stewart would seek redress. The secretary's action was merely to echo the opinion of the court.

The adverse view taken of his beef-tank experiment deterred Captain Stewart's bent for innovation not one whit. Before the year was out, taking advantage of a passing opportunity, he landed four of his carronades and replaced them with two newly cast twenty-four-pounder shifting gunades, one each on the forecastle and quarterdeck in the forward- and aftermost ports. He also requested delivery of a number of multibarreled Chambers swivel guns from Philadelphia, an early form of machine gun capable of firing more than a hundred musket balls with just one pull of the trigger. It isn't clear that any of the swivel guns were delivered, but one English officer prisoner in 1815 reported having seen one resting atop the capstan.

Stewart immediately threw himself into preparing his frigate for sea. Again, many of the same challenges of past efforts now confronted him. In a letter to the Navy secretary, dated 29 May 1814, Stewart reported that he was thirty men, including a gunner, short and that twenty-five additional hands were due for discharge in June. Another letter from Commodore Bainbridge amplified this report. Dated 1 July 1814, Bainbridge informed Secretary Jones that *Constitution* needed sixty to seventy men. In passing, Stewart also mentioned in his log that the British blockade was tight.

Desertion and recruitment apparently came to a head in October and November 1814. In another letter to the Navy secretary, Bainbridge reported that twenty men had deserted in recent days from the yard and from USS *Independence*. He reported that Midshipman Ward, one of the officers looking for the deserters, found a John Baptiste on the privateer *Leo* of Boston. Baptiste had deserted from *Constitution*. The captain of *Leo*, John H. Hewes, knew the man was a deserter but refused to give him up. Captain Stewart ordered an armed party to take two of *Constitution*'s boats and row to *Leo*. Once alongside they were to order the privateer's captain to give up Baptiste. If the captain refused, Stewart directed his men to take the man by force. When one of the boats came alongside *Leo* and identified itself, the privateer's second lieutenant, John D. Carnes, refused to allow any boarding. *Constitution*'s men tried, but were repulsed, with several "severely wounded." After a parley, Lt. Henry E. Ballard was allowed on board, and he successfully negotiated the deserter's return.

On 17 December 1814 Stewart was able to take *Constitution* to sea, unhindered by the British blockade. Word had been passed that the three blockading frigates, HMS *Acosta*, HMS *Leander*, and HMS *Newcastle*, were nowhere to be seen. It was not known at the time, but all three ships left to commence a maintenance period at the Royal Navy Dockyard in Halifax. Only the brig-of-war HMS *Arab* was nearby, and she was at anchor at Provincetown, Massachusetts.[9] Stewart quickly took advantage of this opportunity, and by early afternoon *Constitution* was well out to sea. Certainly Stewart and the crew shared the feelings of the acting chaplain, Asheton Humphreys, who observed in his journal, "We felt no little degree of importance when the circumstance of our being the only American frigate at sea presented itself to our minds. We felt that the eyes of the country were upon us and that everything within the bounds of possibility was expected and we knew that a desperate chance was before us, however we had escaped from port and hope presented bright prospects."[10]

Following the secretary's orders, Stewart sailed to position his ship astride of the convoy routes that stretched south from Canada to Bermuda and then to the West Indies. On Christmas Eve 1814 his actions bore fruit. The ship's log noted that at 8 A.M. *Constitution* commenced pursuit. By 10 A.M. the British brig *Lord Nelson* hove to. She was apparently fooled into thinking her pursuer was a British man-of-war. *Constitution* was flying the Red Ensign, and Stewart had had her repainted a few days out from Boston so that her characteristic American white gun streak was the distinctive yellow band of the Royal Navy. The surprised *Lord Nelson* was taken as a prize. Informed by her captain that she was part of a convoy heading for Barbados,

Considered by some as the *Constitution*'s "finest fight," Stewart and his crew simultaneously defeated two British ships, the *Cyane* and *Levant*, just days after the Treaty of Ghent had been ratified by the United States. (Courtesy of Tom W. Freeman)

Constitution, with the *Lord Nelson* following, began the search. On Christmas Day Stewart hove to and ordered all needed stores to be taken from the British brig to the *Constitution*. The log notes that the crew and cargo (slops, pork, gin, wine, and dry goods) were transferred. Christmas Day was certainly a good one for the ship's company. Later in the day the *Constitution* took the brig under tow. A short time later Stewart ordered Lt. William V. Taylor to board the *Lord Nelson* and cut away one of her masts. Taylor misunderstood his orders and scuttled the ship. Stewart briefly noted this action in his log and then stated he was still looking for the convoy. On 28 December Stewart noted in his log, "berthed 20 sick on gun deck," possibly a result of holiday celebrations. With Christmas behind him, Stewart exercised the ship's great guns and continued south. On New Years Eve 1814 *Constitution* stopped a Spanish brig. The Spaniard failed to offer any intelligence that would improve Stewart's chances to bag a Barbados-bound convoy, and he noted the same in his 3 January 1815 log, which read, "still trying to catch convoy before it reaches Barbados." On that day Stewart was also in chase of another unknown sail, but the log simply stated, "gave over chase at night."

Continuing south, Stewart and the *Constitution* ran into heavy weather. The log noted on 9 and 10 January that the ship was riding with seas heavy on the beam and the "ship wet on gun and berth decks," as she had been in the rolling seas of her first cruise. The next day Stewart also noted the "seas heavy and ship uncomfortably wet." On 14 January Stewart wrote with what seems a great relief, "good weather at last." Then on 16 January the *Constitution* was again in the chase.

The pursuit began early in the morning and continued through the early afternoon, when Stewart wrote in his log, "1:30 P.M. William Herrington fell overboard from the fore chains; gave up chase to rescue him." For the next six days, *Constitution* continued to head east by northward. On 24 January Stewart stopped the French brig *Cassimere* and left the crew of the *Lord Nelson* with her. The rest of January found *Constitution* working north and east until she found herself astride the north-south shipping lanes off Western Europe. However, those days were filled with more disappointment; the only sails seen and identified were neutral Portuguese merchantmen. But on 8 February the winds of change blew upon Stewart and *Constitution*.

On the morning of the eighth the *Constitution* stopped and boarded the barque *Julia*, flying German colors, fifteen days from Cork, and bound for Lisbon. The barque's captain informed Stewart that peace had been signed between U.S. and British negotiators in Ghent, Belgium. Additional credence was given to this report later that same day, when *Constitution* stopped a Russian brig. "Two American masters of vessels, passengers, came on board and brought papers which confirmed the report of peace having been concluded."[11] Stewart had to have realized the end of the war was near. But, two certainties confirmed Stewart's decision to carry on with his war cruise. First, Congress had yet to ratify the treaty. What if they did not? Second, even if Congress did ratify the treaty, Stewart knew that, because of the slow communications, the treaty would have a grace period provision allowed to both sides. He knew the respective governments would uphold legitimate and honorable actions on the part of the belligerents. On 10 February *Constitution* found herself just fifteen miles west of Cape Finisterre, Spain, seeking another opportunity to engage the enemy.

The next week found *Constitution* off the Iberian Peninsula, astride the north-south trade route, and very busy chasing unknown sail. On 12 February action seemed imminent, when out of the squally weather a frigate appeared off the *Constitution*'s weather beam. Chaplain Humphreys made an amusing entry into his journal that describes how this frigate was spotted. The *Constitution* had a terrier dog named Guerriere on board that was owned by the ship's second lieutenant, Beekman V. Hoffman. Apparently, this dog was extremely gifted and knew the workings of a sailing ship, to include knowing his battle station. On this occasion, "the ship's first lieutenant [Lieutenant Henry Ballard] and myself were walking the weather side of the quarter deck lamenting our hard luck . . . and all unconscious of any craft being near us. Guerriere who was playing about the heels of Lieutenant Ballard appeared uncommonly frisky and was rather troublesome. . . . He jumped upon the hammock clothes and stretching his head to windward began to bark most vehemently; upon looking to discover what had attracted his notice lo and behold! There was a great frigate."[12]

The unknown frigate dropped astern of the heavy American frigate, and Stewart wore his ship in chase. Beating to quarters and clearing for action, Stewart drove his ship until, at 8 P.M., the *Constitution* ranged alongside. Stewart ordered the colors to be flown and hailed the frigate but received no answer. By this time, both ships were experiencing heavy seas, rolling the main gun decks of both ships underwater. Stewart could see in the near darkness the other ship's gun deck lit up and her guns manned. He could also see an ensign flying from her gaff, but he could not identify the flag. Ordering his own gunners not to fire unless fired upon, Stewart hailed the ship again and again. Receiving no reply, he then ordered the firing of the carronades and a division of three sent their charges into the unknown frigate. This ship quickly responded by identifying herself as the Portuguese frigate *Amazon* bound for Lisbon from the Canary Islands. The ship hove to as ordered by Stewart, who had every intention to board the ship to verify her claim. But the captain was unable to board, because the seas were running very heavy by now. Seeing this, the Portuguese tacked under double-reefed topsails and headed west and south, breaking contact.

On 16 February the *Constitution* had worked farther south, just off the Rock of Lisbon. The day before Stewart had received word from a passing Portuguese ship that the frigate HMS *Volontaire*, with the duke of Bedford and his family on board, was heading from Lisbon back to Britain. It proved to be a busy day chasing unknown sail and finding no duke of Bedford. Finally, the *Constitution* ran down the British ship *Susan* (*Susanna*). Again the false colors of the ensign at the gaff and the paint along the gun line fooled the British merchant into thinking it had fallen in with one of His

Majesty's Ships. The ship was returning to Britain from Buenos Aires with hides and tallow. In addition, the ship carried two large cats, which were probably jaguars.[13] Stewart ordered them taken on board and chained to one of the ship's boats that were stowed amidships on the spar deck. On 19 February *Susan* was sent off to New York as a prize.

Monday, 20 February started out with moderate breezes and hazy cloud-filled skies. *Constitution* headed northward under easy sail and on the starboard tack. Nothing was seen until shortly after 1 P.M., when the lookout atop the ship's main masthead shouted that a sail was off the starboard bow. Shortly after this sighting, lookouts informed Stewart that another sail was spotted off the port bow. With almost the same breath, the lookout at the masthead shouted the first sail had changed course and was heading for *Constitution*. No merchantman would act this way. Shortly, this approaching ship flew signal flags, which Stewart could not answer. Realizing the *Constitution* was not friendly the unknown ship squared away, added additional canvas to her yards, and headed westward toward the second ship. This first ship began sending additional signal flags aloft followed by the discharge of a number of her guns. Could it be, when Stewart ordered his ship to take up the chase, that he remembered his parting words to his wife Delia's request for a frigate?

If so, this remembrance was short lived, for the *Constitution* quickly added more canvas of her own. The wind was lightening and all of the ship's studding sails were being set. Just after 3 P.M. Stewart ordered his bow chase guns to fire. The rounds fell short. With the chase in full swing, suddenly all on board heard a most distressing sound—the main royal mast snapped and was carried away. Stewart quickly slowed his pursuit by reducing sail and immediately ordered men aloft to clear the wreckage and have the carpenters prepare a replacement mast. All repairs were effected and within an hour the *Constitution* was shortening the distance between herself and the two enemy ships. At 5 P.M. the order was passed for the bow chase guns to fire again. Again, these rounds fell short. By 5:40 P.M. the enemy ships closed one another, signaling between themselves via lamplights. Their subsequent maneuvers made it apparent to Stewart that he would have to face a combined force in the fading light of day. Without hesitation, Stewart ordered his "heavy" frigate cleared for action. He ordered the gun crews to be divided so as to be able to defend the ship from both sides.[14] At this time the *Constitution*'s log read, "1755—they shortened sail and formed a line of wind at half a cable's length from each other."

Having failed to gain the weather gauge on the American, the British ships prepared to receive the *Constitution* and take her under action. The smaller of the two was in the lead. Both appeared to be frigate-type ships. At 6 P.M. Stewart ordered the Stars and Stripes broken.[15] The two enemy ships responded immediately by sending their Red Ensigns and Union Flags aloft. Despite the lightening wind, *Constitution* continued to close the range, and at approximately three hundred yards off the starboard side of the sternmost ship, a single shot boomed out from the American. The British ships firing their broadsides at the American immediately followed this. Stewart fired his port broadside as well. At this point *Constitution* found herself "at the apex of an isosceles triangle, her opponents column forming the baseline."[16]

Stewart had positioned himself on the port-side entry port of the *Constitution* just prior to the opening broadsides. He did this so as to have a better look at his two opponents. The British first broadside killed two of his men stationed nearby with a single ball, which traveled through the ship's waist and smashed into her boat where the chained jaguars were kept. The big cats were also killed instantly. What followed was an intensive exchange of cannon fire from all, lasting between fifteen and twenty minutes. Chaplain Humphreys described the British firing as one that was "returned with great quickness and spirit and some degree of precision."[17] With the sun setting broadly off the port quarter of the combatants, and the sea and air between the combatants choked with smoke, Stewart ordered a ceasefire. He could see that *Constitution* had moved ahead of the aftermost ship and was now alongside the first. The aftermost ship, HMS *Cyane*, luffed into the wind and came to starboard to close the range and bring her carronades to bear more effectively into the *Constitution*'s stern. Seeing this, Stewart quickly ordered his big frigate to fire a full broadside into the smoke and toward the lead ship, the corvette HMS *Levant*. He immediately ordered *Constitution*'s main and mizzen topsails aback. "With topgallants still set, shook all forward, let fly his jib sheet, backed swiftly astern, and unleashed a heavy fire" on *Cyane*.[18] This cannonade caused heavy damage to the British light frigate, and she appeared to be out of control. Seeing the lead ship, HMS *Levant*, reappearing out of the smoke and attempting to steer a course that would put her across the bow of his frigate, Stewart simultaneously ordered his frigate's helm hard to port and the lee braces manned. Amid the choking smoke and deafening sounds of battle, the crew swung the ship's yards around so the sails could catch the wind. Stewart's quick action caused the *Constitution* to leap forward and sail between the British ships. With *Consti-*

tution crossing astern of *Levant*, Stewart ordered two raking broadsides into the British ship's stern. *Levant* was now severely shaken, and she bore away from the American and into the darkness. With *Levant's* disappearance into the darkness, Stewart continued to turn his frigate to port, maneuvering under *Cyane's* starboard quarter and stern. Realizing that Stewart had out-maneuvered him again, and with the range between the two ships down to fifty yards, Captain Falcon struck the Red Ensign and Union Flags, showed a single light and fired one of her carronades to leeward. At 6:45 P.M. the thirty-four-gun light frigate HMS *Cyane* was finished.

Stewart quickly ordered a prize crew of fifteen Marines under *Constitution's* second lieutenant, Beekman Hoffman, to take possession of the crippled *Cyane*. By 8 P.M. Captain Falcon and his surviving officers were on board *Constitution*, and the *Cyane* was firmly under control of Hoffman and the prize crew. Stewart now ordered *Constitution* in search of the fleeing *Levant*. However, *Levant*, under the command of Capt. George Douglas, had not run. Bringing his damaged ship and shaken crew under control, Douglas sailed the *Levant* on a sweeping port turn loop. He intended to return to the fight.

Levant sailed out of the moonlit darkness, and Stewart found his frigate closing with the sloop. At 8:40 P.M., both ships passed each other's starboard side, and, at a range of fifty yards, they exchanged broadsides. Douglas turned *Levant* to port and began to run with the wind. Stewart turned *Constitution* to starboard and fell behind the *Cyane*. A chase now ensued in which *Constitution* began firing her bow chase guns with great effect. *Constitution* set her royals, closing the range between the two quickly. At this point *Levant* was unable to return fire. Seeing that *Constitution* was closing up on his ship, Captain Douglas swung his outmatched ship out of the wind, struck his colors, and fired a single gun leeward. The *Constitution's* third lieutenant, William Shubrick, quickly boarded the new twenty-one-gun ship.

So ended this remarkable action. America's first naval historian, James Fenimore Cooper, wrote in his history of the U.S. Navy, "The manner in which Captain Stewart handled his ship . . . is among the most brilliant maneuvering in naval annals."[19] But, not taking anything away from Stewart's accomplishment, the fight was truly one-sided. He maneuvered a superbly built ship, possessing awesome long-range firepower and a crew that was second to none. Together with Stewart's own finely tuned leadership, his seamanship and seasoned tactical skills made *Constitution* unbeatable in this engagement. The findings of the Admiralty's court-martial of Captain Douglas came to same conclusion. "The court is of the opinion that the capture of the *Cyane* is to be attributed to the very superior force of the Enemy's Ship, aided by his superior sailing."[20] The court passed the same judgment on Captain Falcon. Commander Martin summed it up perfectly when he wrote: "If his adversaries can be said to have done anything 'wrong,' it would have to be having had the temerity to challenge him [Stewart] in the first place."[21]

Both heavily battered British ships were now Stewart's prizes. He was now much closer to fulfilling his promise to Delia. However, a great deal of work had to be done to bring these ships back to America. Most interestingly, Stewart and the crew had to quell the many recriminating outbursts between the prisoners, especially the officers. A few days after the action Stewart entered his cabin only to find Captains Douglas and Falcon bitterly arguing over who was responsible for their defeat. Accordingly, Stewart stopped the argument by saying to both captains that he would be more than willing to return them and their crews to their respective ships, so that they could start the battle all over again. Apparently, this brought the argument between the captains to a quick halt.

Repairs to the captured ships continued, and on 28 February, with the most serious repairs completed, Stewart's little squadron headed toward the Cape Verde Islands. Stewart hoped that during this cruise he would fall upon the frigate HMS *Inconstant*, which, according to correspondence found among the papers obtained from the captured *Susan*, was bringing a large sum of bullion from Rio de la Plata, Argentina. On 10 March they arrived at Porto Praya in the Cape Verde Islands. During the course that day and the next, Stewart had arranged to release at least one hundred of his prisoners, but just after midday on 11 March, through the heavy fog and haze, the sails of a large ship were seen. This single sail turned into three, when two more ships appeared out of the fog and haze. Without hesitation, Stewart ordered his frigate and her prizes underway. Within ten minutes, all three were heading out of the roadstead with the three Royal Navy frigates, HMS *Newcastle*, HMS *Leander*, and HMS *Acasta* in pursuit. Again, Stewart's coolness and experience came to the fore. In his work *The Naval War of 1812*, Theodore Roosevelt later wrote, "Certainly a more satisfactory proof of the excellent training of both officers and men could hardly be given than the rapidity, skill, and perfect order with which everything was done. Any indecision on the part of the officers or bungling on the part of the men would have lost everything."[22]

As Stewart's squadron left the harbor, the released British prisoners manned the town's coastal gun battery and commenced a heavy but ineffective fire on the Americans. *Cyane* was the slowest of the three, and she soon began to drop astern. Stewart saw that if she maintained her present course, the British squadron would quickly run her down. He immediately signaled Lieutenant Hoffman and ordered him to tack. Stewart had hoped this would give Hoffman a better chance to evade his pursuers, while at the same time drawing one of the pursuing British ships off from chasing his own. But this was not the case, for Como. Sir George Collier maintained his squadron's course. Stewart and the crew watched as *Cyane* continued on until she was lost in the fog. Hoffman eventually evaded the British and reached New York City on 10 April 1815.

Now *Levant* began to fall behind. At 3 P.M. Stewart ordered Lieutenant Ballard to tack his prize. Ballard responded immediately, and *Levant* headed back to Porto Praya and Portuguese neutrality. To Ballard and Stewart's surprise, Collier ordered his squadron to tack and take up the chase against the *Levant*, rendering any chance of catching the *Constitution* lost. Not knowing that Ballard had decided to return to port, Stewart sailed *Constitution* into the fog and the open sea. The British captured Ballard and his crew only after Collier's ships and the English shore battery fired into the anchored *Levant*.

Later that day Stewart headed south in the hopes of finding HMS *Inconstant* and the bullion. *Constitution* made landfall off Cabo de Sao Roque, Brazil, without meeting up with the British treasure ship. Stewart turned his ship westward and cruised along the South American coast. Calling into Maranhao, he released 150 of his prisoners and received additional unconfirmed word that peace had been achieved. Turning north on 28 April, he sent a boat into San Juan, Puerto Rico, where Stewart received positive word the war was over. He set course for home.

Six days later Stewart hove to and repainted *Constitution*'s sides to traditional American colors. On 14 May *Constitution* arrived off Sandy Hook, New Jersey, and anchored in the Raritan Bay.

On 16 May Stewart stood his frigate out of the bay and sailed into New York. There the ship received a hero's welcome. On 18 May he received orders to proceed to Boston. Shortly after his triumphant return, Stewart asked for and was granted permission to take a well-deserved leave. He had promised his wife Delia that he would return with two frigates. Although he defeated *Cyane* and *Levant*, he lost the latter. Still, Stewart and the *Constitution*'s crew received prize money for both. Congress awarded the ship's company a considerable sum of $25,000 for the *Levant*. In addition Congress mandated that medals be cast for Stewart and his commissioned officers. Four years later he received a gold medal with his likeness on its face. His officers received silver.

CHAPTER SIX

The Tudors and a
Home in Bordentown

When Stewart left Philadelphia at age thirteen to work on an Indiaman, he would know no home but the sea for twenty years. With the exception of shore duty when he supervised the building of gunboats in New York, Stewart had little time or opportunity for courting. By the time he began courting, Stewart, like Decatur, was recognized as a naval hero in the nascent U.S. Navy, particularly after the heavily publicized exploits of "Preble's boys" off of Tripoli.

The man who returned from the sea had grown and matured.

Stewart, as an adult, stood five feet, nine inches tall.[1] His chestnut hair was offset by large, penetrating, and what were often described as intelligent blue eyes. Contemporaries described him as "erect and well-proportioned," a "dignified and engaging presence," "possessed of great constitutional powers to endure hardships and privations of all kinds," and having a "fair complexion but weather-beaten."[2] To the residents of his nearly lifelong home in New Jersey, his "countenance was Roman, bold, strong, and commanding, and his head finely formed. His control over his passions were truly surprising, and under the most irritating circumstances, his oldest seamen never saw a ray of anger flash from his eye. His kindness, benevolence, and humanity were proverbial, but his sense of justice and requisitions of duty were as unbending as fate. In the moment of greatest stress and danger, he was cool and quick in judgment, as he was utterly ignorant of fear."[3]

His future brother-in-law recounted that Stewart's "manners were coarse and unpolished, though probably not more so than Lord Nelson's, whom he was said to resemble in person." But if Stewart lacked the refinements of the land-based culture of Boston's Beacon Hill residents or Southern plantation owners, it was because he had been reared on the seas among sailors. His focus was more on the law of the sea than the learned manners of high society, and more concerned with maneuvering ships through heavy seas than with the choreography of a contra dance.

Stewart's prominence was not based on familial history or connections. It was, instead, a product of his own hard work, bravery, seamanship, and reputation in the U.S. Navy. He was, in short, a self-made man.

Little is known about Stewart's relationships with women except for two, both of whom appear to have been similar in family background, characteristics, and attitude. Stewart once sought the hand of a Miss Maria D. Mayo of Richmond, Virginia, the eldest daughter of Virginia militia Col. John Mayo. According to one account, Maria "had long been the reigning belle of the fashionable drawing rooms of Richmond aristocracy."[4] Noted for her physical perfections, she could play the harp, sing, write and recite her own poetry, and speak French fluently. Colonel Mayo, protective of his daughter's future and ability to be supported in the fashion to which she had grown accustomed, was not enamored of military suitors given that their earning potential was far less than that of merchants or politicians.

Born in 1789 and about eleven years younger than Stewart, Maria Mayo most likely met Stewart in Washington, D.C. As a young woman, Maria Mayo "got the notice and affection" of Dolly Madison, the wife of President James Madison. Maria was a frequent and extended guest of the first lady during and after the War of 1812. She once boasted that she had received fifty offers of marriage. Other sources state she received over one hundred proposals, including Stewart's. The daughter of Commodore Rodgers recalled that Maria was at the White House and "my father and mother were present at a dinner there, when a letter from Commodore Stewart offering his hand and heart to Miss Mayo was being handed about as a joke. My father folded this letter up when it came near him and handed it back to Miss Mayo, requesting her to put it aside as he could not allow the men present to amuse themselves at the expense of a brother officer. My mother said he looked so angry that she tried to touch him with her foot under the table, but she was too little to reach him. However, Miss Mayo smilingly pocketed the letter, and all was peace."[5]

Her cavalier rejection of proposals was likely not directed at Stewart personally, nor was her treatment of him unique among her suitors. Eventually Maria Mayo succumbed in 1817 to the one man whom she had consistently rejected for years, Gen. Winfield Scott, one of the heroes of the War of 1812, who was "seeking a helpmate to share his glory. In disposing of his heart he had boldly invaded the most exclusive and patrician coterie of his state."[6] Scott had previously proposed three times to Mayo, when he was a lawyer, a captain, and a colonel.

One associate of Mayo recalled commenting to her, "So, you married Captain Scott after all," to which Maria replied, "No—I refused Captain Scott to the last. I accepted the General."[7] General Scott enjoyed a military career as lengthy and successful as Stewart's. Both men were considered presidential material by 1840, and both acquired fame and admiration despite the women they selected as their wives.

While it is not known if Miss Mayo took the opportunity to spurn Stewart's advances directly, the captain did not let his experience with her dissuade him from pursuing further relationships. Perhaps he thought back to years before when a fortune-teller apparently advised him he would marry "the belle of Boston." This was one case in which a seer successfully predicted the future, but the prophecy had a cruel consequence.

The "belle of Boston" was Delia Tudor, a member of one of the most prominent families in New England, if not in the country. Stewart's courtship of Miss Tudor changed his life forever, and not necessarily for the better. As Robert Hallowell Gardiner later wrote of his sister-in-law Delia Tudor and Stewart, "never was a match more ill-assorted."

By the end the American Revolutionary War, the Tudors were one of the most prominent families in Boston and beyond, due primarily to the connections and positions of William Tudor. Tudor's grandfather was from Devonshire, England, and, before his premature death, he had only one son, John, in 1709. When John was five years old, he and his mother immigrated to the American colonies. He grew up to be known as Deacon John Tudor, a witness to many prerevolutionary events in Boston and a diarist. He saw and wrote about, for example, a pivotal event on 5 March 1770, when "a few Minutes after 9 O'Clock a most horrid murder was committed in King Street."[8] He witnessed Bostonians throwing rocks and snowballs at British soldiers, followed with British firing into the crowd, killing five colonists. The tragedy came to be known to every schoolchild as the "Boston Massacre." One of Boston's most famous residents, and a future U.S. president, John

Delia Tudor was the "belle of Boston" and the daughter of Gen. George Washington's judge advocate. On the day Delia wed Charles Stewart, her brother-in-law wrote, "Never was a match more ill-assorted." (Gilbert Stuart; courtesy of the Boston Museum of Fine Arts)

Adams served as the defense counsel at the trial of the British soldiers; by that time he had as his clerk the son of Deacon John Tudor, William.

At the age of eight in 1758, William Tudor entered Boston Latin School, which had seen such colonial era luminaries as Cotton Mather, Benjamin Franklin, Samuel Adams, and John Hancock pass through its doors.[9] Tudor graduated from Harvard in 1769.

During Boston's own early protests against British taxes, William Tudor was already an overt colonial patriot. In a letter to a friend, he wrote, "The cause of freedom is the cause of the whole community, and every man, who is one remove from idiotism, must be at heart a friend to it."[10]

For three years he studied law in the office of John Adams, his mentor. Tudor became a Boston lawyer in his own right on 29 January 1775. Exactly six months later he was appointed by the Second Continental Congress as the army's first judge advocate general, a position he held until 1778. Colonel Tudor was part of the Continental Army during its darkest days. Despite his duties and the dangers of combat, he continued to correspond with a Delia Jarvis whom he was intent on marrying. From New York he wrote, "the Enemy have now almost intirely [*sic*] surrounded Us and are making every

Movement preparatory to an attack. . . . In 3 Days more it is likely New York will be intirely evacuated by the American Troops."[11] A few months later, he wrote from New Jersey to his future wife in Boston: "Do all the young Genius's of Boston still dream and trade on? And are we still to look to every other Place but that, for Liberal Souls and intrepid Spirits, at a Time when our bleeding, ravaged, half conquered Country calls for every exertion—I often blush for my native Town."[12]

John Adams recommended Tudor to be the private secretary to Gen. George Washington while the army was at Cambridge, Massachusetts. And it was William Tudor who handed General Washington his commission as general of the army at Camp Hill. Tudor was made a lieutenant colonel on 9 May 1777 while serving in Col. David Henley's regiment from Massachusetts, a position he kept until 9 May 1778. He later served as the judge advocate on the court-martial of another well-known Bostonian, herald Paul Revere.

Tudor also helped found several significant organizations. He was a cofounder with George Washington and the first vice president of the Society of Cincinnati. He also helped charter the prestigious Massachusetts Historical Society.

During the Revolutionary War, Tudor met and immediately fell in love with Delia Jarvis (also known as Felicia), whom he married on 5 March 1778. But William did not enjoy an easy courtship. Conducted primarily through correspondence while he served with the Continental Army, he struggled with distance and Miss Jarvis's reluctance. In May 1776 he asked her: "Am I only what I was that first charming Hour, an Acquaintance and a Friend?" Her reponse in September 1776 might have indicated her feelings:

> I have no virtues, you only cheat yourself to Apologize for a blind partiality of which you have cause indeed to blush at when it debases the dignity of your character so much as to court *my* Love after a prohibition. . . . I write with plainness prompted by the sincerest friendship. . . . Your *Friend*, Felicia[13]

Despite her seeming ambivalence toward Tudor, they were engaged during the war. William Tudor's devotion to Miss Jarvis was such that while he was stationed with Washington's Army in Cambridge, Massachusetts, he would swim across the Charles River with his clothes atop his head to see her.[14]

After the war, Tudor served in a number of public service positions: magistrate, representative in the Massachusetts legislature, senator from Norfolk

County, Massachusetts state secretary, and clerk of the Massachusetts Supreme Court from 1811 until his death. He was referred to throughout his career as "Judge Tudor." In his private practice, described as both extensive and lucrative, he was known as a popular advocate but not particularly profound. Like his mentor, John Adams, Tudor included among his apprentices noted future Massachusetts citizen, including Fisher Ames and Josiah Quincy.

As the only son and principal heir of Deacon John Tudor, William received a large inheritance upon his father's death in 1795. He made the decision to postpone his career and travel to Europe without his young family, and in 1796 he traveled to France, Flanders, Holland, and then to England. In London, U.S. Ambassador Rufus King presented him at court. "On the mention of his name, the king smiled and observed in his rapid manner, 'Tudor!— What, one of us?'"[15]

Tudor's wife Delia Jarvis was the first of four women in the Tudor lineage named Delia. Delia Jarvis Tudor, born in 1752, also witnessed events in Boston during the Revolution and recalled in a letter that, as a young woman, she saw the British troops pass by on their way to the eventual battle at Bunker Hill and witnessed also the return "of very many of them borne on litters."

Delia, the children, and her widowed mother lived in what is now Nahant, Massachusetts, at their farm, which they called Rockwood. Like Charles and Sarah Ford Stewart, William and Delia Jarvis Tudor had eight children. Delia was committed to preparing her children for societal life in Paris and London.

Their son William Tudor Jr. (1779–1830) graduated from Harvard in 1796, served in the Massachusetts state legislature, continued his father's work in Boston society by helping to found the Boston Athenaeum, and was an advocate of the Bunker Hill Monument to commemorate the early Revolutionary War battle.

On graduating from Harvard, he traveled to Europe and then to the West Indies as a representative of his brother's ice business. From 1815 to 1817 he served as the first editor of the *North American Review,* which included among its contributors early American literary stars such as Edward Channing, Edward Everett, Daniel Webster, and future Navy Secretary George Bancroft, under whom William Jr.'s future brother-in-law Stewart later served. William Jr. became a diplomat and was appointed, through the intercession of John Quincy Adams, U.S. consul in Lima, Peru, coinciding with Stewart's later command of the Pacific Station in the early 1820s. William,

Stewart's brother-in-law, William Tudor Jr., was the son of Gen. George Washington's judge advocate. Tudor later served as a diplomat in Peru and Brazil. (Courtesy of the Boston Athenaeum)

who spent 1811 with other in-laws in the then-Massachusetts colony of Maine, was described as a young man whose "bonhomie and playful wit made him a delightful companion. He was full of the milk of human kindness, and had the warmest affection for [his brother-in-law and sister] and [their] children. He had good taste, was fond of the fine arts, was patriotic and public spirited, and if he had been blessed with fortune would have made himself a useful member of society, as well as being its ornament, but he was wholly deficient in business capacity, and knew not how to live with small means."[16]

William Tudor Jr. was also close with his sister Delia. When he died of a tropical illness in 1830 in Brazil, Delia was plunged "into a grief so profound that her young daughter would movingly recall it fifty years later."[17]

William and Delia Jarvis Tudor's second child, the first to be named Delia, died a day after being born on 21 November 1780.

Their second son was John Henry Tudor (1782–1802), who was born in Philadelphia.

William and Delia's son Frederic, born in 1783, earned fame in his life-

101

time as "The Ice King." In partnership with the Vanderbilts, he had the lofty idea of exporting ice from New England to the West Indies. In 1806 he sent 130 tons of ice to Martinique; by 1833 he expanded his market to Calcutta, India; and by 1856, he was shipping 146,000 tons of ice to the West and East Indies, China, the Philippines, and Australia. Although he also dealt in coffee, his ice trade earned him his fortune. It also allowed fruits from the Northern Hemisphere to reach the warmer climes of India. The amusement park he built on Nahant was one of the first in the United States.

His sister Emma Jane (1785–1865) married Robert Hallowell Gardiner (1782–1864), from an equally prominent but wealthier New England family. Gardiner, born Robert Hallowell in England, changed his name when he became the heir of his grandfather, Dr. Silvester Gardiner, who, in addition to being the only medical practitioner in the colonies with a European diploma, was a major shareholder in over 1.5 million acres of land in New England and a founder of what became Gardiner, Maine. Hallowell was also a first cousin to British Adm. Sir Benjamin Hallowell-Carew, one of Adm. Lord Horatio Nelson's commanders. Robert Hallowell Gardiner built Oaklands Plantation, at which the Tudors were often long-term guests, in Gardiner, Maine. Oaklands later played a significant role in the lives of Charles Stewart's family. Delia Jarvis Tudor remained at Oaklands for the seven years following her husband's death. She was always welcomed at Oaklands, and her final years consisted of rising late, eating breakfast in her room, and never joining the family downstairs, except for dinner. From October to April she never went out of the house except for a short ride on Sundays to service at Christ Church.

James Tudor was born in 1789 and died at the age of eight.

Henry James Tudor was the youngest, born in 1791 and dying in 1864. Known as "Harry," he served as Stewart's secretary on board the USS *Franklin* when Stewart was commodore of the Mediterranean Squadron.

Delia Tudor, the future bride of Capt. Charles Stewart, was the fifth of the six children who survived into adulthood. In his book of recollections, Robert Hallowell Gardiner said that she "was imbued with a most remarkable energy of character and she possessed a perseverance which no difficulties could check. She had a large frame, and her motions were naturally neither easy nor graceful, but by long and unwearied exertions, she acquired the power of moving and dancing with grace and elegance. The same determination for excellence had enabled her to acquire great power both with the harp and piano. Her music was more artistic than [that of Emma Tudor Gardiner], but not so full of expression."

Delia was as accomplished as Maria Mayo. She could read Latin and had some knowledge of German. She was fluent in French, Spanish, and Italian. All served her well when she traveled to Europe as a young woman.

Both Delias joined William Tudor for his second trip to Europe, in the autumn of 1807. Tudor, having recently lost much of his fortune in land speculation in South Boston and other businesses, was desperate for money to finance the trip, so Delia Jarvis Tudor suggested they mortgage Rockwood and sell their possessions. As one historian notes, this pattern repeated itself for several generations. William Tudor hesitated to follow his wife's idea, but nevertheless relented. His deference to his wife's wishes, along with the decision to sell their furniture, added to the Tudor's financially dismal years during which they were not only impoverished but also constantly indebted. The Tudors spent lavishly while abroad and while at home, continuing their downward budgetary spiral.

This is the environment in which Delia was born and to which she truly grew accustomed, particularly to the detriment of her future husband.

While in Paris, one of Tudor's sons joined them as Delia was presented to Napoleon Bonaparte's court.[18] Although the Tudors traveled through much of northern Europe, they spent the majority of their time in England. William remained for about two years and in 1810 chose to return to the United States while both Delias, doubtless wishing to take advantage of exciting high societal life, and not the provincial shadow America, remained behind. Mother and daughter hoped to marry young Delia Tudor to an aristocrat. Delia Jarvis Tudor wrote to her husband that their daughter was "very successful in England. She is intimate with Lord and Lady P. and has rejected a very rich old man" and she "exhilerates [sic] the circle she moves in."[19]

Delia was immersed in the European element for which she and her mother had imagined and hoped. She was the presumably welcome guest of the nobility but her continued stay in England proved costly, including luxurious clothes and other expenses. With her father no longer able to support her, given his own financial difficulties, Delia was forced to seek other means. She wrote to her businessman brother Frederic asking that he send her money. Frederic, replying that he could not meet her request, suggested it was time for her to return to the United States.

By the time Delia realized that she had no choice but to return because of her financial situation, her native country and England were at war. As an American citizen, she was threatened with internment in London. In addition, "lacking a dowry, she had failed in her goal of finding a wealthy and well-connected husband she could happily marry, and who would establish her in London society."[20]

Reluctantly, the younger Delia transited the Atlantic, back to her family's new home in Boston. During her absence, William had mortgaged their home on Nahant and purchased a small home on Belknap Street on Beacon Hill. Unhappy with her new, constricting quarters, she quickly made the whole household miserable, content only in sharing her unhappiness. William Sr. soon determined that the only way of resolving the unbearable situation was to demand that she be married.

At this time the new captain of the USS *Constitution* was introduced to Delia as a potential husband and a "very able and gallant officer, holding high rank in the service, as a man of more than common ability, and at the same time very rich."[21] In the aristocratic circles of England, the young available Delia understood that that country's senior naval officers were respected and prominent in society. Unfortunately, Delia "felt a repugnance" toward Charles who discontinued his visits.

Another of Delia's suitors at the time was Samuel Welles, described by Robert Hallowell Gardiner as a respectable gentleman with "ample fortune who had pressed his suit with great earnestness, but he was neither accomplished nor literary, and for some peculiarity of manner had been made an object of ridicule to the young ladies of Boston. His suit therefore had been rejected."

Again Charles Stewart was considered as a suitor with William Tudor Jr. as his greatest advocate. William made the case for Stewart, reiterating on his wealth and reputed generosity, and finally convincing his sister that she should choose the captain. Charles and Delia were engaged shortly thereafter in the fall of 1813. Their engagement was so soon and so short that even their close relatives, such as Robert Hallowell and Emma Jane Tudor Gardiner, were not aware of it until the day before the wedding.

Charles and Delia were wed on Thanksgiving Day, 25 November 1813, after the morning service at Trinity Church in Boston's Copley Square. Their social differences were apparent immediately: he, a son of the sea and the merchant world of Philadelphia; she, a daughter of refinement with a desire for an aristocratic life. Stewart later admitted to his brother-in-law Robert Hallowell Gardiner that "they quarreled the first night of their marriage, and the more they became acquainted, the more distasteful they became to each other."

One reason for the abbreviated engagement was the impending cruise of the USS *Constitution*. Stewart had delayed the ship's departure for several weeks; his officers complained that they should have been at sea cruising for the enemy much sooner.[22] Given his interaction with his new bride, one might argue that Captain Stewart had already encountered his enemy at home.

In 1815, after the war, Stewart bought a 225-acre estate in Bordentown, New Jersey, called Montpelier. Montpelier was built in 1797 by Francois Frederici, a general of Surinam. It later became known as "Old Ironsides," the nickname of the ship Stewart commanded in the War of 1812. In later years Stewart himself became known as "Old Ironsides" as well. The estate, located on the Delaware River, north of Philadelphia and south of Trenton, cost Stewart $16,000. Bordentown was located almost exactly between Philadelphia and New York City, an important waypoint where the land route from New York ended and the water route to Philadelphia began.

There, the Stewarts began to raise their children. Delia, the third to bear that name, was born in 1816; their son, Charles Tudor Stewart, was born in 1818. Their third child did not survive.

Surrounded by hundred-foot tall white pines on the banks of the Delaware River, Stewart bought the house and 225 acres of his estate immediately after the War of 1812. One of his neighbors in Bordentown was Joseph Bonaparte, brother of Napoleon. (Courtesy of the New Jersey Historical Society)

Bordentown was the summer home of many prominent Philadelphians. Therefore, it was natural that Stewart sought to build his own home there as well. Soon after the Stewarts settled in this small town, another prominent individual built his own mansion there and came to dominate local society.

On 29 August 1815 an American ship carried a Frenchman from Bordeaux to New York. He called himself the Count de Survilliers, but in truth he was Joseph Bonaparte (1768–1844), the brother of Napoleon and the deposed King of Naples and Spain. After living at various places in Philadelphia during the construction of his one-thousand-acre estate Point Breeze, he finally moved to Bordentown in 1817. Joseph Bonaparte "did not wish to make his refuge in America too conspicuous. . . . He proposed to retire to some secluded country place where he could forget the storms of Europe, and end his life in the security and peace of a private citizen."[23] Joseph's choice may also have been influenced by his brother Napoleon, who was reported to have put his finger on a map halfway between New York City and Philadelphia and explained: "If I am ever forced to fly to America I shall settle somewhere between Philadelphia and New York, where I can receive the earliest intelligence from France by ship arrivals from either port."

Point Breeze took three years to complete. In addition to the main mansion, which later housed one of the finest art galleries in North America, the estate had a house a quarter mile away connected by a walled underground tunnel—supposedly for inclement weather—and occupied by one of his

A view from the hill at Bordentown. (Charles Goodman & Robert Piggot; courtesy of the Library of Congress)

daughters and her husband. The property included ten miles of paths for carriages and a half-acre man-made lake.

On the night of 3 January 1826 a mysterious fire engulfed Point Breeze, destroying much of the mansion. The event drew all the citizens of Bordentown, men, women, children, who helped fight the flames. According to rumors at the time, a maid, bribed by a woman at the Russian Embassy, had started the fire. Still, Joseph's funds were sufficient to rebuild the mansion in short time.

Bonaparte's daughters, Princesses Zenaide and Charlotte, and Zenaide's husband Prince Charles Lucien Bonaparte also joined him in Bordentown. His wife, due to ill health, remained in Belgium. While in Bordentown, Joseph had at least one mistress, Anne Savage, who bore him at least one child.

Among the guests at Point Breeze as well as at Stewart's Montpelier were future President John Quincy Adams, Senators Henry Clay and Daniel Webster, Gen. Winfield Scott, and in 1824 the General Marquis de Lafayette and Prince Louis Napoleon, who later became France's Napoleon III.

While Stewart was in the Mediterranean, Delia took advantage of the new society in Bordentown led by Joseph Bonaparte and was a frequent guest at his residence. Reliving her years in England, she struggled to find the money to pay for the accessories necessary to participate in high society. Taking a cue from her mother, she began to sell off the furnishings of Old Ironsides while her husband was at sea. In addition, she borrowed money directly from Bonaparte, which led to rumors of infidelity between Delia and Bonaparte or members of his retinue.

Stewart was a self-made man and, while generous, he was economical. As such, he was "not satisfied with her management of the farm at Bordentown," a problem that did not reach a climax until after he returned from his assignment in the Mediterranean.

CHAPTER SEVEN

Return to the Mediterranean

The War of 1812 brought an abrupt end to American overseas commerce, especially in the Mediterranean. From 1812 to 1815 the once-pacified dey of Algiers threw his lot in with Britain, and his corsairs actively swept the Mediterranean and the eastern Atlantic looking for American merchantmen. But pickings were extremely thin, for only "a brig out of Salem, the *Edwin*, whose master, George E. Smith, and ten seamen were robbed of all they owned and put to hard labor" was found.[1]

When the war ended, President James Madison, who had been President Jefferson's state secretary during the Barbary Wars, realized what needed to be done to ensure that Algiers and the other Barbary States would not resume their piratical activities against America. He knew that offensive naval operations were required before American maritime commerce in the Mediterranean could resume its former "Yankee Trader" prosperity. While Stewart was sailing *Constitution* on her return leg from the frigate's most successful war cruise, Madison acted. The ink had barely dried on the Treaty of Ghent when the president asked for and received from Congress a declaration of war against Algiers, which authorized the president to dispatch another naval squadron to the Mediterranean. Stewart was still at sea when Stephen Decatur was selected to be the new Mediterranean Squadron's commander. Decatur was given broad latitude to accomplish the mission to bring the dey to a treaty advantageous to America. His orders were straightforward. The commander was directed to vigorously prosecute the war to a successful conclusion—a conclusion that would create normal relations between civilized nations. Decatur took the squadron to the Mediterranean that same year and through direct action the sought-after result was quickly achieved. Glenn Tucker wrote that as a result of Decatur's offensive actions, "never again to the present time did Algiers demand tribute from the Untied States and never did she enslave another American seaman."[2]

Upon Decatur's success in Algiers, the American Mediterranean Squadron went on to Tunis to seek similar accommodation, which it achieved in a very short time. Decatur went on with the squadron to Tripoli, obtaining similar concessions. Overall, the squadron established a peacetime naval presence that lasted for almost a century, until the Great War of 1914–1918. But it was Stewart who built upon his friend's success by establishing the operational guidelines of "showing the flag" during peacetime.

At the successful conclusion of the war, Decatur was recalled to the United States. While Stewart was on leave in Philadelphia, "Decatur reached New York on November 12, 1815. He had often been a national hero . . . but he was now taken into the heart of the American people because he had finally handled the task in the Mediterranean with firmness, efficiency, and dispatch."[3] When Decatur returned to Philadelphia, he and Stewart discussed the past three years of their respective lives. Just after their meeting Stewart was appointed as captain of the new ship-of-the-line, the USS *Franklin*, and then, in 1817 after a well-deserved leave, he was selected as commodore of the Mediterranean Squadron, having already graciously declined a presidential appointment to the cabinet.

Which cabinet position is in question. One would think Stewart would have been appointed Navy secretary, but no direct evidence shows that Stewart was considered for that position. Benjamin Crowninshield from Maine had been Navy secretary since January 1815, and he continued in this capacity through October 1817, when President Monroe appointed John C. Calhoun as interim secretary.[4]

However, another Madison appointee, War Secretary William Crawford from Georgia, departed his cabinet position in October 1816, just prior to the presidential election. Madison appointed George Oraham interim war secretary that same month. Possibly, Stewart was offered the office first, but because he declined, Madison appointed Oraham.

At first glance, this post might not have been something a sailor would have been qualified to assume. However, Stewart was well versed in military and naval affairs, and he had shown an astute appreciation of the role of the executive branch outlined in the U.S. Constitution. Also, his knowledge of the Constitution had translated into a deep appreciation of the civilian-military relationship that it set forth, as evidenced when he persuaded a fired-up

Commodore Rodgers to refrain from starting his own war. Further, Stewart demonstrated a sound grasp of naval strategy when he recommended an offensive strategy for the War of 1812. His success in defending Norfolk from British attack can be traced to his understanding of the cooperative and complementary roles that ground and naval forces must maintain to operate successfully within a littoral warfare environment. During that same war, his friend Richard Rush had consulted him as to the assignment of army officers to artillery units.[5] As a successful businessman and merchant, he understood the finer points of acquisition and logistics. All his qualifications aside, had Stewart accepted either cabinet position, his career as a naval officer would have been finished, and the captain had always seen himself first and foremost as a sailor and a naval officer. Regardless of whether he was asked to be either secretary, Stewart served at the pleasure of the president. Because Madison's term expired in a matter of months, the captain had no guarantee that the new president would want him to continue in a cabinet post. Therefore, Stewart opted to continue his career as one of the Navy's senior commissioned officers.[6]

With this decision, Stewart's naval career did not languish, for his credentials and reputation were held in high esteem. Stewart instead garnered the most prestigious appointment of his naval career to date, when an appreciative and astute President James Monroe selected him to command the Mediterranean Squadron.

Stewart must have felt a great deal of satisfaction when he learned that he was to assume command of the nation's premier naval force, which operated on a body of water he knew very well. Along with Decatur, Stewart was one of the most experienced officers in the U.S. Navy in commanding a multiship formation at sea, especially in the Mediterranean. In fact, prior to Decatur's own appointment, only Capt. Thomas Macdonough, who successfully fought a defensive battle at Plattsburg, New York, during the War of 1812, and Capt. Oliver Hazard Perry, who during the same war won the Battle of Lake Erie, had combat experience as a commander of a multi-ship formation; Decatur's was limited at best. Also, prior to Decatur only Perry and Stewart had operated an American naval force offensively. However, the situation in the Mediterranean had altered a great deal since the last time Stewart had sailed its waters a full decade prior. Stewart's gifts as a diplomat, leader, and negotiator soon came to the fore.

The Mediterranean was now an inland sea free of the threat from Napoleon, who was defeated on 18 June 1815 at the Battle of Waterloo. The French and Spanish fleets had virtually disappeared under the Royal Navy's relenting naval campaign. Also, the piratical activity of Barbary States clustered along the North African coast was much reduced. Significant cracks in the ruling structure of the Ottoman Empire were becoming more evident, especially where the waters of the Mediterranean washed the ragged shoreline of Greece. Stewart sailed into that great inland sea on board one of America's latest statements of naval power upon the world's oceans.

Receiving his orders for the Mediterranean, Stewart became the commanding officer of one of America's first line-of-battleships, the seventy-four-gun USS *Franklin*. The *Franklin* was rated a ship-of-the-line, a symbol of the supreme expression of a waterborne war machine. The sheer number of guns found on board ships-of-the-line (such as Admiral Nelson's HMS *Victory*, which exceeded one hundred guns), together with their mobility, represented the greatest concentration of destructive firepower, unmatched by the armies of the world during this time. As the descriptive term ship-of-the-line implies, these warships were to be aligned in a "line of battle" opposite one another, firing broadside after broadside until one fleet submitted. The seventy-four-gun ship-of-the-line was the most numerous and versatile of this type of warship then employed, and at the end of the War of 1812, America entered the capital ship arena with the completion of four seventy-four-gun ships.

Franklin was the third of the 74s authorized in 1813 and the first ship built at the new Philadelphia Navy Yard. Her constructor was Samuel Humphreys, who adapted the design created by William Doughty by updating the 1799 plans of Samuel's father, Joshua, principally by substituting a round bow for the earlier beak-head bulkhead style. The fourth of the 74s, *Columbus*, was burned at the Washington Navy Yard in 1814 to prevent her capture by the British. She was restarted at that yard under an 1816 authorization and to a still-newer design by Doughty.

The *Franklin* was launched on 21 August 1815 before a massive crowd estimated at nearly fifty thousand people.[7] One of the dignitaries in attendance was Charles Stewart. Commissioned in late 1815, her near sisters were the USS *Independence*, commissioned on 3 July 1815, and the USS *Washington*, which was commissioned on 25 August 1815. Both of these ships were also rated as seventy-four-gun ships-of-the-line.[8] These three ships, statements of nineteenth-century America's commitment to the pursuit of global naval power, were of the same design philosophy as the frigate *Constitution*; they were "heavy." *Franklin*'s dimensions were larger than those of her European counterparts: her length measured 187 feet, $10^3/4$ inches between the perpendiculars, with 50 foot molded beam, and she measured 19 feet, 9 inches depth of hold. The *Franklin*'s displacement was also heavier than that of her counterparts across the Atlantic at 2,243 tons. Joshua Humphreys built his "heavy frigates" to dominate their contemporaries in battle, and this could also be seen in the *Franklin*'s armament: sixty-three thirty-two-pound long guns and twenty-four thirty-two-pound carronades. She was indeed a heavy "74," and, although she was much admired for her construction, Stewart's flagship paid a price for her size and was ultimately considered a failure. With their bulk, these ships were unable to carry their lower-deck guns high enough above the water, in service condition, compared to ships of similar rates abroad. "The fault of all of the 74's built for the Navy in these years was that they did not have sufficient displacement to carry the armament placed on board."[9] Failure or not, the *Franklin* was an impressive ship, and she was now awaiting her captain.

Stewart joined his ship in Philadelphia in early 1817. His former first officer of the *Constitution*, now M. Cdr. Henry Ballard, joined him as his first officer. Stewart asked for Ballard to command the *Franklin* when he was notified that he would command the Mediterranean Squadron. While preparing for the deployment, Stewart and Ballard received on board the *Franklin* the newly elected president of the United States, James Monroe, and his entourage. "On coming over the Gangway he was received and saluted by Captain Stewart and the officers of the ship and the Guard of Marines, a salute of 18 guns was also fired. After visiting every part of the ship and partaking of some refreshments in the Cabin with the Officers, he went on shore at 1.30. . . . he was accompanied by Captain Stewart."[10] Shortly after this event, Stewart turned command over to Ballard and both prepared for their fall departure. Prior to the ship's departure, the newly appointed commodore received another honor. On 22 September the *Franklin*'s log read: "These 24 hours commence with light-breezes from the Eastward and cloudy weather, attended with rain. Commodore Stewart came on board, accompanied by Commodore Murray, and several distinguished characters. On this occasion General Duncan presented Com. Stewart with the Sword voted him by the State of Pennsylvania."[11] A grateful state presented this gift to him in recognition for his service during the War of 1812.

When Commodore Stewart stepped on board his flagship's quarterdeck that day, he must have felt a strong sense of gratification seeing his broad pennant hoisted aloft. As the bosun pipes shrilled, and the Marine honor guard presented arms, Master Commandant Ballard received his commodore and guests with all due ceremony and warmth. The ship's company turned out smartly by division to await inspection by their commodore and dignitaries. Some of the midshipmen in charge of their respective divisions were men who became known for their actions during the Civil War: Mid. David Dixon Porter, the son of Stewart's good friend and former first officer who became one of the Navy's great admirals; Mid. Franklin Buchanan, the future commander of the Confederate States Navy; and Mid. Louis Goldsborough, who commanded the Federal Navy's blockading squadron and directed the actions of the USS *Monitor*. Additionally, Charles Stewart's nephew, Mid. Daniel McCauley, was berthed with the rest of the midshipmen. Before the end of his cruise, other future senior naval officers joined the midshipman's berth.

All was correct with the inspection of the ship's company and Marines, and this too would have given Stewart satisfaction, for it made him another step closer to returning to sea. His sense of satisfaction and anticipation would have been balanced by a sense of worry, for he would soon be away from a very troubled married life.

Charles and Delia had moved from Boston shortly after his return to the city on board *Constitution* in the spring of 1815. While still on furlough, the Stewarts packed up and moved south to Philadelphia. Leaving Boston, and her immediate family, must have been difficult for Delia, a mother of two young children. She would be additionally upset about being removed from her connections to Boston society. As a member of a family of prominence, Delia would have had significant connections to Philadelphia society, but because Philadelphia society was not Boston society, it was not a happy prospect for her. For Charles the move was very much the opposite. Although the captain had acquired a tidy sum in prize money and through his business connections, because Delia had expensive tastes, keeping up with Boston society was draining his bank account.

Within a short time of their arrival in Philadelphia, Charles Stewart purchased 225 acres of land situated on a bluff overlooking the Delaware River. The property, a short waterborne excursion up the river from Philadelphia, was located on the New Jersey side near Bordentown. Charles and Delia built a comfortable home and took up residence. But soon their day-to-day interaction demolished what was left of a terribly mismatched relationship. Bordentown was certainly not Boston, and it seems that one of Stewart's reasons for moving there was to make it inconvenient for Delia to immerse herself in the daily activities of Philadelphia society.

On 14 October 1817, the USS *Franklin* sailed with the tide down the Delaware River to the Atlantic.[12] The *Franklin*'s voyage to the Mediterranean was not to be a direct sail. She had been ordered to proceed to Annapolis, Maryland, to await the arrival of the newly appointed American ambassador to the Court of St. James—his friend, Richard Rush.

Born on 29 August 1780, Richard Rush was two years Stewart's junior. He attended the same school as young Charles, Stephen Decatur, and Richard Somers. When Stewart was at sea with the merchant service, Rush entered college at Princeton (now Princeton University) at age fourteen. He graduated in 1797, the youngest of thirty-three classmates. The young Charles Stewart received his lieutenant's commission the following March. Rush worked as an attorney in Philadelphia, and by the spring of 1811 he was the attorney general of Pennsylvania. At that time, he became involved in a form of machismo that all of Stewart's friends seemed hell-bent on pursuing; Rush dueled with another attorney. His opponent missed, and Rush fired his pistol into the air.[13] During the War of 1812, Rush was active in government circles, serving as assistant comptroller of the Treasury. He corresponded on several occasions with his friend Stewart, asking the captain's advice regarding the commissioning of artillery officers. Rush and Stewart remained friends throughout Rush's life. In 1817 President Monroe appointed Stewart's friend to succeed John Quincy Adams as America's new ambassador to Great Britain. In fact, President Monroe had appointed Rush as interim state secretary until Adams returned from Britain to assume the position. Now his friend Commodore Stewart and the *Franklin* sailed Ambassador Rush and his family to Britain.

Another Philadelphian, on board *Franklin* as one of her lieutenants, was present when the new ambassador arrived on that very grey, weather-threatening 19 November in Annapolis, Maryland. This lieutenant was Uriah Levy, who had been born in Philadelphia, which in 1792, at the time of his birth, had the largest Jewish community in the Western Hemisphere. Levy had been with the *Franklin* since 1816, just after he received his lieutenant's commission. As a seasoned master of his own merchant vessel, Levy had joined the fleet as a sailing master during the War of 1812. For his outstanding combat service on board the USS *Argus*, Levy, "in common with other officers, desired that his services should be recognized by promotion, under the rule that 'masters of extraordinary merit and for extraordinary services may be promoted to lieutenants.' His sponsors were Comos. David Porter, Stephen Decatur, John Rodgers, and Charles Stewart."[14] His appointment caused much resentment among the officer corps of the period, in which anti-Semitism was widespread. Additionally, Levy's promotion leapt over the broad expanse of midshipman. Many sailors were resentful of those of "lesser rank" who took away their own chances for promotion. As lieutenant, Levy's Navy life became exceedingly difficult; his departure from Philadelphia, like Stewart's, must have been of mixed emotions. Now on board the *Franklin*, Levy served a commodore who was one of his sponsors, allowing him to show his benefactor he had salt and grit. But this satisfaction would have been tempered by the isolation he felt from his fellow officers in the ship's wardroom. For Levy and his commodore, it quickly became a challenging cruise.

With Lieutenant Levy as the officer of the deck, the *Franklin* received its passengers. As written in the log, "at 4 pm Mr. Rush, his Lady, children, and suite came on board. Fired a salute of 15 guns on his arrival on board."[15] Another source notes: "Boarding at Annapolis on 19 November with the Rushes (and extensive stores) were four children, a secretary, three servants, and a mocking bird (a gift of Secretary Crawford to Lady Auckland). This was the first time Rush had been shipboard. He was not seasick but there was a severe storm only a few days out."[16] The storm severely tested Captain

Faced with anti-Semitism from his fellow officers in the Mediterranean Squadron, Lt. Uriah Levy found support from Como. Charles Stewart. Later a captain himself, Levy fought to abolish the practice of flogging. (Unattributed; courtesy of the Naval Historical Center)

Ballard and the crew of the *Franklin*.[17] On any given day over 10 percent of the crew reported sick. The storm blew the "heavy" liner hundreds of miles off course, and she had to pull into Bermuda for a short respite.

Despite the miserable crossing, Stewart and Rush were able to spend considerable time together. Stewart found his "scholarly guest as eager for instruction as the youngest midshipman."[18] In his biography of Rush, John Powell wrote about a particular time Rush spent with his schoolboy friend:

> In the midst of the raging storm, while hanging on to one of the guns that had been run into the cabin to keep them from banging about the pitching deck, Rush began an investigation of naval warfare. "Commodore," he inquired, "what would you do if we were at war and an enemy of equal force hove in sight?" "Chase him," the Commodore answered. Rush was amazed. Give chase, when for ten hours the whole energy of the crew had been engaged in combating the storm? "Certainly you could not fight him," he shouted. Stewart explained. Not in the storm, he admitted, but immediately [when] it was over.[19]

On 14 December the weather-beaten *Franklin* entered the English Channel.

On 19 December the USS *Franklin*, America's newest capital ship, arrived in Portsmouth, England, the home of the Royal Navy. The officers of the Royal Navy took note of the importance of Rush's arrival in England in the wake of the second war between the British and the Americans in four decades, offering at least one occasion to dine with Rush and Commodore Stewart. In the middle of the dinner, Stewart, likely in conversation about tactics and his prior experience facing British ships, declared to a shocked audience that he could capture the city of London. The British officers found little satisfaction in his response to the question, "How would you do it?"— "The secret I reserved for the benefit of my country, should she require it." Was it audacity, arrogance, or a well-calculated gesture to impress upon those foreign officers that while Rush was there to make peace, Stewart and America would be prepared should peace fail? The British officers in attendance would have found it difficult to contradict the American commodore, for he had been one of the young country's few captains to have never lost in battle or be outmaneuvered when outnumbered. Like John Paul Jones before him, Stewart did not hesitate to command his ship across a cold and unforgiving ocean into the waters close to the British Empire.

Shortly after the dinner, Stewart and Rush parted company. Stewart and *Franklin* remained in Portsmouth through the Christmas season, and the ship became the center of attention, not only of her Royal Navy hosts but also of the commodore of the Russian squadron lying at Spithead. On 30 December Commodore Stewart received his Russian counterpart on board *Franklin* with all honors and courtesy. On the following day, New Year's Day 1818, Commodore Stewart directed his captain to set sail for the Mediterranean, and *Franklin* left with the tide. Her passage to Gibraltar was a relatively quick one for a winter passage down the English Channel and into the eastern Atlantic. Just the same, all on board were extremely pleased to see the Rock. However, their commodore did not wish to linger very long.

Arriving at Gibraltar on 12 January, Stewart went ashore for just six hours, to deliver dispatches to the American consul, receive the latest intelligence from him, introduce himself to the Royal Navy commander as the new Mediterranean Squadron commander, and then he returned to his 74. Stewart departed the next day with the understanding that he would find Chauncey and the squadron at Syracuse, Sicily. *Franklin* arrived at the squadron's primary anchorage in Syracuse on 29 January. This was certainly an important day for Stewart and his flagship. Despite her difficult winter crossing, the new *Franklin* would have appeared better than many of the ships (foreign and domestic) on station as she approached the squadron for the first time. But, as the *Franklin* and Commodore Chauncey's flagship, the seventy-four-gun USS *George Washington*, exchanged a seventeen-gun salute, the *Franklin* ran aground on the western side of the harbor. As Chauncey and the squadron looked on, the embarrassed but undamaged *Franklin* was kedged off the sandbar by the stern, with the assistance of the boats and their crews from the ships of the squadron. By the end of the day, the *Franklin* was warped into the middle of the harbor. All in the squadron must have hoped this incident was not a bad omen for the new flagship and commodore.

On the following day, 30 January, Commodore Chauncey, together with Captains Crane and Gamble and other officers, came on board the *Franklin* for the official change of command. At noon, Stewart assumed command of the squadron from Chauncey, and as Stewart's blue command pendant was hoisted aloft, the entire squadron fired a salute of eighteen guns each. Commodore Chauncey returned to his former flagship, the USS *George Washington*, to become the squadron's second-most senior officer until he and his ship departed the Mediterranean later in the year.

Under Stewart's command, the squadron carried on its normal peacetime duties. "In the half century from the close of the War of 1812 to the outbreak of the Civil War the navy went about its business in peace. . . . The navy's frigates, sloops, and an occasional glowering ship-of-the-line cruised on foreign stations, showing the flag with staunch regularity."[20] Stewart's intention can be seen clearly in his correspondence, dated 3 February 1818, to Richard Rush:

> I am ordered by the government of the United States to apprise your Excellency of my arrival in the Mediterranean in the Ship *Franklin*, and of my having assumed the command of the Squadron of Ships of the United States, employed in this sea. I have to ask the favour of your Excellency to apprise me, if proper, of any changes which may take place, in the relations existing between the United States and the Government at which you reside, which may have any bearing on the employment of the Force under my command, the existing relations between the United States and the Barbary Powers; or the safety of the ships and vessels of war composing the squadron. Should any changes take place in this quarter I shall lose no time in giving your Excellency information of it.[21]

To employ this force, Stewart had to ensure his squadron was ready, and almost immediately he found himself confronted with what would become just the first case of insubordination by his officers. The causes of this particular case of insubordination reflected the norms of nineteenth-century American society, as well as the culture of the American naval officer corps. Ugly aspects of both now confronted Stewart.

Lt. Uriah Levy had accompanied Stewart on board the *Franklin* as one of four supernumerary lieutenants. Upon rendezvousing with the squadron, he and the other three officers were to be transferred to other ships in the squadron. Because he was Jewish, Levy had already experienced the prejudice of his fellow junior officers in the *Franklin*'s wardroom.

> Levy was soon made to feel that the toleration which had been shown the sailing-master, not in the line of promotion, and in time of war, had suddenly changed to a feeling of hostility toward the lieutenant in time of peace. Ostracism, a favourite weapon with religious enthusiasts, was first tried for the purpose of forcing the Jew to resign. The old frigates and line-of-battle ships carried from four to eight hundred men, but Lieutenant Levy found himself always alone. Life aboard ship is at best a sort of voluntary imprisonment. Levy was always incommunicado.[22]

Stewart may or may not have known about this situation. As commodore, he would have been extremely reluctant to interfere with Ballard's authority as *Franklin*'s captain. At the same time, as commodore, Stewart would have been insulated from some of the daily shipboard duties. He may or may not have been prejudiced himself, but, as a native Philadelphian, his interactions with Jewish Americans would have been more frequent than those of many of his contemporaries. Considering his staunch abolitionist stance in later life, it may be safe to say that he was someone who looked at another man more for his character and performance than for his ethnic, religious, or racial background.

Also, as mentioned earlier, Lieutenant Levy's commission was based on the personal recommendations of Stewart and his good friends Decatur and Porter. This would have been widely known among the junior officers, and, as a consequence, the shunning that Levy experienced would probably have been a subtle form, something that could be kept from senior officers. However, when Commodore Stewart issued orders for Mr. Levy to report on board the USS *United States* as one of the frigate's new lieutenants, the captain and officers' objections immediately surfaced, and with them, a challenge to Stewart's command.

In one of the many courts-martial that Levy faced throughout his career, the testimony given by Lieutenant (later Commodore) Jones, who at the time was the frigate *United States*'s first lieutenant, offers a view into what Levy and Stewart had to confront:

> On the arrival of the *Franklin* . . . it was understood that Lieutenant Levy . . . was to be ordered to the frigate *United States*, then short of her complement of lieutenants. Whereupon the wardroom mess, without consulting me, determined to remonstrate against Levy's coming aboard. I was called on by a member of the mess to communicate their wishes to Captain Crane and ask his interference. Astonished at such a proposition, I inquired as to the cause, when I was answered that he was a Jew and not an agreeable person, and they did not want to be brought in contact with him in our then very pleasant and harmonious mess of some eight or nine persons, and, moreover, that he was an interloper, having entered the navy as master, to the prejudice of the older midshipmen, etc., etc. Such was the reply in substance to my inquiry. I then asked the relator if he or any member of our mess knew anything of his own knowledge derogatory to Lieutenant Levy, as an officer or as a gentleman. The answer was no, but they had heard thus and so, and so forth, and so forth.

Jones continued his testimony by saying,

> I endeavoured to point out the difficulties that might result from a procedure so much at variance with military subordination and the justice . . . to sue to a brother officer against whom they had nothing but vague and ill-defined ru-

mours. But my counsel did not prevail; the remonstrance was made directly to Captain Crane, and by Captain Crane to Commodore Stewart. Levy soon after reported on board the frigate *United States* for duty. When Lieutenant Levy came on board he asked for a private interview with me, wishing my advice as to the proper course he ought to pursue under such embarrassing circumstances. I gave it freely and simply: to this effect, viz.: Do your duty as an officer and a gentleman, be civil to all, however reserved you may choose to be to any, and the first man who observes a different course toward you, call him to a strict and prompt account. Our messmates were gentlemen, and having perceived their error before Lieutenant Levy got on board, had, in accordance with my previous advice, determined to receive Lieutenant Levy as a gentleman and a brother officer, and to respect and treat him as such, till by his conduct he should prove himself unworthy. . . . I know that, perhaps with a single exception, those who opposed his joining our mess not only relented, but deeply regretted the false step they had incautiously taken.[23]

So great was the prejudice against Levy, the officers on board blatantly flaunted a challenge to their commodore's authority when Captain Crane ordered Levy to return to the flagship. Stewart could not and would not allow this to stand. However, his approach to resolving this issue said much about his demeanor. Stewart issued a second order to Captain Crane that succinctly stated who was in command:

UNITED STATES SHIP "FRANKLIN,"

SYRACUSE, February 4, 1818.

To William M. Crane, Commanding the Frigate "United States."

SIR: Lieutenant Uriah P. Levy will report to you for duty on board the frigate United States, under your command. It is not without regret that a second order is found necessary to change the position of one officer in this squadron.

Respectfully, your obedient servant,
CHARLES STEWART

For Stewart, this would not be the last episode challenging the absolute necessity of maintaining "good order and discipline."

Concerning America's former adversaries, the rulers of Algiers, Tripoli, and Tunis, Stewart dispatched a single warship to affect communications with the respective American ambassadors. Routinely, he ensured that all of his major combatants sailed as a squadron along the North African littoral, stopping in each principal port. The objective of such operations was twofold. The first was to show the flag, while the second was to maintain communication with the assigned U.S. consular generals. In response to a 28 March copy of a dispatch written by U.S. Consular General to Tripoli R. B. Jones to U.S. Consular General to Algiers William Shaler, detailing the outbreak of a civil war and the threat that it presented to the rule of the bashaw, Stewart led his first sortie along the North African coast. This particular bashaw had signed a peace treaty with the United States. Stewart realized that his overthrow jeopardized the treaty, and that the arrival of a substantial American squadron would convey a powerful message to the usurpers that the U.S. government was "not inattentive to their slightest movements."[24] However, Stewart also realized that the United States must remain neutral in this "civil war," and as such, he had to be careful not to show any outward favor.

Departing Syracuse 6 April, the squadron arrived first at Tunis. Stewart stayed just long enough to convey and receive dispatches, meet with Consular General Jones, and ascertain from him the latest intelligence from Algiers. It was Stewart's first time back to Tunis since he commanded the *Essex*, and his return would have certainly reminded him of the time he had had to inform a former commodore that only Congress, not a naval officer, had the authority to declare war. Commodore Stewart would surely have remembered because this incident, together with his operational knowledge of the Mediterranean, had probably contributed the most to his selection as the squadron commander.

The *Enterprise, Pennsylvania, South Carolina,* and *Hornet*—Stewart commanded these ships or their sister ships throughout his career. (Fred S. Cozzens; courtesy of the Naval Historical Center)

From Tunis, he directed the squadron to proceed westward toward Algiers. At noon on 12 April the squadron anchored in the harbor and exchanged twenty-one gun salutes with the city's fortifications. Stewart met with Consular William Shaler and emissaries of the dey. With the knowledge that American and Tunisian relations were peaceful, Stewart departed Algiers on 14 April and sailed the squadron to Leghorn, passing Minorca on the way.

When Stewart's squadron anchored in Leghorn's harbor, Italy was still far from becoming a unified nation-state. As part of showing the flag and cultivating the several Italian nation-states, Commodore Stewart and his flagship entertained many of his Italian naval contemporaries and members of the governing class. Two weeks after the squadron's arrival, the logbook of the USS *Franklin* stated simply that the duke of Modena and the captain of a Genoese frigate were welcomed on board. Full naval honors were rendered to both gentlemen. Stewart knew well the importance of cultivating those who would influence American trading prospects.

A few days later an outbreak of the plague forced the squadron to depart. After dozens of men from the squadron were hospitalized at Pisa and at least one death was recorded on board *Franklin*, Stewart directed the squadron to get under way for healthier climes.[25] Departing on 28 May with the USS *Peacock*, *Franklin* made sail for Gibraltar to await resupply, fresh drafts of men from the States, and dispatches from the Navy and state secretaries.

Skirting the Spanish coast, *Franklin* arrived on 3 June, and *Peacock* arrived the following day. Stewart, *Franklin*, and elements of the squadron remained in Gibraltar and its environs, waiting for replacements, supplies, and dispatches, and cruised on its adjacent waters through the rest of June. While there, the commodore received dispatches from Rush and from the American ambassador to Spain. Additionally, as senior officer present, he would have interacted with his Royal Navy contemporaries.

The information that Stewart received from the ambassador regarding the deteriorating situation between Spain and her South American colonies, along with his knowledge of the recent series of South American revolutions, would give the commodore the leg up when the U.S. government decided to form the Pacific Squadron.

With their fill of supplies, men, and dispatches, the commodore, the *Franklin*, and the USS *Peacock* set sail from Gibraltar for a return trip to Leghorn on 3 July, and upon arrival on 14 July, the *Franklin*'s log read that the *United States* and *Erie* were at anchor in the roadstead.

With summer passing, Stewart became increasingly concerned about the prospects of a crisis between Britain and the United States over Florida's sovereignty. In a private letter to his friend Richard Rush, Stewart wrote on 9 August 1818 of his concern for developing events, the possibilities of war, and the prospects of his squadron operating in the Mediterranean Sea against a hostile Royal Navy.

> My Dear Sir, I have had the honor to receive your esteemed favour of the 18th May in duplicate copies and return you thanks for the attention. I have also heard from Mr. Erving at Madrid but nothing calculated to excite alarm as regards the Spanish Government. It is towards the Government at which you reside I look with most anxiety, and rumours in this quarter, relative to Florida, the sailing of several ships of the line from England under the pretext of exercising their men. The Government papers speak with a boldness, which excites apprehension, from any other quarter, we have not much to apprehend, but unless timely advised, in case of danger from England, our situation here would be critical, and a considerable part of the nation's force rendered useless in case of a contest. Should you have anything to communicate send your letter to the care of Mr. Thomas Appleton Consul at Leghorn and a copy to Mr. Henry, Consul at Gibraltar. In this way I shall receive your letters more direct and immediately, be pleased to present my best respects to your good lady Mrs. R. and believe me with great respect and esteem.[26]

Stewart was concerned that if a crisis developed and turned into a war with Britain, his squadron and America's premier naval force would be operationally overextended and unable to exit the Mediterranean and return to America. Unless he had a sufficient warning, a superior British fleet could quickly block the Strait of Gibraltar, preventing his squadron from breaking out into the Atlantic. Fortunately, the dispute over Florida was quickly remedied, and it proved a touchstone of the Monroe Doctrine, later forged by Richard Rush, the British government, and the Monroe administration. Not knowing the extent of the crisis, Stewart departed Leghorn as a precautionary measure on 17 August and steered for Messina, Italy. Arriving on the twenty-first, he stayed long enough to ensure messages conveying his appraisal of the current state of the country's affairs were sent to members of the squadron anchored at Syracuse and other locales within the Mediterranean. Stewart then left with *Franklin* for Gibraltar on the twenty-second and arrived on 9 September. Upon hearing the Florida crisis had been averted, Stewart, the *Franklin*, and the USS *Erie* departed eastward to convey dispatches to the American consul at Algiers and show the flag again along the North African coast. Arriving at Algiers on 22 September, he stayed briefly to exchange dispatches and latest intelligence with the American consul. Stewart sailed into Palermo, Sicily, on 9 October, and remained there through 23 October before returning to the squadron anchorage of Syracuse on 1 November.

By 6 November most of the squadron had converged upon Syracuse. Standing in the roadstead were the USS *Franklin,* USS *Erie,* USS *Peacock,* and USS *Spark.* While anchored in the port, Stewart exercised his prerogative as squadron commander to reassign his junior officers. The captain of his flagship and fellow veteran of the *Constitution*'s two war cruises, Master Commandant Henry Ballard, was transferred to the USS *Erie* and assumed command on 17 November. Stewart appointed Lt. Cmdg. John Gallagher, the *Franklin*'s first lieutenant, as the ship's commanding officer.

Throughout November the squadron operated locally. From time to time, Stewart ordered one of his smaller vessels to pick up and deliver dispatches, as well as show the flag about the Mediterranean. On 5 December the new frigate USS *Guerriere* of forty-four guns (actually she carried fifty-three guns) arrived. This ship was the latest statement in America's quest for the "heavy frigate, and it complemented its captain, Thomas Macdonough, the 'Hero of the Battle of Lake Champlain.'"[27] Stewart recognized McDonough for his bravery, but he considered him to be a "bit weak headed."[28] Later events that threw the squadron into chaos confirmed Stewart's opinion. But, Macdonough and Stewart's confrontation did not arise until the spring of the new year—1819. In the interim, the squadron reduced its operational tempo for the winter season and spent Christmas and New Years in the waters of eastern Sicily. In February a very young David Glasgow Farragut, returning to the squadron after taking leave, joined the midshipmen's berth on board the *Franklin.* This was duly noted in the ship's log: "Monday, 15 February 1819: Mid. D. G. Farragut join'd this ship."[29] Robert Schneller wrote the following about Commodore Stewart and Midshipman Farragut's professional interaction:

> Farragut rejoined the squadron at Messina in February 1819, shipping aboard the liner *Franklin.* The *Franklin* had been the flagship of the Mediterranean Squadron the previous summer when the *Washington* sailed for home. Farragut yet again served as aide to the skipper. Impressed by Farragut's ability, knowledge, and deportment, Stewart promoted him as an acting lieutenant and ordered him to the brig *Spark* during the later part of the year.[30]

Farragut received his lieutenancy one year earlier than Stewart received his through John Barry's endorsement. According to Alfred T. Mahan's biography of Admiral Farragut, "this promotion, coming at so early an age, he afterward looked upon as one of the most important events of his life.[31]

However, despite this excellent turn of events for the young officer, Farragut wrote years later that Captain Stewart "could see no justification for the slightest 'insubordination' of a young officer—he is one of the sternest—and I think most illiberal judges I have ever seen."[32] Farragut's judgment was probably correct from the perspective of a young man, but with further reflection upon Stewart's own experience with midshipmen, Farragut's impressions most likely did not take into consideration Stewart's understanding that without a strong sense of good order and discipline among his very young officers, their behavior would likely be unprofessional. The most salient example and the most reprehensible to Stewart was the propensity of the young to duel one another. Furthermore, Farragut might not have been aware that his commodore had been selected to command the squadron in part to restore the good order and discipline that his predecessor, Commodore Chauncey, had been unable to maintain.[33]

Years later, when Adm. David Farragut commanded a Union naval force before Mobile Bay, he paid tribute to his old mentor. Just before the battle, Farragut told his officers and men, "We have no better seamen in the service today than those gallant fellows Bainbridge, Decatur, Hull, Perry, Porter, and Charles Stewart."[34]

Farragut's opinion of Stewart's treatment of midshipmen stands in marked contrast to the recollections of another midshipman in Stewart's squadron. Rear Adm. Charles Wilkes recounted that "the Navy, at the time I am writing of, was in a peculiar and anomalous condition; no school could have been worse for the morals and none so corruptly and so very viciously constituted. . . . The older midshipman . . . were entirely wanting in principles, had all the rude manners of their class and ignorant."[35] He further added that "a midshipman's life on board an American man of war was a dog's life, and in many respects acts of tyranny and a total disregard to the feelings of the young officers were lost sight of."[36]

Wilkes also remembered that his midshipmen's mess was separated into two distinct groups—North and South middies.[37] His appraisal of the division in the midshipmen's mess was probably more than just the recognition that it was based upon cultural and regional lines. After all, the Navy reflected the increasing division within the country that it served, a division along increasingly cultural differences between North and South. However, it seems that Wilkes saw the division more between those who possessed high moral and religious convictions and those who did not. Wilkes stated in his autobiography that "in Messina entertainment was a small theater, an opera house and casino rooms; Com Stuart generally took a Seat at one of the tables and betted largely. Discipline and morals of the Squadron suffered greatly. . . . Crews were intoxicated almost daily."[38] Wilkes provided some insight, albeit indirectly, as to his feelings for his commodore, when he observed that Stewart's second in command, Captain Macdonough, was "a moral and religious man of high tone and character."[39]

With winter conditions diminishing, the squadron's operational tempo increased. Stewart planned for another spring of cruising the Mediterranean, with the intent of visiting major ports and capitals to show the flag. As in the previous year, the squadron also called at Gibraltar to await supplies, fresh drafts of men, and official correspondence. With the smaller warships scattered on their appointed missions to send and receive correspondence to the consular generals in the Mediterranean, Stewart departed Messina on 15 April, in company with the *Erie* and *Guerriere*, bound for Palermo, Sicily. From there, Stewart directed the elements of the squadron to sail to Naples, to Tunis, and westward to Malaga, Spain.

Departing Palermo in early May, *Franklin*, *Erie*, and *Guerriere* sailed for Naples and their prearranged rendezvous with the smaller ships of the squadron. Naples was the capital of the Kingdom of the Two Sicilies and a port at which the commodore and the squadron received many official visitors. All who came on board the flagship were struck by her beauty and efficiency. The young Mid. Charles Wilkes must have been impressed; years later as a rear admiral, he recounted, "The *Franklin* is a beautiful ship both in model and efficiency. She had been recently painted, inside and out, and every bolt and stanchion on her deck was like burnished Silver, and her crew as neat and clean in White and Blue . . . radiant. . . . Royal guests were struck with wonder . . . almost afraid to enter on deck."[40]

Shortly after Stewart's arrival, the *Franklin*'s log recorded such an event.

> May 18, 1819: at 5pm the Emperor of Austria and King of Naples with their suite visited the ship. We rec'd them with the yards manned, the Austrian Colors at the Fore Mast head and the Neapolitan at the Mizzen, when they got on deck fired two salutes of twenty one guns each. After they had visited the several parts of the ship, fired three repeating swivels [probably examples of the Chambers guns] at a target from the launch and 1st and 2nd cutters. At 7:15 manned the yards and the company left the ship.[41]

What was not recorded by the log, but what has been passed on through Stewart's own recollections, was an incident that all sailors recognize in which visitors, not accustomed to the ways of life afloat, can come to harm.

While the squadron lay at Naples the Emperor of Austria and suite visited the *Franklin*. The Grand Master of the Empress—who with other of the Imperial officers was attired in brilliant uniform—being somewhat near-sighted, mistook a wind sail for a mast and fell from the deck to the cockpit, breaking his ankle. The accident occasioned great alarm for a few moments. The Commodore, who was engaged in conversation at the time, not seeing what had happened, asked what the matter was. The old quarter-master of the watch, whose duty it was to see everything, far and near, replied easily: 'Oh, nothing, sir; only one of them bloody kings has fallen down the hatch!'[42]

The American squadron became a major attraction for European nobility, and such were the demands placed on Stewart that the farthermost aft cabin guns were stowed below to provide him with more room to entertain official guests. However, the crush of showing the flag became secondary with the departure of the viceroy of Sicily and his entourage on 26 May. On that same day Stewart ordered signal 297, convene courts-martial, to be sent aloft. Little did he know that this signal would be the precursor to one of his greatest challenges as a naval officer.

The *Franklin*'s captain, Lieutenant Commandant Gallagher, ordered Robert Sloane, a Marine on board the *Franklin*, to be tried by courts-martial. Sloane had "murderously assaulted a member of the *Franklin*'s crew," and, for the common-sense reason of changing the proceeding's location, Stewart ordered Sloane's court-martial to be held on board Macdonough's ship, the *Guerriere*.[43] While the commodore was receiving the viceroy of Sicily, Macdonough, as senior officer, presided over the court, which consisted of those commanding officers present at Naples, including Captain Ballard of the *Erie*, Master Commandant Nicholson of the *Spark*, and Lieutenant Commandant Gallagher and Lieutenant Page of the *Franklin*. The court finished the day without reaching a verdict, but they and Macdonough decided to reconvene the proceedings the next day ashore in Naples. Macdonough "preferred to sit at a hotel in Naples, where the man was tried and convicted."[44] After meeting the following day, Macdonough sent the decision of the court to Commodore Stewart, who promptly declared the court illegal and released Sloane from custody. Stewart knew that (1) any session of a court-martial held at any place other than that directed by orders was illegal and (2) the second session of Sloane's court-martial was not conducted on American soil. Had the second session been conducted as ordered on board *Guerriere*, a U.S. warship and thus sovereign U.S. territory, the illegal ruling would have been avoided. In his letter to Macdonough, Stewart wrote: "The foregoing proceedings of the court being illegally held on the last day of the meeting of the said court in the city of Naples, where the U. States of America have no jurisdiction, and it being there held in violation of the order contained in the warrant dated May 26, 1819, directing the same to be held on-board the U.S. frigate *Guerriere*, directs the prisoner to be released and considers the proceedings null and void."⁴⁵

Before the court-martial officers could respond, and knowing there could be trouble, Stewart correctly and prudently ordered the squadron to sea.

Through the rest of May and the entire month of June, the squadron scattered throughout the Mediterranean on its mission of showing the flag. *Franklin* and elements of the squadron sailed to Tunis and Malaga, and eventually, Stewart and Macdonough arrived on board their respective ships at Gibraltar during the first days of July. On 5 July Macdonough convened the officers of Sloane's court-martial back on board *Guerriere*, and at the conclusion of the meeting "was of the opinion that the language used by the commander in chief in his communication was virtually a censure upon its proceedings—an unjustifiable interference with the deliberations of the court."⁴⁶ The officers did not think the court had been dissolved and resolved to reconvene. While on board *Guerriere*, the officers signed, "a resolution embodying the court's opinions as to its rights as a body and its status with relation to the authority of the commander in chief was passed and sent to Commodore Stewart."⁴⁷ Stewart immediately wrote back to the officers that he found the "resolution grossly disrespectful and an attempt to impugn his personal and official motives."⁴⁸ The officers responded to their commodore saying, "The members of the court disavow such an intention and offer their tribute of respect . . . but sustain the opinion of their corporate rights and the resolution founded therein."⁴⁹ That very same afternoon Stewart acted and in the *Franklin*'s log stated: "At 1.45 pm made signal 297 for court martial which was answered by the squadron consisting of the flagship, *Erie* and *Spark*."⁵⁰ The next day the officers of Sloane's court-martial board were remanded on board the flagship to account for their collective insubordination. Macdonough's own account, dated 8 July, stated that he "was suspended from my command by Commodore Stewart and agreeably to his order gave the ship up to the command of the next senior officer on board. . . . At the same time were suspended with myself, Captain Ballard, Captain Nicholson, Lieutenant Commandant Gallagher, and Lieutenant Page for alleged improper conduct observed towards the commander-in-chief as members of a court-martial."⁵¹

Two days later the *Franklin*'s log duly recorded the following event, on 10 July 1819:

> At 10am call all hands to muster when the following General Order from the Commander in Chief was publicly read on the Quarter Deck: "US Ship *Franklin* Gibraltar, July 8, 1819—The Commander in Chief of the Naval Forces of the United States, in the Mediterranean, impelled by the high obligations of duty he owes to his government and the Laws of his Country, finds himself reduced to the heart-rendering necessity of suspending from their duty, Capt Thomas McDonough, commander of the Frigate *Guerriere*, Master Commandant Henry E. Ballard, Commander of the Ship *Erie*, Master Commandant. J. J. Nicholson, commander of the Brig *Spark*, Lieut. Commandant John Gallagher, commander of the Ship *Franklin* and Lieutenant Benjamin Page of the Ship *Franklin*, of which the officers, seamen and Marines employed in the Squadron above named and all other officers concern'd will take due notice. . . . The Commander in Chief finding himself reduced to this serious measure whereby the Naval Forces under his command, will be materially reduced on a Foreign Station, in effective officers of a superior grade; he trusts the remaining officers will and he calls on them in this Public manner, to cooperate and individually, to give their unremitted attention to the preservation of Good order and discipline in the squadron, and while they carefully superintend the conduct of those under them, they will be careful in guarding efficiently their own."[52]

With Macdonough relieved of command, Stewart appointed the young Lt. Robert Stockton to command Macdonough's *Guerriere*. Stewart ordered Stockton to return to the United States with the dismissed officers— Macdonough, Ballard, Gallagher, and Nicholson. Years later, Stockton's understated accounts of these events were recorded in a biography, published in 1856. He simply recounted "some unfortunate difficulties that led to numerous courts-martial. Several post-captains were suspended from their commands and placed under arrest by Commodore Stewart, for the purpose of being sent home."[53] However, Lieutenant Page did not return with the other officers; he stayed on board the *Franklin*. Stewart recognized that as the most junior of the officers on the Sloane courts-martial board, Page was probably not in a position to challenge the authority of such officers as Macdonough and Ballard. Stewart gave Page the benefit of the doubt, allowing the young lieutenant to remain, and in November of that year Page and Farragut were transferred. Page rose to the rank of commodore in 1841, and in 1855 he and other senior officers were forced to retire in the congressionally mandated purge of older naval officers.

Stockton served under Stewart in the Mediterranean and was ordered to take command of the *Guerriere* when Stewart relieved its commander, Thomas Macdonough, and the rest of the squadron's commanders. (Carruth & Carruth; courtesy of the Naval Historical Center)

Stewart's own recollection of the results of his action was typically understated: "This summary proceedings at once restored a healthy state of feelings throughout the squadron."[54]

Later that year, when the *Guerriere* returned to New York, Macdonough and his fellow officers officially admitted to the Navy secretary and the president that they were wrong and that Stewart was correct in taking the action that he did. In fact, Charles Wilkes said as much in his autobiography that recounted a meeting he had as a young midshipman with Macdonough shortly after his dismissal. Macdonough told the young Wilkes that he had relied on the judgment of his purser Mr. Bourne, "of the Boston bar," rather than on his own.[55]

The incident quickly came to the attention of President Monroe and the entire cabinet. Monroe felt that Stewart had acted appropriately, and at the same time he forgave all of the dismissed officers. Macdonough returned to sea in 1824 as commander of the U.S. Navy's Mediterranean Squadron.

Again, Stewart's understanding of the Constitution, military regulation, and federal law helped establish and, in this instance, reaffirm the process that U.S. naval officers could legally take in situations surrounding courts-marital. Navy regulations also defined the responsibility each officer had for maintaining "good order and discipline." In the remaining months of Stewart's command, good order and discipline became the stay of the U.S. Navy's Mediterranean Squadron.

On 29 October Stewart received bad news relating to the passing of one of the U.S. Navy's greats, and one of his contemporaries. The *Franklin*'s log read, "at 9 hoisted the colours half mast in respect to the late Capt O. H. Perry."[56]

During the following year Stewart also received dispatches informing him that his mercurial old friend, Stephen Decatur, had been killed in a duel on 22 March 1820 near the town of Bladensburg, Maryland. Ironically, Decatur had fallen at the hands of another naval officer, Capt. James Barron. All three, Stewart, Barron, and Decatur, had sailed together on their first commission on board Barry's *United States*. When he killed Decatur, Barron was still on furlough by the Navy secretary for questionable actions, including leaving the country without the permission of the government and working as a foreign agent. One of Stewart's first duties upon returning to the United States was to preside over the court of inquiry that investigated Barron's activities outside of the country.

The court was held on 10 May 1821 at the Brooklyn Navy Yard, and Barron's appeal to return to active duty was rejected by Stewart and the court that same summer. Barron had to wait three years before another board restored him to active duty.

Before this unfortunate chapter in his life, Stewart still had a squadron to command. Through the remaining months of 1820 and the first few months of 1821, Stewart continued to direct naval operations in the Mediterranean. Upon his relief as commodore, he sailed home on *Franklin*, landing at Philadelphia during the early spring days of 1821.

CHAPTER EIGHT

≈≈≈

On Pacific Station:
Commodore Stewart

"Southern seas are calling you, Lord of the sea."

—Pablo Neruda

After the War of 1812, and America's naval victories against the domi-
nant British Empire, the United States elected to pursue a more expan-
sionist policy out west, into territory the Lewis and Clark expedition had
explored a decade before, and into foreign waters. To avoid repeating the
inconclusive Barbary Wars, the United States quickly established a squadron
of premier ships-of-the-line and frigates to secure commerce against the
Barbary States' depredations. The success of Como. Stephen Decatur's
squadron in the Mediterranean indicated that the presence of U.S. naval
warships on other distant stations might benefit America as well.

With the Mediterranean situation secured, the U.S. government found an
arguably more difficult diplomatic situation to its south. During the War of
1812, U.S. warships began to frequent the Pacific Ocean, especially along
the west coast of South America. Stewart's former first officer David Porter,
for example, cruised against the British in that area on board the frigate
USS *Essex*. After the war, the frigate *Macedonian*, with Capt. John Downes
commanding, was one of the U.S. ships that witnessed the changing political
landscape in the Pacific. In 1810 Latin American territories began asserting

133

their independence from their European rulers—Spain and, in the case of Brazil, Portugal.

Although U.S. Navy ships patrolled the waters of the South Pacific, they did so individually, not in a squadron like the one sent to the Mediterranean. The case for establishing a Pacific Station rested on three primary criteria. First, distance considerations in the Pacific were markedly different from those in the Mediterranean. Whereas the transit time between ports for Mediterranean-based merchant ships was only a matter of days, transit between ports in the Pacific took weeks, if not months. Far East traders from Philadelphia completed a round-trip in a year or more. Even along the western coast of South America, substantial ports were few and far between, in contrast to ports along the coastlines of Spain, France, Italy, and North Africa. This meant that U.S. merchant ships were on their own for extended periods, more subject to adverse weather or threats from marauders, and isolated from timely assistance from other merchant vessels or friendly naval warships.

In addition, the Pacific trade routes were new to many U.S. sailors. Thus, establishing routes to South America and the Pacific meant hiring pioneering captains unfamiliar with the territory and potential sailing dangers. Not until 1820 did a U.S. sloop, the *Hero,* find land to the south of Cape Horn, which was later recorded as Antarctica.

Finally, a naval squadron was certain to face difficult logistical and operational problems in an age when word of mouth and letter transmittal were its only means of communication with Washington, D.C. A ship on Pacific Station could expect a lag time of five months between the issuance of an order from the president or war or Navy secretary and its receipt by the captain.

The second reason for establishing the Pacific Station was to keep tabs on the volatility of South American governance. The independence movements were by no means firmly established by 1821. The revolutionary leaders Bernardo O'Higgins in the south and Simón Bolívar and José San Martín to the north had made great strides to lift the yoke of Spanish rule, but Spanish Royalists maintained some strongholds. In 1819, with the Adams-Onis Treaty, Spain renounced its claims to the Oregon territory and ceded Florida to the United States. Only forty years had passed since America's war for independence and only six years since the War of 1812, what some considered America's second war for independence. The U.S. government had to balance its support for independence movements and its relationship with a government with which it had just ratified a major territorial treaty.

The conclusion of the War of 1812 coincided with the end of Europe's decades-long wars, the end of Napoleon, and the beginning of regional stability throughout the Mediterranean. For that reason, Decatur's—and later Chauncey's and Stewart's—Mediterranean Squadron found its diplomatic mission in the relatively stable post–Congress of Vienna era a less complicated task than it would have contended with in a volatile, revolutionary region such as South America. The end of Napoleon's wars also meant that the European powers were free to turn their attention to other regions of the world. Even France, under the restored Bourbon monarchy, continued to exert itself as a world power.

In August 1821, just before the first Pacific Squadron sailed, U.S. Ambassador to England Richard Rush met with England's foreign minister, George Canning. Both were concerned about potential French involvement in the South Pacific. Canning may have had some foresight, because two years later, in 1823, a new Holy Alliance of European nations (less England) was formed to oppose revolutionary movements and either return to Spain its South American possessions or claim them for their own.

Canning asked Rush about the possibility of a joint U.S.-English effort to prevent French involvement in South America, given that a simple statement of policy might deter France.[1] This possibility was later rejected with additional developments in U.S. foreign policy after the Pacific Squadron set sail.

The third major reason for establishing the Pacific Station was to capitalize on the growing economic importance of the Pacific trade routes. In addition to continuing the Far East trade, whose birth Stewart had witnessed as the *Canton* and other ships left Philadelphia in great fanfare, the United States was benefiting from new markets along the west coast of South America as well as from the thriving whaling industry vital to New England, particularly to Massachusetts, the home of the country's new Secretary of State John Quincy Adams.

Between 30 June 1818 and 30 June 1819, thirty-three American ships passed through the port of Valparaiso, Chile, including twenty-seven whalers and four merchant ships. This compared to three British whalers and twenty merchant ships. The actual number of ships throughout the Pacific was growing. In 1820 the U.S. consul in Valparaiso reported some eighty English whalers and fifty merchant vessels.[2] Although England dominated trade, the United States was more than competitive compared to other nations, such as France. The value of imports from Valparaiso in 1820 totaled $1.2 million for the British, $240,000 for the United States, and only $120,000 for the French; exports were $732,000 for the British and $413,000 for the Americans.

Protection of American commerce was paramount to the U.S. Navy mission. Privateers commissioned by the Spanish Royalists as well as the nascent South American navies threatened American merchant ships.

The Pacific was swarming with buccaneers claiming the protection of Spain, who were depredating on our commerce, and the 'Patriots' pretexts for plunder and sweeping our shipping from the ocean, to interpose his forces and efforts in restraining the piracies and robberies of the buccaneers claiming the protection of the Spanish flag, were the duties devolved upon [Stewart].[3]

Because of the volatility of the South American governments, the United States did not establish formal embassies there. Instead various agents and consuls were assigned in ports and major cities.

The U.S. government had to select a commodore for Pacific Station who could rely on significant sailing experience in unknown waters, who would understand commercial interests, who had experience in diplomacy, and who, in response to potential threats, had experience in combat. A likely choice would have been Stephen Decatur, particularly with his success as the first commodore of a permanent Mediterranean Squadron. His was a name of national and international renown—at least in naval circles—and he dealt swiftly with the North African threats to American commerce. But Decatur was now dead, the victim of his own recklessness and obstinacy.

There were others among the two dozen or so active-duty Navy captains who had some relevant experience, including Chauncey, Morris, and Rodgers, even Barron, and Biddle and Porter had both commanded the West Indies Squadron. But one now stood above the others—Charles Stewart. Since his commission as a lieutenant in 1798, he had fought the Barbary pirates, distinguished himself on the *Constitution*, and served ably as commodore of the Mediterranean Squadron. In his merchant career he had also rounded the Horn at least once across the Pacific. And he was the third-most senior captain in the U.S. Navy.

The decision to send Stewart must have been made only in early 1821. When he returned from the Mediterranean in the summer of 1820, he thought his next assignment would be in the capital, where, unlike many of his peers, he had never served, and an appointment he did not seek nor apparently desire. His sister-in-law Emma Tudor Gardiner suggested in a letter that Delia would be sorely disappointed at not living in metropolitan Washington, vastly different from Bordentown. Emma wrote that Stewart "must see the president before he can decide on anything."[4] After attending ceremonies to receive an honorary degree at Princeton, Stewart accepted the offer to serve as the first commodore on Pacific Station.

Selected as the flagship of the Pacific Squadron, on which would fly the commodore's pennant, was Stewart's former flagship, the USS *Franklin*. After a refit in New York, she was ready to put to sea again. Although the *Franklin* was rated a 74, Stewart continued his tradition of carrying more guns on his ships, including bow chasers, than were intended; the *Franklin* carried eighty-two guns. Stewart also directed two other modifications. First, he had a fifteen-hundred-volume library constructed on the gun deck, which was supervised during the voyage by Mid. Charles Wilkes, the ship's librarian. Thus, the *Franklin* had the U.S. Navy's first shipboard library. Although Stewart approved the effort, the idea originated with William Wood, a New York philanthropist.[5]

The major renovation, however, entailed accommodations for his wife Delia, who dreaded the cruise as nothing less than imprisonment for what she felt was simply living according to the standards to which she had grown accustomed in Boston and Europe—and deservedly so, in her mind—but Charles feared that leaving his wife for another extended period would propel him into bankruptcy. The excursion on board *Franklin* was, for Delia, three very long years at sea, traveling into unknown and relatively uncivilized territory. If her husband would confine her to a ship for three years, then she would take as many creature comforts as possible and try to shine on an otherwise dark coast. Delia's mother wrote a letter to her in September 1821, stating her opinion that despite the voyage destination far from the courts of Europe, Delia's prospects of receiving social privilege and acclaim were most brilliant. Before she departed, the noted New England painter Gilbert Stuart completed portraits of both Delia and her mother. That the two most prominent portrait artists of the era—Sully and Stuart—were commissioned by the Stewarts and Tudors underscores the position the families held in society.

As the commodore of a squadron, Stewart would have rated a captain in command of the *Franklin* herself, much like Henry Ballard, who had served in that capacity during the *Franklin*'s Mediterranean cruise. (Although Ballard held the rank of master commandant in 1818, he was the captain of the ship.) Because Stewart, out of financial necessity, brought his wife and children on board for the cruise, he chose to command the ship himself and use the captain's spaces for his family and retinue. An extra cabin was constructed on the upper deck to accommodate Delia and her maids, including Mrs. Banister, the wife of the ship's sailmaker. According to Midshipman

Wilkes, the light deck was thrown over from side to side with iron stanchions to better secure it.

Delia's wardrobe alone was nothing less than "extensive" and the subject of conversation even before the voyage began. One of Stewart's officers later recalled that her wardrobe "amused the New York society not a little"; her outfits were "enumerated and laughed over. . . . The bills were the astonishment of the Com but they were paid, though the baggage which encumbered the cabins greatly moved his equanimity."[6]

When Delia took her place on board the *Franklin,* her reputation for nearly ruining Stewart financially preceded her. Like Delia's brother-in-law Robert Gardiner, who wrote in his memoirs that the two were ill-suited, the officers of the ship had already heard that their marriage was rocky, that Delia was ambitious, and that the "glitter of his name and position is said to have had its influence." But Delia was immediately recognized as beautiful with a tall and fine figure, though seemingly advanced in years, exceedingly nearsighted, and having a rather slouchy walk.

Stewart's wardroom knew the real reason for her presence on this extended voyage, and Delia herself proceeded to reinforce the notion of her fiscal irresponsibility. The matter played out on ship and shore at nearly every port, where she constantly asked the officers themselves for money, often simply to distribute among the less fortunate of South America, as if she were a noble dispensing the alms. In the wardroom, she quickly earned the nickname "La Commodora," a reference to the Spanish nobility she shallowly imitated.

In contrast, the children, young Charles and young Delia (named for her mother and grandmother), proved a welcome change of pace on the ship. Charles, only three at the outset of the voyage, and Delia, just a few years older, were "lively and spirited and great favorites on board."

On 12 August 1821 the *Franklin* lay at anchor in New York's East River because it was shorthanded by seventy crewmen. The Age of Sail's equivalent to a twentieth-century battleship or aircraft carrier, ships-of-the-line had difficulties in manning because they were crew intensive. Eventually the Navy recruited additional crew from state prisons.

Stewart walked the deck of his anchored ship, awaiting orders to sail, the holds filled with enough stores for six months, 74,000 gallons of water, and an abundant supply of potatoes in bins on the deck. Stewart had also ordered a light wagon painted yellow with black molding and six horses stored on the deck and used on the west coast of South America when he and his wife were on shore.

One day while he was awaiting his departure, Stewart witnessed the future of the U.S. Navy—the steam ship USS *Robert Fulton*, just six years old, was nearby exchanging officers with the *Dolphin*.

Along with the numerous merchant ships in the river was the USS *Cyane* lying alongside the *Franklin*. The sight of the old British 34 brought back fond memories for the commodore, the recollection of his greatest victory, when the *Constitution* had taken on the *Cyane* and *Levant* simultaneously. Though the *Levant* was retaken shortly after the battle, the *Cyane* was a clear prize and now in service with the U.S. Navy. The *Cyane* would have been a welcome addition to accompany the *Franklin* on Pacific Station as a tribute to Stewart's initiative, boldness, and skill. She could also have served as a gentle reminder to foreign ships, particularly British warships, that U.S. warships could win battles and keep her trophies. But the *Franklin* would not have *Cyane* as her escort.

The Pacific Squadron actually consisted of only two ships—the massive ship-of-the-line *Franklin* and the schooner *Dolphin*. The schooner was one of the newest ships in the American Navy, launched on 23 June 1821. With a length of eighty-eight feet, a beam of twenty-three and a half feet, and carrying twelve six-pound guns, she displaced nearly two hundred tons. She had a twenty-two-foot bowsprit and a mainmast seventy-four feet high. She had as her commander the able Lt. David Conner, first commissioned in 1809 and promoted to lieutenant in 1813. Conner later commanded the Gulf Squadron and achieved amphibious victories in the Mexican-American War. Serving as *Dolphin*'s first officer was Isaac Mayo, who had been commissioned ten months after Conner and who was promoted to lieutenant in 1815.

Upon completion, the *Dolphin* was destined for patrol in the West Indies, but her orders were changed at nearly the last minute. So little time did Conner have before the unexpectedly lengthy and distant voyage—in fact, he did not receive official orders until shortly before she sailed—that he prepared her himself. Despite his efforts, there was insufficient time to change out any equipment. For example, the signal flags with which the *Dolphin* had been outfitted were so small that other vessels could not make them out. Conner presumed that the fitter thought the *Dolphin* was such a small ship that she should have flags only half the regulation size.[7] Estimating individual usage at 60 gallons per day, she had onboard 5,800 gallons of water, twelve 30-gallon casks of whiskey, and eleven 20-gallon casks of whiskey.

The situation between the two ships was similar, and there were deficiencies in what the Navy supplied to the *Franklin* as well. For example, from the perspective of one of the officers, the new chronometers were problematic and the new Board of Naval Commissioners was hesitant to supply them. "Chronometers had been but little used and little confidence was placed in them. The largest vessels had only one and often a very indifferent instrument and those Masters who had charge of them were often ignorant of their use and had to depend upon others."[8]

The largest warship in New York Harbor received visitors both welcomed and uninvited. On one occasion a large boat pulled alongside the 2,257-ton *Franklin* late in the afternoon asking to see the commodore. The passengers, a church committee, sought to come on board, meet the crew, and pray publicly. Stewart was reluctant to allow them on board given that the crew had been working all day and dinner was about to be called away. But the boatload of preachers would "listen to no refusal" and Stewart finally relented. An old adage says that no man who goes to sea returns an atheist after witnessing the forces of nature over man and the prayers men say to keep themselves safe through a storm far from shore and home. Stewart had lived most of his life at sea, but he was a practical sailor who continued to put the well-being of his crew above speeches.

On 8 September 1821 Commodore Stewart received his official instructions for the Pacific Station from Navy Secretary Smith Thompson. The first directive was to pay the usual civilities to the authorities of each country, as due from a friendly station. The second was to ascertain whether belligerents had molested American commerce. Third, Thompson clearly stated that the U.S. policy was to observe strict neutrality and that Stewart must maintain that neutrality. Fourth, Stewart's squadron would act, unless otherwise ordered, defensively. Finally, Stewart was instructed to decline receipt of additional men, money, and provisions, except specie, which he would be allowed to bring to the United States.

Before the ship set sail, it encountered a storm that quickly grew to a hurricane. The ship dropped two anchors to secure it but had to set out yet a third anchor to keep her from drifting and running aground. Three of *Franklin*'s crew died in the storm, unnerving for those believing it a portent of the voyage to come.

After a calm and cloudy night, Commodore Stewart made the signal for the squadron to get under way at 5 A.M. on Sunday, 7 October. Though the officially rated ship's complement was 786, the *Franklin* had 738 souls on board including 56 Marines. It took another three days for the great ship and her escort to stand out to sea. As one of the *Franklin*'s Marines reflected, "Some were doomed, alas, to see their homes no more."[9]

Stewart's choice as first lieutenant was William Weaver. However, Weaver was commissioned as a lieutenant only in 1816 and with at least five officers senior to him, the Navy selected another. Stewart's preference may have harkened back to his own days as a lieutenant. Given that he had been selected for command over some other officers with more time in the Navy, he may have sought someone with merchant ship experience, potential, and, most importantly, character. Stewart never learned if Weaver could fulfill the role of first officer; the lieutenant was detached at his own request, as Midshipman Wilkes recalled, with the possibility of joining the *Franklin* in the Pacific later. But Weaver never returned to the squadron as he was cashiered from the Navy in 1824. Nevertheless, his name remained on the logbooks, a point of future contention.

Instead, the Navy chose for first lieutenant an officer with similar experience to Lieutenant Conner on *Dolphin*. William M. Hunter served as both first lieutenant and acting captain, neither of which the other officers felt he could manage. Hunter displayed a gentlemanly manner but had a slight speech impediment that caused him to speak with "a hesitancy followed by a gust of words that few could understand."

Like Stewart's last cruise to the Mediterranean, during which he trained Levy, Buchanan, DuPont, Farragut, and Porter Jr., the Pacific cruise had a wardroom of future naval leaders. Many of Stewart's officers had over eight years commissioned service in the Navy. At least two, Edward Preble and James Alexander Perry, came from illustrious Navy families.[10] At least six eventually rose to the rank of captain, another one (his nephew, Charles Stewart McCauley) became a commodore, and four more reached the rank of rear admiral. Stewart was able to follow each of their illustrious careers because he outlived nearly all of his former junior officers. The wardroom on the *Franklin*, like that on *Dolphin*, exceeded the required number of officers and was, therefore, crowded. Wilkes, normally critical of fellow officers, recognized that Stewart "stood very high in the estimation of the Service," an opinion shared by the officers who served under him. But Wilkes also criticized Stewart for being reticent, paying little attention to his officers, and not enforcing discipline on his ship, noting that "punishments were few and generally of light kind."

The wardroom was divided into five messes, each a room of ten square feet with a total of forty-three midshipmen and lieutenants. The mess, with no light except the allotted two candles a day, had a small pantry and a table in the center. The essentials in the mess were coffee, tea, sugar, butter, and flour. For the midshipmen on their first cruise, "there was no part of the ship where they were not lying about" because of seasickness.

If there were extended periods of labor under trying circumstances in Stewart's wardroom, the young officers also found moments of levity and amusement that have always been characteristic of shipboard life. Mid. Frederick Jarrett, for example, brought a pet monkey named Jaco on board. The monkey, prone to imitation, found a likely target in the black-haired Lt. Ebenezar Ridgeway. Jaco's repetition of Ridgeway's long sighs and use of his toothbrush and pen were a source of delight to the midshipmen, but not to Ridgeway, who swore he would use his pistol on Jaco when the opportunity arose.[11] Jaco's fate was not recorded, but Jarrett was one of the few of the *Franklin*'s officers who did not enjoy a lengthy career, dying only a few months after his promotion to lieutenant in 1825.

Lt. William Ramsay, fair haired, florid, and possessing small feet and hands had "a good deal of Miss Nancy about him."[12] According to a shipmate, Ramsay had a great regard for outward appearances and "lived to show." During one inspection, Wilkes later recalled, Ramsay reported wearing a Turkish morning robe, red slippers, and a small, fanciful smoking cap on his head with a large gold tassel.

Another lieutenant, John D. Sloat, was an object of ridicule among the young midshipmen. Midshipman Wilkes described him as of "medium height and ungraceful, fearful of responsibility, nervous, timid and undecided, issuing orders and then countermanding them almost in the same breath." Few had served in the Navy as long as had Sloat. Only three years younger than Commodore Stewart, he was made a midshipman in 1800 and was promoted to lieutenant in 1813. Sloat was known by the midshipmen as "Grandmother," and, when he would call down the hatchway for the young officers, they would blow out the candles and launch anything at hand at him.[13] Wilkes also noted that discipline on the *Franklin* was exceedingly lacking, a seemingly supportable contention. Stewart rarely, if ever, disciplined his men for minor incidents like this, in contrast to disciplinary measures common on other ships in the Age of Sail.

Sloat succeeded Lieutenant Hunter, who later left the ship because of ill health. Sloat may have proven false the additional criticisms of being an "inefficient officer, exceedingly conceited, and deeming himself as if he were the wisest." Like his fellow officer, Lieutenant Conner, who commanded the *Dolphin*, Sloat eventually became a Navy commodore and commanded the Pacific Squadron early in the Mexican-American War.

The wardroom had other future naval leaders including Charles Wilkes himself, who later commanded the exploring expedition in the Antarctic from 1838 to 1842; Louis Goldsborough, who commanded one of the Civil War's blockading squadrons; and Joshua Sands, who commanded a ship and captured six cities during the Mexican-American War and commanded the Brazilian Squadron during the Civil War.

Stewart established the rules for the ship, which included:

> No officer whatever is to inflict punishment upon any petty officer. Should a petty officer in any manner misbehave, he is immediately to be reported to me, or in my absence [put in irons]. The Midshipmen are strictly forbidden to strike or punish any person whatever. . . . The ship is never to be left without two LTS or one LT and the Master. The 1st and 2nd LT must never be absent from the ship at the same time without my special permission. . . . In port on Mondays and Thursdays are the correct washing days. The cloathes [*sic*] in port to be hung between the fore and main rigging. . . . No person is to hang cloaths in the rigging without permission. . . . The crew are to have their dinner exactly at noon. . . . on Sundays one hour and an half will be allowed for dinner, on other days one hour only. . . . At sea the gunner is to examine the guns every morning and evening.[14]

The *Franklin* and the *Dolphin* steered well clear of Bermuda due to the former's close encounters with its reefs during its previous cruise to the Mediterranean. Upon nearing the Cape Verde Islands, the squadron sighted an unidentified fleet of men-of-war. As was standard practice, the ships beat to quarters and the decks cleared for potential action. The fleet was soon revealed to be Portuguese, and the two forces passed each other quietly and without incident.

On an excessively hot Sunday, 18 November, at 10 A.M., the crew of the *Franklin* enjoyed a long-held tradition on Navy ships that continues through this writing. At twenty-six degrees west longitude, the squadron "crossed the line," a momentous occasion that separated the "shellbacks" from the "pollywogs," or just "wogs." Crossing the equator meant neophyte sailors had joined the ranks of countless sailors before who had proven themselves on the high seas.

Lieutenant Hunter, appropriately attired as King Neptune, and a party departed *Franklin*, and when at a short distance the lieutenant called back to be allowed on board the warship. After proceeding aft to the poop deck and saluting the commodore and his wife, Neptune paraded around the main deck in a car that was "provided by using the Spar deck Fire Engine for his deck out in true nautical style."[15] Then the commodore "made his Majesty a short speech in return, scarcely able to keep his countenance at the grotesque appearance before him, and gave his consent that he might hold his court and Baptise [*sic*] those whom he thought were novitiates."[16]

The squadron maintained her course for Brazil, and along the way the new sailors saw, for the first time, flying fish that soared some twenty feet in the air alongside the ships and dolphins that, after being caught, changed their hues quickly upon dying.

On 30 November, at 3 P.M., the *Franklin* arrived at its first port of call, Rio de Janeiro, which was recently liberated from Portugal. The *Dolphin* arrived the next day to find, in addition to the *Franklin,* an English frigate at anchor.[17] A series of blunders then occurred. Upon arrival or departure from a port, it was naval custom to fire a salute, with the number of guns fired dependent on the seniority of the official being recognized. For example, a full admiral rates a seventeen-gun salute. In Rio de Janeiro the senior official was the head of state, the newly-installed Emperor Dom Pedro I, who, the crew could see, merited a twenty-one-gun salute.

Although the guns were reported ready, in some instances the powder had, for some unknown reason, been in the guns for several days. As a consequence, they did not fire at the precise interval and number of shots; three guns fired in sequence, then silence, a misfire, two more guns fired, and then another long interval of silence. Stewart might have been embarrassed enough to replace the captain of the gun deck, but he apparently gave him another chance at the next port of call.

While at anchor in Rio, the *Franklin* was found to be listing heavily to starboard, another miscalculation quickly corrected by shifting stores to the nearly empty port-side storage areas. Although minor, it is curious that Stewart himself did not notice the list, which certainly affected the ship's maneuvering and the readiness of her guns. Stewart's slip might be an additional indication that the ship truly needed a captain, and not a first lieutenant simultaneously serving as acting captain, or that Stewart himself should have been in command.

The lack of crew discipline, particularly during the Age of Sail, might have also resulted in the next incident. With ten days in port, the crew had opportunities to go ashore. According to Midshipman Wilkes, more than a few midshipmen returned in a state of "beastly intoxication" and literally had to be hoisted on board. Other officers suggested that since they had disgraced the ship, they ought to be sent back to the United States. Stewart agreed and gave the order, probably made easier because the wardroom already had an excess of officers.

144

The ex-viceroy of Peru paid a visit to the ship on 2 December. He spoke highly of the naval officers under Captain Biddle, to whom he had given a sword.

According to her brother-in-law, Delia was received by the court in Rio with the greatest distinction, not simply because she was the wife of Commodore Stewart. "Her graceful manners, and the fluency with which she spoke both Spanish and Portuguese, excited the greatest admiration. Mrs. Stewart was much surprised, when presented at Court, at meeting negro officers in full uniform holding positions of equality with the notions prevalent in the United States as to the coloured races."[18]

Before departing on the tenth, the squadron replenished its stores. Stewart ordered sweet meats, preserves, and enough cabbage to be "strung from one end of the Ship to another." Wilkes's mess had so much tapioca pudding daily that the members became nauseated and had to trade its supply for different foods from the other messes.

On 15 December the squadron began preparing for its first true test of seamanship when it approached the often arduous transit round Cape Horn, known for its heavy seas and dangerous gale-force winds. In 1788 Captain Bligh of the *Bounty* was thwarted by the cape and had to reach the Pacific by way of the Cape of Good Hope. Joshua Slocum, sailing round the world in his sloop, the *Spray*, nearly eighty years later wrote that, "in no part of the world could a rougher sea be found than at this particular point." Capt. David Porter, on board the frigate *Essex* during the War of 1812, warned on making the trek, "our sufferings . . . have been so great that I would advise those bound into the Pacific, never to attempt the passage of Cape Horn, if they can get there by another route."[19]

At Cape Horn the *Franklin* lost another crewman but not because of the sea. Porpoises and dolphins were swimming alongside the bow. Like several other crewmen, Boatswain's Mate Haines tried to harpoon one of the escorts, but he lost his balance and fell into the ocean. If Wilkes is to be believed, Lieutenant Ridgeway, who had command, was accountable for Haines's death. While there was still time to save Haines, Ridgeway "lost his presence of mind and ordered the helm put up instead of down. . . . There was not a dry eye in the Ship. [Haines's] life was a Sacrifice to ignorance and incapacity."

The *Dolphin*, which had lost sight of the *Franklin* off of Terra del Fuego on 7 January 1822, was located the next day eighteen miles north-northwest of the Islands of Diego Ramirez. Five days later, they could finally turn north into the Pacific and rendezvous at a site preselected by Commodore Stewart.

An experienced sailor like Stewart would have known about the best rendezvous site after rounding the Horn. The Island of Juan Fernandez, actually a small archipelago of three main islands, is located at eighty degrees west longitude and thirty-three degrees south latitude, fewer than four hundred miles from Valparaiso, Chile. European explorers discovered the islands in 1574. Stewart also knew the legends of Juan Fernandez. More than a hundred years before Stewart set foot on its shore, the main island, fourteen miles long and eight miles wide, for four years was the home of sailor Alexander Selkirk. The author Daniel Defoe later wrote a novel based on Selkirk's experience and called his protagonist Robinson Crusoe. The crew of the British privateer *Speedwell* was marooned on the islands in 1719; the *Speedwell's* adventures later inspired the poet Samuel Taylor Coleridge to pen "The Rime of the Ancient Mariner."

The islands, with their wooded and fertile valleys, streams, and calm bay, were a welcome sight to all sailors in the weeks following their voyage around the cape. In 1896, when Joshua Slocum saw its blue hills from thirty miles off, he was overcome by gratitude. "A thousand emotions thrilled me when I saw the island, and I bowed my head to the deck." To others, the island's five-thousand-foot-high mountain from seventy miles off rose "ahead like a deep-blue cloud out of the sea."

The crew of the *Dolphin* was disappointed when it arrived on 25 January to find Robinson Crusoe's island inhabited, albeit by only a small Chilean population. But its disappointment was soon diminished by the island's plenty, rich soil, trees, figs, peaches, wild horses, and hogs. Five days later Stewart and the *Franklin* arrived.

Conner had charted the bay before the *Franklin's* arrival and anchored a buoy for her. He later piloted her into the safety of Cumberland Bay on the north side of Juan Fernandez, the largest of the three islands. Conner had gained some experience piloting another ship in when, ninety-four days out of New York, the *Canton,* under the command of Captain O'Sullivan, arrived at Juan Fernandez and requested his services on the afternoon of 26 January.

Stewart joined his escort and saw the other familiar vessel, the merchant ship *Canton*, which forty years before had been the Philadelphia merchantman that had set out for profitable voyages to the Far East. The *Canton* now stayed in the Western Hemisphere. Although commanded by O'Sullivan, merchant Eliphalet Smith was on board as the cargo master. Stewart and Smith were acquainted with one another. Before the War of 1812, when Stewart was in the merchant service, he and Smith had a business partnership purchasing Merino sheep in Cadiz, Spain.

Eliphalet Smith played a pivotal role in Stewart's tour as commodore of the Pacific Station. Their relationship was often criticized and later resulted in charges. Stewart, however, relied heavily on Smith's several years' experience operating in the merchant business along the west coast of South America during its most tumultuous years.

The U.S. Navy had no formal intelligence officers during the Age of Sail. Instead, "quite often the commander had to use great initiative in developing his own local sources of general and intelligence information for, even though there were such items coming to him from his superiors, they were relatively infrequent and insufficient."[20] This was particularly true in Stewart's case. The latest information from Washington, D.C., was always at least five months old. There were no U.S. embassies on the west coast of South America and the various agents' information was not completely reliable.

Intelligence in that era was primarily based on individuals' observations. Normally those individuals were "prisoners of war, returning prisoners of war, deserters, neutrals (including fishermen and merchants), paid spies, and 'friendly' enemy nationals."[21] Absent prisoners of war and a spy network, Stewart relied heavily upon experienced American merchants such as Eliphalet Smith. The *Canton* had been to every port along the coast and had been boarded by all sides of the respective conflicts. Since Stewart had been a business partner with Smith, he felt he could trust the man. Unfortunately for Stewart, his trust was not shared by some of his crew or U.S. government representatives in South America.

Stewart's replenishment opportunity at Juan Fernandez also allowed two midshipmen on the *Franklin* to resolve a months-long quarrel. Mids. Robert Marshall and John Cramer, commissioned in 1815 and 1816 respectively, agreed to duel at the first land they reached; that land was Juan Fernandez. Quarreling seems to have been endemic on the *Franklin* during the voyage, but perhaps no less so than on any other ship with cramped quarters. "Fights were of frequent occurrence and, in those days, I think were rather encouraged. There was no discipline and, in fact, no attention was paid to these men."[22]

Stewart was no stranger to dueling. Although there is no record of his ever participating, he had attended duels, and, of course, he had lost his friend Stephen Decatur to a duel only the year before. Stewart was consistently and completely opposed to the practice. When it came to his attention that Marshall and Cramer planned to duel, he ordered that if any officers engaged in this, he would send them out of the squadron and back to the United States. This order put an end to midshipmen's dueling plan. Later events suggest that the two men eventually reconciled their differences.

After filling their stores on the island, the squadron, with the *Canton* in company, set out on a southeast course for Valparaiso, a port with no wharves and where "none remained longer than their necessities required." On 6 February the three ships entered the Bay of Valparaiso, and Stewart's ship underwent the same embarrassment as it did in Rio de Janeiro when the gun deck failed to properly render honors. The U.S. squadron received a more proper salute with thirteen guns fired from the sloop-of-war HMS *Blossom*, eleven guns from the Chilean commodore, and twenty-one guns from the city itself.[23]

Given the volatility of the region, the U.S. squadron faced the potential of battling new forces as swept up in revolutionary fervor as U.S. naval forces themselves had been forty years before, when the North American colonies struggled against Britain.

Landing at Valparaiso gave Stewart and his crew more news about the local political environment. More importantly, the commodore learned the number and status of U.S. merchant ships there. The crew also heard the shocking account of the Nantucket whale ship *Essex*, commanded by George Pollard, which had been struck at sea by a great whale and sunk during the previous year. In the wreck, her crew was dispersed among three small boats three thousand miles from South America. By the time two of the boats were discovered three months later, only a few crew members were found alive, having resorted to cannibalism. Decades later the story inspired another sailor, Herman Melville, to pen *Moby Dick*.[24] During a cruise of one of Stewart's Pacific Squadron boats, the crew encountered the whale ship *Two Brothers* commanded by a Captain Pollard. Midshipman Wilkes had only the day before read an account of a whale ship that had been struck by a whale. Pollard "at once said he was the person. . . . I cannot state the narrative of this, it is too horrible to be related as it was told to me."[25]

Sixteen days after entering Valparaiso, the squadron welcomed the arrival of two more U.S. ships, the whale ship *Maryland*, seven months out of Havre de Grace, Maryland, and the brig *Hermaphrodite*, 104 days out of New York, bringing vegetables. Upon the ships' arrival, Stewart ordered they be boarded. On 7 March an officer and sailors from the squadron boarded the Boston schooner *Wasp*, Captain Smith commanding. The schooner was a tender to another ship from which she had parted company in a gale three months prior. The British brig *Cesco* of Plymouth arrived from New South Shetlands with sealskins and oil. The following day Stewart's men boarded the brig *Anna*, commanded by Captain Williams, sixty-five days out of Buenos Aires. At 2 P.M. on the clear-weathered 10 March, the squadron received in Valparaiso and exchanged salutes with the British frigate *Creole*, the flagship of Rear Admiral Hardy, who had been Nelson's loyal aide and captain of the *Victory* at Trafalgar.

Stewart's voyage to Valparaiso had carried him into a hotbed of political intrigue, where he encountered potential enemies, not only in foreign powers but also in U.S. State Department officials and appointees, continuing the perpetual struggle between the military and diplomatic communities.

After arriving in Valparaiso, the squadron received many invitations by U.S. and foreign government officials. The U.S. consul at Valparaiso, Michael Hogan, was an "Irish Gentleman of the old school and a very polished one" who was familiar with Mid. Charles Wilkes's family. Later, in 1833, he died in the arms of Wilkes's father after telling the younger Wilkes, during his illness, about the persons he knew, "praising many but finding great fault with others and begged me to beware of them. . . . One in particular whom he designated as one of the worst of men, though outward pretending good friendship, he likened him as a 'snake in the grass.'" It is likely this snake was the U.S. special agent for commerce and seamen in Chile, Jeremiah Robinson. Had Stewart been aware of this man's activities earlier, he could have saved himself, the squadron, and the U.S. government much embarrassment and difficulty. In Stewart's case specifically, Robinson became his bane. Other government officials, as well, proved themselves to be Stewart's enemies and detractors.

Because of U.S. merchant and warships' logistics needs on distant shores, the United States assigned requisition agents to various ports. These positions often led to higher positions in consulates when such diplomatic credentials were needed. For example, the special agent for commerce and seamen in Valparaiso, Michael Hogan, was appointed in November 1820 and was named consul in 1823 as the revolutions abated.[26]

The agent to Chile and Peru, John B. Prevost of New York, had been appointed in July 1817, after the commission for one Jeremiah Robinson of Massachusetts had been issued and almost immediately revoked, an issue that later played a significant role in Stewart's cruise. The new agent appointed 21 August 1821 was William Tudor Jr., Delia's brother, in his first diplomatic post. Tudor, well traveled as a result of his business dealings, was close not only with his sister but also his brother-in-law, who was only a year older. He had also worked on a literary magazine with George Bancroft, who in two more decades served as Navy secretary and worked closely with Commodore Stewart. Unfortunately, Tudor did not depart the United States

When his attempts to gain a prestigious diplomatic position in South America were thwarted, Jeremiah Robinson's rumormongering led to some of the court-martial charges levied against Stewart. One diplomat described Robinson's "personal habits in every respect so low, groveling and filthy, as to be in unison with the rest of his character." (By Maine artist Anthony Shostak; courtesy of the artist)

with Stewart and the *Franklin*, and so he did not arrive on station for another two years, at which time he was appointed consul to Peru.

Jeremiah Robinson, in his early forties when Stewart arrived at Valparaiso, was a native of Essex County, Massachusetts, and by the time of Stewart's arrival was already biased against Navy captains. As a student traveling in Europe a decade before, he was caught in Britain at the outbreak of war in 1812. He communicated regularly with another American resident in Britain, Navy Capt. James Barron. Robinson returned to the United States in 1814, and, during travel to Pacific islands such as Marquesas, Tinian, and the Galapagos, he formed a negative opinion of Capt. David Porter of the *Essex*. He wrote of Captain Porter, "During that period he fired on the unarmed, inoffensive inhabitants."[27] Robinson's criticism of Navy captains extended to every one who served on Pacific Station from the time of his arrival. A letter he wrote to John Quincy Adams in August 1822 revealed his opinion that the conduct of "Captain Biddle, Captain Downs [*sic*], and Captain Ridgely, has at once been mercenary, anti-neutral or hostile to the patriots and injurious to the victors. . . . I am obliged to add that that of Commodore Stewart is questionable if not positively censurable."

Throughout his adult life, Robinson was constantly in search of government appointments and seems to have spent more time corresponding with U.S. government officials asking for jobs than fulfilling the responsibilities of his post. In 1817 he requested an appointment as consul to Malta, and barring that, an appointment to Peru.

When he returned to Washington in 1823, he wrote to John Quincy Adams regarding his "wishes in relation to an employment under the Government as a Special Agent of the U.S. at Mexico, Peru, the Brazils or some other part of South or Spanish America; if not, then Consul General of some part of that region." A year later he took another opportunity and again wrote to Adams: "I saw the death notice of the Special Agent in Guatumala [*sic*], I beg leave to offer myself to your consideration as a candidate to fill that vacancy . . . or any other destination."

When he was not pursuing a position with the United States, he was soliciting jobs with foreign governments. In mid-1822, for example, the Chilean governor of Valparaiso informed Hogan that Robinson had been at the government seat in Santiago seeking an appointment as an agent for Chile in Washington, apparently with the knowledge of Captain Ridgely. Robinson was said to be in the pay of Chile and spying on U.S. actions in the eastern Pacific. This charge was never confirmed, but Robinson can at least be tied to the Chilean government by a letter he received in which the head of Chile, Bernardo O'Higgins, personally wrote: "You possess the talents which is [*sic*] required to foreigners for the acquisition of public esteem."[28]

By the time Stewart arrived in Valparaiso, Robinson had acquired a reputation as a troublemaker, an untrustworthy scoundrel, and a rumormonger. Commerce agents in foreign ports, like Robinson, were important because they were supposed to provide much-needed intelligence services far from the United States. They were agents of trust. This was not a position for Robinson. One example of his troublemaking was the case of Señora Maria Isabel Vidal of Chile, who had expected Robinson to deliver her eighteen doubloons from Lieutenant Aulick of the USS *Ontario*. Months passed and the lady had not received the money, so Hogan intervened at the request of Captain Biddle to uphold "the Honor of the Naval officers." After a series of denials that he had ever received the doubloons from Aulick, Robinson finally returned them to Senora Vidal.

The vice consul at Conception said Robinson could be of no use, except to himself. Hogan reported to the State Department that Robinson was "corresponding with many on political and other subjects, and meddling with everyone's affairs," that the president was "certainly ignorant" in recommending him for positions, and that his appointment to any public office in South America "would dishonor the American name."

> I would not compromise the honor of the U.S. by any such appointment—a total destitution of character in him would prevent it—his talent for writing is the only one he possesses and that in the same eminent degree a plausible sicophancy of manners, the most disgusting while always acting against the person he found upon making two words of conversation with any one who gives him an opinion aided by a futile brain the subject of a long letter on the political affairs of this country.[29]

For a diplomat, this was a surprising and damning indictment, but it appears to be consistent with the views others held of Robinson throughout his career. Even ten years later in Cuba, where Robinson had found a minor government position, Nicholas Trist, the U.S. consul, wrote to another official that Robinson's "mode of living, his personal habits in every respect were so low, groveling and filthy, as to be in unison with the rest of his character; than which, in whatever light it be considered, a more disreputable one to represent the U. States in any capacity could not well have been found."[30] Such was the man who would level direct and indirect, overt and covert accusations against Stewart throughout his tenure as commander of the Pacific Squadron.

Throughout their mission, Stewart's squadron encountered several fleets—the Chilean fleet, a Peruvian Patriot fleet, and a Peruvian Royalist fleet. If some spark had set off a new conflict, especially with Chile, Stewart would have been faced with a capable opponent that he likely could not have defeated in battle. The Chilean Navy commander was the legendary Thomas Lord Cochrane, perhaps the finest frigate captain in history, described even by local American agents as one of the greatest naval commanders and ablest of men. However, one agent, Jeremiah Robinson, opined differently that "I have never considered General San Martin as a pure patriot inspired by philanthropy, but rather as an ambitious, unprincipled, military chief in pursuit of renown, and influenced by cupidity—my opinion of Lord Cochran [sic] is not much different."[31]

152

Following a court-martial and other difficulties in England, Cochrane sought other naval opportunities. This was not unusual. A few years later, for example, Capt. David Porter was court-martialed, found guilty, and became commander of the Mexican Navy. Chile's liberator, José de San Martín, convinced the former British naval commander to join his forces because he planned to liberate Peru by sea and needed an effective naval leader. Cochrane arrived in Chile in 1818, replacing the surprisingly able twenty-eight-year-old Blanco Encalada. As the vice admiral of the Chilean Navy, Cochrane led a far more effective force than Stewart's. Cochrane had the *San Martin* (rated as a 50-gun ship but later reported as a 64), *Lautero* (50), the *O'Higgins* (54), and four other ships. All were commanded by British officers loyal to Cochrane.

Cochrane was a visionary who saw the power of steam in naval warfare. In England, he supervised the building of the five-hundred-ton *Rising Star*, "one of the world's first steamships, confident that the Chilean government would pay for it when he brought it across."[32] Ultimately, the ship never saw combat. Cochrane also tried to reshape South American politics by devising a plan to extract Napoleon Bonaparte from exile and install him as an emperor of South America.

Before Stewart departed on his three-year voyage, he received the most recent political and military information about his new area of operations; in this case, the most recent news would have been five months old. He had information as of April 1821 primarily from government commerce agents and consuls. Stewart would have been advised on Cochrane's activities, especially because of the admiral's renown and potential threat.

Cochrane was already familiar with American naval officers. As a British commander, he had encountered them in the Mediterranean during the Napoleonic Wars, but in South America he made it a point to meet them face-to-face. Such was the case in December 1818, when he met with Captain Biddle to discuss the blockade of Lima's port of Callao.

In 1819 the U.S. vice consul in Valparaiso, Henry Hill, wrote to the war and navy secretaries in Chile that the merchant Eliphalet Smith of the *Macedonian* had filed a complaint about money taken from him by the Chilean Navy commander, Lord Cochrane, and that the merchant's detention on the frigate *O'Higgins* was "unjustifiable." According to State Department Commerce Agent Jeremiah Robinson, Cochrane had established a naval system to exact contribution on board his ship and others under his command off the port of Arica, in violation of neutral rights and oppressive to neutral commerce. Prior to entering Arica, Cochrane required neutral vessels to pay an 18.5 percent duty on the value of their cargo.

Robinson was, at the same time, highly critical of American ships. In August 1822 he wrote to Secretary of State John Quincy Adams that "the Brigs *Canton* and *Macedonian* were for more than three years constantly violating blockades, neutral and belligerent rights, and supplying the royalists and flew the Spanish flag."

Stewart's criteria for judging his Anglo-Chilean counterpart are unknown as the commodore kept no record of their meeting. He only wrote later to his government that Cochrane and San Martín were "two of the greatest rogues ever existing."[33]

On 16 March Stewart ordered Lt. David Conner to proceed to the coast of Conception, cruise for ten days, and ascertain whether any real danger threatened the *Franklin*'s forthcoming voyage. The escort would also acquaint itself with the harbors and coastline. The *Dolphin* departed on 17 March for patrol duties, arriving at the port of Arauco on the twenty-eighth. She returned to Valparaiso on 4 April.

After the *Dolphin* departed on her mission, Lord Cochrane invited Stewart and a retinue to his estate, called Quintero. He specifically requested the presence of Mid. Charles Wilkes, to whom he was related by marriage through his uncle, Sir Alexander Cochrane. As a boy, Lord Cochrane had visited his distant family in New York. At a dinner given by Cochrane, Wilkes was "struck with [Cochrane's] want of enthusiasm in the Cause of Chile and a doubt seemed to exist with him whether they could maintain the independence they had achieved." Quintero had a good landing site and was replete with quail. Cochrane invited the officers to hunt on his property during the *Franklin*'s stay in Valparaiso, an invitation that was gladly accepted but soon regretted.

A few days later, on 20 March, a hunting party left the ship and made sail on one of the *Franklin*'s small boats to a beach. On board were the potential duelists, Midshipmen Marshall and Cramer. Joining them was Midshipman Pinkham and two officers from notable and historic naval families—Lt. James Alexander Perry and Mid. Edward Preble (appointed only five years before).[34]

The small cutter set out on a beautiful day with a good breeze. The participants planned an overnight trip. Approaching the shore, the boat was caught in rollers and flipped several times, entangling most in the sails and rigging. All were drowned except for Pinkham, who found himself washed up on the beach. Still dazed, he was robbed of his possessions and stripped by a passing

Chilean. Preble and Perry, both of whom appeared to be living up to their respective family's reputations, were included in those souls lost. The List of Navy Officers records their deaths on 22 March, but both the logs of the *Franklin* and the *Dolphin* document the tragic day as 20 March.

The other tragedy was that of Marshall and Cramer. Only a few weeks earlier they were prepared to duel. When their bodies were found, it appeared that they had "died together in a struggle to free each other from entanglement and subsequent drowning."

Stewart must have sensed futility in stopping the duel between Cramer and Marshall only to lose them in what was anticipated to be an enjoyable shore leave. He might have felt responsible somehow, particularly in contemplating what he would say to the Perry and Preble families.

A few years later in the Pacific, sailor Richard Henry Dana recounted the shipboard feeling of such a loss: "When a man falls overboard at sea and is lost, there is a suddenness in the event, and a difficulty in realizing it, which gives it an air of awful mystery. . . . See no forms and hear no voices but their own, one is taken suddenly from them, and they miss him at every turn. It is like losing a limb. There are no new faces or new scenes to fill up the gap. There is always an empty berth in the forecastle."[35]

On 21 March the *Franklin* displayed her colors at half mast, which was answered by all foreign ships in port.

On 29 March the USS *Constellation*, Capt. Charles G. Ridgely commanding, arrived in Valparaiso to a thirteen-gun salute. Stewart knew the *Constellation* as well as any ship because twenty years before he had served as her executive officer and briefly as her commander. Ridgely and Stewart exchanged information on the situation in the South Pacific, and Eliphalet Smith was seen on board the *Constellation* with the two captains more than once. (According to one of the *Franklin*'s officers, unattributable, the Chilean José de San Martín said Smith had done more injury to the Patriot cause than any other individual in South America.) One week after Ridgely's arrival in a change-of-command ceremony, Stewart became the first commodore of the Pacific Station.

CHAPTER NINE

On Pacific Station: Revolutions

Valparaiso was a welcomed respite for the officers, crew, and passengers of the *Franklin,* none more so than "La Commadora"—the prima donna of the voyage, Delia Tudor Stewart. Delia was more accustomed to fine homes in Boston, Europe, and Bordentown than to the close quarters of a ship-of-war in near-perpetual motion. During the months preceding the stop at Valparaiso, Delia had earned the whispered derision of the ship's company, though they continued to pay her the respect due the wife of their commodore and incorrectly obeyed her at one of the voyage's defining moments. Perhaps because her husband refused to allow his wife to squander any more of his money, she was forced to turn to other sources, just as she had turned to Joseph Bonaparte back in Bordentown.

According to Midshipman Wilkes, Delia

did not fail to give [the officers] a good deal of amusement, particularly in the way she contrived to borrow money, & empty our pockets, which she at once dispensed to the beggars surrounding her. We used to laugh greatly at her sharpness of hearing—a chink of coin inaudible to many, was detected by her and when she became aware of the officer having any change, She would quickly decide on the Manner of getting it from him. It was borrowed for a time, but rarely, if ever, returned. . . . One time I pulled out all I had in hand and offered it supposing she would take a few shillings, but she at once grabbed the whole, about five dollars, and began deliberately to distribute it to those beggars. . . . I never saw a farthing of it again but the fun it created among us all was worth the amount.[1]

Five dollars was not an insubstantial sum in 1822, especially to an officer for whom it was at least a week's pay. Although events like this amused the officers, had they continued unabated the amusement would have been overtaken by discontent. Fortunately, Commodore Stewart became aware of his wife's behavior and directed his aides, Lt. Joshua Sands and Mid. William Weaver, to keep a meticulous account of all the money his wife took from the officers. Stewart repaid these overly accommodating, patient, and dutiful officers.

While in port, Stewart was not averse to spend money himself, though not on the civilian population's disenfranchised, as his wife was wont to do. He gambled—surprising behavior for a merchant who had amassed his own fortune and might be considered thrifty—though the extent to which he was willing to gamble and the amount he was willing to risk is not known. Of Stewart's two aides, Lt. Henry Henry (who preceded Weaver) shared Stewart's pastime, but he was known to go a step further with his apparent gambling addiction. Henry was described as "tall and well-proportioned with bright red hair and whiskers and a florid complexion and his temperament was quick and hasty." Together he and Stewart directed themselves to the Monte tables.

Stewart's other aide, Joshua Sands, was the junior lieutenant on board the *Franklin*. Sands was a "slight figure" with "extremely agreeable manners, frank and pleasant in his speech and good expression, a great deal of vivacity, exceedingly polite and attentive and fond of ladies' society among whom he was always a great favorite" and might be called "a great Ladies' Man." He was "generous to a fault and free to lend and give" and a "better selection could not have been made as an aide."[2]

Meanwhile, Delia basked in the appreciation of Valparaiso's poor as she distributed other peoples' money. She contented herself with the parties held for her and the commodore by the diplomatic community, such as it was, and on Lord Cochrane's estate. In the spring of 1822 Stewart remained on Cochrane's estate in Valparaiso with his wife while the admiral cruised along the coast. Delia likely spent time with Kitty, Lord Cochrane's twenty-six-year-old wife.

Kitty was the antithesis of Delia in many ways. She was sensitive and compassionate, beautiful and intelligent. Kitty grew up "a penniless orphan with no social standing."[3] Delia was raised in one of New England's most prominent families and always had money, though not always her own, to spend.

Delia likely may have been jealous of Kitty and eager to find a way to distinguish herself from Cochrane's wife as the preeminent socialite in the region. Perhaps for this reason Delia pursued a course that ultimately sullied Stewart's reputation and resulted in severe charges upon his return to Washington.

Delia and Charles also met the unfortunate widow of Captain Graham, the captain of the British forty-four-fun frigate *Doris* who died in March 1822 while rounding Cape Horn. The *Doris* arrived in Valparaiso on 28 April, her colors flying at half-mast. "As soon as Commodore Stewart saw the *Doris* approach the harbour . . . he came to offer every assistance and accommodation the ship might require."[4] Stewart and his wife, as well as Baron Macau, the captain of the French frigate *Chlorinde*, often visited and consoled Maria Graham, who was in her late thirties.

La Commadora's gaiety and enjoyment of the limited Valparaiso society was interrupted on the beautiful moonlit evening of 5 May 1822, sometime between 7:00 and 9:30 (various eyewitness reports and *Franklin*'s logbook differ on the exact time). Delia was being entertained on the second floor of the Main Street home of the U.S. consul, Michael Hogan, when a massive earthquake struck Valparaiso. It was the first of several earthquakes Stewart and his crew would experience during the next two years. Seeing the havoc wrought upon the city, Charles Wilkes described the devastation: "Scarcely a tenement was left standing. . . . Many buildings lay like a pack of cards with the walls fallen in overlapping each other."

The months in Valparaiso offered time for Stewart, the officers, and the crew to form opinions on the warring Patriot and Spanish Loyalist factions. Stewart's squadron served a young nation that had twice in the previous forty years fought the British Empire for independence. Stewart and his crew might logically have sympathized with the so-called Patriots under the leadership of Bolívar, O'Higgins, and San Martín, and if the views of Captain Downes's *Macedonian* crew are any indication, American support leaned toward the Patriots. Before the arrival of the Pacific Squadron, a flotilla of fourteen boats under Lord Cochrane rowed past the British frigate *Hyperion* and the U.S. frigate *Macedonian*. Many of the U.S. warship's officers "hung over the bulwarks, cheered [the Patriots] in whispers, wishing [them] success, and wishing also that [the Americans] could join [the Patriots]."[5]

The majority of Americans did support the independence causes of other nations, but a significant number still harbored the aristocratic notions of Tories, like those who opposed the American Revolution. Delia's brother-in-law, Robert Hallowell Gardiner, for example, was the heir of Dr. Silvester

Gardiner, a prominent Tory and landowner in New England during the Revolution, who was forced to escape to England and abandon some of his holdings.

The division of opinions between the Patriots and Loyalists did not escape the officers of the *Franklin*. According to Midshipman Wilkes: "There were two parties on board the Ship, One in favor of the Royalists, the other strongly Patriotic, which caused a great deal of Animosity. . . . [The] right-minded were for the Patriot cause, while the Dissipated and gambling (including the Commodore) were intent upon . . . Gambling & trade." It is unclear how or why Wilkes associated gambling and trade with supporting the Loyalists since either activity would have continued regardless of the government in charge.[6]

If Stewart found Pacific Station initially less active than the Mediterranean, he did not have to wait long to encounter other warships. As a waypoint for Pacific traders, established empires, struggling powers, and emerging republics, Valparaiso offered Stewart the opportunity to assess a part of the commercial, political, diplomatic, and military prowess, capability, and intent of several foreign powers. The Chilean Navy under Cochrane was based in Valparaiso, and the Peruvian squadron visited occasionally. In mid-May 1822 alone, the French frigate *Chlorinde* and the British frigate *Doris* anchored in the harbor with the *Franklin*. The operations of his European counterparts convinced Stewart that America was not the only nation with interest in these newly independent nations. Moreover, he could surmise that the operations of the *Franklin* were under the watchful eye of the Europeans.

The struggling new countries' naval power was not dissimilar to the U.S. Navy of only a quarter-century before, when Stewart was a young lieutenant. According to local U.S. diplomatic officers, Chile had twelve ships-of-war, including three frigates; Peru had thirteen ships including three frigates; and Panama had three ships of its own.

Stewart was clearly concerned about foreign ship activity, and he relied on a variety of intelligence sources for information. As author Steven E. Maffeo pointed out in *Most Secret and Confidential: Intelligence in the Age of Nelson*, British diplomats provided information to the British Admiralty on terms of treaties, details of French defensive positions, and the number and condition of ships. "British diplomats posted around the world made constant observations. . . . This was the best and chief source of peacetime intelligence."[7] Like the British, U.S. Navy officers also relied on diplomats as well as department special agents who reported on political conditions abroad, public opinion, and investigations of various kinds. Sometimes these intelligence sources were unreliable, and their reports were occasionally inspired by their own personal and political agendas. Jeremiah Robinson, for example, was a civil servant and prolific correspondent in both official and private letters who provided extensive reports and updates on domestic and foreign activity in the eastern South Pacific. On 21 February 1823 Robinson wrote to Secretary of State John Quincy Adams that "Spain has neither a ship nor a cannon in the Pacific. France manifests the strongest inclination to established intercourse and connexions [*sic*] with these new states. She has at present in the Pacific two Frigates, probably the largest in the world, each mounting sixty-six cannon, and other ships."

The inherent weaknesses of Robinson's correspondence, and of other reports based on human intelligence, were the reporter's ability to determine his information's accuracy and the reporter's intent for the report. Robinson's reports ultimately proved to be strategically unreliable to Washington and, more importantly from an operational standpoint, to Stewart.

More than the inaccuracy of his information, Robinson's motives were debatable. Prior to the *Franklin*'s voyage, Robinson had been issued a position as U.S. consul to Lima, a position later retracted and offered to William Tudor Jr. As a native of Massachusetts well integrated in society gossip, Robinson was likely aware of the relationship between Tudor and Stewart.

Not only did Robinson detest Stewart and Stewart's fellow captains, as evidenced by other public and private correspondence, but he consistently attempted to ingratiate himself with those domestic—or foreign, for that matter—officials who might provide him with future employment. Robinson had lived most of his life outside the United States and always claimed that his inability to secure a government position was due to not having the benefit of personal friends in Congress. At one time or another, he sought the new foreign ministerial positions in Chile, Peru, Argentina, Mexico, and Colombia. To that end, he engaged, quite simply, in endless letter writing.

His correspondence was always biased, usually negative, and self-ingratiating. It is difficult to find any positive comments about individuals of whom he writes, except the recipients of the letters, whom he praises. Robinson's correspondence and subsequent meetings in Washington became one of the causes of Stewart's woes when he completed his tour as the commander of the Pacific Squadron two years later.

The Navy secretary had ordered Stewart to preserve U.S. neutrality while on Pacific Station, but he did not restrict Stewart from protecting the squadron or U.S. commercial ships. The U.S. consul at Valparaiso, Michael

Hogan, made the U.S. position clear when he wrote to Joaquim de Echarvaria, Chile's state secretary:

> I pray you to be convinced, and request you to assure his Excellency the Supreme Director that however desirable it may be to Commodore Stewart to preserve a course strictly neutral, his high mind and exalting situation places him far above the insinuation contained in the information given to the government of his affording protection to the merchant vessels of his country engaged in trade.[8]

Strict neutrality meant that the U.S. Pacific Squadron, unlike Decatur's Mediterranean Squadron, was constrained in its choice of courses of action. The Pacific Squadron was also in a different position from its commercial counterparts and fellow countrymen. U.S. merchant ships had been trading throughout the South American conflict without regard to either party so long as their customers could pay. Most ships maintained legitimate commerce, but other ships pursued more profitable trade by violating blockades or by trafficking in arms. The *Pearl*, for example, was reported to have swords, muskets, and pistols on board destined for the Sandwich Islands. On 5 January 1823 John Prevost, U.S. consul to Chile and Peru, wrote to Stewart that he thought it proper for the commodore to decline the *Pearl*'s request for protection. Stewart chose otherwise.

British and North American merchants also financed the purchase of arms and ammunition for both the revolutionaries and the Royalists, knowing that the expulsion of the Spaniards would create a vacuum ripe for new U.S. commercial and military opportunities. But it was the U.S. merchant ships that caused difficulties for Stewart. Specifically, the *Canton* was apparently known up and down the west coast of South America as a blockade-runner and had been boarded by Cochrane on at least one occasion. When in Valparaiso, the *Canton* had muskets and "other implements of war" to sell to the Royalists at Lima, Peru. Moreover, Stewart himself appeared to undermine his orders to maintain strict neutrality by frequently meeting with Eliphalet Smith, beginning with their meeting with the Spaniards on the *Constellation* before Captain Ridgely's frigate departed Pacific Station.

Rumormongering by individuals like Robinson led foreign officials themselves to believe that the American naval presence in the Pacific was less than neutral. Regarding the connection between Stewart and Smith's *Canton*, Robinson wrote, "some illiberal remarks of [the *Canton*] having some illicit connextion [*sic*] with the *Franklin* are circulated in which the Commodore's name has been disrespectingly mentioned." There is no doubt that much of the disrespect and illiberal remarks originated with Robinson. Yet the *Canton* did carry arms with the intent to sell them to Royalists at Lima. On 7 May 1823 Smith visited Stewart on the *Franklin* as the *Canton* hove to aft. The following year an unsigned letter that can be attributed to Jeremiah Robinson by language and penmanship stated that Smith and Stewart "were ancient friends and partners in trade and their former intimacy was only to be assumed" and attacked Smith, who was "the daily and hourly companion of the Commodore and his evil genius still maintains its swagger."[9] Robinson charged additional improprieties when he wrote that Stewart received a percentage of the *Canton*'s profits and a gratuity for protecting the merchant ship.

The insinuation that a nefarious relationship existed between Smith and Stewart had no foundation other than the fact that the two men did indeed have some commercial partnership prior to the War of 1812.

On 13 January 1823 Stewart lost his first officer, Lieutenant Mayo. The surgeon's mate on *Franklin* found the climate had an ill effect on Mayo's health and recommended to Stewart that Mayo be released from duty. Subsequently, Mayo left for Washington with dispatches. Stewart lost another officer when Lt. Horace Sawyer was arrested and suspended from duty after making "intemperate remarks" when he had been refused permission to go ashore. At a shipboard court of inquiry Sawyer was found guilty of having violated the law and discipline of the service. The lieutenant soon requested that he be allowed to return to the United States.

Stewart wrote to the court saying that it was free to make its own decision about Sawyer but that it ought to consider the possible ramifications of its decision. Were Sawyer granted return to the United States, other crew members may similarly want to "go home and avoid duty." Further, Stewart was concerned about the efficacy of the Navy to conduct courts-martial if sailors used the system simply for this end. His thinking on Sawyer's case was a far cry from his "draconian" rulings during the Mediterranean cruise, when he sent many commanding officers home. Even though the *Franklin* had ordered some of her officers back to the United States during the squadron's visit to Rio de Janeiro, she still had more than ample officers. Nevertheless, by the time Sawyer was tried, it was only 1822, and the squadron still had two years left on Pacific Station. How many more officers could the squadron afford to lose?

During the *Franklin*'s stay in Valparaiso, Stewart unintentionally created hostility in yet another civil servant. Prevost complained to the secretary of state that he remained two months in Lima awaiting the *Franklin* without receiving any information from the new commodore. On 25 April 1822 Prevost set out for Valparaiso but "had the mortification to reach within sight of the Port, just as [Stewart] was going out of the Harbor."[10] Prevost assumed that Stewart was intentionally avoiding him, a confusion that reflected a communication obstacle inherent during the Age of Sail.

One of the great difficulties for a naval commander on a distant station was maintaining communication with Washington and the Navy secretary. Letters and orders issued from Washington took as long as five months to reach the squadron and, then, only if it happened to be in port. Captains were aware of this obstacle and accepted it. Some suggested methods of reducing the time. Thomas ap Catesby Jones, for example, who arrived on Pacific Station in September 1825, found this method of communication a "time-consuming and harrowing journey." In a letter to the Navy secretary, he suggested that the Navy "should station small ships on each side of the Panamanian isthmus to provide timely information."[11] The Navy Department, however, chose not to follow his suggestion.

Perhaps Catesby Jones, arriving so soon on Pacific Station after Stewart's departure, had acquired the idea from Stewart himself.

With only the *Franklin* and *Dolphin* under his command, Stewart had arrived on Pacific Station with no means of communication other than in-port government officials or U.S. merchant ships. In-port officials, having no special ability to convey a letter more rapidly to Washington, were subject to the availability of passing ships as well, while merchant ships might make several port calls plying their trade and lengthening the delay before returning to the United States.

From his experience with small boats in the Mediterranean during the Barbary Wars, his defense of Norfolk, and his command of the Mediterranean Squadron, Stewart recognized the value and utility of small boats, particularly after the *Dolphin*, under Conner, parted with the *Franklin* on 7 May 1822. The *Franklin* was left alone for the rest of the summer as the *Dolphin* sailed for Arica and later Callao.

While accompanying the *Pearl*, Stewart found that the merchantman was carrying the frames of three small boats—two Boston pilot boats and one schooner. On 18 May 1822 in Valparaiso, Stewart purchased the frames, planning to construct the small boats to use as couriers. Although the *Franklin* probably had sufficient funds, Stewart made the purchase with his own money so as not to deplete the squadron's financial resources against unforeseen challenges during the two years remaining in the tour. Stewart considered the boats to be his private property.[12] His decision to use personal funds for the boats had repercussions when the squadron eventually returned to the United States.

On 20 May 1822 Valparaiso welcomed the French frigate *Chlorinde*, as the British frigate *Doris* departed. Two days later the *Franklin* got under way with the *Canton* and *Pearl* joining her the following day, after Stewart ordered provisions laid in, including sweet potatoes and plantain oranges to avoid scurvy.

The ships made for the Island of Juan Fernandez where the crew of the *Franklin* began construction on the small boats. Stewart directed that stores of the ship—rigging, sails, carpenters, etc.—be made available for construction. Jeremiah Robinson, upon learning that the crew was directed to build the boats, wrote to the State Department, questioning if a crew on foreign relations duty should be employed in such capacity. He relayed that "the circumstance has suggested many remarks and speculation, not any favourable to the naval service or credibility, the government which permits such transactions."

The three dispatch boats, built intermittently during the next six months, were named the *Peruvian*, the *Water-witch*, and the *Robinson Crusoe*, aptly named after Daniel Defoe's protagonist. Lieutenant Henry was given command of *Water-witch* with now-Lieutenant Wilkes as his second in command, plus eight sailors, a cook, and a quartermaster.

Stewart himself worked on the construction of the boats and spent a great deal of time on Juan Fernandez. Wilkes recalled him driving spikes and assisting in various ways. Stewart likely had as much familiarity with boat construction as his ship's carpenters, thanks to his experience supervising the construction of Jefferson's gunboats twenty years before and to the technological recommendations he had made to previous Navy secretaries. According to Wilkes, Stewart seemed to take a great interest and pleasure in their assembly.

When the schooner *Water-witch* was completed, she displaced forty-five tons. During her launch, Stewart's uniform became drenched and all that could be found to replace it was a midshipman's uniform that Stewart gladly wore. In fact, he seemed amused by the uniform, which he had never worn before, having bypassed midshipman to be commissioned as a lieutenant directly.

Stewart's enjoyable but all-too-brief respite on the island was far removed from the machinations of diplomacy. Months passed before he learned that

Colombia, including modern-day Venezuela, Ecuador, and Panama, under Simón Bolívar had been granted recognition by the United States.

Stewart arrived in Arica on 5 June 1822 for a two-week port visit and an audience with the governor of Peru. Arica was a town of four thousand inhabitants, which Jeremiah Robinson described in a 25 July letter as a "small dangerous port." On 6 June at 11:30 A.M., a Peruvian Patriot man-of-war schooner approached the town and began to fire upon it for the following three days. The *Franklin* stayed clear while the town's artillery responded against the schooner. The exchange seems to have gotten the better of the schooner; her commanding officer requested medical assistance from the *Franklin*, which Stewart approved. On 9 June the belligerent schooner, the *Castillian*, departed.

Shortly thereafter the *Franklin*, along with the *Pearl*, set sail for Quilca. The ships celebrated the Fourth of July with a twenty-one-gun salute. The *Franklin*, according to one account, was decorated with all the flags on board, and the crew received an extra allowance of grog. The celebrations ended with a ball that concluded at midnight.

On 2 August, under light breezes and clear weather, the *Franklin* and *Canton* arrived in Callao, Peru's port city, for a two-month visit. As the ship-of-the-line doubled the point of the Island of San Lorenzo, she was saluted by the *Dolphin* with thirteen guns. The British frigate *Aurora* also saluted the commodore and hoisted an American ensign. The British frigate *Doris* was also in port and was followed eight days later by the French frigate *Chlorinde* as well as forty assorted vessels from various countries. On 20 August the Americans saw one of the revolutionary leaders for the first time when José de San Martín arrived on a Peruvian brig-of-war. "Callao was the key to Lima, because it supplied all the food and luxuries for the city, as well as exporting Peru's huge mineral treasures back to the mainland."[13]

John Prevost continued to have concerns about Stewart. He wrote to Jeremiah Robinson that he still had not met with Stewart but that the ship's reputation had reached him. Specifically, while the *Franklin* had visited what were called the intermediate ports, she had "excited some irritation" toward the U.S. government from the local governments. "It is a fact," Prevost wrote, "that infinite mischief from the Patriot camp has grown out of this intercourse. I regret that our Commodore should have thought proper to disregard a Blockade which Sir Thomas Hardy felt himself bound to respect." This assessment probably arose out of the *Canton* neutrality issue as well as other incidents, including one involving the U.S. merchant ship *Ocean*. U.S. Consul Michael Hogan wrote to Secretary of State John Quincy

Adams that the *Ocean* had encountered difficulties with the local authorities, presumably running a blockade, and both Hogan and Stewart demanded restitution from the Peruvian government. Unlike Prevost and Robinson, Hogan supported Stewart's efforts. He noted to Secretary Adams that the *Ocean*'s "protection under our Flag will render it unnecessary to pay tribute to the exclusive monopoly established by the Protectorial Government of Peru."

Both Michael Hogan and Judge John Prevost visited Maria Graham, who spent most of 1822 among the elite of Valparaiso. She recalled that Prevost was originally from a Genevan family. She believed Prevost was "wrong in endeavouring to impress on the government that Chile has no business with ships of war, or of trade, for these hundred years to come, and that she should hire the former, and employ foreign carriers in lieu of the latter . . . but the simple-minded Chilenos are no match for Genevese sagacity, united to North American speculation."[14]

Joining the *Franklin* in the summer of 1822 was a passenger apparently known to all but Commodore Stewart himself. The passenger was an officer, Madrid, who served in the Royalist Army in Peru and who had presented himself to Mrs. Stewart while she was ashore. With letters of recommendation from two of her new socialite friends, the Countess of Valle Esmola and Dona Rosita de Paneiro, Madrid fed Delia a compelling tale. He had been a passenger on the Genoese ship *Diana* from Rio de Janeiro, which was taken by a Patriot cruiser and escorted to Callao. Having not obtained a passport, he expected to be imprisoned. Consequently, he implored Delia to allow him to remain on board the *Franklin*. "Her lively imagination at once converted the supplicant into a hero of romance, fleeing from the vindictiveness of a hard-hearted usurper. Her feelings, always alive to those in distress, did not allow her to turn a deaf ear to his petition."[15]

At least part of the story was true. Lieutenant Conner recorded that on 14 June 1822 the *Dolphin* had boarded a Genoese ship, the *Diana*, eighty-three days from Rio, having last made port in Arica. The *Diana* had been seized and brought in by a Peruvian brig, the *Nancy*.[16]

Delia considered Madrid's story to be "lamentable" and could not bear to turn him away. Perhaps her effort was less one of compassion than one of competition. Kitty Cochrane, the young wife of Admiral Cochrane, had the year before aided Dona Angela Pezuela, the wife of the deposed viceroy, in securing safe passage to Europe.[17] Robert Hallowell Gardiner believed that Madrid was actually the president of Peru who had been deposed and branded a traitor with a prize on his head. Gardiner probably based his belief on information from Delia herself. Delia, as a product of high society, aspired to the higher elite of royalty. She probably heard of Kitty Cochrane's adventures in saving the viceroy's wife, and, inspired by a spirit of one-upmanship, she initiated and embellished her own activity.

Delia consulted on her plans with American merchant Eliphalet Smith, who advised her that she make no decision before speaking with the commodore. Regrettably, Delia pursued her own path. She directed the ship's steward, Peter Birch, to take care of Madrid and provide him with food. She also directed Birch to refrain from telling anyone about the passenger, especially her husband.

Birch obeyed La Commadora and gave Madrid a space in the captain's pantry to take his meals, some of his own clothes to use as a disguise, and some duties in the wardroom. That Eliphalet Smith, the officers, and the crew of the *Franklin* knew of the passenger but chose not to inform Stewart was one of the most curious, egregious, and harmful decisions made during the voyage. Did they assume Stewart already knew if Delia was behind it? Did they fear the reaction of the commodore? Or did they fear retribution by La Commadora more?

Along with the dispatch boat, the *Peruvian*, the ships set sail on 30 September and arrived in Quilca on 23 October 1822, the same day as the *Chlorinde*. At the first opportunity, Madrid slithered out of one of the gun ports and away from the ship not to be seen or heard from for another year.

On 27 October the ships were rejoined for four days by the *Dolphin*, which they had not seen in over five months. A few days later the *Peruvian*, now under the command of Lieutenant Henry, departed while Lieutenant Wilkes was given command of the *Water-witch*. On 1 December the *Franklin* and the *Water-witch* led a convoy out of Quilca including the *Canton*, the *Dick*, the *Chauncey*, and an English brig, the *Lady Collier*. The ships arrived at Valparaiso before the new year and before the *Franklin* returned to Cumberland Bay at Juan Fernandez Island to construct the *Robinson Crusoe*.

The year 1823 began with Stewart in no better stead with his diplomatic counterparts. The Patriot blockade of the Peruvian coast continued to pose a threat not only to American shipping but also to U.S. diplomatic and military relations with both the Patriot and Royalist forces. On 19 January 1823 Stewart forcefully wrote to Prevost that had the squadron known about the blockade of the Intermedios—the coastal cities, towns, and ports along the Peruvian coast—and had Prevost entertained any ideas at that time on the subject, he should have made them known to Captain Ridgely, who was then on station in Lima, the year before. In addition, Stewart told Prevost that the consul's ideas were not in unison with those of the U.S. government. Stewart also corrected Prevost about the previous summer—Stewart hadn't offered the *Canton* protection, nor was the merchantman under any imminent or apparent threat by the Peruvian naval force.

Stewart's report to Prevost differed from Consul Michael Hogan's report to John Quincy Adams the following month, in which Hogan advised that had Stewart not "wisely determined to protect [U.S.] commerce at the Intermediates, where protection was wanted, National property would have been lost in immense amounts, and these Governments would laugh at [U.S.] imbecility."

As was customary, the commodore welcomed local government dignitaries on board his ship-of-the-line in the interest of diplomacy but more importantly for a show of military strength. Among the retinue of senior officials was a Spanish Royalist officer whose face was familiar to many of the crew. After the party of dignitaries departed the *Franklin*, Stewart received a complaint from the Patriot government charging him with transporting a Spanish Loyalist spy. Stewart refused to believe the allegation and gave his word of honor against the claim. One of Stewart's officers later noted that one of the visiting officers who had come on board the ship was Madrid, the same Madrid who had been transported the prior year. Stewart, who had no prior knowledge of Madrid's transport, became enraged (indeed, this is the first time recorded that the normally even-tempered Stewart reacted in this manner). Upon receiving the Patriots' complaint, he approached Birch and struck him, demanding the truth. He then learned that Delia was behind the entire episode.

> He felt that his professional reputation was put in jeopardy, that the complaints of the ruling powers in Peru would subject him to be tried by a court-martial by whom he might be dismissed from the navy with disgrace, or unpleasant complications might be produced between the new republic and his own country. His rage against his wife became unbounded, and he adopted a most original mode of showing it. He determined never to open his lips again to her during the remainder of the voyage, but she was compelled to take her usual seat at table without the least notice from her husband, and, difficult as it is to understand, no change was made during the long voyage from the Pacific to New York.[18]

The *Franklin* departed Quilca on 2 May 1823 and arrived in Callao on 9 May 1823. While the *Franklin* was in port, Prevost had another opportunity to meet with Stewart, and, as he wrote to Adams in late May, he hoped to reestablish at least a courteous intercourse between Stewart and the current government of Peru. Prevost reported that during the issue of *Canton*'s neutrality and the Madrid affair Stewart had treated the Peruvian government officials with the "utmost disrespect."

In July the Peruvian squadron sailed into port, and the *Canton* was seized at Callao for running the blockade. On 9 July Stewart wrote to the local governor, William Psenier, that the *Canton* was a private vessel belonging to U.S. citizens. The blockaders, who were now the Patriots, stated as one of their issues that the *Canton* bore a pennant that implied it was part of the U.S. squadron and, therefore, a military ship. Stewart responded that no U.S. law or practice prohibited the use of pennants by private armed vessels belonging to North America.

The next day Psenier announced that his government's instructions offered sufficient motives to detain the ship. On 11 July Stewart became more forceful: "I am sent into the Sea with the naval Forces of the U.S. under my command to protect the Citizens (and their property) of the U.S. in all their lawful pursuits. The *Canton* violated no laws." Psenier wasted no time in making his case to the *Canton*'s protector and insisted that the government of Peru had formally declared the coast under a rigorous blockade and that the *Canton* was in violation.

Commodore Stewart achieved no resolution with Psenier. He, therefore, wrote an appeal to Psenier's superior, a twenty-eight-year old general named Antonio José de Sucre. The *Franklin* had no judge advocate on board (unlike some later U.S. Navy ships) nor any diplomat with whom Stewart could consult. The commodore's disagreements with Prevost made his assistance unlikely and Hogan, with whom he shared better relations, was too far away to help.

Stewart's letter to Antonio José de Sucre was logical, at times even flowery, and bespeaks much of the man who is considered by some historians to have come from near-illiteracy. Chief Justice John Marshall "called it the best statement of the principles of blockade that he had ever seen."[19] Because of its importance and its demonstration of the commodore's logic, the 14 July 1823 letter to Sucre is provided in its entirety:

> The letter your Excellency did me the honor to write me on the eighth instant, in reply to mine of the thirtieth ultimo, has been duly received. It does not, perhaps, belong to me to discuss the principles your Excellency contends for, with respect to the declared blockade of the western coast of Peru by the

Patriot Government; it may only belong to me to notify my respectful protest against its illegal and injurious operations, so far as the commerce of the Republic of North America is concerned, and in compliance with my orders to guard it against those effects, leaving principles and points contended for to the discussion of the two Governments. But the Government of Peru may have been led into an error on that subject, by the infraction of those principles of the laws of nations, during the late wars in Europe, between France and England, and then for the first time adopted by Great Britain, and, as your Excellency states, not opposed by her commanders on this station. If I bring to the notice of your Excellency some important facts, out of the strict line of duty attaching to my command, I hope and trust your Excellency will do me the favor to believe that it only originates in a strong desire to safeguard our respective rights, and to preserve a lasting harmony between the Governments.

After the commencement of hostilities between Great Britain and France in '92, so long as it was the interest of England, and during the existence of the marine [influence of] several European powers, that Government observed and applied the principles of the laws of nations to all the blockades instituted. But when she had destroyed, in turn, the marine of the other European powers, her policy was then changed. International law was rejected, honor and common honesty were abandoned; power gave right, and a war of destruction was waged against the unoffending neutral; commerce was given up to its cormorant rapacity, and that which escaped its talons, she forced her open enemies to prey on, under pretext of retaliation. Against such principles, I need not now remind your Excellency, the United States resisted, even with England, successfully, and as the Republic of the North was the first to contend for just principles in the late war, she was also found the last in the field defending them.

The conclusions your Excellency has drawn from the tacit conduct of the British Naval Commanders on this station, are not applicable to the United States, and perhaps those commanders may not be instructed to interfere with any kind of blockade the Patriot Government may deem proper to impose, especially one founded on principles so lately and newly exercised by themselves. England, the most politic nation, has always been guided in her conduct towards others, by principles of policy and interest often times just, but as often at variance with justice and previous conduct. She may reserve to herself the right of discussing and demanding indemnification of the Patriot Government hereafter, for any violation of her rights, to preserve a future cause of quarrel with these governments, to obtain some exclusive commercial advantage as indemnity hereafter, to apply the same rule to the commerce of this country in her future wars. Whatever infraction of her rights she may deem proper to tacitly acquiesce in now, does not and can not constitute a reason that the government of the United States should also yield theirs. Your Excellency very justly observes that a blockade declared by the commanders of a ship of the line or a schooner, legally commissioned for war, does not import less in the one case than the other, and it will be but just to add that the declaration of a blockade, originating in their will, imports nothing.

The commander of a ship of war, or commander in chief of a squadron, can institute a blockade in very distant seas—the urgency and necessity of the case renders it legal. The act of a belligerant [*sic*] involving certain rights of a friend is an act of sovereignty; it belongs to that authority to declare it, and only to the commanders to carry it into effect. But the belligerant's right and will, to do so, and the declaration of it, does not constitute the act, unless combined with an object that is legitimate, and a force competent to sustain it. With respect to the legitimacy of the object, that can only exist in depriving your enemy of all external means of annoying you, and external resources of continuing the war, and is in a great measure dependent on their actual situation; hence the right of the neutral to introduce all articles of a perfectly innocent nature, and which do not contribute anything towards carrying on the war. It would be preposterous to blockade a port, by sea, against the entrance of provisions, which has an extensive and abundant country adjoining to supply it. In such a case the belligerent would only be injuring a common friend, without prejudice to his enemy: this the law of nations forbids his doing; but on the other hand, where a possibility exists of your reducing your enemies to terms, by excluding such provisions, your right is legitimate to do so, and the injury done the neutral is accidental.

With respect to the competency of the force, it will depend on the localities of the port or ports blockaded; and the force applied is of such description and so stationed, as to render it extremely hazardous to enter: so also with respect to the force of your enemy; if he possess a thousand ships of war more than the blockading power, and does not see proper to drive it from his ports, it is effectual against the neutral so long as that blockade preserves and does not voluntarily abandon its stations.

A blockade originally legitimate and legally instituted, may derive an opposite character from the conduct of the belligerant blockading. Thus the forces stationed to carry it into effect, negligently and partially executing it, the Government contravening its legitimate object, and by partiality or licence permitting one or two neutral flags to trade while all others are excluded, thereby rendering it a subject of convenience to themselves, or a source of tribute to their coffers. Admitting, in consequence of the localities of the Western coast of Peru, that it be susceptible of blockade by as small or a smaller force than the same extent of coast in any other part of the world, yet the whole naval force of Peru, even if actually engaged in that service, is not a competent force for the blockade of a coast, eight hundred miles in extent, and containing very many ports and harbors. I, however, believe very little of the naval force of Peru has been employed on that service, and in fact this extensive blockade has often been left for months, with no other vessel beyond a schooner; and also there can no doubt exist, of exclusive privileges having been given by the Government of Peru to particular persons and flags, to trade by licence, with this coast declared under blockade.

The principles here contended for, the United States are also contending for with Spain in the North Atlantic, where they operate in favor of the Patriot Government. It would be absurd for the government of Spain, to declare under blockade, and the operation of the laws of the Indies, the whole coast of Chili, Peru and Mexico; and as the most susceptible and convenient mode of sustaining that declaration, to cause a naval force, superior to that of the Patriots, to cruise to the westward of Cape Horn, and there arrest every vessel coming or going, under pretext of violating the laws of the Indies and blockade of an extensive coast by the Patriots, without anything like an adequate force to sustain it.

Sucre, as a result of the letter, released the *Canton*.

In October the logbook of the *Franklin* shows a series of floggings for about two dozen crewmen for various incidents. What makes this unusual is that this is the first recorded use of corporal punishments under Stewart's command on Pacific Station or, for that matter, any other of his many commands. Corporal punishment aboard U.S. naval vessels was standard procedure during the Age of Sail. The practice was eventually banned in 1850 by advocates such as Como. Charles Stewart and Capt. Uriah Levy, who testified before Congress on the "anti-flogging" bill.

On 8 October Stewart's junior lieutenant and aide, Joshua Sands, was placed under arrest for starting a fight with one of his fellow officers—Lt. Thomas Hamersley. After fighting in the wardroom, the two went ashore for a duel. They exchanged three shots without effect and agreed only to resume the duel the following morning. Stewart, upon hearing of the duel, could not have helped but to recall his younger days in the Navy when he tried to stop Decatur from dueling. He might have also recalled that only three years earlier he had lost his childhood friend on the fields of Bladensburg in a pointless duel.

When the lieutenants rowed ashore the following morning, Stewart ordered the two back to the ship. Sands, by letter, refused the order but eventually returned to the *Franklin*. "The following day Sands, under suspension, again insulted Hamersley. There were not enough officers in the squadron to form a court-martial, since the three officers on the court of inquiry had already formed an opinion and five officers were needed."[20] Eventually a court-martial was convened when the *Franklin* was relieved by Isaac Hull's *United States*. Consequently from 9 October 1823 to 13 April 1824, Joshua Sands remained confined to his stateroom.

In December 1823 the United States adopted a new foreign policy, engi-neered in part by Stewart's old friend and Minister to Britain Richard Rush, that opposed European intervention in the Western Hemisphere. A few months before, the British foreign secretary, George Canning, "proposed to Rush that [the U.S. and Great Britain] unite in a joint declaration against European intervention in the Spanish American revolutions."[21] Stewart did not receive word of the new policy, the Monroe Doctrine, for another five months.

That same month the ship left Valparaiso and arrived three days later in the Bay of Coquimbo. On shore, the local governor honored Stewart and his wife while the ship's band provided the entertainment. The following day the commodore reciprocated and "invited the Governor and principal of the rich inhabitants on board for a grand feast which lasted till late at night."[22] These activities throughout the voyage were common for a major warship visiting ports on diplomatic missions, but they added fodder to the accusations by those who opposed Stewart. Jeremiah Robinson charged that Stewart counted his money in his cabin while Delia enjoyed the benefits of being a commodore's wife, accepting presents, such as elegant silver filigree work, from officers of the Royalist Army. Robinson recounted one story in which an individual offered Stewart $3 million for the *Franklin* including the crew, and Stewart considered the offer.

In late December 1823 the squadron found another issue to occupy its attention. Stewart received reports from Quilca that Spanish privateers had been acting against American merchant ships including the brigs *Winefred* of Alexandria, Virginia, and *Frederick* of Stonington, Connecticut. Upon learning that two vessels were attacking U.S. ships, Stewart ordered the squadron out to sea to lure the attackers. He sent the *Dolphin* to pursue one of the belligerents, the nineteen-gun Peruvian brig *Belgrano*. He intended to pursue the other belligerent himself.

On 24 January 1824 the *Franklin* found the U.S. brig *Amanda,* which had been boarded a few days prior by one of the privateers. Stewart ordered 110 sailors and Marines from the *Franklin*, under the command of Lieutenant Hamersley, to ride the *Amanda* in the hope that she would again be boarded by the privateer, whose men would be surprised by the additional cargo. Stewart also ordered all four cutters, the gig, and the barge under the com-mands of Lieutenants Ridgeway and Ogden to search for the privateer.

The boats returned to the *Franklin* the following day with intelligence from the port of Molliendo that the privateer had left there only the day before, bound for Arica. On 28 January Stewart sailed into port and found the American schooner *Adonis* of Baltimore, which had recently been captured by the privateer and was under the command of a prize master. Stewart seized the craft and seven pirates and then prepared another trap for the privateer. The boats were remanned under Lieutenant Ogden and pulled alongside the *Adonis* on the far side of the privateer so as to remain unnoticed. The privateer approached what she thought was her prize when unexpectedly "one of the pistols went off in one of the boats thereby causing the whole of the powder to ignite and explode and wounding mortally a petty officer and a marine and a number were disabled and disfigured for life. . . . the privateer immediately after altered her course from the land."[23] Stewart pursued the privateer, the *General Quintanilla*, but never found her again.

On 11 March Stewart welcomed William Tudor Jr., the newly appointed consul to Peru. Tudor had left 120 days prior from New York City, reporting back to the secretary of state that the news from Peru was "disastrous in the extreme, but perhaps exaggerated." With Tudor on board, the *Franklin* got under way from Valparaiso on the 15 March for Callao and found the town back in the possession of Spanish forces on the twenty-seventh.

General José Ramón Rodil, in command of the fortress at Callao, immediately sent an emissary to the squadron. The prisoners from the *Adonis* were handed over to Rodil. Tudor was the only U.S. diplomat present, as John Prevost had departed with the Patriot refugees when the Spanish forces took control. Tudor parted company from his sister and his brother-in-law and went on to Lima. The new consul recognized the difficulty in the territory to which he was now assigned. After a land battle between the Patriots and Royalists, he wrote to John Quincy Adams that it "seems to promise only a prolongation of evils to this unfortunate country. If the Spanish armies are to succeed only to conquer the country for a despotic monarch and the Inquisition, it will be only to reduce it once more to the butchering bigots and monopoly of their ancient system; and if the Colombian army succeeds, the consequence will be a further exhaustion of the inhabitants by a protracted civil war."

A few months after he departed the *Franklin*, Tudor also recognized the leverage area warships afforded him, noting that the three vessels currently on station were inadequate. Conversely, he believed that the area was of little use to the United States with the value of the trade worth little more than the cost of a single warship.[24]

After a final rendezvous in Valparaiso with the *Dolphin* on 8 April, the *Franklin* was relieved on 14 April by Capt. Isaac Hull and the *United States*, the first Navy ship on which Stewart had served. Stewart's Pacific Squadron had made an impact in Valparaiso throughout its mission. According to the U.S. minister to Chile, Herman Allen, Chile's minister of state said that Chile had experienced nothing but the utmost satisfaction with U.S. presence.[25]

Even John Prevost seems to have reconsidered his prior hostility toward Stewart. On 9 June he wrote to John Quincy Adams of the infinite regret he felt about his relationship with Stewart. Prevost admitted that his initial view of Stewart was based on several factors, including Stewart's failure to defend or dispute the circumstances surrounding the Madrid affair to his satisfaction or to the satisfaction of the South American officials.

Fellow Americans also expressed their thanks to Stewart for his command and conduct. "We are grateful to acknowledge the readiness with which you have at all times listened to the complaints or wishes of your countrymen, and the promptness with which you have afforded them all the protection your situation would permit."[26]

The *Franklin*'s departure from the Pacific also meant that it missed another incident by only days. On 7 June 1824 the U.S. whale ship *Globe* arrived in Valparaiso flying a distress signal. Six months prior, one of the whale men had organized a mutiny and murdered the captain and several officers. After the mutineers had abandoned the ship, the remnants of the crew made their way to Valparaiso. The mutineers were hunted first by David Conner and then by the *Dolphin*'s new commander, John "Mad Jack" Percival.[27]

The *Dolphin* never returned to her homeport in the United States; she continued to serve on Pacific Station until 1835 when she was sold.

The *Franklin* continued her return journey alone but not without incident. At 10 P.M. on 25 June, the ship narrowly escaped destruction. According to *Franklin* Marine William Augustus Von Vuldee, "the watcher stationed on the forward part of the ship suddenly reported breakers ahead. . . . The Commodore took command who had rushed on deck with nothing but his shirt on. . . . [At] the moment of clearing them we were not more than twice the ship's length off, and had the look been asleep, our doom of destruction would have been inevitable as we were going at a good rate." The breakers were not recorded on any chart. It is likely that they appeared during the many severe earthquakes in the region. There was no record of the event in the ship's log.

On 15 July the ship arrived in Rio de Janeiro and received a visit from Admiral Cochrane who, after leaving the Chilean Navy, had been offered a position as head of the Brazilian navy. During the port visit, Cochrane received a seventeen-gun salute from the *Franklin*. The commander of the British squadron in South America, Adm. Sir George Eyre, also visited Stewart's ship. Eyre's flagship was the *Spartiate* whose commanding officer was none other than Capt. Gordon Thomas Falcon. When Stewart and Falcon had last met nine years prior, the latter was a prisoner of Stewart's after the battle between the *Constitution* and the *Cyane* and *Levant*.

On 21 July 1824 the *Franklin* left for the final leg of her journey, arriving five weeks later in New York City. At noon on 5 September, she saluted General Lafayette's arrival in the United States. The *Franklin* was finally transferred to New York Navy Yard. Those crew and passengers who began the journey three years before enjoyed the benefits of their return home; Stewart, however, found his troubles were only beginning.

CHAPTER TEN

≈≈≈

Court-Martial

Commodore Stewart arrived in New York City at the end of his tour on Pacific Station in 1824. Since 1818 he had been overseas for five of six years. He returned to the United States to find forces at work against him. His problems began when his brother-in-law, William Tudor Jr., was appointed U.S. consul to Lima, Peru, taking the offer made initially to Jeremiah Robinson but then rescinded; Robinson subsequently found himself without a position. Unable to secure another appointment in the U.S. government and or Foreign Service, Robinson returned to the United States and became instrumental in bringing forth matters that led to Stewart's court-martial.

Captain Caldwin, commander of the merchant brig *Cora*, was another likely source of charges against Stewart. He provided testimony concerning Stewart's handling of money on board the *Franklin*. The *Franklin* housed money from several American merchant ships to protect their finances from pirates or other adversaries. Some $60,000 of the *Cora's* money was on the *Franklin*, and, for a reason lost to history, Stewart refused to release the money to the *Cora's* captain upon his request. Caldwin threatened to prosecute Stewart if the situation was not immediately resolved to the captain's satisfaction, and given the nature of some of the charges, the issue was never able to be resolved between Caldwin and Stewart.

The decision to court-martial Stewart was based initially on complaints by at least one new South American government and later on rumors likely circulated by Jeremiah Robinson. Stewart "returned to find the Peruvian government had made official complaint against him and that this complaint had been seconded by American consular officials."[1] On 21 September 1823

179

Robinson wrote to the president that he must "speak with the Executive, and communicate privately, on a delicate nature." Through his extensive correspondence and private journals, Robinson had already sown the seeds of discontent against Stewart, sharing his unique perspective of the commodore's activity in South America with anyone who would listen to or read the accounts. The responses to Robinson's narratives of this period are not known,[2] but the charges appeared to have some corroboration in a 29 November 1823 letter to State Secretary John Quincy Adams from the envoy to Colombia. Adams recalled: "I observed that we had received a direct complaint from the Government of Peru against Captain Stewart, which we should directly answer; that we had proofs that the complaint was unfounded; and had causes of complaint against the Governments of Peru and Chili."[3]

On returning to the United States and after the *Franklin*'s crew were paid, Stewart and his wife Delia remained in New York City to visit with acquaintances. Several months at sea seemed to have abated Stewart's anger at his wife at least temporarily. The commodore was soon called to Washington, D.C., and Delia and the children went to stay with relatives in Gardiner, Maine.

Stewart became aware that he should expect charges shortly after he arrived in Washington, charges that would receive the government's highest attention, given that another Navy captain, David Porter, had recently been charged with unauthorized activities in the Caribbean. Porter, Stewart's friend and one-time first officer, and father of one of Stewart's young officers, was facing his own court-martial. In January 1823 Porter took command of the West Indies Squadron, which was assigned to suppress pirates amongst the islands. When Spanish officials in Foxardo (Fajardo), Puerto Rico, charged the commanding officer of the *Beagle*, one of Porter's ships, for being a pirate and jailed him, Porter responded by landing a force of two hundred men and demanding an apology. The U.S. government court-martialed Porter on 11 August for not waiting for authority or instructions. Porter was found guilty and was suspended from service in the U.S. Navy for six months. Rather than accept this decision and punishment, Porter resigned from the service and found employment as the commander of the Mexican navy.

The Navy then turned its attention to Stewart's court-martial. The charges against Stewart were the subject of discussion at a cabinet meeting on 10 November 1824. In attendance were President Monroe, Secretary of State John Quincy Adams, Treasury Secretary William H. Crawford, War

Secretary John C. Calhoun, and Navy Secretary Samuel L. Southard. Southard discussed several Navy courts-martial, including that of Porter and of Lt. James Ramage, the commander of the *Porpoise*, whose charges insinuated cowardice, but the particular focus of the meeting was on Stewart's court-martial.

Southard "was uncertain whether in the charges should be included that of violating the blockade declared by the Peruvian Government," inasmuch as the U.S. government utterly denied the legality of that blockade in all its parts.[4] As secretary of state, Adams understood the difficulty such charges could pose in the world of diplomacy. As president-elect and with his own inauguration only weeks away, Adams recognized that these courts-martial reflected the principles of justice on which the Navy and the nation would be judged by other nascent countries, particularly in South America. On the morning of 20 December 1824, only a few weeks before his inauguration, Adams met with Stewart. Stewart had already been placed on suspension from active duty until the court-martial was resolved. On 6 January 1825, at another cabinet meeting, Crawford, Calhoun, and Southard reviewed further correspondence that accused both Stewart and Consul John Prevost of impropriety in foreign affairs. The secretaries deliberated on whether it was proper to share the correspondence with the House of Representatives, as was prescribed, with the potential of prejudicing against either side. They unanimously decided not to disclose the information and President Monroe agreed.[5]

Stewart prepared for the trial by selecting two counsels. The first, Joseph Hopkinson, was the son of a signer of the Declaration of Independence. In addition to being a prominent attorney, he had written the first national anthem, "Hail Columbia!" in 1798. Like Stewart, Hopkinson was a Philadelphian and owned another home in Bordentown.

As Hopkinson's cocounsel, Stewart selected Brig. Gen. Robert B. Taylor, the commanding officer of the Norfolk Military District when Stewart and the *Constellation* defended Norfolk during the War of 1812. Taylor was an experienced attorney and was also defending Captain Porter. Taylor's involvement in this case gives yet another example of the small size of the U.S. Army and Navy community at the time, when there were barely two dozen Navy captains and corresponding Army field grade officers. Taylor had also defended Capt. James Barron during his court-martial after the *Chesapeake* affair.

In the role of opposing counsel was Judge Advocate Richard Coxe, an equally experienced attorney to Hopkinson and Taylor. Like General Taylor, Coxe was involved with the Porter court-martial, but he had the role of pros-

Joseph Hopkinson, son of a signer of the Declaration of Independence, served as Stewart's attorney during the commodore's court-martial. (Charles Fenderich; courtesy of the National Portrait Gallery)

ecutor. Coxe later represented "Star-Spangled Banner" composer Francis Scott Key before the Supreme Court.

The four general charges against Stewart were unofficer-like conduct, disobedience of orders, neglect of duty, and oppression and cruelty. These charges included forty specifications, one of which required Delia Tudor Stewart's testimony concerning the Madrid affair. The commodore wrote to Delia that he was to face a court-martial for "offences of which she was really the guilty person." Emma and Robert Hallowell Gardiner in Maine advised her to go to Commodore Stewart's aid immediately, but "she was like a timid animal in presence of a powerful foe ready to devour it, against whom it has no power of resistance, and whom fear has deprived even the power of flight."[6] Delia could not even bring herself to reply to her husband's correspondence.

She did not remain in the new state of Maine. Instead she sought sanctuary with other family members in Boston, Newport, and Nahant, a small peninsula north of Boston near Swampscott and Lynn, where Stewart had once sailed the *Constitution* and where her brother Frederic had an estate.

Often Delia would return to Emma's mansion, Oaklands, in Maine, never finding the sanctuary she sought from her husband's desperate pleas. Rumors were whispered "about Delia accepting a bribe or of being in love with the Spanish spy."[7]

If Stewart could not rely on his wife through his troubles, he could certainly rely on his colleagues and friends. In early August 1825 Stewart's ties to the Adams administration were further cemented when his longtime friend Richard Rush was named treasury secretary. The Adams administration continued to follow the court-martial. On 5 August the president met with his cabinet and "remarked to Southard the difference in the indications of public sentiment upon the trials of Porter and Stewart."[8] On the evening of 13 August Stewart's cocounsels, Hopkinson and Taylor, visited President Adams at the White House to bring him up to date on the charges.

After a reading of the charges on Tuesday, 16 August, the court-martial convened on 18 August 1825 in a building on the corner of First Street and Maryland Avenue. The *Washington Gazette* questioned the legality of the proceedings, particularly in the aftermath of the Porter trial, in an editorial published that day, stating that courts-martial have always blended "the principles of ancient chivalry with those of the Roman courts, as altogether unfit forums, before which questions of complicated facts and laws could be safely tried."

A number of notables served on the court-martial, including Stephen Cassin and George Campbell Read, both of whom were only recently promoted to the rank of captain. Another captain, Jesse Elliot, was a longtime friend of James Barron and was allegedly an outspoken rival of both Oliver Hazard Perry and Stephen Decatur. Elliot had been the commanding officer of the USS *Niagara* during the War of 1812 and the *Ontario* with the Mediterranean Squadron. Capt. Alexander Wadsworth served as a midshipman under Barron on the *Chesapeake* and was an uncle of literary great Henry Wadsworth Longfellow. Capt. James Renshaw, until May, had served as the commanding officer of Norfolk Naval Shipyard, when Capt. James Barron succeeded him. During the War of 1812, Renshaw commanded the fourteen-gun brig *Rattlesnake*. Renshaw's ship had been captured off Nova Scotia in July 1814 by the HMS *Leander*, which had unsuccessfully pursued Stewart's *Constitution* after his battle with the *Cyane* and *Levant*. The coincidence of all these men coming together to proceed over the fate of a fellow officer was not really striking after all.

In another coincidence, or, more appropriately, an indication of how few senior officers were in the early Navy, Como. James Barron presided over the court-martial proceedings. Only five years before, Stewart had presided over Barron's own court of inquiry, and both had been shipmates twenty-seven years before on the *United States*. When asked if he had any objection to any of the officers on the court, Stewart stated that he had none. And although he had the benefit of two experienced counsels, Stewart himself directed questions toward the witnesses.

Stewart's first charge of unofficer-like conduct included twenty-nine specifications, ranging from carrying specie aboard a U.S. Navy ship (also part of the second charge) to aiding and protecting U.S. commercial ships carrying contraband and violating the blockade imposed by a foreign nation.[9]

The second charge of disobedience of orders included an additional seven specifications. The thirty-six specifications in the first and second charges were broken into five groupings. The first group of charges stated that Stewart had interfered with the laws of neutrality, supported the transport of contraband, and assisted the ship *Canton* in those actions. The second stated that Stewart was associated with the merchant Eliphalet Smith in the engagement of private commerce. The third stated that Stewart supported the transport of specie. The fourth stated that Stewart used Navy resources to outfit schooners for his own private interests. And the fifth, the most serious grouping of charges, stated that the commodore had carried a Spanish spy on board his ship.

As to the specifications that Stewart had interfered with the laws of neutrality, the specifications most likely arose from complaints issued by the Patriot government of Peru, claiming that the *Canton* had violated the Patriot's blockade of Peru's coastline, which was still under Spanish control. The specifications stated that Stewart had interfered with a foreign government and transported contraband.

Specifically, Stewart was charged with aiding the ships *Canton* and *Pearl*, the English brig *Sarah*, and the French merchant ship *Telegraph*, all of which carried contraband in the summer of 1822. In his defense against these charges, Stewart said his primary concern was for the safety of the ships and their wares in the interest of protecting American and other commerce. According to one of the *Franklin*'s Marines, Von Vuldee, on at least one occasion Stewart was concerned that the *Canton* would be boarded. The *Telegraph* had been seized previously under the pretense that it had violated the blockade, and the probability of subsequent seizure was one of the reasons Stewart gave for assessing that the *Canton* was at risk. While at anchor preparing to escort a convoy, Stewart had ordered the *Franklin*'s Marines to be supplied with ammunition and ordered to the main deck, ready for any emergency.

Lieutenant Hunter testified that Stewart initially refused the *Pearl* as part of the convoy because she carried arms on board. The logbook of the *Franklin* shows the *Pearl* having joined the convoy, and, therefore, one could assume the ship had likely complied with Stewart's direction to dispense with the arms in return for safe passage.

Other specifications charged that Stewart purchased for the *Canton* bolts of canvas, casks of wine, and other supplies; that Stewart employed naval carpenters and other *Franklin* personnel on other ships; and that Stewart had directed musket cartridges to the *Canton*.

The logbooks of the *Franklin* and the *Dolphin* clearly show that the ship did, on several occasions and for several American ships, provide various forms of assistance. In June and July 1822 *Dolphin* carpenters were employed on board the *Mirror* and the *Magnet*. The *Magnet* received sheets of log paper in July. Later that year, the *Franklin* sent working parties aboard the *Chauncey*, *Dick*, and *Canton*. Other ships also benefited from the *Franklin*'s presence, such as the merchant schooner *Wasp*,[10] which received thirty-seven gallons of whiskey, and the *Constellation*, which received twenty bolts of canvas. Edward Fitzgerald, the *Franklin*'s purser, noted during the trial that he received permission to send some officers' clothes, such as white drilling pantaloons and vests, ashore. During the court-martial two former captains on Pacific Station—Downes and Biddle—stated that it was perfectly acceptable for the crews of U.S. Navy ships to provide assistance to other ships.

Regarding the issue of giving musket cartridges to the *Canton*, John Blight, a gunner on the *Franklin*, noted one discrepancy. Lieutenant Hunter testified that he had no knowledge of musket cartridges being exchanged, yet Blight noted that in 1822 over 370 cartridges were drawn on Hunter's verbal requisition specifically for the *Canton*.

On these specifications, the court found that the charges were proved, but that the assistance provided by the *Franklin* was proper and correct and that there was no impropriety. Stewart and the ship had performed in fulfillment of public duties to render assistance when necessary to other ships.

The second group of specifications involved the merchant Eliphalet Smith, the subject of Jeremy Robinson's suspicions, innuendos, and gossip. Robinson linked Smith and Stewart together as conspirators in the illicit traffic of goods in the South Pacific. One specification charged that Stewart offered protection and aid to only those ships with which they were tied but ignored other vessels, which were engaged in legal commerce. Another specification claimed that Stewart employed Smith to carry dispatches to help the former benefit from private commerce. The court accepted that Smith was employed in carrying dispatches, but it was proved that they were in the aid of the public interest and common good and not in the engagement of private commerce.

Smith testified that Commodore Stewart had no interest in the cargo of the *Canton*, a quarter of which Smith owned, and did not participate in trade. He had offered Stewart an interest in a number of speculations, especially in wool, but Stewart had rejected the offers, stating he "legally could but morally speaking he could not free" himself to accept the offer. The court found Stewart had in no way profited from his association with Smith.

The third group of specifications centered on the practice of carrying specie on U.S. Navy ships. Ship captains could earn a fee amounting to a percentage of the specie carried on board, and this could be a lucrative venture. Stewart was charged with permitting specie in violation of the law and of defending and protecting persons and property smuggling specie bullion.

The U.S. Navy officially sanctioned the practice of carrying specie in October 1818 "when acting Secretary of the Navy gave Commodore Daniel T. Patterson, stationed at New Orleans, permission for ships under his command to transport specie belonging to U.S. merchants."[11] More than one Navy officer who commanded ships on Pacific Station prior to Stewart supported carrying specie. Capt. Charles Ridgely noted that it was part of his duty to take specie. In fact, he had carried some $200,000 of specie back to the United States on behalf of Eliphalet Smith. Capt. John Downes of the *Macedonian* also stated that it was customary to have specie so long as it did not belong to belligerents. Capt. James Biddle of the *Ontario* suggested that the charge of shipping specie was simply another in a series of charges against Stewart by the Peruvian government. "I believe it is impossible," he said, "for any commanding officer to be in the Pacific without giving offense to the one side or to the other. The Royal party of Peru, knowing the general feeling of our country, is jealous of them. The Patriots on the other hand expecting too much are dissatisfied."[12]

Some U.S. government officials believed that no U.S. ship should carry specie regardless of whether it belonged to neutral or warring parties. In 1821, prior to Stewart's arrival, U.S. Consul John Prevost wrote to the U.S. government that the conduct of Captain Downes during his cruise in the Pacific Ocean in carrying money was disgraceful to him as an officer. Prevost noted that he was opposed to the practice in principle because it was neutral money.

Members of Stewart's own crew knew that trading specie on behalf of neutrals was legal, but some nevertheless suspected their own captain was participating in an illegal practice. Von Vuldee wrote in his journal that he saw money carried to the *Franklin* that belonged to American citizens. He believed that Smith and a local merchant named Gotera engaged in the contraband trade of evading the duties on the exportation of specie.

Lieutenant Henry stated that he had no knowledge of goods or specie on board the ship but that the commodore had given orders to receive "none but only neutral property." Hunter did acknowledge that the director of the mint in Peru, a Spaniard, wanted to deposit bullion, but Stewart refused because the Spaniard was a belligerent in the regional crisis. Lieutenant Ogden recalled that the Baron de Macau of the French *Chlorinde* requested to transship money via the *Franklin*. Commodore Stewart had no objection if it was neutral money, which the Baron assumed since one merchant was an American and the other a Prussian.

Stewart, however, did not appear to be interested in benefiting from the transport of specie. Lieutenant Henry noted that the *Peruviano,* owned by Commodore Stewart, was treated as a public vessel like the other schooners. Stewart told Henry that it was not the object to make money but that money received for deposition of freight and specie would be paid to Henry. "You have taken all the responsibility and are consequently entitled to it all," Stewart had told Henry.

By all accounts provided during the court-martial, the transport of specie was acknowledged but nowhere could it be proved that it belonged to anyone other than neutral parties. Therefore, the court determined that the charges were partially proved but unobjectionable since Stewart had carried out a standard and sanctioned practice.

The fourth major grouping of specifications in the first two charges concerned Stewart's decision to buy the frames of three schooners and construct them. Stewart was charged with employing two of the schooners in the merchant trade and with using naval assets to construct the three schooners. After a thorough review, the court determined that the squadron commander used the schooners in the faithful exercise of an unquestioned right to carry out his mission.

If any issue affected Stewart and his reputation the most, it was the sixth specification of the second charge. The specification noted that Stewart received spies and officers in the Royalist Army on board the *Franklin*, specifically a man named Madrid who was a spy in Lima. There was no debate about whether the *Franklin* did indeed transport the officer, one "Madrid," from Peru during a three-week transit from Lima's port of Callao to the port of Quilca. The charge focused instead on what Stewart knew, when he knew it, and how involved he was in its prosecution.

The charge was discussed a few weeks before Stewart's court-martial, during the trial of First Lt. William Hunter, which began on 10 August. Commodore Stewart brought Hunter up on a single charge—neglect of duty. Specifically, Stewart charged that Hunter had permitted Madrid on board without informing his commanding officer as he had been required to do. Testimony during Hunter's court-martial was vital to Stewart's. Delia had refused to respond to her husband's pleas to come to Washington to testify on his behalf. Her only response came via an attorney in Boston, not in response to her husband's court-martial, but in response to a request from Hunter's court-martial. Her response was in the presence of and signed by Justice of the Peace Elijah Downing in Boston on 9 August, only the day before the trial began several hundred miles to the south.

The first interrogatory asked if Delia knew whether a certain Spaniard named Madrid had come on board the *Franklin* and if so, under what circumstances. Delia denied much involvement, claiming that he was an entire stranger to her. She testified that she had no authority to allow him to remain, but finally she "yielded to the recommendation of the two friends . . . to his own innocence and to his impressive appeal to my humanity."[13] Believing that his story appeared to be lamentable, she did not believe she could "summon sufficient resolution to request him to depart."

The second series of questions asked were, who helped him get on board, how long did he remain on board, and where did he stay? Delia claimed that she did not know who helped him on board. All she knew was that Madrid lived in the pantry with the steward and that she had ordered the steward, Peter Birch, to take care of Madrid and give him something to eat. According to Delia, she spoke with him for only about ten minutes and never spoke with him again while he was on board. She testified that she did not know how he left the ship or with whose help.

While Madrid was on board, Delia "did not inform [Commodore Stewart] of it supposing that if he were entirely ignorant of the said Madrid being on board no censure could probably be attached to him." In addition, she realized that if Stewart had been aware of Madrid's presence, the commodore would have found himself "under painful obligation of surrendering an unfortunate human being."

In her responses to the interrogatories, Delia recalled that Madrid wore no uniform and did not inform her that he had been in the military of either opposing factions in South America. Neither did her friends advise of this.

During Lieutenant Hunter's court-martial, he pled guilty, though not guilty of the charge. He stated that a stranger was reported as being in the pantry cabin and that Stewart had been informed. Hunter testified that Delia had directed him to take care of the stranger and believed the order would not have been given without the express knowledge and consent of the commodore; therefore, he did not report it to Stewart. Hunter admitted, however, that almost every person on board knew of Madrid's presence. Incredibly, Hunter bore no ill will toward his commander for bringing him up on charges. He testified that for the rest of the cruise Stewart did not appear to attach blame to Hunter for the incident.

Wilkes also testified at Hunter's court-martial. He said that the colonel of engineers at Quilca was on board and that the first lieutenant—Hunter— must have been aware of it, but Hunter was greatly in favor of the Royal cause and very much opposed to the Patriots.[14] Wilkes later saw someone escaping through one of the lower deck ports into a boat. Assuming the individual was a sailor attempting to escape the ship, he reported it to the officer of the deck who seemed aware of it but "took no notice" of Wilkes's observation. The officer of the deck seemed to be Lieutenant Ridgeway, who admitted that he knew Madrid was on board when the *Franklin* got under way and that, later, Mrs. Stewart requested that he help Madrid ashore.

Many years later, in his memoirs, Wilkes recalled that when he reached Washington he told Stewart's cocounsels about his upcoming testimony in the Hunter trial. He noted that he "knew too much" and did not desire to testify as he "felt very friendly to the Commodore for his kindness" toward him. Wilkes felt uncomfortable in having to speak "the whole truth."[15] In the memoirs, he suggests that his testimony was interrupted and the court cleared before he could recount his full interpretation of the events. According to the testimony of Stewart's officers, a Spaniard had been seen speaking with Mrs. Stewart ashore. Delia first approached Lieutenant Mayo and asked him if he wanted a servant, introducing Madrid as a "poor man trying to meet family in the Intermedios." According to her own testimony, she then directed the ship's steward, Peter Birch, to "take care of that poor man, and give him to eat and not to let him suffer from anything to eat or drink."[16]

On the day Madrid arrived on the ship, as Lieutenant Ogden noted during the court-martial, an interpreter pointed to Madrid and told Ogden that the Spaniard wanted to see Mrs. Stewart. Ogden proceeded to tell Delia about the visitor on the quarterdeck. When Delia saw Madrid and his retinue, she hurriedly scampered off to the poop cabin without speaking to them.

When Birch took the stand, he told the court that Mrs. Stewart had sent for him, and he made his way immediately to the captain's cabin and confirmed the statement Delia provided on this issue. Once the ship reached Quilca, he continued, Madrid asked to go ashore several times, and Mrs. Stewart told Birch to do what he could to help Madrid off the ship. Birch gave him some clothes and was helping him to the deck, but, when he saw the commodore, he directed Madrid to leave the ship by one of the ports. A year later in Callao, he saw Madrid again, but, instead of wearing the poor clothes of a ship's steward, he wore a coat with gold lace. When the commodore heard about Madrid, he asked Birch about him, and then hit him. Birch's only response was the truth—Mrs. Stewart told him not to let anyone know Madrid was there, especially Stewart, and plenty of officers knew about Madrid. In one testimony before the court, Lieutenant Mayo testified that he mentioned the issue in the wardroom at mess.

Birch's testimony continued, stating that Mrs. Stewart had then approached the merchant, Eliphalet Smith, and asked his advice. Smith told her to take no action without the consent of the commodore. Smith added in his own testimony that he understood from Delia that Madrid was a deserter. Commodore Stewart found out only later, by accident, that he had transported a foreign national.

All signs of responsibility for the incident clearly pointed to Delia. But conspicuously absent from the court-martial was none other than Delia Tudor Stewart. Delia had lied to her husband and placed his and his officers' careers at risk. So too, the officers and the steward Birch were partially to blame, although as Lieutenant Hunter put it, "believing the orders would not have been given without the Commodore's knowledge, I did not report it to him."[17] The court found Stewart not guilty.

The seventh and last specification of this second group of charges suggested that Stewart had intelligence of a contemplated expedition prepared by the Patriot government of Peru against the Intermedios. This specification was not proved and Stewart was found not guilty of the entire charge.

The third group of charges, neglect of duty, consisted of three specifications. The first concerned the absence from duty of a Lieutenant Weaver, and was addressed and resolved in the first charge. The second specification, not proved, was that, under Stewart's command, Lt. Horace B. Sawyer made a charge against Lt. David Conner but that Stewart chose not to investigate the charge.

More important than the first and second was the third specification of this charge, which addressed Stewart's competence in maintaining a proper ship, ready for action. The specification stated that Stewart was negligent in regularly exercising his men at quarters. The origin of this accusation is unknown, but according to the ship's logbooks, the great guns of the *Franklin* were exercised.[18] Furthermore, while there were minor inconsistencies among their statements, several individuals offered testimony in support of the commodore. The always well-dressed Lieutenant Ridgeway took the stand and testified that the guns were always kept in a state for action. Lieutenant Hunter and gunner John Blight noted that the crew was exercised every day or so but not while in port.

Thomas Hamersley, the ship's third lieutenant, had a large burly frame standing about six feet in height, according to his shipmate Mid. Charles Wilkes.[19] With bushy red hair and whiskers, Hamersley's manners were coarse "and all his tastes low." He apparently was also ignorant and overbearing. But when he testified, he reported simply that both the crew and guns were exercised by divisions, weather permitting, as frequently as on any ship that he had ever been on board. He did admit, however, that the guns on the lower deck were not as regularly exercised since the roll of the sea prevented it. The commodore's coxswain, William Warner, noted the cabin gun in the commodore's quarters was not exercised. Finally, Captain Ridgely of the *Constellation* stated that he was frequently on board the *Franklin* at Valparaiso and considered her in very superior order. Conspicuous in its absence was the failure of the guns to properly fire when they entered Rio de Janeiro and Valparaiso.

Given this testimony, the court found that this specification was not proven. Stewart was found not guilty of the third charge.

The fourth and final charge against Stewart consisted of only one specification—that Stewart confined Lt. Joshua R. Sands in an "unusual and unnecessary manner" on board the *Franklin* from 9 October 1823 to 13 April 1824 without trial for alleged misconduct.

Sands claimed that his confinement was cruel. Lieutenant Ogden testified in Stewart's court-martial, that Sands's "floor was frequently covered with water two inches deep and he complained very much of rheumatism in his face and had a tooth extracted in consequence of it,"[20] although as he also noted, Sands never requested to be, nor was he, placed on sick report.

Ogden also stated that the officers of the ship had made application to Commodore Stewart that "no unfriendly feeling existed" on their part toward Sands. Stewart, in a near reprisal of the incident in the Mediterra-

191

nean several years before in which he relieved all the commanders in the squadron, construed their motives into disrespect and interference with his duty. If Stewart harbored any notion of relieving these officers, it was muted by the reality that he had no other officers to replace them.

According to Wilkes, Ogden was always very attentive to his duties and had a quiet disposition. Rarely, if ever, did he enter into any of the frolics on board or ashore. A "small and spare figure" with peculiar falling shoulders, he rarely laughed but read a good deal. Perhaps because of his quiet disposition and aversion to join the shipboard fraternity, he withdrew his name from the application the officers sent to Stewart, not wishing, as he testified, to be disrespectful to his commander.

On the same day that the Madrid affair was exposed on the ship, Sands—who had begun his cruise as one of the commodore's aides—reached out to his mentor by sending a letter to Stewart that evening in which he tried to make concessions. The correspondence ultimately failed when Stewart asked Sands to settle the matter with Hamersley and Sands refused.

There were not enough officers in the squadron to form a court-martial for Sands because three officers on the court of inquiry had already formed an opinion and five officers were needed. Further delays occurred when Sands understandably refused the judge advocate appointed to him—Stewart's brother-in-law, William Tudor Jr. A court-martial was convened, however, when Capt. Isaac Hull arrived to relieve the *Franklin*. However, Stewart ultimately dismissed the court's sentence, a decision that was not reversed by the government.

According to the testimony in Stewart's court-martial, Sands harbored no ill feeling toward the commodore. Sands understood that Stewart considered the young man an "officer of promise" despite the events that occurred on the *Franklin*.

The fact that Sands had predicated the charge against Stewart on the accusation that he had been held under cruel circumstances was undermined by the testimony that he had never requested medical attention. Lieutenant Hunter noted that Sands never reported to him that his health was affected. In addition, several officers testified that Sands had been offered the use of the gun deck to walk about, which Sands refused to accept.

The court returned a not-guilty verdict on the fourth and final charge.

This particular charge must have been difficult for Stewart, who was training a generation of young officers to lead the future Navy. Acting Lieutenant Goldsborough stated that Stewart admitted regret to him in confining Sands and spoke of him flatteringly as a very fine young man, a praise that seemed to apply to most of the officers whom Stewart was leading. According to Goldsborough, Commodore Stewart's conduct toward his officers in general was unusually kind; he allowed them indulgences that were not customary.

Public sentiment supporting Stewart appeared to have only strengthened throughout the court-martial ordeal, if local papers were any indication. In the middle of the trial on 27 August, the *Washington Gazette* wrote that "as the trial of the gallant Commodore Stewart progresses, the belief is every day strengthened that he will be acquitted of every charge brought against him."

In his closing statement Stewart's cocounsel General Taylor told the court, "This entire nation awaits your decision with intense anxiety. The most precious of her gems, is her naval renown. To it she owes that elevation of national sentiment that lofty tone of conscious worth which constitute the chief power of every government and without which republics perish."

The court rendered a verdict of not guilty on every charge and laid the responsibility of the trial on individuals irresponsibly trying to tarnish Stewart's accomplishments and reputation. President Barron's statement read, in part:

When rumors and reports are unduly and industriously disseminated calculated to impair the high standing and usefulness of an officer in whom great trust and confidence have been reposed, it becomes the duty of the Executive to afford to such officer by the convention of a proper tribunal an ample opportunity of vindicating himself before the world. . . . [The court] is impelled by a sense of duty to go farther and to make unhesitatingly this declaration to the world, that so far from having violated the high duties of neutrality and respect for the laws of nations, so far from having sacrificed the honor of the American flag or tarnished his own fair fame by acting upon any motives of a mercenary or sordid kind; so far from having neglected his duty or betrayed the trust in him by proper protection subservience to individual interests, no one circumstance has been developed throughout the whole course of this minute investigation in the various occurrences of a three year cause calculated to impair the confidence which the members of this court, the Navy and the nation have long espoused in the honor, talents and the patriotism of this distinguished officer, or to weaken in any manner the opinion which all who knew him entertained of his humanity and disinterestedness. These virtues only glow with brighter luster from their ordeal of trial like the stars he triumphantly displayed when valor and skill achieved a new victory to adorn the annals of our naval glory.

After all was said and done, perhaps the experience on board the *Franklin* fostered something positive in the quarrelsome Sands. Of the lieutenants and

Stewart's association with Barron began in 1798 when the two served together on the frigate *United States*. Stewart served on Barron's court of inquiry after the commodore killed Stephen Decatur in a duel; Barron later presided over Stewart's own court-martial. (Unattributed; Courtesy of the Naval Historical Center)

midshipmen on board the *Franklin* during her Pacific years, five rose to the rank of captain, one to commodore, and three to rear admiral—including Rear Adm. Joshua Sands.

John Prevost, the U.S. consul with whom Stewart had so many disagreements, never returned to the United States, having died in Peru.

So too, William Tudor Jr., Delia's beloved brother, was never to return. After serving in Peru, he became U.S. consul in Brazil and died in 1830.

Jeremiah Robinson was one of the few government officials in Washington who could give testimony on the events surrounding Stewart's Pacific cruise. No records support that he was called to testify in Stewart's court-martial. Perhaps Robinson stayed far away from the center of the storm because he had grown accustomed to causing strife from the shadows rather than coming face-to-face with his self-created adversaries.

Robinson continued his never-ending quest for a government position, which he believed had been hampered by insinuations of his involvement with the court-martial. Four years later he wrote to Congressman John Varnum, a Federalist from Massachusetts, about "the injustice of certain unfriendly representations which it is understood were made concerning me about the year 1825."[21] Robinson pleaded with numerous public officials in trying to clear his name, diminish the negative reputation he had earned, and find employment with the government. In response to one of his letters in 1830 about the events in the Pacific, former President James Monroe wrote that he had no recollection of the incident.

Eventually Robinson found a position. He was sent to Havana in 1833 as commissioner for claims of the Florida Archives, a position to resolve official correspondence related to the transfer of the Florida territory from Spain to the United States. Less than eighteen months after arriving at his long-awaited post outside of the United States, Robinson died of cholera. It fell upon another official, the U.S. consul in Havana, Nicholas Trist, to expose Robinson for what he was.

Trist was the antithesis of Robinson. Whereas Robinson had to beg for government positions, they came easily to Trist. Robinson desperately sought connections in government; Trist was well connected. Trist had married well, choosing for his wife the granddaughter of Thomas Jefferson. Trist had attended West Point and served as private secretary to President Andrew Jackson. Later in his career he was tasked by President Polk to negotiate the Treaty of Guadalupe Hidalgo, ending the Mexican-American War.

After Robinson's death, Trist wrote several letters to Secretary of State John Forsyth informing him that he had found and reviewed Robinson's journal and memoranda. After an investigation, Trist heard from several individuals that Robinson had been in the practice of obtaining vouchers for expenses beyond those that he had actually incurred.[22] Further, Robinson had left numerous creditors. More importantly, he found Jeremiah Robinson had kept a diary, which Trist suggested, "must have occupied most of the little of his time which was not lost either through physical infirmities or in gossiping with every one who would listen to him." Robinson, Trist declared, lied and distorted and falsified facts.

Trist recommended that Robinson's successor be "a very different character." Of Robinson, Trist wrote that his "personal habits in every respect were so low, groveling and filthy, as to be in unison with the rest of his character; than which, in whatever light it be considered, a more disreputable one to represent the U. States in any capacity could not well have been found. How he ever came to be selected for any such purpose must have been a subject of new wonder to the Caballeros here every time he came near them."

And what of Stewart's wife? Delia learned the result of the trial only from public announcements in the newspapers, with five hundred miles of safety between her and the man whom she married a dozen years before.

195

CHAPTER ELEVEN

Tudor versus Stewart: The Second War of the Roses

I n September 1825 Stewart was honorably acquitted of all charges stemming from his court-martial. From 1821 to 1824 he had commanded 10 percent of the entire U.S. Navy on a distant station, and during the past year he had focused solely on defending himself in a highly publicized trial. At forty-seven years old, he had spent most of his life at sea and had very few possessions at the home he had built in Bordentown. Any illusions that he would return to an idyllic mansion with a loving wife and welcoming children were shattered during the long months of his trial. Despite Stewart's ordeal, Delia had not visited Stewart in nearly a year, nor had she given their children the opportunity to see their father.

Delia remained in hiding among family members in New England during the trial, and upon its conclusion she immediately wrote to her friend Mrs. Bright, a wealthy woman from Elizabethtown. Delia anticipated Stewart would be wrathful on his arrival home, so she appealed to Mrs. Bright to act as her ally and begged her friend to meet her at Montpelier, the Stewart's estate in Bordentown.

Delia made her way to Bordentown immediately but decided to keep her children far away from her husband. On 10 September Anne Hallowell Gardiner, Delia's niece by her sister Emma, wrote to her brother, Robert Hallowell Gardiner II, to relay the latest family news. Gardiner at that time was at the Round School in Northampton, Massachusetts, where future Navy Secretary George Bancroft was a teacher.

I suppose you read Mr. Hopkinson's and General Taylor's speeches at Uncle Stewart's trial. They are very fine and "tout le monde" says that he will come off with great honor. . . . Delia [Commodore Stewart's daughter] is going to remain with Madame Canda a French lady who has been giving drawing lessons [in Nahant] for a fortnight and is going to keep a boarding school in Boston. Charles [Stewart's son] may go there also.[1]

Charles Stewart arrived in Bordentown to find Montpelier already occupied by his wife and Mrs. Bright. Stewart demanded that Delia leave immediately, an act that some of her Tudor and Gardiner relations considered barbarous. Delia also enjoyed the staunch support of many society friends rallied by Bright. Robert Hallowell Gardiner, who owned the mansion where Delia had stayed, did not consider Bright a "judicious advisor" as she failed to keep an open mind with regard to Delia's own role in the dispute. Bright saw only Commodore Stewart's alleged ill treatment of his wife and was Delia's most ardent defender.[2] Delia refused to leave.

For twenty-five years Stewart was the indisputable commander of his own ship; but, on shore facing Delia, he could not even go on board the mansion he had built and paid for himself. Stewart proclaimed that he would never live under the same roof as Delia again. Consequently, Commodore Stewart found refuge one mile down the road at White Hill Mansion, the home of Mr. and Mrs. Field, founders of Fieldsboro, New Jersey. Soon accusations surfaced that Stewart had "tender relations" with Mrs. Field.

The separation was, to some who knew both parties, inevitable. As early as Charles and Delia's wedding day Robert Hallowell Gardiner had said, "Never was a match more ill assorted." Even years later his daughter Anne admitted that the separation was something the family had long dreaded, especially Delia's mother, Delia Jarvis Tudor.

Anne Gardiner wrote again to her brother just prior to Christmas 1825, saying that though Charles and Delia were separated at present, they might reconcile in the future. Anne, who had just turned eighteen, suggested to her younger brother by two years that one reason for the separation was that the couple had been acquainted with each other for only a month before being wed. More importantly, she wrote, "Aunt Delia spends money as if the mines of Peru were at her command,"[3] further testimony to her lack of fiscal restraint.

Stewart himself seems to have fared better than Delia in the eyes of his in-laws. Anne wrote that Stewart tried in vain to restrain Delia's spending, and she implied that he managed a great deal of civility and dignity in his letters to Delia's brother Frederic during that difficult autumn.

Delia also wrote to Frederic begging him to join her in Bordentown, but he was otherwise occupied in his struggling business. As a result, the task of assisting Delia fell to the Gardiner family patriarch, Robert Hallowell Gardiner, who only reluctantly agreed to represent Delia in her defense or at best reconcile the two, though he bore no ill will toward the commodore.

When Gardiner arrived at Montpelier, he found the presence of Mrs. Bright, whose views were tainted by both Delia and the now village-wide scandal alleging involvement between Stewart and Mrs. Field, to be an immediate problem. Over a decade later, two correspondents noted that Stewart had been "particularly loose" in the matter of women and had a mistress "who is said to be a relative left under his guardianship and debauched by him."[4] Other accounts suggest Delia herself may have initiated the scandals. Little evidence indicates the allegations against Stewart and Mrs. Field were true, at least during the initial time of the Stewarts' estrangement.

In 1826 Delia visited with another potential ally, a female relative of Mr. William Meredith in Harrisburg who wrote of her visit:

> The poor afflicted creature was snuggled up into the study where I was doomed to pass the evening with her. . . . I was the patient listener to the low vices of the naval commander [Stewart] and if my patriotism was ever doubted, it is redeemed by this action of my life. . . . I could not gaze upon the poor mourner without sympathy, nor hear her tale of aggravated woes, without doing my best to comfort her. . . . his treatment of her, in the Pacific, was horrid beyond belief and argued against a murderous intent. . . . at Valparaiso he commanded her to leave the ship with her children.[5]

Delia claimed to her visitor that Stewart stood her and the children on the shore at Valparaiso in the middle of the night in a violent thunderstorm and ordered them to return to the ship in such conditions. "I cannot but feel glad," Meredith's relative wrote, "that she is likely to be safe from his tyranny."

Such was the likely opinion of Stewart in Bordentown in the fall of 1825. Delia told Gardiner that she would never consent to a separation because of the negative connotations of divorce. He found Stewart "equally determined against a reconciliation and . . . he would never consent to hear a word upon the subject."[6] Finding no way to agree with Delia, Stewart recommended that Gardiner speak to his attorney, Joseph Hopkinson, who had ably defended Stewart earlier that year during the court-martial.

Gardiner's hope to make peace between the two rested on his insistence

199

that Delia cede the commodore's house to him; Gardiner himself admitted that Stewart had a "perfect right" to the house. He advised Delia, knowing she had no means of supporting herself, that the only way she could keep the house was if she bought it from Stewart—or had Mrs. Bright purchase it for her. But Mrs. Bright had neither the inclination nor the means to do so.

Gardiner initially assessed Hopkinson as a keen but not unscrupulous lawyer. What Gardiner failed to realize was the extent of Mrs. Hopkinson's influence over her husband. Bordentown, the summer home of the Philadelphia elite, boasted its own social circles (enabling prominent portrait artist Gilbert Stuart access to many of the elite), and Mrs. Hopkinson had been overshadowed in these circles by Delia, leading to a jealously of and hostility against the commodore's wife that shaped the opinions Mrs. Hopkinson shared with her husband.

Joseph Hopkinson proposed a legal separation with the children remaining with the commodore at his estate in Bordentown. In return, Stewart would pay off Delia's existing debts, but pay no others, and give her $800 per year in quarterly installments, nearly a third of his salary as a captain in the U.S. Navy. If the issue of Stewart's then-alleged involvement with another woman arose, Hopkinson was prepared to respond with evidence that Delia "was not a suitable person to have charge of her minor children." He suggested that the money Delia borrowed from Bordentown resident and former monarch Joseph Bonaparte implied an inappropriate relationship since Stewart had known nothing of it. Furthermore, Hopkinson claimed that he had evidence that Delia had "gone late in the evening to a house of ill-fame."[7] Delia claimed she had no idea what kind of establishment she had walked into but outright denied borrowing money from Bonaparte. When confronted with her denial, Hopkinson told Gardiner that his source was Bonaparte himself, whom the attorney had represented in other matters.

Clearly frustrated by his sister-in-law's consistency in denying charges that later proved true, Gardiner told Delia he would seek help from a prominent Philadelphia lawyer, William Meredith. But, when Gardiner appeared at Meredith's residence, he found Delia already there, and quickly realized that Delia had no confidence in his ability to cousel. Nevertheless, he felt a familial obligation to remain engaged in the affair, which would drag on for nearly three years.

Gardiner returned to his own mansion, Oaklands, in Maine but continued to correspond with Meredith. In February Delia asked Gardiner to take the children back to Maine, and, when he left on 10 February, Charles Stewart charged Gardiner with abduction. Regardless, the children, Delia and

Charles, remained at Oaklands. Gardiner advised Meredith by mid-year that Mrs. Stewart was "too much agitated to take any rational view of her situation."[8] Commodore Stewart, he wrote, "was under the advice of his counsel Joseph Hopkinson, attempting to starve Mrs. Stewart into terms."[9]

Stewart told Gardiner that as long as the children were in Maine, Gardiner would have to pay for their needs. Finally in 1828 Delia allowed Stewart's nephew Lt. Daniel Smith McCauley to come for young Charles.

That same year Delia and her daughter went to the Washington residence of Delia Jarvis Tudor, Delia's mother. Together they visited President John Quincy Adams, the son of William Tudor's old mentor in Boston. Delia also took this opportunity to consult on her divorce with one of the best minds in the country—Daniel Webster.

The following year Delia accepted the terms of the divorce: their daughter would remain with Delia while Charles stayed with his father; Stewart would pay all of Delia's debts incurred prior to 1825, and he would pay her $800 per year. Delia would take up residence at her mother's home on I Street in Washington near Lafayette Square, where they attended services at St. John's Episcopal Church, the church attended by generations of U.S. presidents. When Delia Jarvis Tudor died in 1843 at age ninety-two, she left her home and belongings to Delia. Mrs. Tudor also created a trust for her daughter, which included an allowance for a Reverend Charles S. Stewart, an early missionary to the Sandwich Islands and later chaplain of the Navy. If her mother's obituary is any indication, Delia, who continued to refer to herself officially as Mrs. Commodore Stewart, was troubled by the stigma of her divorce long after the settlement.

Stewart fought a battle at home that was longer and harder than any of his forty naval engagements, yet when the matter was finally resolved, he refocused on Montpelier.

Stewart turned to farming, an endeavor common to landowners and to many sailors on returning to their homes. Perhaps because he had spent so much time on ships passing over the ever-changing sea, he now sought more stable ground with roots and the opportunity to watch something grow. Stewart's contemporaries, like Capt. Thomas ap Catesby Jones, also tried their hand at farming after or during a life at sea. Stewart always took the opportunity to bring back unusual seeds or animals from his many overseas travels.

The only disagreements with his neighbors, in what were otherwise amiable relationships, stemmed from the problem of local pigs, who had overrun

Stewart's land to "make havoc in his turnip patches." Shortly after Stewart ordered all trespassing pigs shot, his neighbors took him to court to curb the practice. Though he was defeated, one nearby landowner supported Stewart's case, testifying that the commodore was perfectly within his authority to protect his crops. In return for this gesture, Stewart found and sent the best of his own pigs to that neighbor.[10] According to local narratives, "a good sailor never made a good farmer." When Stewart was home, the farm did poorly, but, when he was away, it did worse.

Montpelier, or "Old Ironsides" as it was more commonly called, was surrounded by hundred-foot tall white pines. In front of the house was an Italian marble bathtub, a gift from Joseph Bonaparte, used for flowers. Inside, the mansion resembled a museum, housing such items as the rhino-tooth handle dirk that a Barbary pirate once aimed at Stephen Decatur's heart on the deck of the *Philadelphia*.[11]

To the general population of Bordentown, Stewart attracted a following—they regarded him as a hometown hero. It was known that his "sense of justice and requisitions of duty were as unbending as fate." He was also known as a storyteller, famous for his repartee and ever-ready, pleasant wit. He was described as polite, distinguished, and a generous host, as well as a man of dignity.[12]

In 1834 Lord Powerscourt and his maternal cousin, John Parnell of Ireland, traveled to the United States, and in Washington met Charles's daughter Delia. Delia captivated the two cousins but it was John to whom she gravitated.[13] The following year, John Parnell asked for Delia's hand in a letter to the commodore:

> Sir, I feel some hesitation, least you think it presumption in me an entire stranger thus abruptly writing to you upon so delicate a subject, but I should consider that I did not do myself justice, if I delayed any longer communicating to you my feelings and wishes. I met your daughter Miss Stewart for the first time about 12 months since, and was very much struck with her, we subsequently met at West Point, Boston, and here again last winter. . . . I shall have no difficulty in obtaining her own and her mother's consent to our union, and only wait your favorable answer, when I shall forthwith do myself the pleasure of waiting upon you and shall be happy to give any explanations you may require.[14]

Stewart consented, and two weeks later, on 31 May 1835, Delia married John Parnell at Grace Church in New York. After spending a week at Montpelier, Stewart and his son accompanied the newlyweds to Charleston, South Carolina, where they boarded a ship bound for London. Delia bore ten children, including Charles Stewart Parnell, the late-nineteenth-century Irish statesman.

Young Charles was less successful in marrying, perhaps due in part to his own sister. In 1842 Charles was engaged to a Miss Bruce, reportedly from a wealthy Virginia family from the inference of the value of their plantation. In a letter to her father, Delia described Miss Bruce as unacceptable, unequal to her brother, and very short with an ugly nose. The letter inferred that a $500,000 dowry was at stake based on her family's property. Charles never married.

The inference by some that Stewart himself was in a relationship during his separation and divorce appears to have some validity. U.S. Census Records for Stewart's home show an interesting pattern. In 1840, for example, Montpelier housed one free white male between five and ten years old and two white females of the same age group. In 1850, the first time individual names are provided, the residents aside from the commodore were Margaret Smith (age fifty), Charlotte Smith (age seventeen), Julia Smith (age fifteen), and an employee. In 1860 there is a Charlotte Smith (age twenty-eight) and an Edward Smith (age twenty-four), along with a farm laborer and a cook.[15]

While Captain Stewart proved to be the bane of the British on the high seas, his grandson, Charles Stewart Parnell, challenged them as a member of Parliament. (Courtesy of the Avondale House, Wicklow, Ireland)

Later local records show a Charlotte Smith who died in 1882 and who had a brother, Edward L. Stewart of Bordentown, and a sister, Julia Stewart Laguerenne, of Philadelphia. The evidence that these three individuals were Stewart's children is also supported by two additional clues. The Philadelphia gravesite of Como. Charles Stewart contains the remains of only one other body—a six-day-old child interred in 1874, the son of Edward and Mary Stewart. In addition, another gravesite in Bordentown has two sisters laying side by side—Frances Stewart Cocke (born in 1882) and Elizabeth B. Tudor Stewart (born in 1875), both children of Edward.[16]

The puzzle of Stewart's second family received a final piece in a short obituary in a Newark, New Jersey, newspaper in 1903 announcing the death of Edward Livingston Stewart, son of Commodore Stewart and uncle of Charles Stewart Parnell. The rumors of the 1830s leading up to Stewart's failed presidential bid were true, but there is no evidence that Stewart was involved with any women prior to his separation from Delia.

CHAPTER TWELVE

A Changing Navy

With the court-martial behind him, Charles Stewart found himself without orders for the next five years. As the U.S. Navy struggled to keep up with rapidly changing technology during the five decades after the War of 1812, Stewart personally struggled with a rapidly deteriorating marriage, while competing with his fellow senior officers for active postings.

The U.S. Navy had difficulty keeping up with the revolutions that the steam engine, armor plating, and gunnery improvements brought to the world's navies. Although the U.S. Navy lagged behind other navies in adopting these innovations, it did experiment with steam-powered propulsion systems, armor plating, shell guns, and telegraph after the War of 1812. This period also marked a change in the Navy's culture, which improved the daily life of its sailors and midshipmen. In 1850 flogging was discontinued as the primary means of maintaining discipline in the ranks. The rum ration was discontinued in 1862, and the Navy finally officially banned the practice of dueling between its officers. In an effort to enhance the professionalism of the officer corps, the Navy established an engineering-oriented naval academy in 1845, thus taking the schoolroom out of the ship's gunroom and placing it ashore.

The establishment of the U.S. Naval Academy was just one part of a growing effort to reform the Navy and its officer corps. Operationally, the fleet's presence expanded abroad as American commercial interests reached around the world. Also, through naval expeditions, Japan, China, and Southeast Asia were opened to American trade. A half-hearted attempt to suppress the slave trade along the west coast of Africa also commenced during the period after the war with Britain. In 1816 the Board of Navy Commissioners was established to handle the increased administrative burden accompanying expanded operations, but it could not keep up with the rapid changes brought about by the industrial revolution. Ultimately the board was replaced by the bureau system in 1842, which the Navy operated under well into the twentieth century. As one of the most senior officers on the Navy's list, Stewart found himself in the center of all this change and controversy, often as the senior officer present.

While his personal life was filled with turmoil, Stewart maintained an active professional life as a naval officer, a businessman, and an American patriot who never failed to offer his opinion on the Constitution and the state of the Union. In all of his professional endeavors, he was a staunch supporter of the Constitution and the Union. Stewart conveyed his feelings in a letter that he wrote to Mr. Harrison Gray Otis on 23 April 1829:

> I have received your letter . . . and in reply beg leave to state that while I was in command of the Frigate Constitution, then fitting in Boston for a cruize [*sic*], in 1814, I met you in State Street a short time after the New England States had decided on holding a Convention at Hartford, and I think it was two or three days after it was announced that you were to be one of the Delegates from Massachusetts. On meeting you as above I asked if you had been appointed to the convention, to which you said you had. I stated to you that some anxiety was felt by many with respect to the objects of the convention, and that apprehensions were entertained by some that a separation from the Union was contemplated—you assured me the Convention had no such object—I stated that I was glad to hear you say so, as nothing in my opinion could be more injurious to the town of Boston than such an event, as it would render Boston little more than a fishing town—its commercial advantages and resources derived from the middle and southern states would be cut off, the Merchants, Seaman and Mechanist dependent on commerce would emigrate to the southward. You then observed you could have no desire to aid a possibility of bringing on your native town such a consequence, to make myself ease on that score, as the convention had nothing more in view than to adopt some general measures of cooperating defense, and to ascertain whether the means raised in the New England States, for prosecuting the invasion of Canada: aught not to be applied under the circumstances to the Defense of those states, or what other measures might be necessary, as the General Government did not seem disposed to afford any protection, and the enemy appeared determined to prosecute the war with vigor along the maritime sea board. This is the substance of what passed on that occasion, which you are at liberty to use as you deem proper.[1]

Earlier, Stewart recounted to his friend and attorney Joseph Hopkinson a conversation he had had with Harrison Gray Otis on the street:

> Stewart: "My God, Mr. Otis, what are you going about? What is to be done by this convention? Do you intend to separate from the Union?"
>
> Otis: "That is too rediculous [*sic*] to be imagined by anybody."
>
> Stewart: "What then is the object of the meeting?"
>
> Otis: "To take measures to defend ourselves against the enemy, as the general government cannot do it."[2]

The proceedings and corresponding declarations issued by the Hartford Convention turned out to be more than just New England's reaction to the scourge of war. Stewart's letter shows an appreciation of that.

The Hartford Convention was actually one of two other early regional efforts sponsored by a grouping of states that tried to assert their states' rights in an attempt to counter the actions of the federal government. In the case of the Hartford Convention, the New England states that faced economic ruin banded together on 15 December 1814 (only two days before Charles Stewart took the *Constitution* to sea) to condemn the Madison administration and Congress for abuses and the bad administration of the War of 1812. The convention declared, "'The right and duty of a state to interpose its authority' in cases of 'deliberate, dangerous, and palpable infractions of the Constitution.'"[3] The delegates to the convention did state "that it would be unwise 'to fly to open resistance' upon every offense."[4] However, the convention's declaration contained seven provisions proposed as amendments to the U.S. Constitution. If, under the duress of a protracted war, these provisions had found their way into the Constitution, they would have severely limited the power of Congress to declare war, admit new states, enact embargoes, and restrict commerce. The remaining provisions were aimed at the Virginia dynasty—the Madisons, Monroes, Masons, etc.—and they foretold the future of American history. One provision attacked the three-fifths compromise that gave southern states the right to count slaves as three-fifths of a person when apportioning congressional districts. Another provision directly attacked the southern orientation of previous presidents, stating that presidents should not be reelected and that successive presidents should not be from the same state. One can see what the Hartford Convention produced that so troubled Stewart. His advocacy for the Union carried him forward to a point when he was considered as presidential candidate, albeit an unwilling one. His fervor for the Constitution and the Union continued to his dying day.

Even without orders, Stewart continued to be consulted on naval matters. On 1 March 1830 the U.S. Senate directed the Navy to provide an assessment on the utility of Marines being assigned to U.S. ships-of-war. Two days later John Branch of the Navy Department wrote to Stewart asking him to provide his opinion on the subject.

Stewart responded to the four issues raised by the Senate. First, on whether it was necessary that Marines compose part of the force on a warship, Stewart answered that it was proper and necessary. Second, the Senate asked if Marines could be dispensed with and replaced by seamen trained in small arms instead. Stewart responded that seamen could be instructed for the purposes of battle and, to answer the third question, that seamen already had been training in small arms, though small-arms battle was not their primary function. Lastly, the Senate inquired whether petty officers and seamen could replace Marines as station guards; Stewart responded that he thought not.[5]

In July 1830 the commodore received orders assigning him to the Board of Navy Commissioners, and on 31 August Stewart attended his first meeting of the board. Also present at the meeting were Como. Daniel T. Patterson, a hero at the Battle of New Orleans, and Stewart's senior, Como. John Rodgers, the president of the board.[6]

When Charles Stewart was appointed to the board, it was the principal advisory body to the Navy secretary. It remained so until 1842, when Congress established the bureau system. The board was created in response to the experiences of the War of 1812, during which the Navy expanded rapidly, straining its supporting bureaucracy beyond its limits. The Navy secretary needed the help and expertise of professional naval officers to manage the growing fleet, so in 1815 a three-member board was comprised of three senior captains selected by the president and confirmed by the Senate.[7] The law that created the board was written specifically stating that the Navy secretary was solely responsible for controlling and directing the U.S. naval forces. The uniformed officers of the board, who answered to the secretary, were responsible for the "procurement of naval stores and materials and the construction, armament, equipment, and employment of vessels of war as well as all other matters connected with the naval establishment of the United States."[8]

This division of labor did not suit the officers on the first board, who believed they were best qualified to direct the operations of the fleet. It took the intervention of President Madison to reiterate to the board its responsibility. In his directive, the president stated that the board's responsibility lay on the material side and the logistics of the Navy, while the Secretary's responsibility lay with the naval operations of the fleet.

In fact, Stewart's friend Richard Rush most likely provided President Madison with the legal interpretation buttressing his presidential directive. As attorney general, Rush offered his legal opinion of the congressional act creating the board: "The entire context bespeaks the board to be, not an original, but an auxiliary institution."[9] The act of Congress creating the board stated, "the President shall appoint three officers of the Navy whose rank shall not be below a post captain, with the power to form rules for government of their own meetings and shall be attached to the office of the Secretary of the Navy." Rush offered his opinion of the wording in the act to President Madison: "If it had been intended to confer an independent or coordinate power, a mode of expression less equivocal would have been chosen. . . . It no where appears to be contemplated that they were to act upon their own views."[10]

Over time, the officers of the board became more involved in the Navy secretary's responsibilities; these responsibilities eventually evolved into the chief of naval operations's duties. With Charles Stewart's appointment, the Board of Navy Commissioners, through its logistical charter, influenced the operations of the fleet.

For most of the board's existence, Commodore Rodgers held the position of president. President Madison had selected him to be the board's first president in 1815, and, except for a three-year hiatus when he was commodore of the Mediterranean Squadron between 1824 and 1827, Rodgers held the reins of power until 1837. During his service on the board, Rodgers established a rapport with and was well respected by all of the presidents from Madison to Jackson, their respective Navy secretaries, and members of Congress.[11] Senator Thomas H. Benton, an influential senator from Missouri and a contemporary of Rodgers and Stewart, wrote appreciatively about Rodgers in his book *Benton's Thirty Year View*. Benton later offered his support, through the creation of the Thomas Hart Benton Club, to draft a silent and unwilling Charles Stewart as a presidential candidate.

The first day that Commodore Stewart sat as a member, the board drafted correspondence ranging from a request to the treasury secretary for supplemental funding for the board to a letter responding to the Navy secretary's inquiry into the material condition of the USS *Macedonian* and the USS *John Adams* and a request for additional supplies for the Navy as a whole.[12]

This flurry of administrative activity continued the next day, 1 September 1830, when Rodgers, Stewart, and Patterson wrote to Capt. Alexander J.

Dallas, ordering him to repair the Navy hospital in Philadelphia without delay and directing him to charge $500 for the repairs. This correspondence was followed by a series of letters to naval officers of note such as Commodores Morris, Chauncey, and Hull.[13]

Stewart's experience came to the fore later that fall, as can be seen in the board's 6 September correspondence. Commodore Rodgers received a letter, dated 31 March 1830, from Capt. Alexander Wadsworth complaining about the use of cotton, laden pitch caulking to pay the seams in the deck of the USS *Constellation*. Stewart replied for the board stating "that cotton caulking should not be payed with pitch but with white lead ground in oil and as stiff as it can be that the seams should be filled with it. That paying with [cotton] pitch cracks, water gets it and forces it out. This explains the Constellation's problem."[14]

On a lighter and celebratory side, the board's minutes for 28 October 1830 noted, "This day, the citizens of Washington celebrated the late revolution in France, which has resulted in the establishment of a system of Government, favoring, as conceived by them, the progress of universal Liberty—all business was suspended."[15]

During Stewart's first year on the Board of Navy Commissioners, two significant events occurred indicating the future direction of the U.S. Navy. First, the return of the beautiful sloop-of-war USS *Vincennes* on 8 June 1830 from her around-the-world cruise signified that the U.S. Navy now had global responsibilities. Six months later the Naval Observatory, America's first national observatory, was established in Washington, D.C., on 6 December. The observatory's role helped to meet the celestial navigational requirements of a fleet that now found itself in almost every one of the world's oceans. Both events represent benchmarks for the fleet that Charles Stewart championed. By the time of his departure from the board, the Navy had successfully negotiated diplomatic and commercial treaties with countries as distant as Siam (March 1833). On 17 June 1833, under the board's sponsorship, the first public dry dock for refitting U.S. Navy ships and craft was completed at Gosport Navy Yard, Norfolk, Virginia. On that day the USS *Delaware* became the first warship laid up in dry dock.

The year 1831 found the Board of Navy Commissioners directing the Navy's chief constructor, fellow Philadelphian Samuel Humphreys, to prepare a draft for a steam-powered battery that would be employed as harbor-defense craft. In a letter dated 7 October 1831, the board instructed Humphreys to assess the cost for design of the engines and boilers being manufactured in Baltimore.[16] Humphreys, an unabashed supporter of the U.S. Navy's use of steam-powered ships and craft, had prepared a draft describing a steam battery prior to receiving the board's orders. His draft was dated September 1831 and described the vessel's dimensions as 125 feet in length and with a 34-foot beam.[17]

Critics of the board felt Rodgers and the others were disingenuous when they commissioned Humphreys to design and build the steam battery the USS *Fulton II* and accused the captains of delaying the ship's construction. These critics held the view that the conservative board members were only paying lip service to pressures from Congress, and the young bucks within the naval service felt the board would do everything in their power to frustrate the vessel's completion.

Charles Stewart has been labeled obstinate and conservative regarding the introduction of new technology, especially steam-powered warships, to the fleet. Steam power was introduced into the U.S. Navy in the 1830s and 1840s. Although Stewart characterized steamships as "Monsters," at this early time in the evolution of steam-powered warships, the commodore, like many others, considered the new boats' prowess against the traditional "wooden walls" exaggerated from both a tactical and operational perspective. He shared the view of Navy Secretary James K. Paulding, who espoused practical reasons for forestalling the introduction of steam at the time Stewart was commandant of Philadelphia Navy Yard. "Paulding as well as senior officers were skeptical about the utility of naval steamships for deep-sea operations had yet to be demonstrated."[18] However, Paulding bowed to political pressure from the steam enthusiasts in and out of uniform; "a quiet compromise was affected that allowed for three steamships."[19] Two were built in Philadelphia: the USS *Mississippi* and the USS *Missouri*.

As such, Stewart's reaction to the steamships was not based solely on an aesthetic perspective but also on his judgment of the practicality of steam. First, from a tactical perspective, the conundrum confronting both the sailing and the early steam-driven warships was the rapid advance in gunnery. Around this time, the French Navy, followed by the Royal Navy, experimented with explosive ball-shaped projectiles fired from large caliber guns, sitting on gun carriages that were center-lined on the main deck and could be swiveled 180 degrees or more. All wooden ships, regardless of whether they were sail or steam powered, were extremely vulnerable to these new projectiles. With the larger guns, these explosive canon balls could blast through the "wooden walls" with catastrophic effect. A shell penetrating a steam warship's hull and then exploding in the boiler room would certainly be more destructive than a shell penetrating a sailing warship. Second, Stewart and others felt the large cumbersome side-wheels used to propel steam-ships were vulnerable to gunfire.[20] Stewart certainly knew artillery and the tactical implications of the newer weapons. After all, he was not shy about experimenting and improvising with naval gunnery. During the War of 1812 he had directed the *Constitution* to be fitted out with a pair of captured British shifting gunades and perhaps with multiple barreled swivel guns.

As a man of practical business skills, Charles Stewart likely held the opinion that steam warships were an extremely expensive and unproven proposition, especially for this era of extreme financial belt-tightening overseen by presidents and congresses who disfavored keeping an expansive military organization during a time of global peace and continental expansion. From an operational perspective, the steam-powered ships and craft of the 1820s, 1830s, and 1840s had limited endurance, because they were veracious consumers of coal; they needed to operate within range of ports that could provide adequate coal-bunkering facilities. Few ports provided such facilities at this time.

Additionally, all things mechanical have a tendency to break down, and the early steam-power plants were not very reliable. The ability of early steamships to cross the great expanse of the Atlantic Ocean and carry their crews into battle was not held in very high esteem by the Navy's senior leaders, including Charles Stewart. Also, early steam-powered warships struggled to maneuver under sail with monstrous side-wheels and protective wheel housings retarding the ship's advance, by placing additional drag on the vessel's hull and by disrupting the air flow for the lower sails. Knowing the operational reality of stationing steam-powered warships overseas, Stewart had written a directive instructing captains of these warships under what circumstances to employ steam while operating in European waters.

Fuel conservation was paramount because of both the expense and the necessity of keeping a sufficient supply of coal on board at all times so the captain could outmaneuver his enemy in battle or save his ship from a storm-tossed sea. Therefore, a steam-warship captain had to conserve his ship's coal supplies, and he had to ensure its boilers and engine were functional throughout a cruise, so as to be ready for any tactical eventuality. A squadron commander possessed certain tactical advantages by having one or two of these warships under his command. Como. Matthew Calbraith Perry knew as much when his composite squadron, consisting of the Navy's first major steam frigates together with his sail-powered sloops and frigates, entered Japanese waters in 1854. But Perry also realized the operational limitations of commanding two different types of powered ships.

Stewart's conservative viewpoint regarding steam was a practical one, not just a reaction to what these "monsters" did to his beautiful sailing men-of-war. Had his view been superficial, he would not have advocated what certainly was a radical idea for a new type of steam-powered warship, nor would he have commented so favorably on the Navy's steam transformation during the Civil War.

During the second Jackson administration, relations between France and the United States were again strained. War was a possibility between the two powers, so on 4 February 1835 the House Committee on Naval Affairs recommended to the full House an appropriation of $75,000 for the construction of a steam-powered "prow"-configured warship proposed by Charles Stewart.

> This strange craft, two hundred or two hundred and fifty feet long, and seventy or eighty feet wide, built of solid timbers, was to comprise three hulls, the center one of which was to contain three steam engines, of 150 horse power, driving side paddle wheels to revolve between the hulls. Protected by impenetrable wooden bulwarks, and a heavy deck overhead, with the whole exterior sheathed in such manner as to be 'comparatively incombustible by ordinary means,' she would attack hostile ships by striking them 'two or three feet above the water and six or eight feet below its surface,' with her solid 'pyramidal prow,' formed of hard wood logs covered with iron plates four to six inches thick in such fashion as to 'produce a saw-shaped space upon the prow, and prevent the glancing of the vessel from her object.' This ram, solidly incorporated by extending back at least fifty feet into the mass of the three vessels, so that no concussion even at a speed of eight or ten miles an hour might wrench it from its base, would be withdrawn from the enemy's side by reversing the paddle wheels.[21]

Congress failed to act on the recommendation. But one can assume that had Stewart's "prow ship" been funded, his "conservative" reputation would have been erased from history.[22]

If signatures on official Board of Navy Commissioner's correspondence are any indication, Charles Stewart's role on the board was a prominent one. His background as a merchant and sailor born in one of America's centers of maritime commerce and shipbuilding came to the fore thanks to several inquiries by the Navy secretary as to the status of the Navy's live oak inventory. Again, requests for the "fleet in being's" status occurred periodically to help the Navy Department determine, through its inventory of live oak, how quickly a fleet could be built in response to a war emergency. The series of inquiries were far ranging, and they give insight into Charles Stewart as an administrator.

A Navy commissioners' correspondence to the Navy secretary, dated 12 November 1832 and signed by Charles Stewart, spelled out in excellent detail the prices paid by the U.S. government for live oak, broken down by year and ship type. Apparently, Secretary Levi Woodbury needed the price of live oak prior to 1800 for a congressional inquiry. Stewart's response to the secretary's request went beyond that: "the Navy Commissioners respectfully state, that this office, not having been established till the year 1816, the records furnish no information as to the prices paid for live oak timber prior to 1800."[23] Realizing that no records existed, the board found a contract made by the Navy Department in 1799 for the furnishing of 120,076 cubic feet of live oak at seventy-five cents per cubic foot. Using this metric, the board was able to project the cost up to the point when records were finally kept. With the establishment of the Navy Board of Commissioners in 1816, accurate records were kept and Stewart incorporated both sets of information into a comprehensive report.

Five days later Stewart and the board responded to the secretary's inquiry as to how much live oak was bought and used to repair U.S. Navy vessels since 1797. The board's response projected "there would probably be required to keep in repair a given force afloat, until it should become necessary to rebuild the vessels, about 2 per cent, per annum of the live oak which was necessary for their frames originally; and, to keep up perpetually such a given force afloat, about six per cent, per annum."[24]

The effort Stewart and the members of the board, to include the small number of civilian bureaucrats, put into this detailed response to the secretary's directive can be seen in a letter to the Secretary dated just one week later, 24 November 1832.

Sir: To enable the commissioners appointed under the act of 19th May, 1832, to execute the duties assigned to them, an appropriation will be necessary. The sum that may be required cannot be ascertained with any precision; but the Commissioners suppose it may be $15,000, and would respectfully submit that sum as their estimate upon the subject. I have the honor to be, with great respect, sir, your very obedient servant.[25]

In 1833, during President Andrew Jackson's first administration, Charles Stewart's stewardship on the Board of Navy Commissioners expired, and he was again without orders. Jackson's presidency had inherited the Republican Party's Jeffersonian lack of enthusiasm for the perceived aristocratic naval establishment, and so the president moved to cut that aristocracy. Politics played a hand "in the selection of commandants, mechanics and laborers" who remained to serve at the pleasure of the president.[26] Stewart's background was incompatible with Jackson's, and his chances of receiving the position at the Philadelphia Navy Yard came to naught. Como. James Barron, a southerner, a Jacksonian Democrat, and a duelist, was selected instead, as the president preferred a man who possessed comparable credentials. Later, when Jackson left the White House, Stewart relieved Barron.

From a policy perspective, the Jackson administration reduced the expenditures on large ships and, instead, allocated funding to the purchase and storage of enough materials to build ships in case of war. However, when the possibility of war with Great Britain arose, this policy changed, and, at the end of Jackson's second administration, naval expenditures actually exceeded those under the navalist administration of John Quincy Adams.[27] This upturn in the Navy's fortunes coincided with Charles Stewart receiving orders in 1837.

Stewart was returned to active duty with orders to report to the Philadelphia Navy Yard as its new commandant. He relieved Como. James Barron, who at the time of his relief had the Navy yard in the throes of preparations for the launch of America's, and probably the world's, largest sailing man-of-war, the 120-gun USS *Pennsylvania*.

Fifteen years passed between November 1822, when this great ship-of-the-line's keel was laid down, and her launch in 1837. This was not unusual for the Navy's sailing capital ships, for traditionally successive presidential administrations maintained ships like the *Pennsylvania* in a state of suspended animation. For the ever cost-conscious federal government, it was cheaper to maintain the ten ships-of-the-line ordered between 1816 and the early 1840s either in ordinary (not fully manned or ready to sail) or partially completed and sitting on stocks. As a matter of course, the Navy secretary submitted as part of his annual report to Congress "the vessels on stocks and in ordinary, and often cited estimates of the time and cost required to ready them for service."[28]

Stewart's influence in determining the status of these ships cannot be discounted, for as one of the Navy's senior officers, he was often asked to provide his estimate of the composition of the fleet, including the ratio of ships-of-the-line to smaller classes of warships. As an early advocate for a balanced

With four gun decks and mounting 120 guns, the USS *Pennsylvania* was the largest ship-of-the-line ever built. Stewart supervised her construction and later commanded her for her only short voyage to Norfolk. (Lithograph by N. Currier; courtesy of the Naval Historical Center)

fleet, his estimates included the number of ships-of-the-line necessary to provide a deterrent to any potential European aggressor. He also saw the value of possessing a battle fleet "in being," in which these ships could be prepared for service within a few months rather than kept fully operational.[29]

As the commandant of the Philadelphia Navy Yard and senior officer present, Charles Stewart was on hand when the USS *Pennsylvania* was launched on 18 July 1837. It was a huge event for the city of Philadelphia. An estimated 150,000 people lined the Pennsylvania and New Jersey shorelines of the Delaware River or crowded aboard various craft to witness the launch, overseen by John Lenthall, the *Pennsylvania*'s naval constructor. The ship's hull slid down the ways in a "slow, easy and graceful" manner.[30] The *Pennsylvania* was then towed to the Navy yard's fitting-out quay, and Stewart prepared to supervise her fitting out. By November the *Pennsylvania* was placed into commission. Stewart later commanded this great ship, and the following year he sailed her into Norfolk, Virginia, where the embodiment of the "wooden walls" remained in ordinary until 1842, becoming a receiving ship up through the early days of the Civil War.

While Philadelphia's citizens felt pride upon seeing this symbol of national power and the embodiment of their city's patriotism, sliding down the ways, the following year brought mourning. A favorite son returned home for burial. On 1 August 1838 Como. John Rodgers died while still on active duty as the president of the Board of Navy Commissioners. As senior officer present, Charles Stewart arranged for a funeral befitting one of the stalwarts of the "Old Navy." "In compliance with the orders of Commodore Charles Stewart, the commandant of the Philadelphia Navy Yard, Rodgers's funeral was attended by all the naval officers in the city, in full uniform."[31] Stewart was one of Rodgers's pallbearers, a duty he had performed for Capt. James Lawrence of the *Chesapeake* in 1813.

With USS *Pennsylvania* now part of the fleet, Stewart turned his attention to other matters of the yard, which ranged from the physical expansion of the yard to new construction and authorized ship maintenance. Despite his immense popular appeal up and down the Delaware Valley, Stewart had considerable difficulty expanding the yard, as its location had become an increasingly controversial subject among Philadelphia's citizens, who saw it as impeding the city's progress. The Navy Department questioned its location because it was far up the Delaware Estuary where the Delaware River was too shallow for larger warships to be built or refit.

As for new construction and maintenance, the constructor, John Lenthall, remained at the Navy yard under Stewart's command and played a dual role. For his commandant, he designed and supervised the building of the swift sloop-of-war, the sixteen-gun USS *Dale*. In addition, Lenthall promoted the development of naval steam engines. He joined the Southwark Foundry entrepreneurs Merrick and Towne to secure a Navy Department and Board of Naval Commissioners contract to build an experimental two side-lever steam engine and the machinery for the authorized side-wheel steam sloop, the USS *Mississippi*.[32]

However, the USS *Dale*, authorized by the Navy Department for use in the U.S. commitment to the suppression of the slave trade, was a priority of the commodore's. "The next year, 1838, saw the construction of a new class of ship sloops, which were intended to be economical cruisers particularly suited for distant stations, and were to rate as 16-gun sloops."[33] These were beautiful and popular among the fleet, possessing very good sailing qualities to boot. Of the five built during this period, only the *Dale* lasted, being sold in 1906.[34]

A recent history of the Philadelphia Navy Yard criticizes Stewart's decision to focus on the *Dale*. Authors Dorwart and Wolf interpret Stewart's decision solely on his prejudice for sail over steam, failing to take into account Stewart's strong sentiments against the slave trade. In fact, the national controversy over slavery increased significantly after the brig-of-war USS *Washington* seized a small, Spanish merchantman named *Amistad* near Montauk Point, New York, on 26 August 1839, and the subsequent events surrounding the *Amistad* played a larger role in Stewart's decision than his "prejudice."

When the USS *Washington* seized this Baltimore clipper–type vessel, it carried fifty-three enslaved Africans, who had killed most of the ship's crew in freeing themselves from their captors. The Africans had taken over the *Amistad* shortly after she departed Havana, Cuba, and, at the time of her seizure, she was proceeding aimlessly up the East Coast. The vessel and her Africans were interned, and, because "Congress outlawed the African slave trade in 1808 and declared it to be piracy punishable by death in 1820,"[35] interest in the subsequent legal proceedings, which would decide the Africans' fate, spread across the country like wildfire. The *Amistad* affair enflamed abolitionist and pro-slavery sentiment and even became a factor influencing presidential politics.

Stewart considered the USS *Dale*'s importance from two perspectives. As an officer in the U.S. Navy, Stewart saw the *Dale* as an instrument to enforce federal law against slave trading. From a personal perspective, the *Dale* and her role symbolized his own beliefs as well as the beliefs of his friend John Q. Adams, who successfully defended the fifty-three Africans in the U.S. Supreme Court. Like the court, Stewart believed "all people born free must remain free."[36] His personal beliefs reflected those of the majority of his fellow Pennsylvanians, especially those of an influential group from his hometown. His decision to proceed with the construction, fitting out, and commissioning of the *Dale*, "endeared himself to the antislavery Quaker community in Philadelphia. On October 8, 1839, Charles Stewart presided over the launching of the *Dale* from the Philadelphia Navy Yard."[37] As commandant, he oversaw the vessel's fitting out and commissioning.

Because of his past actions in support of the Constitution and the Union, during Stewart's first years as commandant of the Philadelphia Navy Yard, his name was suggested as a possible presidential candidate for the 1840 elections. A campaign to maneuver him toward consideration began in 1838, when "the Democracy of Pennsylvania sought to bring out the Commodore as a candidate for the Presidency."[38] This maneuver had its genesis in the admiration of Stewart's friends and grew throughout his tenure as commandant until "an earnest and formidable movement was made" to launch the reluctant naval officer into the candidacy for President of the United States.[39]

In 1838 a lengthy article, written under the penname Gen. Anthony

During Stewart's brief pursuit of the presidency, one political caricaturist suggested in 1844 that the commodore was "better fitted to govern the helm of old Ironsides than the helm of State." (Unattributed; courtesy of the Library of Congress)

Wayne of the Revolutionary War era, appeared in the *Spirit of the Times*, a Philadelphia paper. Actually the writer was Charles Stewart's friend, the lawyer and long-time public servant Richard Rush. The article was addressed "to the Democratic Party of Pennsylvania on the next Presidential election," and Rush urged that the Pennsylvania Democrats unite in a campaign to put Como. Charles Stewart in the White House in 1845.[40]

Richard Vaux, Robert K. Scott, William Bradford, and Richard Rush's son, J. Murray Rush, commenced an earnest and formidable movement for Charles Stewart's candidacy. These young men were members of the Philadelphia bar and leading Democrats of the state of Pennsylvania. Vaux and Scott later became mayors of Philadelphia. In 1841 they privately strategized together and agreed to pay the *Spirit of the Times* a certain sum for its advocacy of Stewart's candidacy. Vaux then took over writing pro-Stewart editorials for the newspaper. The group's advocacy took hold and soon an organization called The Old Ironsides Club was formed, comprising the leading Democrats from Philadelphia. A wood cut showing the fight between the *Constitution* and the *Cyane* and *Levant* was placed in the paper. Pamphlets with this woodcut and a brief Stewart biography were printed and distributed throughout the city, the surrounding areas of southwest Pennsylvania, and across the river in Stewart's adopted home state of New Jersey. Within four months of the first articles, sixty-seven Democratic papers declared for Stewart.[41]

Although grateful for the consideration, Stewart was nonetheless silent to the prospect and would remain so through the six-year effort that his friends expended on his behalf. Stewart's silence is understandable on two levels. First, he was a serving officer in the U.S. Navy and, as such, his silence was a requirement of his position. Also, Stewart realized that his private life could be used against him if he campaigned. In fact, in a letter written around 1839 by a fellow Philadelphian, Henry S. Patterson, to Orestes A. Brownson, Patterson recognized that Stewart supporters were becoming organized and that "arrangements are being made to organize a [Senator Thomas Hart] Benton Club. The friends of [James] Buchanan in the interior are urging his claims. He is probably the most popular man so far as [Pennsylvania] is concerned."[42] Patterson continued by describing Commodore Stewart:

> He is about 60, in tolerable health, but with an iron frame terribly shaken by a life of dissipation. He has some mind and his information is superior in both to General [William Henry] Harrison. As a sailor he stands deservedly high. He is separated from his wife. In the matter of women he had been particularly loose. He now has a mistress who is said to be a relative left under his guardianship and debauched by him. He is also far from select in his male associations. The nomination has been brewing for some time but is generally laughed at. A Captain Henry, a man of arrogance, insolence and dissoluteness, is Stewart's constant companion and the reputed author of the articles in the Spirit of the Times, which is now their recognized organ. Stewart has generally voted a democratic ticket, but for several years past has been looked upon as a conservative. If nominated he will be regarded in Pennsylvania as the candidate of that party which looks for a perpetuation of the present abuses. The only paper, which actively supports him, is the Spirit of the Times, long known as a merchantable article. Another is to be established at Camden, NJ under the editorial charge of Dr. English, backed by Captain Robert Field Stockton who, if they may believe him, elected Harrison by his individual exertions.[43]

Indeed, William Henry Harrison was elected president in 1840, and with his election came a sweeping victory that gave the Whig Party control of both houses of Congress. The Whigs inherited many of the philosophies and political aspirations of the old Federalist Party, including the belief in a strong Navy.[44] This belief turned into political action, even after Harrison's death placed his Southern Democrat vice president, John Tyler, in the presidency. Action for a stronger Navy began to take shape when President Tyler asked the Virginian Abel P. Upshur to be his Navy secretary. After his Senate confirmation, Upshur threw himself into reforming the administration of the Navy.[45] "Upshur spent November preparing his first annual report, consulting with the navy commissioners along with Marine Colonel Archibald Henderson; Captain Beverley Kennon, an old friend; his brother, Lieutenant George P. Upshur; Captain Charles Stewart, to command the Home Squadron; Captain Thomas ap Catesby Jones, to command the Pacific Squadron; and reform-minded junior officers."[46]

One of the first changes Upshur made was reorganizing the fleet by creating the Home Squadron in 1841. The rationale for this change was twofold: First, Upshur determined the United States required a squadron "from which vessels could be quickly dispatched to other areas when needed."[47] Second, a continental-based squadron could patrol the Atlantic and Gulf Coasts. It can be said that the present-day U.S. Navy's Atlantic and Second Fleets, both located at Norfolk, Virginia, can trace their linage to the Home Squadron.

The Home Squadron's first commander was one of its most experienced officers who had previously commanded the Mediterranean and Pacific Squadrons—Charles Stewart. At the time of Stewart's appointment, the U.S. Navy "kept small squadrons in the Mediterranean, the Caribbean, off the West African coast, and in the Pacific. While its ships supported commerce and diplomacy in the far flung corners of the world and suppressed piracy in the Caribbean and the slave trade off the African coast, as before, the navy was limited to support of the merchant class, and it was still not assigned any broad national roles during peacetime."[48]

As commander of the Home Squadron, Stewart was directed to take the USS *Independence* as his flagship. The *Independence* was built at Charlestown Navy Yard, Boston, as a seventy-four-gun ship-of-the-line. Commissioned in July 1815, this near-sister ship of the USS *Franklin* was 188 feet between the perpendiculars and had a 50-foot molded beam. Like the *Franklin*, the *Independence* carried a much heavier armament than any contemporary European 74. Her original battery consisted of eighty-seven guns: the thirty-two-pound long guns were on the lower deck and twenty-four-pounders were on the upper decks. This was subsequently changed to all 32s with twenty-four of them being carronades.[49]

The first American capital ship to sail European waters, the *Independence*, under the command of Captain Bainbridge, was sent to the Mediterranean.

Upon her arrival there, she became the flagship of Stephen Decatur's squadron, and her appearance did much to persuade the Algerians that a final treaty between them and the United States was in their best interest.

Bainbridge reported that she possessed many fine sailing qualities, and he considered her to be the fastest and best sea boat he had ever sailed.[50] However, as with her sister, she sailed very low in the water. When fully provisioned, the height of the lower gun ports to the waterline was just a little over three feet. However, when Charles Stewart stepped on board her in 1841, this twenty-six-year-old warship had been considerably altered.

Alterations began in Boston in 1836 to cut her down to a large frigate—a "Razee." The Royal Navy first conducted this practice of reducing seventy-four-gun ships-of-the-line to large frigates in 1794 to counter existing similar units in the French Navy. The work, involving the removal of the *Independence*'s upper deck, was completed well within a year. When Stewart was piped on board as commander of the Home Squadron four years later, this "heavy" frigate was much admired for her handling and speed. The *Independence* would have been a choice command for an aspiring captain, and it is ironic that on the day Commodore Stewart stepped onto the ship's quarterdeck in New York, Capt. John Gallagher greeted him. Twenty-one years earlier, Stewart had relieved Gallagher, together with other senior officers of the Mediterranean Squadron, for insubordination. Apparently, the incident in the Mediterranean did not adversely affect Gallagher's career.[51]

One of the most profound incidents influencing the culture of the "Old Navy" of the U.S. Navy occurred during Stewart's tenure as commander of the Home Squadron. The U.S. brig-of-war *Somers* was placed into commission on 12 May 1842, with Cdr. Alexander Slidell Mackenzie in command. Como. Matthew Perry had selected the *Somers* to be a training vessel for midshipmen, and he charged the spit-and-polish Mackenzie with providing for their schooling at sea. Within the complement of handpicked midshipmen, many of whom were well connected in public life, was one who arrived on board just before the brig sailed with dispatches for West Africa.

His name was Philip Spencer, and he was the son of a domineering father, John Canfield Spencer, war secretary for President Tyler. The eighteen-year-old Spencer was temperamental and a maverick compared to his shipmates occupying the *Somers*'s midshipmen berth. This was Spencer's second chance; he had been relieved of his duties on another naval vessel for drunkenness and insubordination. It did not take long for Philip Spencer to find himself an outcast in the midshipmen's berth of the *Somers*.

This unruly teenager turned to the crew for companionship and soon fell under the influence of two sailors of questionable character: Samuel Cromwell and Elisha Small. Spencer stole alcohol and cigars from the wardroom for these sailors by bribing the brig's steward. By the time the *Somers* made her way back from Africa, Midshipman Spencer was thoroughly enthralled with the two sailors and their stories of adventure, debauchery, and piracy. At the same time, Spencer conveyed to his shipmates his hatred for the captain and his officers.[52] Spencer's fate and those of his two shipmates turned on what might have been an alcohol-induced conversation with a crew member outside of the trio of confidants. According to the testimony of the purser's steward, Midshipman Spencer said that he was part of a conspiracy of twenty other members of the *Somers* crew, who wanted to murder all of the officers and take control of the brig. The steward passed along Spencer's comments, which in short order reached the ears of Commander Mackenzie. The next day at evening muster, Mackenzie confronted Spencer, whose manner of response only enraged the brig's captain. He ordered the midshipman to be placed in double irons, and he directed that Midshipman Spencer's personal artifacts be searched for incriminating evidence. Pieces of paper with Greek writing were found among his belongings. The writing was translated and revealed that Spencer had written down the names of some of the brig's crewmen. Upon this discovery, Mackenzie ordered his officers to arm themselves, an action that increased the tension among all on board.

The breaking point came when the brig's first lieutenant mistakenly thought the crew had gathered aft to commence the mutiny. Actually, they were responding to a lawful order to form a working party to repair some damaged rigging. The first lieutenant charged his pistol and ordered them to stop, and, although this action was unjustified, Mackenzie felt increasingly threatened and ordered the arrest of several crew members. The arrests added fuel to the burning embers of discontent among the crew who now had to man the brig under the constant watch of armed officers, brandishing their charged pistols at any suspicious-looking movement. On 1 December Mackenzie determined that the safety of the ship required that the suspected mutineers be executed and ordered Midshipman Spencer and his two cohorts to be hanged on that day. Spencer, Cromwell, and Small were hanged from the brig's lower yardarms.

On 15 December the *Somers* sailed into New York. Mackenzie did not report to Stewart, nor did he feel that it was necessary. During this period, subordinate commanding officers felt the need to report to their commodores only when actively engaged on a foreign station. No administrative reason seemed to exist for Commander Mackenzie, who knew his squadron's commander would be nearby, to immediately report to Stewart. Mackenzie decided on a different course. Instead of reporting to the senior officer present in New York, he sent a dispatch to Washington and Navy Secretary Upshur, reporting the mutiny and directly requesting a court of inquiry. Upshur quickly ordered Commodore Stewart to convene the court. As commander of the Home Squadron with his flagship, the *Independence,* anchored at New York and under orders to sail, Stewart was directed by Upshur to be the court's president. Stewart, together with two other senior officers—Como. Jacob Jones, port captain of the New York Station and commanding officer of the *North Carolina,* and Como. A. J. Dallas, commandant of the Pensacola Navy Yard—convened on board the ship-of-the-line, now receiving ship, USS *North Carolina.* The judge advocate general charged with presenting the evidence to the court of inquiry was Ogden Hoffman, the U.S. district attorney for the Southern District of New York. Hoffman was a former junior officer who had served with Stewart during the War of 1812.[53] All arrived on board the *North Carolina* on 28 December, and Stewart declared the proceedings open precisely at 11 A.M.

As the president of the *Somers*'s court of inquiry, Charles Stewart would have been mindful that the ugly incident in question occurred on board a ship that was named in honor of his boyhood friend, who died before the shores of Tripoli. Additionally, Stewart must have felt his sixty-four years at some point during the inquiry, and the court-martial that followed, because the court carried on through the bleak New York City winter. Also, public interest grew daily and, with it, heated controversy.

On the first day of the proceedings, the New York press, led by Horace Greeley's *Tribune,* arrived in force on board the *North Carolina.* As the leading voice of the fourth estate, Greeley exercised his influence in the controversy that resulted from the court's findings. Another New York paper, the *Herald,* in its commentary observed: "There never has been any case . . . whose examination has awakened such universal and pervading interest. . . . It is the great topic of the day. . . . Immense crowds have visited the *Somers* and inspected her with all the closeness and interest of jurymen."[54]

On that cold December day two of the most prominent writers on maritime affairs and fiction during the era, James Fenimore Cooper and the young Richard Henry Dana, joined the throng of newspapermen and interested citizens who were crammed into the broad captain's cabin on the *North*

Carolina. They had come to the city to witness and comment on the proceedings, and the two men would find themselves on opposite sides of the issue. Cooper, a former midshipman himself and a voice in favor of sweeping Navy reform, was also the father of a schoolmate of the executed Spencer. He proved to be a vociferous critic of Mackenzie. He wrote extensively against Mackenzie's decision to execute Spencer and the two seamen. Dana, the author of *Two Years before the Mast,* championed Mackenzie's side. He felt strongly that the captain had acted properly.

Stewart's court of inquiry simply took testimony and no one stood accused. "Almost everyone told their story, except ten of the twelve men still under arrest—and of course the three who had been hanged."[55] Mackenzie was not called to testify, but he had provided an extensive written report to the Navy secretary, which was recited first. This report immediately became public record, and its aristocratic, condescending tone did much to explode the issue in the public's mind. Mackenzie, who was a known writer of eloquent and imaginative travelogues for the reading public, later admitted that he wished he had written his statement differently.

Stewart allowed Commander Mackenzie the opportunity for cross-examination of each witness after District Attorney Hoffman finished his questioning. However, Mackenzie was ordered to present his questions in writing, and he was prevented from speaking to the witnesses. The board members presented the questions.

Although this inquiry was a straightforward proceeding, it lasted through most of January. The pressure on the board must have been considerable, as the executed midshipman's father was a member of the president's cabinet. However, Stewart staunchly continued to ensure the investigation proceeded in the most thorough manner possible. All aspects of the proceedings became excellent stories for the public. Daily accounts ran in all the papers, and, by the time Stewart announced that the proceedings had concluded, the *Somers* mutiny was the biggest story in the land. Interest in the story only grew when Navy Secretary Upshur "ordered a court martial of Commander Mackenzie. The charges were murder, oppression, illegal punishment, conduct unbecoming an officer, and general cruelty and oppression."[56] The court would consist of twelve senior officers, excluding Stewart, Dallas, and Jones, and would convene on board the *North Carolina* immediately at the conclusion of Stewart's inquiry, on 1 February 1843. Actually, Mackenzie himself requested the court-marital. For one thing, he and his advisers saw that public opinion was not going to be satisfied with a favorable finding by the court of inquiry.

On 20 January 1843 Stewart convened the court's last session and simply stated "that the testimony being now closed the Court would be cleared. . . . The Court will deliberate and frame their decisions in secret, and it will then be sent to Washington for approval."[57]

Upon receipt of this report, Secretary Upshur made public the opinion of Stewart's court of inquiry: "Commander Mackenzie, under these circumstances, was not bound to risk the safety of his vessel, and jeopardize the lives of his crew, in order to secure to the guilty the forms of a trial—and that the immediate execution of the prisoners was demanded by duty and justified by necessity. The court is further of the opinion that throughout all of these painful occurrences, so well calculated to disturb the judgment and try the energy of the bravest and most experienced officer, the conduct of Commander Mackenzie and his officers was prudent, calm, and firm—and he and they honorably performed their duty to the service and their country."[58]

Stewart's and his fellow officers' official statement that "immediate execution of the ringleaders [was] demanded by duty and justified by necessity" brought out the cynics, some of whom, for many reasons, held a deep-felt conviction that the republic's navy needed immediate reform and considered the decision of the board and the subsequent decision by the court-marital a whitewash.[59]

The board's decision and the immediate commencement of Mackenzie's court-martial brought out America's most recognized literary notables of maritime interests. James Fenimore Cooper took up the cause of Midshipman Spencer and the two seamen. However, it was written, "he is rather anti-Mackenzie than pro-Spencer. Though trained as a naval officer, and proud of the Navy, he does not stand in closed ranks with the officers in defense of the clan."[60]

Cooper severely criticized Mackenzie for the hangings. He was the nation's first naval historian, and, adamant in his criticism of the way the Navy conducted its business, his voice contributed to changes in how the Navy approached discipline. Cooper wrote the first history of the U.S. Navy, which was published after the *Somers* mutiny. He does not slight Stewart's findings, but levies accolades upon Stewart's many notable accomplishments as a naval officer.

Other reporters, like Dana, strongly sided with Mackenzie, which at first glance seemed unusual. After all, Dana had spent "two years before the mast" as a common sailor in the merchant service and experienced the harsh conditions under which the average sailor lived. What seemed to convince

Dana of Mackenzie's innocence was his personal inspection of the *Somers*, during which he concluded that on such a small vessel with a large, tightly berthed crew, a conspiracy among just three disciplined conspirators could easily go unnoticed. In an instant, they could overwhelm the vessel's watch standers with hardly a warning. The slightest indication of such an act, if observed by the watch, would have to be met with an immediate response by the officer of the deck, or the vessel would be carried away by mutiny.

The *Somers* Affair can also be viewed from a larger perspective, and, in his book *The* Somers *Mutiny Affair*, Harrison Hayford wrote,

> This case occurred at the full flood of Jacksonian democracy. Conservative Whigs confronted radical Democrats, in the newly opened "era of the common man." A major ground of the affair was the way in which the case seemed to array principles against each other: aristocracy against democracy (perhaps Jeffersonian against Jacksonian democracy); discipline against popular rights; security of property against security of life; the safety of society against the right of individuals to due legal process. No one, of course, wanted either anarchy or arbitrary government; everyone looked to the law for assurances of rights and saw "justice" on his side; but some saw the *Somers* case as a manifestation of law and order triumphant over mutiny and piracy, whereas others saw it as a display of privileged military arrogance overriding human rights.[61]

As for Stewart, his decision can be understood in light of his devotion to maintaining good order and discipline, and it appears consistent with his previous decision in a court of inquiry that occurred three years earlier.

In 1839 Charles Stewart presided over a court of inquiry that investigated several charges levied against Como. Jess Duncan Elliott. The court was informed that Elliot had abused his authority while he was in command of the Mediterranean Squadron. Stewart and the members of the court took testimony during a three-month-long investigation, which ended in late July. Aspects of Elliott's case must have reminded Stewart of his own experience commanding the Mediterranean Squadron eighteen years earlier. Stewart, ever mindful of the need to preserve good order and discipline, did not see the charges levied against Elliott as serious enough to warrant a court-martial. He saw a judgment against Elliott as detrimental to the authority a senior commander must maintain in the execution of his duties. Stewart stood by the letter of the law in his decision on the Elliot court of inquiry, as he had when he informed Commodore Rodgers that only Congress could declare war and when he suspended Captain Macdonough over his decision to convene a court martial on non-American soil. As such, when the court of inquiry on the Elliot case announced its findings, Stewart was the lone dissenting vote; the rest of the board found sufficient evidence to proceed. Elliott stood before a court-martial in 1840 and was subsequently found guilty. He was suspended from the service.

Before the *Somers* Affair, Charles Stewart held a stalwart belief that a prospective U.S. Navy officer could learn his profession only through service at sea. Objecting to a formal school, Stewart shared the opinion of one of his former midshipmen, later Confederate admiral, Franklin Buchanan, who thought that "within the navy hierarchy a successful cruise on a merchant ship was deemed a valuable experience for an ambitious young naval officer and furlough for such purposes were not only approved but encouraged."[62]

However, Stewart's experience on the *Somers* court reshaped his opinion regarding the need for a formal school for midshipmen. Although he had been from the old school of thought, "Charles Stewart, who presided on MacKenzie's court martial, concluded that future crises of this nature could be prevented if a single national shore-based school for midshipmen were established."[63] Stewart now exerted his influence to establish a naval school.

The first rudimentary school had opened while Stewart was commandant of the Philadelphia Navy Yard. "In 1838 a naval school of much more importance than any of its predecessors was organized at the Naval Asylum," located in Philadelphia. "Secretary Paulding . . . established there a school of preparation, at which midshipmen were permitted to pass a year—an academic year, however, of only eight months—in the study of mathematics required at the examination. Commodore Biddle and Stewart were directed to establish the school, with Biddle selected its superintendent. Professor David McClure was appointed to take charge of the class in mathematics and navigation, and a teacher of the French language was added."[64] The school was beset with many difficulties, ranging from poor accommodations to a failure to discipline the young gentlemen, who found it more interesting to experience the many diversions that a seaport town the size of Philadelphia offered than to work at their studies. However, the naval academy in Philadelphia was a beginning, and Stewart and others later continued to advocate formal schooling.

Stewart wrote a report, which Secretary Upshur delivered to Congress, reflecting this advocacy. In it "Commodore Stewart advocated a school with a limited course of instruction, with special reference to mathematics, language, international law, and the principles and mechanism of the steam-engine."[65]

The need for a school was just part of a greater need to reform the Navy. In the years following his tenure as a member of the Board of Navy Commissioners, Charles Stewart became increasingly dissatisfied with the board's conduct. There were many critics in and out of uniform who blamed all of the problems that beset the Navy on the board. Much of this criticism stemmed from a generational split, with the younger officers lacking promotion opportunities and good pay, while realizing the need for maintaining good order and discipline in the fleet. Among the older naval officers Charles Stewart was the most "unsparing critic" of the board.[66]

In March 1842, shortly after the conclusion of the *Somers* inquiry and Mackenzie's court-martial, Commodore Stewart wrote a letter to Navy Secretary Upshur, stating that the Board of Navy Commissioners failed the Navy and the country. He was very much aware of the secretary's perspective on the issues, because both men had worked on the secretary's annual report to Congress the previous fall.

Stewart continued by saying that the individual members of the board lacked responsibility for their decisions and that the "absence of economy in the construction, equipment, and repair of our vessels; the diversity in their models, classes, and qualities; the incapacity of some and the worthlessness of others; the excessive waste by continual experiments, have never been surpassed, if ever equaled, in any other naval establishment of the same limits."[67]

The debate, in and out of the Navy and through the halls of Congress, continued through the spring and summer months. Secretary Upshur submitted his plans for reform to President Tyler, who concurred and sent the bill to Capitol Hill. Congress made some slight modifications to the bill, and on 31 August 1842 passed the act that replaced the Board of Navy Commissioners with the bureau system Secretary Upshur recommended.

The new system created five separate bureaus with a senior naval officer heading each one, except the Bureau of Provisions and Clothing, which could be led by a civilian. The bureaus were divided into the following technical divisions:

1. The Bureau of Navy Yards and Docks
2. The Bureau of Construction, Equipment, and Repairs
3. The Bureau of Provisions and Clothing
4. The Bureau of Ordnance and Hydrography
5. The Bureau of Medicine.

Each bureau chief was appointed by the president and confirmed by the Senate. Each chief received his orders from the secretary and reported directly to him.[68] This technical breakdown of the bureaus remained in place until the Civil War, when the demands of modern war stretched the fleet along the entire American coastline and into the world's oceans, requiring that the organization be modified.

This restructuring did not affect the relationship of the secretary to the various squadron commanders. The Navy secretary was still responsible to the president for fleet operations, and as such he was the administrative and operational head of the Navy; there was no chief of naval operations. However, Stewart was the most senior squadron commander, and, as commander of the Home Squadron, he was responsible for operations in home waters and for providing ships and craft to the deployed squadrons. Additionally, the close proximity of the Home Squadron to the secretary meant that Stewart could be consulted for his recommendations on all aspects of fleet operations. One such inquiry occurred shortly after the creation of the bureaus.

Secretary Upshur next tackled the officer corps structure. He asked Stewart for his recommendation as to the total number of officers per grade that the Navy should maintain. Stewart responded that he estimated the current number of ships in the fleet would require 18 captains, 18 commanders, and 185 lieutenants. He added that for shore establishments an additional 18 captains, 13 commanders, and 92 lieutenants would be required for the dockyards and bureau chiefs. This first major attempt to reform the officer corps came to the forefront thirteen years later.

CHAPTER THIRTEEN

Senior Officer Present

While Charles Stewart was in his last year as the commander of the Home Squadron, another presidential election campaign year began. Momentum for Stewart's candidacy continued to grow within the immediate Philadelphia area, and it reached its peak at the national party level during the 1844 presidential campaign year. National party conventions had become the mechanism for nominating candidates for the presidency, and, by this time in its evolution, the nomination process usually decided a candidate's fate through the horse-trading found within the "smoke-filled room."[1] Stewart's political future was decided in this environment.

By the spring of 1844, Charles Stewart was home in Bordentown, New Jersey. He had not only completed his tour as commander of the Home Squadron the previous November, but he had just come off the longest stint of active duty he ever performed—seven years. Without orders, he resumed his Philadelphia-based business interests and continued his efforts to make his beloved estate "Old Ironsides" into a successful farm. But, the spring also brought both major political parties, the Whigs and Democrats, to their respective conventions in Baltimore, Maryland. For the Whigs, there was little horse-trading; Henry Clay had the nomination sown up. However, the Democrats had several horses to consider, and this despite Martin van Buren's apparent lock on the nomination.

The most outstanding and divisive political issue in American politics at the time was the question of whether the independent state of Texas should be annexed into the Union, and if it were annexed, whether it should be a slave or free state. Slavery was Martin van Buren's Achilles heel, because he had publicly declared years earlier that annexing Texas would divide the Union. Declaring Texas a slave state after annexation would tip the balance in Congress in favor of the southern, slave-holding states. However, van Buren underestimated annexation fever, and so the Democrat nomination for president remained up for grabs.

> Lewis Cass of Michigan, a hero of the War of 1812 . . . considered van Buren's strongest challenger, was a fervent advocate of annexation. . . . Other rivals were John Calhoun, the South's Ancient of Days and 'the sleepless guardian of slavery;' Silas Wright of New York, popular but believed to be too free with the bottle; James Buchanan and Commodore Charles Stewart of Pennsylvania, the former a veteran of both House and Senate and onetime minister to Russia, the later a comparative unknown.[2]

Eventually, the former Speaker of the House of Representatives, James Knox Polk, from Tennessee, was added to the list of nominees.

Van Buren's apparent unbeatable lead dissipated after the first ballot, and, with the results of the seventh ballot, he lost his position. The convention was deadlocked, and that night, the members maneuvered to find another horse. The future Navy secretary, George Bancroft of the Massachusetts delegation, weighed in on the struggle. It was probably at this point that Stewart's name was considered. Bancroft conferred with the New York delegation, and, during the discussions, Polk's name was mentioned as a vice-presidential candidate to either Martin van Buren or Charles Stewart.

Polk's supporters sent word that if the Philadelphians supporting Stewart would support Polk on their ticket as vice president, they would, in turn, support Stewart for the presidential nomination. But, Stewart's supporters failed to agree to this proposal in time, and thus lost the assistance of those who later nominated Polk for the presidency. The older politicians of the country were jealous of the Philadelphia movement. This was the time when James Buchanan and Alexander J. Dallas, a prominent Philadelphian lawyer and old Jeffersonian Republican, were gaining prominence as candidates. Most of Stewart's friends were Dallas men, and when Polk took Dallas on his ticket, the Stewart movement was injured. "But never before in the history of the country, it has been remarked, was so much accomplished for a man not in politics as was done for Stewart at this time."[3] What is interesting is that for unknowns, Stewart was at the time placed alongside Polk, who after all had been twice speaker of the House of Representatives.

"Had Stewart himself been anything of a politician, the result might have been different. As it was the movement was carried forward, from first to last, without consultation with him."[4] In a letter to another Stewart supporter, R. Watson Gilder, Richard Vaux wrote: "It is just to say, that all this time Stewart never came to see us to talk about the matter. He dined with me several times, with leading statesmen of the country, but never said a word about it. During the agitation of the subject Stewart was unusually nervous and fidgety. He regained his usual equanimity only when his name ceased to be bandied about by the political press."[5]

The hesitation on the part of Stewart's supporters proved decisive, because, in the early morning hours of the next day, Bancroft and the New York delegation agreed to push Polk. This protégé of Andrew Jackson and a fervent annexationist stymied the morning ballots. "On the eighth ballot, van Buren sank to 104 and Cass rose to 114. The deadlock had deepened. But James Knox Polk had received 44 votes. That not only ended the stalemate, it started a stampede: on the tenth ballot the dour little man from Tennessee became the Democratic candidate for president."[6] The moment passed for Stewart—a moment that he really didn't want. His family life was certainly a consideration. But, after all, he always considered himself just a sailor, and during this time in his life when he was considered for the highest elective office in the land, Stewart was awaiting the call from the profession that he loved so much.

Stewart had been without orders since November 1843, but, with the election of President Polk, the opportunity to serve again presented itself. In 1845, when he was sixty-six years old, the commodore received temporary orders assigning him to Philadelphia. From his hometown as well as in Washington, Stewart spent the year supporting the initiatives of the Navy secretary.

With the new administration came a new Navy secretary, George Bancroft. This appointment surprised everyone within naval circles, and Bancroft as well, who possessed no expertise in naval affairs and who had wanted to be the ambassador to Great Britain. However, Bancroft was a well-respected historian, and, as Stewart recognized given the previous presidential election year, a political force. Doubts aside, Bancroft threw himself into the job. "Bancroft was a whirlwind of activity in the doldrums that otherwise afflicted naval policy from 1845 to 1852, and left an important legacy for officer personnel even though he stayed but a short time."[7]

As Navy secretary, Bancroft had two interrelated objectives: First, he pursued the Navy's budget to wring out economy in its expenditures. Second, he sought to reform officer personnel administration.

Almost immediately, Bancroft partially succeeded with his second objective. As a result of his deft maneuvering within his legal authority as Navy secretary, Bancroft provided a fait accompli to those in and out of uniform, as well as those in Congress, by simply creating the U.S. Naval Academy in the summer of 1845. Stewart's influence in this process was surprising because the commodore had originally believed the best place for instruction of future officers was at sea. However, by 1838, he had changed his mind and was a strong proponent for a naval school. In October 1860, the elderly Stewart was invited to help dedicate the newly assigned *Constitution* as the Naval Academy's school ship.

As it concerned Bancroft's first objective, in March 1845, he submitted a budget that was two-thirds that of the previous Navy secretary's budget. Bancroft's budget was part of his only annual report (he left office the following year after the Senate confirmed him as America's ambassador to the Court of St. James), and in it he "urged retrenchment and economizing across all fronts."[8] Prior to submitting the report, Bancroft consulted several reform-minded officers, with Stewart taking an active role in supporting the secretary's effort to reform the officer personnel structure. For the previous twenty years, commissions had been based on political patronage and not the needs of the service. "On April 24, relying upon Captain Charles Stewart's counsel, Bancroft transmitted a letter discussing the structure of the personnel problems in greater detail and proposing solutions."[9]

Stewart submitted his recommendations to Bancroft for the number of officers by grade that the Navy required for sea duty and for "disability from age, sickness or other causes, and for the support of all proper stations on shore."[10] Using the recommendations he offered to Secretary Upshur in 1842 as a baseline, Stewart examined the requirements for sea officers from the operations of the previous year and concluded the fleet could reduce the number of captains, commanders, and lieutenants. Stewart also recommended that the number of midshipmen allowed be "fixed for that class of officers, the diminution would impose upon them more duty, instruct them better in their profession, and open to them the way for more rapid promotion."[11] The reductions in all grades were significant.

Bancroft moved ahead with his officer-reform effort. In 1846 Stewart assumed command of the Philadelphia Navy Yard for the second time. The same year also saw Mexico and the United States at war.

In January, when Stewart assumed command, the yard was rebuilding after having fallen into decay. The Navy facility was not benefiting from its neighborhood in a city suffering from "terrible labor, ethnic and religious unrest and violence that convulsed Philadelphia from the working class neighborhoods of Kensington to the ship-building and industrial community surrounding the government compound in Southwark."[12] Philadelphia, as well as New York and Boston, were absorbing the effects of another European wave of emigration. Eighteen months earlier, anti-Catholic rioting had broken out in the city, which could only be quelled by the state militia. Actual rioting nearly reached the entrance to the yard, compelling the commandant at the time, Commodore Read, to take measures to protect the federal property from attack. He augmented the guard and improved the main entrance to the yard by extending the guardhouse to the edge of federal property. However, in 1845 the city's fortunes brightened, when the new Polk administration directed shipbuilding and repair operations to the yard.[13] The Philadelphia Navy Yard played a major supporting role in the war with Mexico for the Navy and the officers whom Stewart had lead and mentored in previous years.

Stewart's attention was divided as a result of Navy Secretary Bancroft's tasking. In July 1846, two months after the United States responded to Mexico's declaration of war with its own, Bancroft appointed a twenty-member officer selection board and appointed the sixty-eight-year-old Charles Stewart as its president. The board was directed to fill the twenty vacant captain and forty-seven vacant commander billets that were created as a result of Stewart's recommendations. Per Bancroft's direction, Stewart convened the board of senior officers in secret—the Navy, Congress, and the general public were caught unaware. Rumors abounded, but gradually the word got out and the criticism became heated. When the board's selections to fill the spots became known, the Senate refused its consent, because it considered the selection process subjective and certain to produce distrust and jealousies within the officer corps. The Senate held that seniority was the only fair mechanism for promotion within the Navy, and, although Stewart was the senior officer present on the board and had carried out the secretary's direction, he agreed with the Senate's conclusion. Stewart saw that it was the Navy's prerogative to determine how many officers it required, but he felt the next senior officer should fill any vacancy. Reform-minded officers placed Stewart squarely in the conservative camp for his support of promotions by seniority. This was especially unfortunate, because Stewart's initial recommendations as to the number of officers required and Bancroft's decision opened the door for future officer reform—reform that influenced the future positioning of officers who excelled during the Civil War.

With his responsibilities to the board completed, Stewart returned to the

Philadelphia Navy Yard, which was now in the throes of fitting out ships of the Home Squadron for duty in the Mexican War. Stewart was responsible for completing the last pure sail-powered warship built at the Southwark yard, the twenty-gun sloop-of-war USS *Germantown*. Christened at launching on 22 August 1846 by Miss Lavinia Fanning Watson, the USS *Germantown* she was placed in commission that fall.

Stewart was also responsible for fitting out the sail-powered frigate, USS *Brandywine*; and the steam sloop-of-war USS *Princeton*.[14] In addition, the experimental steamer, USS *Water Witch*, was in the Southwark yard for the purpose of improving her engineering plant, to include the fitting out of twin screw propellers—the first vessel in the world to be so configured. The older Stewart must have found the steam-powered vessels daunting compared to the sailing vessels, but they were his responsibility nonetheless.

Stewart's connections with the Polk administration also became more apparent. He was the most senior naval officer and held a position of esteem within the elite of Philadelphia. With the commencement of hostilities, Gen. Winfield Scott was the senior-most general in the U.S. Army, directing operations in the field. For the Navy, only Stewart was his contemporary in status. "Because of Scott's rank Polk, for a while, considered sending the Navy's senior officer, Commodore Stewart, to assume temporary command of the naval forces for the landing."[15] Instead, a younger man, "brave, able, accomplished from handling a frigate in a storm to looking after the health of his men" was chosen; a man similar to a younger Stewart and one of the commodore's former junior officers on Pacific Station—Como. David Conner, the commander of the Home Squadron.[16]

During the war, the Navy demonstrated for the first time its ability to operate on two oceans and confirmed the value of sea power. Along the California coast operations progressed quickly. While Stewart wrestled with Bancroft's directive over officer selection, another one of his former midshipmen, Como. John D. Sloat, landed at Monterey and claimed California for the United States on 7 July 1846. Two days later, on 9 July, sailors and Marines landed from USS *Portsmouth*, and successfully occupied San Francisco. On 29 July sailors and Marines from the sloop-of-war USS *Cyane* captured San Diego, California. On 4 August sailors and Marines from the USS *Congress* captured Santa Barbara, California, while on the thirteenth Robert Stockton led an assault and captured Los Angeles. Although ground combat continued into the following year, California was, for all practical reasons, lost to Mexico.

On the Atlantic side of the war, the ships refitting in Philadelphia played major roles in blockade and amphibious operations along the Mexican Gulf Coast. At President Polk's direction, Maj. Gen. Winfield Scott's army moved by sea to land at Veracruz, Mexico, in 1847. On 6 March 1847 Commodore Conner met with General Scott and his staff, which consisted of Robert E. Lee, Joe Johnston, and George Meade. Conner recommended landing Scott's troops just south of Veracruz. The young commodore was responsible for selecting the landing sites, the method of transportation, and directing the landing itself. Another one of Stewart's former midshipmen, Cdr. Josiah Tattnall, commanded the flotilla of light-draft steamers and gunboats that provided direct support to the landing force. Under Scott, men such as Robert E. Lee honed their trade much as those senior officers who had served under Stewart had. On 9 March Commodore Conner lead the largest and most successful amphibious assault in U.S. naval history to date. From there, Scott marched inland on Mexico City, ultimately forcing an end to the war.

During the war, President Polk visited the Philadelphia Navy Yard. He reviewed the USS *Princeton*, which had just returned from operations in the Gulf of Mexico. Shortly after his visit, "work started on a floating dry dock and a contract arrived to build the powerful side-wheel steamer USS *Susquehanna*."[17] Stewart supervised the construction of the dry dock and most of this great ship's construction as well. He also oversaw the improvements in the yard's infrastructure until he was relieved in October 1849. Charles Stewart was seventy-one years old when he was relieved of command.

The next year saw the old sailor without orders. Stewart returned full time to his home Old Ironsides in Bordentown, New Jersey. However, between October 1849 and September 1850 many changes occurred in the Navy, ranging from technological improvements and scientific expeditions to a major reform of the manner that the Navy meted out punishment to its sailors. Stewart's influence on this cultural sea change with how the Navy functioned cannot be understated.

The completion of the USS *Susquehanna* and the improvements in the Philadelphia Navy Yard embodied the technological changes occurring in the Navy.

Completion of the Susquehanna in 1850 marked an institutional watershed of sorts for the Navy Yard. Over the next decade the facility adjusted to new technologies and larger, more complex steam and sail-powered warships. . . .

Water pipes, gaslights, and a telegraph system were added between 1850 and 1851, while the work force climbed to over 300 to rebuild wharves, timber shed, and craft shops. . . . The Navy Department installed new machine shops, while private contractor A.B. Cooley of Philadelphia used his patented steam dredging machine to cut a 38-foot channel in front of the ship houses and a basin for the new sectional dry dock.[18]

The cultural sea change that began in 1850 with the abolition of flogging as a method of punishment was part of a greater morass confronting the Navy. "Morale in the old navy was often poor, but the most pervasive crisis in leadership occurred during the 1850s, which began with the abolition of flogging, continued with a clumsy attempt to purge the officer corps and ended with the entire nation drifting toward disunion and civil war."[19] Two of Stewart's former junior officers, Uriah Levy and Robert Stockton, fought to abolish the lash. Their attitude toward flogging was probably influenced by Stewart's own record.

Stewart was one of the rare officers who came to naval service from years as a merchant sailor and captain. As such, his approach to discipline was influenced by his experience in merchant ships. Christopher McKee's analysis of the ship's logs of the pre-1815 Navy is telling for what it does not show. McKee admits that figures on the number of floggings are based on log entries that are certainly incomplete because flogging was considered so routine that it was not necessarily recorded. But, the list of officers who used the lash does not include Charles Stewart.[20] This does not mean that Stewart didn't use corporal punishment (though there is no clear evidence that he did), but McKee's analysis does show that Stewart did not appear to be a flagrant user of the lash during the period that he analyzed, that is, Stewart's formative years as a naval officer.

Levy and Stockton were friends and protégés of Stewart. Both men maintained a close correspondence with the old sailor, which continued until their deaths. As such, Stewart certainly was aware of Levy and Stockton's philosophy, because both men "were reformers and experimenters who gave much thought and effort to the task of trying to liberalize, rationalize, and humanize the naval justice system."[21] Levy was the first officer to publicly reject flogging as a method of disciplining sailors, an action that led to his court-martial and suspension from duty for five years. President Tyler overturned his sentence, and the movement continued to build in and out of the Navy.

A naval hero of the Mexican War, Robert Stockton resigned his commission in 1849 and successfully ran for the Senate. Senator Stockton helped "to mastermind the campaign to outlaw flogging and defeated repeated attempts to get the practice reinstated. It was Stockton who helped devise the summary court system and several other major naval administrative reforms that were adopted between 1850 and 1862."[22] Through the efforts of two of Stewart's protégés, President Millard Fillmore signed into law the abolition of flogging on 2 September 1850.

That same month, the seventy-two-year-old Stewart returned to active service. The Navy secretary selected Stewart to be the president of the Board of Rank from September 1850 to June 1853. On this assignment, Stewart was involved in placing officers within the fleet, to include deciding which officers would be retained or retired. Coincidentally, upon the election of President Franklin Pierce in 1852, the new Navy secretary, James Dobbin, commenced a reform movement that culminated in the establishment of a Naval Efficiency Board, a board designed to purge the officer ranks of those incapable of performing their duties afloat or ashore.

When Stewart's tenure as president of the Board of Rank concluded, he remained without orders for only two months. In August 1855 Secretary Dobbin ordered the seventy-five-year-old commodore to his third tour as the commandant of the Philadelphia Navy Yard.

Stewart's return to the yard found the facility prospering. The new generation of screw-propeller, steam-powered frigates and sloops, armed with John Dahlgren's heavy-shell guns, were now being built at the yard. The *Merrimack*-class frigates and the *Hartford*-class sloops were the backbone of the Union Navy at the beginning of the Civil War. However, shortly after his return, Stewart's tenure as commandant was interrupted by the reforms of Secretary Dobbin.

In 1853 Secretary Dobbin's first report to Congress emphasized the need to reform the Navy's officer personnel system. The upper ranks of the officer corps were now overstocked with old and incapacitated men, who restricted the flow of promotions. "In 1854, of the 68 captains, the youngest was 56 years of age; and of the 97 commanders, 74 were between 50 and 55 years; the lieutenants were between 30 and 50 years; and the 198 passed midshipmen, from 21 to 37 years."[23] Through the secretary's efforts and those of key members of Congress, an act passed on 28 February 1855 gave the Navy secretary the power to establish the Naval Efficiency Board, which would report to the secretary those officers "incapable of performing promptly and efficiently all their duties both ashore and afloat."[24] This act of Congress was the most important legislation affecting the officer structure of the Navy since the creation of the Naval Academy.

On 5 June 1855 Dobbin appointed fifteen naval officers, comprising five captains, five commanders, and five lieutenants, to the board. One of the captains was Stewart's nephew, Charles Stewart McCauley. After determining which officers could not perform duties afloat and ashore, the board was instructed to place the "incapable" officers into three classes. "Those officers who were incompetent by reason of their own fault were to be discharged from the Navy; certain other officers were to be retired on furlough pay; and still others on a leave-of-absence pay."[25] The board began its work on 20 June and completed its task one month later, finding that 201 officers were not fit for duty. Forty-nine officers were recommended for dismissal from the service; eighty-one were to be retired with pay, while seventy-one officers were to be retired on leave-of-absence pay. On 5 September 1855 President Pierce approved the findings of the board, and orders were immediately issued. At seventy-seven years old, and as the most senior officer, Charles Stewart was placed on the retired list.

In response to the secretary's letter informing him that he had been found unfit for continued service and placed on the retired list, Stewart wrote to a friend: "On receipt of the Secretary's letter my natural impulse was to resign my commission immediately, but to this course my friends would not assent, but advised any memorializing Congress on the subject."[26] The public reaction throughout the country to Stewart's and his fellow officers' dismissal or retirement was profound. The New Jersey State Legislature passed a resolution and sent it to the U.S. Congress asking that Stewart's name be placed back on the active list. When Congress reconvened in December 1855, it faced numerous petitions and testimonials from the affected officers and their supporters, who saw their new status as punishing judgment that discredited their professionalism. Almost half of the 201 officers affected submitted memorials to friendly senators—Stewart's memorial was one of the seventy-eight submitted. The memorials forced Congress to reconsider President Pierce's action, and thirteen months later, Congress amended the act, allowing officers to appeal to the Navy secretary.

Not only did Stewart appeal his own status, but also he personally supported his fellow officers in their appeals. Of particular note was his outspoken support of his friend and "fiery former lieutenant," Capt. Uriah Levy. On 14 November 1857 the seventy-nine-year-old Stewart traveled down from Philadelphia to testify at Levy's court of inquiry. After witnesses testified against Levy, Stewart testified on Levy's behalf. In full dress uniform, "the man who had captained 'Old Ironsides' in its great victories . . . took the stand wearing the gold-hilted sword presented him by the Pennsylvania legislature, and he proceeded to give his opinion of Uriah—and the Board of Fifteen—in terms allowing for no misunderstanding."[27] Sitting before the board the elderly Stewart was still an imposing figure.

Stewart began his testimony by stating that when Levy was under his command on board the USS *Franklin* in 1817, he had recommended Levy for a commission. Stewart continued by stating that while serving together on board the *Franklin* in the Mediterranean Sea, Stewart promoted him and transferred the young Uriah to the frigate *United States*. Stewart then spoke of how Captain Crane and some of the officers treated Levy while he was on board the frigate, and the commodore "left no doubt of his disgust at Crane's actions."[28] When the prosecutor stated that Stewart's comments were irrelevant and asked if the senior officer present thought that Captain Levy was competent at this time to serve on active duty, Stewart snapped back at the judge advocate, "I thought he was competent in 1818 and I think he is competent now. . . . I'd be glad to have him on any ship under my command."[29] The board recommended to President Buchanan that Levy and his former skipper should be reinstated to full duty, and in March 1858 the president authorized that Stewart, Levy, and other officers recommended by the board be returned to active duty.

The following year, just before Stewart's eighty-first birthday, Congress reinstated him to full duty. From his home in Bordentown, Stewart wrote a reply to the Navy secretary, dated 23 April 1859. The letter shows the character of the man, and it is quoted in its entirety:

> I had the honor to receive your communication of the 20th Inst. Accompanied by a Commission from the Presdt. Of the United States, authorized by a joint Resolution of the Congress of the U. States, on the 2d day of March 1859. Feeling and appreciating most sensibly this effort on the part of the late Congress as well as your good self and the President to repair and render innoxious [*sic*] as far as could be done, the Act of Congress approved February 28, 1855 as well as the action had under its authority, by the Board of Naval Officers, which that act had authorized. For this noble effort in behalf of those officers of your Navy, who had been so wantonly wronged, I beg to tender my most grateful thanks, and to assure you that could I do so with due regard to honor, the Commission should be accepted. It is gratifying to me to observe in the Resolution of the late Congress, the flattering compliment; the 'cognition of some meritorious & distinguished services' rendered to the Republic through a

period of fifty seven years, up to the time of the action of the Retiring Naval Board in 1855, by whose decision I was placed at the head of a Retired list of officers, thus degraded, in accordance with the Law, for inefficiency to perform the duties of a Captain in the Navy. The notification of this fact should have put a period to any future services in the Navy on my part, but the occasion seemed to call on me as the senior naval officer, not to abandon two hundred brother Officers who like myself had fallen under the ban of the Retiring [sic] board, but to do for them all I could through a memorial to the Congress, to relieve them from the distressed and degraded situation in which the Board had placed them. The 34th Congress passed an amendatory act for the relief of such as would voluntarily ask for it through a Court of Enquiry into all their antecedents for the Government and when prepared to hand them in to resign at the same time my employments in the Navy—This I contemplated doing last winter prior to the adjournment of Congress, but prostrated by a severe spell of sickness a great portion of the last session, I was obliged to postpone it until their next assembling, when I shall at the same time transmit to the Executive Government the Commission I hold as a Captain in the Navy. The present Commission you have sent to me, I shall have the honor to place in your hands on my first visit to Washington.[30]

That same year a special act of Congress was passed, which conferred upon Stewart the title of "senior flag officer" on the active list. However, Stewart refused to receive the commission, claiming that he already held that rank, and, in a follow-up letter to the Navy secretary regarding his commission as senior flag officer in the U.S. Navy, Charles Stewart wrote:

> I feel most sensibly their distinguished and marked kindness towards me by the President and your good self for its transmissions and I most sincerely beg leave to assure you and the President that not the slightest disrespect was intended toward yourselves in my declining its acceptance but as one whose whole life has been spent in honor and honorable service I could not reconcile to that innate sense to accept a new contract for the service after the original one of fifty seven years of meritorious services under it, had been so cavalierly and necessarily degraded by a special act of Congress and your predecessor in the department. I do trust and hope that your good selves will concur with me that it is not worthy of me to spend any few remaining years allotted me by a kind Providence in dishonor. I beg to assure you that I shall carry with me through the residue of life a most grateful sense of yours and the Presidents kind intentions in transmitting it unaccepted by your obliged and obedient servant.[31]

Later that year in September, the old commodore received orders to resume command of the Philadelphia Navy Yard. Just one month later, on 18 October 1859, U.S. Marines reached Harper's Ferry, Virginia, and successfully assaulted the arsenal that was seized by John Brown and his followers. The U.S. Constitution and the Union were on the verge of being torn asunder.

CHAPTER FOURTEEN

"*They Are Gone—*
All Gone . . ."

O n 20 December 1860 South Carolina seceded from the United States of America. Loyal federal troops and sailors responded by rallying to their respective bases and forts. Those officers and men possessing strong sympathies for their southern roots responded by returning to their home states.

U.S. Army Maj. Robert Anderson commanded the defenses of the city of Charleston, South Carolina. He ordered his troops to repair to Fort Sumter on the day after Christmas, abandoning the other coastal fortifications. Fort Sumter commanded the approaches to Charleston's port, and secessionist forces quickly isolated the fort from the mainland. Other commanders faced similar difficulties.

Stewart's nephew, Capt. Charles Stewart McCauley, was commandant of the Gosport Navy Yard in Portsmouth, Virginia. This yard was one of the main naval facilities of the Old Navy. The sixty-eight year old McCauley was responsible for volumes of naval stores and many valuable ships moored there in ordinary or as receiving ships. He faced an increasingly difficult situation, resulting from desertions, resignations, and an increasingly hostile civilian population that threatened to isolate the yard.

Although his command was not located in a secessionist leaning state, McCauley's uncle, the commandant of the Philadelphia Navy Yard, experienced the same loyalty issues among his sailors and Marines. The situation facing Stewart, his command, and the city of Philadelphia was a microcosm of what the country at-large faced. "Quasi-military clubs known as Wide Awakes, who supported Republican presidential candidate Abraham Lincoln and a protective tariff to aid local labor and industry, battled violent Democratic [Philadelphia] city gangs called Minute Men, who sympathized with the Southern agrarian slave-holding states and regarded Lincoln and the Republicans as threats to states' rights."[1] With Abraham Lincoln's election in November 1860, events began to rapidly unfold.

Inside the walls of the Philadelphia Navy Yard and other Navy facilities, officers loyal to their southern roots resigned their commissions and returned to their home states in hope of obtaining a commission in what would become the Confederate States Navy. Those officers with southern sympathies on foreign stations prepared to do the same at the first opportunity. Some of Stewart's former midshipmen, such as Buchanan and Tattnall, resigned their commissions and headed south. In fact, fifteen captains, thirty-five commanders, ninety-nine lieutenants, six masters, and eighty-five midshipmen resigned their commissions.[2] At the same time, the senior officer in the U.S. Navy saw most of the other former midshipmen remain loyal to their commission to "uphold and defend the Constitution." Officers such as Du Pont, Goldsborough, Porter, and Farragut rose to prominence within the Union Navy.

Charles Stewart turned eighty-two years old in July 1860. Although his spirit was full of fervor for the cause of the Union (he told one listener "I am as young as ever to fight for my country"), Stewart was no longer physically able to take up the cause against succession.[3] On 31 December 1860 he submitted a request to be relieved of his command of the Philadelphia Navy Yard.

One reason for his decision to resign may be found in the opinion of Stewart's relief, Capt. Samuel Francis Du Pont: "I presume he thought himself too old to be ordering out Marines to put down bread riots or to keep Wide-Awakes and Minute Men apart."[4] However, Du Pont does not seem to take into account Stewart's knowledge of the law or his determination to uphold it. Stewart understood fully that his sailors and Marines had no authority outside of the yard's walls. Unless otherwise directed by President Buchanan to support the governor of Pennsylvania's request for federal troops, Stewart knew his jurisdiction rested only within the yard's walls.

During previous years the Philadelphia Navy Yard had been threatened by segments of the city's population. For reasons ranging from lack of employment opportunities within the yard to food or race riots that threatened to

In his fervent support for maintaining the Union, the eighty-two-year-old Stewart proclaimed in 1860: "I am as young as ever to fight for my country." (Washington Lafayette Germon; courtesy of the National Portrait Gallery)

spill onto the grounds of the yard, sailors and Marines had been ordered to prepare to "repel boarders." Stewart would have responded with such a command if he had seen the yard directly endangered in such a manner. More likely, Stewart realized that the months and years to follow would require younger officers. Old age and his overall health had finally caught up with him.

On 9 January 1861, less than two weeks after Stewart asked to be relieved, South Carolinian forces fired on a steamship trying to resupply Fort Sumter. Shortly thereafter, the Pensacola Navy Yard in Florida was abandoned, and its commander ordered his sailors and Marines to occupy Fort Pickens. As with Fort Sumter, Fort Pickens controlled the approaches into Pensacola and its Navy yard. Secessionists had isolated this fort, and its only hope was relief from the sea. By the end of the month, six more states seceded from the Union. In February the Confederate States of America was formed.

Abraham Lincoln's inaugural address on 3 March 1861 left no doubt as to his intentions. Lincoln declared that he would fulfill his duties as chief executive and enforce federal law in all of the states, declaring that he would "hold, occupy and possess the property and places" belonging to the federal government of the United States. He further stated that "there needs to be no bloodshed or violence; and there shall be none, unless it be forced upon the national authority."[5] With lines drawn, Lincoln now needed to find the right men in his cabinet to support his stance.

Fortunately for the Union and the Navy, the president quickly filled the position of navy secretary with Gideon Welles, whom he gave tremendous administrative leeway.[6] Welles was no stranger to the Navy or to Stewart, because he had been appointed by President Polk to be the chief of the Navy's provisions and clothing in 1846, a capacity in which he served until April 1849. "His bureau tenure gave him more direct experience with navy issues, procedures, and personalities than his predecessors."[7] Secretary Welles quickly took the reins. Not only did he commence major administrative changes, but also he threw himself into determining a comprehensive naval strategy and overseeing the operations of the fleet. Welles looked to his most senior naval commanders for their professional opinions.

The most pressing issue was relieving the isolated federal forts and naval establishments, especially Forts Sumter and Pickens. Upon the relief of Fort Sumter, President Lincoln and Secretary Welles asked Stewart for his advice on how best to succor the besieged fort and its garrison of federal troops. Lincoln and Welles probably also asked Stewart to offer his opinion about Fort Pickens and the Pensacola Navy Yard, because Stewart was very familiar with that yard, having previously assessed the yard's capabilities. He possessed considerable experience, especially as it concerned logistical support and the role of the fleet in enforcing a tight blockade. The blockade of the Confederacy was the first blockade of its kind attempted by the U.S. Navy (Union Navy) since Preble's blockade of Tripoli, in which Stewart was second in command. Additionally, as the senior flag officer, Stewart would have been consulted, because his contemporary, the most senior officer in the army as well as in age, Gen. Winfield Scott, was actively participating in the initial operations of the Union Army.

Secretary Welles acted quickly to improve the Union Navy's situation at the besieged naval facilities located in the southern states. Unfortunately, circumstances and indecisiveness, bordering on incompetence, hindered his efforts. On 31 March 1861 Welles ordered Captain McCauley to transfer seamen to Gosport to reinforce the Navy yard there and speed up the return to service of the several ships that were laying in ordinary. McCauley did not immediately accomplish this task. Welles then directed McCauley to take action to return the steam frigate USS *Merrimack* and the sailing sloop-of-war USS *Plymouth* to service. With the surrender of Fort Sumter, the Gosport Navy Yard was now besieged, and Welles ordered that the facility be destroyed. "Welles orders were direct, but he was dealing with an aged, veteran officer. . . . As Commandant of Gosport, the 68-year old officer proved indecisive in the first days of the Civil War."[8] McCauley mishandled the yard's destruction, leaving the dry dock and its pumping equipment intact; these actions contributed to a coming revolution in naval warfare. The Confederates took the almost totally destroyed steam frigate USS *Merrimack* into the dry dock and converted her into the steam ironclad, CSS *Virginia*.[9]

Also burned was the ship-of-the-line USS *Pennsylvania*, which Stewart had supervised in construction and later commanded in her only voyage from Philadelphia to Norfolk twenty years before. The frigate *United States*, the first Navy ship on which Stewart had served, was captured in the harbor by the Confederates and broken up when the Union retook Norfolk.

Welles continued to face critical administrative issues that he could not ignore and that had to be solved quickly. One was preparing the fleet for war. Of the ninety warships in the Union Navy, less than half were in commission. Many of the remainder were away on foreign station and most were obsolete. Welles needed to expand the fleet's numbers immediately. In addition to expanding the number of warships, Welles had to expand the fleet's infrastructure, to include providing logistical support to the blockade force that would be strung along the entire southern coast, ranging from Virginia down along the Gulf of Mexico's western shoreline, to include Texas and portions of the Mexican coast. Finally, Welles had to have a number of "competent," vigorous officers and sailors to run this expanded naval force. This final measure led to Charles Stewart's retirement.

The Lincoln administration and Congress moved quickly to act on Gideon Welles's recommendations for restructuring the Union Navy and its officer corps. As expected, Stewart and other older officers were deemed unable to carry out their duties and were placed on the retired list by an act of Congress, dated 24 July 1861. Therefore, Charles Stewart's active service of sixty-three years came to an end only two days before his eighty-third birthday.

However, this same act of Congress established flag ranks in the Union Navy and the rank of rear admiral and commodore were formalized.

On Welles's recommendation to Lincoln, and of the latter to Congress, votes of thanks had been rendered to Flag Officers Louis M. Goldsborough, Samuel

F. Du Pont, David Glasgow Farragut, and Andrew H. Foote. Accordingly, they were nominated as active-list rear admirals. Captains Charles Stewart, George C. Read, William B. Shubrick, Joseph Smith, George W. Storer, Francis H. Gregory, Elie A. F. Lavalette, Silas H. Stringham, and Hiram Paulding were sent for confirmation as rear admirals on the retired list.[10]

For those officers named from the retired list, this was a one-time selection that recognized the service they performed for their country and Navy. Stewart was the only surviving captain from the War of 1812 and was selected for promotion to rear admiral. It was unfortunate that Capt. Uriah Levy missed the selection, as he had died earlier in 1862. As a provision in his will, Stewart's fiery lieutenant left his old captain and friend a funeral ring as a keepsake of their comradeship.

On 16 July 1862, twelve days before Charles Stewart's eighty-fourth birthday, his former midshipman David Glasgow Farragut was promoted to rear admiral on the active list, while his old mentor, Charles Stewart, was promoted to rear admiral on the retired list. However, the senate did not confirm the retirement list until the following session.

In the meantime, as the war remorselessly churned through its first bloody year, Charles Stewart's pen was very active. He constantly wrote to friends and politicians expressing his uncompromising loyalty to the Union. In a letter dated 4 May 1861 and addressed to a friend, George W. Childs of Philadelphia, Charles Stewart wrote that southern leaders had long thought of dissolving the Union. Stewart detailed a conversation that he had with John C. Calhoun fifty years before, in 1812, the same time that he was in Washington, fitting out the USS *Constellation* and lobbying President Madison to send the fleet to sea. To Childs, Stewart quoted Calhoun's conversation: "It is through our affiliation with that party in the middle and western states, we control, under our Constitution, the government of the United States. But when we cease thus to control this nation, through a disjointed Democracy, or any material obstacle in that party which shall tend to throw us out of that rule, we shall then resort to a dissolution of the Union."[11] Childs was the editor of the newspaper, *The Ledger*, and Stewart's reflections were printed and carried widely across the North by other publications.

From his home in Bordentown, New Jersey, Stewart kept up with the war news. Additionally, his home, Old Ironsides, sat on a hill above the main rail line between Philadelphia and New York, and Stewart often watched as the

David Porter was Stewart's first officer on *Experiment* and a lifelong friend. His son, David Dixon Porter, was a midshipman under Stewart. (Portrait in oils, possibly by John Trumbull; courtesy of the Naval Historical Center)

troop trains sent regiment upon regiment to the war front. Charles Stewart was aware of the human wreckage returning on that same railway, and he offered the government twenty acres of his land and one of his houses for a hospital.[12]

Despite his advanced age, Charles Stewart was still able to get about from time to time. In 1862, Commodore Stewart was asked to christen the Philadelphia-built ironclad steam frigate, the USS *New Ironsides*, upon its launching, becoming the penultimate male sponsor of a U.S. man-of-war.

In November 1863, while he was back at his home two New York journalists interviewed Charles Stewart. Both men were returning from the newly consecrated cemetery for Union dead at Gettysburg. They were very surprised to know that the old commodore was still involved in affairs of state. Stewart offered his opinion as to current naval and military operations, to include the aftermath of the *Trent* Affair, in which his former midshipman, Capt. Charles Wilkes, seized two Confederate diplomats from the neutral British steamer *Trent*. Britain had threatened war over Wilkes's action, but diplomacy prevailed.

Early in 1865 America's most dreadful war came to an end. Stewart, who had witnessed the birth of the country, lived to see both the Union and the Constitution survive. He also saw the tremendous growth of the Navy that he served for so long and so well. At war's end the Union Navy had over 58,000 men in service and a force of over six hundred ships, and Stewart witnessed the revolution in naval operations that the arrival of the steam-powered ironclads brought about as the result of the battle between the USS *Monitor* and the CSS *Virginia*. In August 1865 the Naval Academy returned to Annapolis, having been moved to Newport, Rhode Island, in 1861.

Edward Yorke McCauley, Stewart's grandnephew by Charles Stewart McCauley, who had accompanied Perry on his second voyage to Japan, served honorably throughout the war and lived up to his great-uncle's early exploits by successfully engaging and capturing numerous ships attempting to run the blockade of the South. And, like his great-uncle, McCauley was eventually promoted to the rank of rear admiral.

Stewart's officers whom he had trained as midshipmen and lieutenants decades before had risen to prominence in both navies. The *Franklin* had served as the incubator for most of the Civil War admirals and senior officers. R. Adm. Franklin Buchanan served as commander of the Confederate Navy. V. Adm. David Farragut was his counterpart in the Union Navy. V. Adm. David Dixon Porter commanded the Mississippi River Blockading Squadron. R. Adm. Louis Goldsborough commanded the North Atlantic Blockading Squadron while R. Adm. Samuel Du Pont commanded the South Atlantic Blockading Squadron. Even Joshua Sands, whose stubbornness and propensity for fighting kept him confined for six months on Pacific Station, rose to rear admiral commanding the Brazil Squadron.

Stewart's children sought different paths. His son pursued business interests in France. A trained civil engineer who helped plan the Reading Railroad, Charles Tudor Stewart also had other interests such as naval lumber. Pursuing this interest, he negotiated contracts through Prince Murat, an old friend whom the family had known in their early Bordentown days, with his cousin, the Emperor Napoleon III. Commodore Stewart himself continued to maintain a correspondence with Louis Napoleon, whom he had "reason to think more favourable . . . both as a man and a ruler than some do." In reply to one autograph seeker, Stewart wrote: "The attachment and intimacy we formed more than twenty years ago in the days of his exile and friendlessness were never forgotten and one still maintained by a not infrequent . . . exchange of letters. Since he has become Emperor, I only have two of six now in my possession.[13]

Charles Tudor Stewart negotiated similar contracts with the British government through his nephew, Charles Stewart Parnell. Stewart later studied

As a young man, Franklin Buchanan was one of Stewart's midshipmen. He later became the commander the Confederate Navy. (Rembrandt Peale; courtesy of the Naval Historical Center)

law in New Orleans. He died in Paris in 1874 and left the Bordentown estate to his sister Delia.

Edward, Stewart's son by his mistress, lived most of his life at one of the cottages on the grounds of Old Ironsides, but did not fully benefit from being the son of one of America's greatest officers. Edward made his way as a steamfitter, eventually moving away from Bordentown and establishing a business in Newark. He had five children: a baby who died and was buried with the commodore; May S. Stewart, who died at age sixteen in 1888 at Ironsides; Elizabeth B. Tudor Stewart; Frances Stewart Cocke; and Charles Stewart. His youngest was named after Edward's father and his half-brother, with whom he was close. Commodore Stewart had been dead for twenty years before another Charles Stewart was born. Since the commodore died intestate, his estate went primarily to his legitimate son, Charles, but some agreement within the family appears to have been made to allow Edward and his family to remain at Ironsides. Still, no mention of Edward was made when his half-cousin, Fanny Parnell, died at the estate. Of the family members and friends attending the funeral mentioned in the local newspaper, there was no account of Edward. Subsequent local histories likewise largely failed to mention Edward, Julia, or Charlotte.

After the death of her husband, John Parnell, Delia found herself in a similar position to that of her mother and grandmother. She "would think nothing of dispossessing herself of all her most prized possessions in order to find ready cash for whatever new project she had in mind."[14] Delia eventually returned to Bordentown, where she died in 1892. Despite the estates of both her father and brother, Delia died in poverty.

Charles Stewart increasingly struggled with the advancement of old age during his last few years. He was gradually fading, but he refused to sit still. According to family members and friends he remained "cheerful, and hopeful, busied with affairs, dictating letters, cracking jokes, expecting soon to be well again."[15] By 1869 Stewart was confined to bed and he had difficulty speaking due to cancer of the tongue. He tried to write his needs and thoughts, but after a time, even this became too difficult. The old commodore lingered on for many weeks, unable to speak or write, before his death.[16] Stewart, a shrewd businessman and one who followed the letter of the law throughout his life, died intestate.

On 6 November 1869 R. Adm. Charles Stewart, U.S. Navy, died at his home, Old Ironsides. The family, the city of Philadelphia, and the Navy Department made arrangements for his funeral and internment. The Navy dispatched a small steamer up the Delaware River from the Philadelphia Navy

COMMODORE STEWART'S SON DIES IN NEWARK

Uncle of Charles Stewart Parnell
Had Been a Resident of This
City for Ten Years.

Edward Livingston Stewart died at his home, 76 Elizabeth avenue, on Saturday night in his sixty-seventh year. He had been ailing for nearly eight years, but it was only during the past week that his condition became serious. The death, which was not unexpected, was caused by heart trouble.

Mr. Stewart was born in Philadelphia on August 10, 1836, was a son of Commo-

While Charles Stewart had one son with his wife Delia, he later had another with his companion, Margaret Smith. Edward Livingston Smith later assumed the surname of his famous father. (From the *Newark Evening News*, 1903)

Yard to bring Stewart's body back to Philadelphia. On its return from Bordentown, the steamer carrying his body, family, and dignitaries inadvertently grounded on one of the many shifting bars in the river. Stewart's coffin was taken off the vessel and transferred to a train that carried it to the city. At the station, the coffin was met by a naval escort and under a moonless night sky

Stewart's daughter Delia married John Parnell of Ireland. Among their children was Charles Stewart Parnell, the advocate of Irish freedom. (Courtesy of the Avondale House, Wicklow, Ireland)

the procession carried Charles Stewart's body to Independence Hall to lay in state. While Independence Hall's bell solemnly tolled its notes, thousands of Philadelphia's citizens paid their respects. This continued through the night and into the next day, when amidst the boom of cannon, the muffled notes of the church bells, and the funeral music from several military bands, Stewart's funeral began.

His funeral was the largest Philadelphia had seen to date and the second largest one for the nation, surpassed only by Lincoln's funeral. Thousands of Civil War veterans escorted his coffin to the cemetery. The admirals and generals that led them to the victory that preserved the Union and the Constitution accompanied them. Stewart was laid to rest nearby in the part of Philadelphia he knew as a boy and from whose port he sailed toward his dreams and sixty-two years of service to his country. A monument was placed over his grave the following year, and its inscription reflected the man it memorialized: Charles Stewart, U.S.N.

Stewart had outlasted most of his ships with the exception of the *Constitution* and the *Independence*. He outlived all of his junior officers from the *Franklin* with the exception of Farragut, Goldsborough, Wilkes, and Sands. His death was the occasion of one of Edmund Clarence Stedman's poems, entitled "The Old Admiral":

256

He was the one
Whom Death had spared alone
Of all the captains of that lusty age,
Who sought the foemen where he lay,
On sea or sheltering bay,
Nor till the prize was theirs repressed their rage.
They are gone—all gone:
The rest with glory and the undying Powers;
Only their name and fame and what they saved are ours!

EPILOGUE

In January 1869, just a short four years after the end of the American Civil War, three writers made their way to the Old Ironsides estate in Bordentown, New Jersey. It was months before R. Adm. Charles Stewart's death, but he had already been diagnosed with tongue cancer. His condition was terminal and word had been spreading quickly that he would not last long. The writers came in the hope of obtaining enough personal information to compose the old commodore's biography. They considered his biography a literary prize, because all of Stewart's contemporaries—Decatur, Bainbridge, Somers, and Hull—had their biographies. Of those who contributed to the early successes of the U.S. Navy, only Stewart's life remained to be caught on paper. A brief sketch had been written about him in 1838 by friends who wanted him to become president of the United States. But this sketch was not a sufficient testimony for those who came to visit Old Ironsides during that cold January day; something more needed to be written.

The writers found the octogenarian in poor health, because the cancer increasingly affected his ability to speak. However, his mind remained sharp, and he communicated with his guests mostly through pencil on paper. The old sailor declined to have his life story written and in the end the biographers left disappointed. As consolation, Stewart provided them with a few recollections to be published in the local newspaper after his death. It was the last act of public humility from a man who had declined a presidential cabinet post and the full pursuit of the presidency of the United States itself. After all, he was a sailor first, and, more importantly, Stewart was an officer in the U.S. naval service.

During the Quasi-War, Stewart commanded his first warship at twenty-one, and, with his ship, the schooner *Experiment*, Stewart's own experiment as an officer in the U.S. Navy showed promise. At age twenty-four, he commanded a brig-of-war and at the same time became Commodore Preble's deputy squadron commander against the Tripoli pirates. At age twenty-eight, his solid, staunch service brought Stewart to the then-highest rank in the U.S. Navy. He commanded almost every class of sailing warship the Navy possessed, from sloop to schooner to frigate to ship-of-the-line. Stewart held more sea commands (eleven) than any other U.S. Navy captain before or since, and he served longer (sixty-three years) than nearly anyone else in U.S. naval history. In his hometown of Philadelphia, and at the founding of the American Republic, the young Charles Stewart found himself at the knees of Gen. George Washington. Only a few years later President Thomas Jefferson recognized the young Stewart for his Mediterranean exploits. Stewart went on to advise President James Madison at the outset of the War of 1812. He advised Congress on issues such as the utility of Marines on U.S. warships, the numbers and classes of warships the U.S. Navy should build, and the appropriate number and ranks of officers. He personally trained most of the future senior naval officers in three of America's wars— the War of 1812, the Mexican War, and the American Civil War.

Stewart and two men that he led and trained, Commodores Levy and Stockton, spearheaded the fight to eradicate flogging as a means of disciplining the crew on Navy ships. He also promoted the equality of officers, including America's first Jewish naval officer, Como. Uriah Levy, regardless of backgrounds. Stewart judged a fellow officer on his ability rather than on his background and heritage. He supervised the construction of warships from gunboats to ships-of-the-line and not only oversaw the technological changes that the Navy experienced but made recommendations to improve weapons, ship designs, and the Navy's dockyards.

Stewart's recommendations were the products of a sound naval operational and tactical mind. Some historians have wondered how Stewart and his contemporaries fared so well, because there was no formal school for them in which to learn their profession. Perhaps the basis for their successes can be found in their backgrounds, their maritime experiences, as well as their own insatiable quest for professional improvement. That quest included personal interactions with Royal Navy counterparts and avid reading of current naval publications. First and foremost, Charles Stewart was a craftsman. He understood how a sailing ship worked in the varying conditions of the sea, from the faintest zephyrs to a raging gale. Stewart knew the interactions of water, wind, wood, canvas, and rigging. But, for all his formidable technical prowess, skill that witnessed the pinnacle of sail upon the world's oceans, Stewart first and foremost knew how to command men at sea.

The foresight that made Stewart the consummate naval commander, sailor, and warrior did not carry over into his personal life. This was especially the case with his marriage. Desperate for marriage, he selected poorly, and his career and reputation suffered as a result of his wife Delia's actions and temperament. His marriage was a disaster, and the subsequent divorce raised many an eyebrow among the elite of nineteenth-century American society. Stewart's subsequent decision to take up house with another woman, to whom he was not married, only added to the opinion of many a contemporary that "in the matter of women he had been particularly loose." However, this personal decision was apparently a good one.

Despite the turmoil with this part of his life, Stewart's character came to the fore. He proved to be a caring father for the two children he had with his wife, as well as for the three he fathered with his mistress. Stewart could have readily dismissed the three younger children and their subsequent families, but he didn't.

Although he was not a trained legal mind, Stewart wrote a significant letter on laws of blockades and the role of neutrals during time of war, which Chief Justice John Marshall considered a standard to be followed. Through his many years of naval service, Stewart served on some of the most significant and controversial courts-martial and courts of inquiry in U.S. naval history. Stewart's decisions were based on his uncompromising belief that good order and discipline were paramount for a well-functioning navy.

Stewart did not pursue personal glory. He was, instead, a skilled sailor, a successful merchant, but a mediocre farmer. Stewart firmly believed he could best contribute to the success of the United States and its Constitution by providing for its defense and its commerce at sea. His actions under fire personified courage, his refusal to use his position to further his later commercial enterprises showed integrity, his understanding and support of the U.S. Constitution demonstrated a devotion to the republic and its democratic ideals with which he matured. Stewart was a diplomat and an unflappable warrior, a prosperous merchant and a dedicated father. His life exemplified the principles of sailors in today's U.S. Navy: duty, honor, and commitment. Charles Stewart was a sailor first, last, and always.

In the end, his life was summed up best by the epitaph on the headstone of his grave, which is remarkably absent of the exploits that his contemporaries instructed to have placed on their headstones. In the same Philadelphia cemetery where Stewart rests, the graves of his contemporaries are adorned with their respective naval accomplishments. Instead, Stewart's headstone simply reads, "Charles Stewart, U.S.N."

NOTES

Chapter 1

1. Jeffrey M. Dorwart, *The Philadelphia Navy Yard*, with Jean K. Wolf (Philadelphia: Univ. of Pennsylvania Press, 2001), 14.

2. Charles Lyon Chandler and others, eds., "Early Shipbuilding in Pennsylvania, 1683–1837," in *Philadelphia, Port of History, 1609–1837* (Philadelphia: Philadelphia Maritime Museum, 1976), 10 and 23.

3. Alexander Slidell MacKenzie, *Life of Stephen Decatur: A Commodore in the Navy of the United States* (Boston: Little and Brown, 1846.)

4. Edna Miriam Hoopes, *Richard Somers: Master Commandant of the United States Navy* (Atlantic City, N.J., 1933).

5. H. D. Smith, "Rear-Admiral Charles Stewart, United States Navy," in *The United Service*, vol. 1 (Philadelphia: L. R. Hamersly, 1889), 264.

6. MacKenzie, *Stephen Decatur*. See also Charles Lee Lewis, *The Romantic Decatur* (Philadelphia: Univ. of Pennsylvania Press, 1937).

7. Edgar P. Richardson, *Philadelphia, 1800–1824* (n.p., n.d.), Library of Congress.

8. Thomas F. Doerflinger, *A Vigorous Spirit of Enterprise: Merchants and Economic Development in Revolutionary Philadelphia* (Chapel Hill: Univ. of North Carolina Press, 1986), 77.

9. Marion V. Brewington, *Maritime Philadelphia, 1609–1837* (n.p., n.d.), Library of Congress.

10. K. Jack Bauer, "The Golden Age," in *America's Maritime Legacy: A History of U.S. Merchant Marine and Shipbuilding Industry Since Colonial Times*, ed. Robert A. Kilmarx (Boulder, Colo.: Westview Press, 1979), 27.

11. File 226 78.58 Ship *Canton* from 3 May 1791, Independence Seaport Museum, Philadelphia.

12. Richard Henry Dana Jr., *Two Years before the Mast: A Personal Narrative* (New York: Signet Classics, 2000), 12.

13. E. M. Woodward, "Bordentown and Its Environs," unpublished manuscript, Bordentown Library Association, 1967.

14. Woodward, "Bordentown."

Chapter 2

1. Christopher McKee, *A Gentlemanly and Honorable Profession: The Creation of the U.S. Naval Officer Corps, 1794–1815* (Annapolis, Md.: U.S. Naval Institute Press, 1991), 3.

2. McKee, *Gentlemanly and Honorable Profession*, xi.

3. *Captain Barry of the United States* (n.p., n.d.), 23.

4. Charles Lee Lewis, *The Romantic Decatur* (Philadelphia: Univ. of Pennsylvania Press, 1937).

5. Naval Historical Center, www.history.navy.mil (accessed January 2002).

6. Anthony Irvin, *Decatur* (New York: Charles Scriber's Sons, 1931), 63.

7. Charles also received a tidy sum of $221.71 in prize money (Statement of Prize Money from Prize Agents Keen & Stillwell to the Officers, Crew, and Marines of the USS *United States*, 14 October 1799) when he captured three merchant ships and recaptured three American merchant ships. The Barry-Hayes Papers, series I, John Barry Papers, box 1, JB51, Philadelphia Maritime Museum.

8. Howard I. Chapelle, *The History of the American Sailing Ships* (New York: W. W. Norton, 1935), 94.

9. "In this arduous and protracted engagement the *Experiment* was fought with spirit, and handled with skill." James Fenimore Cooper, *The History of the Navy of the United States of America* (Annapolis, Md.: U.S. Naval Institute Press, 2001), 144–45.

10. Donald L. Canney, *Sailing Warships of the U.S. Navy* (London: Chatham Publishing, 2001), 169.

11. David Long, *Nothing Too Daring: A Biography of Commodore David Porter, 1780–1843* (Annapolis, Md.: U.S. Naval Institute, 1970), 14.

12. Gardner W. Allen, *Our Naval War with France* (Boston: Houghton Mifflin, 1909), 183.

13. See Naval Historical Center, www.history.navy.mil. The Web site provides an excellent historical overview of the Quasi-War and the operations of the U.S. Navy.

14. Smith, "Rear-Admiral Charles Stewart," 264.

15. National Archives and Records Administration, Naval Records Collection of the Office of Naval Records and Library, Naval Documents Related to the Quasi-War between the United States and France, Naval Operations, June 1800–November 1800, RG 45.

16. David D. Porter, *Memoir of Commodore David Porter of the United States Navy* (Albany, N.Y.: J. Munsell, 1875), 35–36.

17. Porter, *Memoir*, 36.

18. Porter, *Memoir*, 36.

19. James Grant Wilson and John Fiske, *Appleton's Encyclopedia of American Biography*, vol 5 (New York: D. Appleton, 1888).

20. NARA, Naval Documents Related to the Quasi-War, December 1800–December 1801, 100.

21. Glenn Tucker, *Dawn Like Thunder: The Barbary Wars and the Birth of the U.S. Navy* (New York: Bobbs-Merrill, 1963), 131.

22. NARA, Naval Documents Related to the Quasi-War, June 1800–November 1800, John Barry to Benjamin Stoddert, letter, 198.

23. President Jefferson sent a letter to the bashaw of Tripoli with the squadron stating the United States was sending the squadron to attend to the safety of American commerce through naval strength, not tribute.

24. Tucker, *Dawn Like Thunder*, 130.

25. Joseph J. Ellis, *American Sphinx: The Character of Thomas Jefferson* (New York: Vintage Books, 1995), 89.

26. Ellis, *American Sphinx*, 89.

27. Ellis, *American Sphinx*, 89.

28. Ellis, *American Sphinx*, 90.

29. Cooper, *History of the Navy*, 155.

30. McKee, *Gentlemanly and Honorable Profession*, 215.

31. Lord Keith was the commander of the British Mediterranean Fleet. In 1801 Keith and Gen. Sir Ralph Abercromby conducted the first successful amphibious expedition of the war against Napoleon when they defeated the remnants of the French Army that Napoleon had abandoned in Egypt. One cannot discount the possibility that Charles Stewart was informed about this operation and as such he would have been exposed to British operational and tactical thought—useful information for someone about to be sent against the Barbary Pirates.

32. McKee, *Gentlemanly and Honorable Profession*, 157.

33. Tucker, *Dawn Like Thunder*, 157. The *Chesapeake* mainmast was badly sprained during the crossing.

34. Tucker, *Dawn Like Thunder*, 158–59.

35. Cooper, *History of the Navy*, 158

36. An excellent model of the USS *Syren* is on display at the U.S. Naval Academy's ship model building center.

37. Canney, *Sailing Warships*, 172.

38. Chapelle, *History of American Sailing*, 128.

39. NARA, Naval Records Collection of the Office of Naval Records and Library, Records of Citizens of the United States, 1775–1908, Logs, Journals, and Diaries of Officers of the U.S. Navy at Sea, March 1777–June 1908, vol. 28, PC30, entry 392, Journal kept by Midshipman F. Cornelius DeKraft on board the U.S. Brigs *Siren* and *Scourge*, 6 August 1803–13 February 1805, RG 45.

40. Canney, *Sailing Warships*, 173.

41. Canney, *Sailing Warships*, 173

Chapter 3

1. Tucker, *Dawn Like Thunder*, 191.

2. Tucker, *Dawn Like Thunder*, 249.

3. Fletcher Pratt, *Preble's Boys: Commodore Preble and the Birth of American Sea Power* (New York: Sloane, 1950), 317.

4. NARA, DeKraft journal, 6 August 1803–13 February 1805.

5. NARA, DeKraft journal, 6 August 1803–13 February 1805.

6. Tucker, *Dawn Like Thunder*, 202.

7. Tucker, *Dawn Like Thunder*, 250.

8. NARA, DeKraft journal, 6 August 1803–13 February 1805.

9. Tucker, *Dawn Like Thunder*, 253.

10. James Fenimore Cooper, *The History of the Navy of the United States of America* (Annapolis, Md.: U.S. Naval Institute Press, 2001), 175.

11. Cooper, *History of the Navy*, 175.

12. Cooper, *History of the Navy*, 269.

13. NARA, DeKraft journal, 6 August 1803–13 February 1805.

14. Cooper, *History of the Navy*, 177.

15. Cooper, *History of the Navy*, 183.

16. Cooper, *History of the Navy*, 184

17. NARA, DeKraft journal, 6 August 1803–13 February 1805.

18. Tucker, *Dawn Like Thunder*, 279.

19. Tucker, *Dawn Like Thunder*, 281.
20. Tucker, *Dawn Like Thunder*, 281.
21. Tucker, *Dawn Like Thunder*, 286.
22. NARA, DeKraft journal, 6 August 1803–13 February 1805.
23. William Fowler, *Jack Tars and Commodores: The American Navy 1783–1815* (Boston: Houghton Mifflin, 1984), 110.
24. NARA, DeKraft journal, 6 August 1803–13 February 1805.
25. Tucker, *Dawn Like Thunder*, 310.
26. Edward Callahan, ed. *List of Officers of the United States Navy and the Marine Corps, 1775–1900* (New York: L. R. Hamersly, 1901), 43.
27. Tucker, *Dawn Like Thunder*, 321.
28. Cooper was the first one to reference Preble's thoughts about using such a weapon. Subsequent historians, beginning with Tucker, picked this up too.
29. Edna Miriam Hoopes, *Richard Somers: Master Commandant of the United States Navy* (Atlantic City, N.J., 1933), 8–9.
30. Cooper, *History of the Navy*, 207–208.
31. Tucker, *Dawn Like Thunder*, 327.
32. NARA, DeKraft journal, 6 August 1803–13 February 1805.
33. Tucker, *Dawn Like Thunder*, 339.
34. Tucker, *Dawn Like Thunder*, 341.
35. The Papers of the Rodgers Family, Library of Congress.
36. Eliza Cope Harrison, ed., *Philadelphia Merchant: The Diary of Thomas P. Cope, 1800–1851* (South Bend, Ind.: Gateway Editions, 1978).
37. Woodward, "Bordentown," 927–28 (see ch. 1, n. 13).
38. Tucker, *Dawn Like Thunder*, 441.
39. Cooper, *History of the Navy*, 232–33.
40. Charles Oscar Paullin, "Building the Navy, 1801–14," in *Paullin's History of Naval Administration, 1775–1911: A Collection of Articles from the U.S. Naval Institute Proceedings* (Annapolis, Md.: U.S. Naval Institute, 1968).
41. Fowler, *Jack Tars*, 183.
42. One could argue that the construction of the gunboats was one of the first major "pork barrel" acts by the federal government on behalf of the navy and those maritime states of the Union.
43. Canney, *Sailing Warships*, 196.
44. Spencer C. Tucker, *The Jeffersonian Gunboat Navy* (Columbia: Univ. of South Carolina Press, 1993), 57.
45. Gene A. Smith, *For the Purposes of Defense: The Politics of the Jeffersonian Gunboat Program,* (Newark: Univ. of Delaware Press, 1995), 85.
46. Tucker, *Jeffersonian Gunboat Navy*, 57.
47. Tucker, *Jeffersonian Gunboat Navy*, 57.
48. Smith, *For the Purposes of Defense*, 85.
49. Tucker, *Jeffersonian Gunboat Navy*, 57.
50. Cooper, *History of the Navy*, 231.

Chapter 4

1. Hull and Stewart were in at least one joint venture in French merchandise including cognac, wine, and whole pipe. Charles Stewart to Isaac Hull, letter, July 1811, box 8, letter 53, USS *Constitution* Library and Archives, Boston.
2. *Bordentown Register*, 19 November 1869. After Stewart's death, the *Borden-*

town Register published a three-part biographical sketch of Stewart, which the paper described as the only authentic biography of the sailor, perhaps to negate the other biographers who descended upon Stewart's estate in January 1869 after learning of his illness.

3. Theodore Roosevelt, *The Naval War of 1812* (Annapolis, Md.: U.S. Naval Institute Press, 1987), 31.

4. Richard Rush to Charles Stewart, letter, 12 April 1812, Charles Jared Ingersoll Collection, box 4, F-15, Historical Society of Pennsylvania.

5. The National Gallery of Art, www.nga.gov (accessed 30 January 2003).

6. "England's Glory" was the name of a famous brand of English wooden matches. The matchbox displayed a fanciful picture of a British warship with the name "England's Glory" emblazoned above it.

7. Cooper, *The History of the Navy.*

8. NARA, Naval Records Collection of the Office of Naval Records and Library, Paul Hamilton to Charles Stewart, letter, 22 June 1812, RG 45.

9. NARA, Hamilton to Stewart, letter, 22 June 1812.

10. Cdr. Tyrone Martin, U.S. Navy (Ret.), in discussion with the authors, 21 April 2002. Commander Martin said that Stewart was Hamilton's second choice for *Constellation* and that Bainbridge had lobbied the secretary for the *Constitution.* Bainbridge was left cooling his heels when news reached him that Hull had taken his command to sea. Commander Martin suggested, "Perhaps his [Bainbridge's] pout had something to do with the non-progress of the refit."

11. Geoffrey M. Footner, *USS* Constellation: *From Frigate to Sloop of War* (Annapolis, Md.: U.S. Naval Institute Press, 2003), 62–63.

12. Cdr. Tyrone Martin, discussion, 21 April 2002.

13. Charles C. Jones, *The Life and Services of Commodore Josiah Tattnall* (Savannah, Ga.: Morning News Steam Printing House, 1878).

14. Jones, *Life and Services*, 13.

15. Footner, *USS* Constellation, 74.

16. Footner, *USS* Constellation, 74.

17. Cooper, *History of the Navy.* Cooper writes that a senator made the comment, but the "Biographical Sketch and Services of the Late Commodore Charles Stewart," *Bordentown Register*, 12 November 1869, attributes the comment to the Navy Secretary Paul Hamilton.

18. Footner, *USS* Constellation, 84.

19. Footner, *USS* Constellation, 84.

20. NARA, Naval Records Collection of the Office of Naval Records and Library, Charles Stewart to Navy Secretary William Jones, letters, 23 January 1813, MF125, RG 45.

21. Wade G. Dudley, *Splintering the Wooden Wall: The British Blockade of the United States, 1812–1815* (Annapolis, Md.: U.S. Naval Institute Press, 2003), 71.

22. Dr. Dudley's book provides an excellent assessment of the British difficulties in establishing an effective blockade of the America's maritime frontier.

23. Hamilton resigned on 31 December 1812. Footner, *USS* Constellation, 82.

24. Accounts differ. Stewart reported that he faced two ships-of-the-line and three frigates. What apparently showed up that morning were four frigates. Regardless of the types of ships confronting the *Constellation*, Stewart was outnumbered.

25. Footner, *USS* Constellation, 84–85. Footner references the journal of the *Constellation*'s sailing master, George de la Roche, which says the frigate stood out to sea on 3 February and was chased back into the Chesapeake Bay. Ship's logs in

1812 (and until the 1840s) were kept on a noon-to-noon basis, with the day-date being on the concluding hour, while civil time, of course, went midnight-to-midnight. In this situation, an afternoon occurrence would not be recorded in the later half of day one ashore but rather at the beginning of day two aboard ship. This may account for the noted date difference.

26. Cdr. Tyrone Martin, discussion, 21 April 2002.

27. NARA, Naval Records Collection of the Office of Naval Records and Library, Charles Stewart to William Jones, letter, 10 February 1813, MF-125, RG 45.

28. Today, Craney Island has disappeared and is part of a great artificial extension of the shoreline—a landfill.

29. William C. Davis, *Duel between the first Ironclads* (Baton Rouge: Louisiana State Univ. Press, 1975), map illustration, 109.

30. Davis, *Duel*, 142–43.

31. Cooper, *History of the Navy*. James Fenimore Cooper was the first historian to describe Charles Stewart's imaginative defensive arrangements for his ship that added immeasurably to the overall defense of Norfolk.

32. Cooper, *History of the Navy*, 302. It should be noted that all these actions were undertaken in the heart of an American winter. Those who have sailed upon the Chesapeake Bay during the winter will readily recognize that the feat of seamanship displayed by Charles Stewart has been rarely equaled in U.S. naval history.

33. Charles Stewart to John Warren, letter, 20 May 1813, Naval Historical Center, Washington, D.C.

Chapter 5

1. Reference the orders sent by Navy Secretary Jones to Stewart.

2. Cdr. Tyrone Martin, discussion, 21 April 2002. Commander Martin said Stewart had actually had beef storage tanks built for the USS *Constellation*.

3. Navy Secretary Jones's orders to Capt. Charles Stewart dated June 1813.

4. Tyrone Martin, *A Most Fortunate Ship*, rev. ed. (Annapolis, Md.: U.S. Naval Institute Press, 1997).

5. Nathaniel Silsbee, "The Chase of the Frigate Constitution," *Salem Register*, 28 July 1879.

6. Silsbee, "The Chase."

7. Silsbee, "The Chase."

8. Silsbee, "The Chase."

9. Tyrone Martin, *The USS* Constitution's *Finest Fight, 1815: The Journal of Acting Chaplain Assheton Humphreys, U.S. Navy* (Mt. Pleasant, S.C.: Nautical and Aviation Publishing, 2000), 4.

10. Martin, *The USS* Constitution's *Finest Fight*, 5–6.

11. Logbook of the USS *Constitution*, Franklin Delano Roosevelt Presidential Library, Hyde Park, N.Y.

12. Martin, *The USS* Constitution's *Finest Fight*, 20–21.

13. Martin, *The USS* Constitution's *Finest Fight*, 25.

14. Martin, *Most Fortunate Ship*.

15. *Constitution*'s log.

16. Martin, *Most Fortunate Ship*.

17. Martin, *The USS* Constitution's *Finest Fight*, 28.

18. This description by Commander Martin is the most elegant rendition of Charles Stewart's brilliant tactical move that split the British ships and allowed the

Constitution to quickly sail between the two and cross their tees; the stern of *Cyane* and the bow of *Levant*.

19. Cooper, *The History of the Navy*, 425.

20. NARA, Naval Records Collection of the Office of Naval Records and Library, Area File (Atlantic and Mediterranean), 1775–1910, Record of the Court-Martial of Captain, The Honourable George Douglas, 28 June 1815, RG 45.

21. Martin, *USS* Constitution.

22. Theodore Roosevelt, *The Naval War of 1812* (Annapolis, Md.: U.S. Naval Institute Press, 1987), 378.

Chapter 6

1. Stewart's seaman's certificate states that he was five foot, four inches; however, this discrepancy may be a result of normal growth between the time his certificate was issued and adulthood, when he was recalled as being five foot, nine inches.

2. J. Harding, *Biographical Sketch of Commodore Charles Stewart* (Philadelphia, 1838), 49.

3. Woodward, "Bordentown," 243.

4. Charles Winslow Elliott, *Winfield Scott: The Soldier and the Man* (New York: Arno Press, 1937), 212. Two portraits of Maria Mayo can be found on p. 214.

5. Charles Oscar Paullin, *Commodore John Rodgers: Captain, Commodore, and Senior Officer of the American Navy, 1773–1838.* (Annapolis, Md.: U.S. Naval Institute, 1909), 381–82.

6. Elliott, *Winfield Scott*, 212.

7. Timothy D. Johnson, *Winfield Scott: The Quest for Glory* (Lawrence: Univ. Press, Kansas, 1998), 74.

8. John Tudor, *Diary of Deacon John Tudor* (Boston: Press of W. Spooner, 1896).

9. Boston Latin would also count among its graduates Henry Knox, a soldier in Washington's Army who entered with Tudor in 1758, as well as John "Honey Fitz" Fitzgerald (mayor of Boston and grandfather of John F. Kennedy), Joseph P. Kennedy, and conductors Arthur Fiedler and Leonard Bernstein.

10. William Tudor to Parsons, letter, 7 May 1773, Collections of the Massachusetts Historical Society, series 2, vol. 8, Massachusetts Historical Society, Boston.

11. William Tudor to Delia Jarvis, letter, 14 September 1776, Tudor Family Papers, 1773–1822, Massachusetts Historical Society, Boston.

12. William Tudor to Delia Jarvis, letter, 7 February 1777, Tudor Family Papers, 1773–1822.

13. Delia Jarvis to William Tudor, letter, 17 September 1776, Tudor Family Papers, 1773–1822.

14. Robert Hallowell Gardiner, *Early Recollections of Robert Hallowell Gardiner, 1782–1864* (Hallowell, Maine: White and Horne, 1936).

15. Collections of the Massachusetts Historical Society, series 2, vol. 8, 299.

16. Gardiner, *Early Recollections*.

17. Jean Cote, *Fanny and Anna Parnell: Ireland's Patriot Sisters* (New York: St. Martin's Press, 1991), 19.

18. Cote, *Fanny and Anna Parnell*, 301.

19. Delia Tudor to William Tudor, letters, 19 May 1811 and 12 December 1812, Tudor Family Papers.

20. Cote, *Fanny and Anna Parnell*, 20.

21. Gardiner, *Early Recollections*, 168–69.

22. Gardiner, *Early Recollections*, 169.

23. William S. Walsh, "The American St. Helena, A Reminiscent Sketch of Old Bordentown," *Frank Leslie's Popular Monthly* 37, no. 2 (1894).

Chapter 7

1. Tucker, *Dawn Like Thunder*, 460.

2. Tucker, *Dawn Like Thunder*, 461.

3. Tucker, *Dawn Like Thunder*, 464.

4. U.S. Congress, *Biographical Directory of the United States Congress, 1774–1989*, bicentennial edition (Washington, D.C.: U.S. Government Printing Office, 1989), 12–13.

5. This account comes from Richard Rush.

6. Pratt, *Preble's Boys*, 337 (see ch. 3, n. 3).

7. Dorwart, *Philadelphia Navy Yard*, 60 (see ch. 1, n. 1).

8. Canney, *Sailing Warships*, 87–88.

9. Howard I. Chapelle, *The History of The American Sailing Navy* (New York: W. W. Norton, 1949), 310–15.

10. NARA, Records of the Bureau of Naval Personnel, Logs of Ships and Stations, 1801–1946, Logs of US Naval Ships, 1801–1915, *Franklin* 7 July 1815–13 June 1820, E118, vol. 1, RG 24.

11. NARA, *Franklin* 7 July 1815–13 June 1820.

12. NARA, *Franklin* 7 July 1815–13 June 1820.

13. Richard Rush, "Memoir of Richard Rush" (undated manuscript, Princeton Firestone Library), 1–4.

14. James Morris Morgan, *The Century Illustrated Monthly Magazine* 58 (1899): 796–800.

15. NARA, *Franklin* 7 July 1815–13 June 1820.

16. John Harvey Powell, *Richard Rush: Republican Diplomat, 1780–1859* (Philadelphia: Univ. of Pennsylvania Press, 1942), 81.

17. As commodore, Stewart would have observed the workings of Ballard's command, and he would have intervened only if Ballard asked for his advice or if Ballard had shown himself unable to command under such circumstances.

18. Powell, *Richard Rush*, 82.

19. Powell, *Richard Rush*, 82.

20. Canney, *Sailing Warships*, 64.

21. Correspondence of Richard Rush. Letters received: Miscellaneous A-Z 1818, box 17, Letters received by Richard Rush Q-W, folder 6, Rush Family Papers II, Special Collections, Princeton Univ. Library.

22. Morgan, *The Century Illustrated Monthly Magazine* 58 (1899): 796–800.

23. Morgan, 796–800.

24. R. B. Jones to William Shaler, letter, 20 April 1819.

25. NARA, *Franklin* 7 July 1815–13 June 1820.

26. Correspondence of Richard Rush, Princeton Univ. Library.

27. Rodney MacDonough, *Life of Commodore Thomas MacDonough* (Boston: Fort Hill Press, 1909), 231.

28. Woodward, "Bordentown," 938.

29. NARA, *Franklin* 7 July 1815–13 June 1820.

30. Robert J. Schneller Jr., *Farragut: America's First Admiral* (Washington, D.C.: Brassey's, Inc., 2002), 17.

31. A. T. Mahan, *Admiral Farragut* (New York: Appleton, 1892), 55.

32. The Papers of David G. Farragut, Naval Historical Foundation Collection, Library of Congress.

33. "In the U.S. Mediterranean squadron, commanded by Commodore Chauncey, a widespread spirit of mutiny had manifested itself. So far had it gone that the malcontent officers had actually 'threatened' to draw their swords on their Commanders. Commodore Stewart was sent in the ship-of-the-line *Franklin* to supersede Chauncey and restore the proper discipline. It was a difficult and delicate task, but he was exactly the right man to do it." Woodward, "Bordentown," 938.

34. Mahan, *Admiral Farragut*, 60.

35. Charles Wilkes, *Autobiography of Rear Admiral Charles Wilkes, U.S. Navy 1798–1877*, ed. William Jarrett Morgan, et. al (Washington, D.C.: U.S. Government Printing Office, 1978), 44.

36. Wilkes, *Autobiography*, 45.

37. Wilkes, *Autobiography*, 49.

38. Wilkes, *Autobiography*, 66–67.

39. Wilkes, *Autobiography*, 66.

40. Wilkes, *Autobiography*, 77–78.

41. NARA, *Franklin* 7 July 1815–13 June 1820.

42. Woodward, "Bordentown," 938.

43. MacDonough, *Life of MacDonough*, 237.

44. Woodward, "Bordentown," 938.

45. MacDonough, *Life of MacDonough*, 237.

46. MacDonough, *Life of MacDonough*, 235.

47. MacDonough, *Life of MacDonough*, 236.

48. MacDonough, *Life of MacDonough*, 236.

49. MacDonough, *Life of MacDonough*, 236.

50. NARA, *Franklin* 7 July 1815–13 June 1820.

51. MacDonough, *Life of MacDonough*, 237.

52. NARA, *Franklin* 7 July 1815–13 June 1820.

53. Samuel Bayard, *A Sketch of the Life of Commodore Robert F. Stockton* (New York: Derby and Jackson, 1856), 36.

54. Woodward, "Bordentown," 938.

55. Wilkes, *Autobiography*, 79.

56. NARA, *Franklin* 7 July 1815–13 June 1820.

Chapter 8

1. Richard Rush, journal entry, 16 August 1821, C0079 Rush Family Papers I, Writings of Richard Rush, Manuscripts: "Residence at Court of London," box 2, Princeton Library Rare Books and Special Collections.

2. NARA, Records of the Department of State, Dispatches from U.S. Consuls in Valparaiso, Chile 1812–1906, M-146, roll 1, RG 59.

3. Woodward, "Bordentown," 938–39.

4. Emma Gardiner to letter, 19 October 1820, Tudor Family Papers 1773–1822, Massachusetts Historical Society, Boston.

5. Naval Historical Center, www.history.navy.mil.

6. Wilkes, *Autobiography*, 114.

7. Journals of Commodore Conner, Synopsis of the Cruise of the U.S. Schooner Dolphin around Cape Horn, Naval and Maritime Collection, Franklin Delano Roosevelt Presidential Library, Hyde Park, N.Y.

8. Wilkes, *Autobiography*, 132.

9. William Augustus Von Vultee, unpublished journal, Naval Historical Center, Washington, D.C., 47.

10. James A. Perry (born 26 June 1801) was a son of Capt. Christopher Raymond Perry and brother to Oliver Hazard and Matthew Calbraith Perry.

11. Wilkes, *Autobiography*, 110.

12. Wilkes, *Autobiography*, 122–23.

13. Wilkes, *Autobiography*, 118.

14. Journals of Commodore Conner, Synopsis of the Cruise.

15. Von Vultee, unpublished journal.

16. Wilkes, *Autobiography*, 134.

17. NARA, Records of Naval Personnel, Decklog of USS Dolphin, 7 October 1821–17 January 1823, E118, RG 24.

18. Robert Gardiner, *Early Recollections*, 170.

19. Nathaniel Philbrick, *In the Heart of the Sea: The Tragedy of the Whaleship Essex* (New York: Penguin Books, 2000), 62.

20. Steven E. Maffeo, *Most Secret and Confidential: Intelligence in the Age of Nelson*. (Annapolis, Md.: U.S. Naval Institute Press, 2000), 179.

21. Maffeo, *Most Secret and Confidential*, 159.

22. Wilkes, *Autobiography*, 111.

23. NARA, Records of the Bureau of Naval Personnel, Logs of Ships and Stations 1801–1946, Logs of U.S. Naval Ships, 1801–1915, *Franklin* 21 July 1821–31 July 1822, E118, vol. 2, RG 24.

24. For a complete account of the story of the *Essex*, we suggest you read Philbrick's *In the Heart of the Sea*.

25. Wilkes, *Autobiography*, 168.

26. See NARA, Records of the Department of State, List of U.S. Consular Officers, 1789–1939, Toronto-Vlaardingen, NL, M-587, roll 20, RG 59; see also NARA, Records of the Department of State, List of U.S. Consular Officers, 1780–1939, Lima-Maracaibo, Venezuela, M-587, roll 11, RG 59.

27. The Peter Force Collection, series 8D, items 148.10–155.2, reel 62, item 148, 7–9, Library of Congress.

28. Bernardo O'Higgins to Jeremiah Robinson, letter, 7 February 1822, The Peter Force Collection.

29. NARA, Records of the Department of State, Michael Hogan to John Quincy Adams, letter, 20 January 1822, RG 59.

30. NARA, Records of the Department of State, Dispatches from U.S. Consuls in Havana, 1783– (29 March 1833–8 December 1835), Nicholas Trist to John Forsyth, letter, 14 June 1835, M899, roll 6, RG 59.

31. NARA, Records of the Department of State, Dispatches from Special Agents to the Department of State, 1794–1906, Jeremiah Robinson to John Adams, letter, 2 August 1821, vols. 5–6, M-37, roll 3, RG 59.

32. Robert Harvey, *Cochrane: The Life and Exploits of a Fighting Captain* (New York: Carroll & Graf, 2000), 225

33. David Long, *Gold Braids and Foreign Relations* (Annapolis, Md.: U.S. Naval Institute Press, 1988), 83

34. In addition to the Wilkes account, see NARA, *Franklin*, 21 July 1821–31 July 1822.

35. Dana, *Two Years before the Mast*, 31 (see ch. 1, n. 12).

Chapter 9

1. Wilkes, *Autobiography*, 165.
2. Wilkes, *Autobiography*, 122.
3. Harvey, *Cochrane*, 265.
4. Lady Maria Calcott, *Journal of a Residence in Chile, during the Year 1822; and a Voyage from Chile to Brazil in 1823* (New York: Praeger, 1969), 114
5. Harvey, *Cochrane*, 251. See also Thomas Cochrane Dundonald, *Narrative of Services in the Liberation of Chili, Peru and Brazil from Spanish and Portuguese Domination* (London: J. Ridgway, 1859).
6. For evidence, consider the Asian territory of Macau, controlled by the Portuguese from the sixteenth century until the latter half of the twentieth century, when it was known for its casinos. When Macau came under Chinese control in 1997, the casinos continued to operate, and indeed flourished.
7. Maffeo, *Most Secret and Confidential*, 9.
8. NARA, Records of the Department of State, Dispatches from U.S. Consuls in Valparaiso, Chile, 1812–1906, Michael Hogan to Joaquim de Echarvaria, letter, 19 March 1822, RG 59.
9. Unsigned letter, 23 August 1823, The Peter Force Collection, series 8D, items 148.10–155.2, reels 60–63, Library of Congress. The language used in this unsigned letter is similar to other letters signed by Robinson. In addition, the letter can be found in an extensive collection of Robinson correspondence.
10. NARA, Records of the Department of State, Dispatches from Special Agents to Department of State, 1794–1906, John Prevost to John Quincy Adams, letter, 12 June 1822, vols. 5–6, M-37, roll 3, RG 59.
11. Gene A. Smith, *Thomas ap Catesby Jones: Commodore of Manifest Destiny* (Annapolis, Md.: U.S. Naval Institute Press, 2000).
12. Robert Erwin Johnson, *Thence Round Cape Horn: The story of United States Naval Forces on Pacific Station, 1818–1923* (Annapolis, Md.: U.S. Naval Institute, 1963).
13. Harvey, *Cochrane*, 236
14. Calcott, *Journal of a Residence*, 183
15. Robert Gardiner, *Early Recollections*, 170.
16. NARA, Records of the Bureau of Naval Personnel, Decklog of USS *Dolphin*, 7 October 1821–17 January 1823; 22 April 1824–19 January 1827, E118, RG 24.
17. Harvey, *Cochrane*, 276.
18. Gardiner, *Early Recollections*, 171–72.
19. Johnson, *Thence Round Cape Horn*, 32.
20. Claude G. Berube and John Rodgaard, "The Court-Martial of Charles Stewart," *Naval History*, October 2002.
21. Powell, *Richard Rush*, 1 (see ch. 7, n. 16).
22. Von Vuldee, unpublished journal, 15 December entry.
23. Von Vuldee, unpublished journal, and NARA, Records of the Bureau of Naval Personnel, Logs of Ships and Stations, 1801–1946, Logs of US Naval Ships, 1801–1915, *Franklin* 7 July 1815–13 June 1820, E118, vol. 1, RG 24.
24. Tudor anonymously wrote the analysis in the *National Intelligencer*. William Tudor Jr. to the Editors of the *National Intelligencer*, letter, 24 September 1824, C. E. French Collection, 1823–26, Massachusetts Historical Society, Boston.
25. NARA, Records of the Department of State, Dispatches from U.S. Ministers to Chile, 1823–1906, Herman Allen to John Q. Adams, letter, 29 April 1824, M-10, roll 11, RG 59.

26. Daniel W. Celt, et. al to Charles Stewart, letter, 2 May 1824, in the *Bordentown Register*, 26 November 1869.

27. Thomas Farel Heffernan, *Mutiny on the Globe: The Fatal Voyage of Samuel Comstock* (New York: W. W. Norton, 2002), 137.

Chapter 10

1. Johnson, *Thence Round Cape Horn*.

2. Some government officials' opinions of Robinson are only available in relation to Robinson's later public service.

3. John Quincy Adams, *Memoirs of John Quincy Comprising Portions of His Diary from 1795 to 1848*, ed. Charles Francis Adams (Philadelphia: J.B. Lippincott, 1878), 218.

4. Adams, *Memoirs*, 429.

5. Adams, *Memoirs*, 461–62.

6. Robert Gardiner, *Early Recollections*.

7. Cote, *Fanny and Anna Parnell* (see ch. 6, n. 17).

8. Adams, *Memoirs*, v, vii, 40.

9. Berube and Rodgaard, "The Court-Martial of Charles Stewart."

10. National Archives and Records Administration, Records of the Bureau of Naval Personnel, Logs of Ships and Stations, 1801–1946, Logs of U.S. Naval Ships, 1801–1915. *Franklin*, 31 July 1822 to 14 September 1824, E118, vol. 3, RG 24.

11. Bernard D. Cummins, "The United States Navy in the Pacific: A History of the Pacific Station before the Mexican War, 1818–1846" (master's thesis, Wichita State Univ., 1975), 29.

12. Cummins, "The United States Navy."

13. NARA, Records of General Courts-Martial and Courts of Inquiry of the Navy Department, 1799–1867, 21 June–5 September 1825, M273 R19.

14. Wilkes, *Autobiography*, 185.

15. Wilkes, *Autobiography*, 213.

16. NARA, Records of General Courts-Martial, 21 June–5 September 1825.

17. NARA, Records of General Courts-Martial, 21 June–5 September 1825.

18. NARA, Log of USS *Franklin*, 31 July 1822–14 September 1824.

19. Wilkes, *Autobiography*, 118–19

20. NARA, Records of General Courts-Martial, 21 June–5 September 1825.

21. Robinson's extensive correspondence and journals can be found at the Library of Congress in the Peter Force Collection, series 8D, items 148.10–155.2, reels 60–63.

22. NARA, Records of the Department of State, Dispatches from U.S. Consul in Havana, 1783– (29 March 1833–8 December 1835), Nicolas Trist to John Forsyth, letter, 14 June 1835, M899, roll 6, RG 59.

Chapter 11

1. Anne Hallowell Gardiner to Robert Hallowell Gardiner II, letter, 10 September 1825, The Yellow House Papers: The Laura E. Richards Collection, file 1825, no. 5, Gardiner Public Library.

2. Robert Gardiner, *Early Recollections*, 174.

3. Anne Hallowell Gardiner to Robert Hallowell Gardiner II, letter, 18 December 1825, Yellow House Papers.

4. Henry S. Patterson to Orestes A. Brownson, letter, 1839, University of Notre Dame Archives.

5. Mother or daughter of William Meredith to Delia Tudor Stewart, letter, 1826, Meredith Papers, boxes 36 and 37, collection 1509, Historical Society of Pennsylvania, Philadelphia.

6. Gardiner, *Early Recollections*, 174.

7. Gardiner, *Early Recollections*, 176.

8. R. H. Gardiner to William Meredith, letter, 3 July 1826, Meredith Papers, box 37.

9. R. H. Gardiner to William Meredith, letter, 25 September 1826, Meredith Papers.

10. Woodward, "Bordentown," 945.

11. Earle W. Huskel, "Montpelier: The Home of Commodore Charles Stewart," *Proceedings of the New Jersey Historical Society* 69, no. 2 (April 1951), 86.

12. Woodward, "Bordentown," 944.

13. Margery Brady, *The Love Story of Charles Stewart Parnell and Katherine O'Shea* (Dublin: Mercier Press, 1991), 16.

14. Letter, 10 May 1835, *Bordentown Register*, 26 March 1964.

15. See National Archives, Census Records, 1840, Burlington County, Mansfield Twp., reel 248, 348; 1850, Burlington County, Mansfield Twp., reel 443, 189; and 1860, Burlington County, Bordentown, reel 685, 699.

16. The two gravesites referred to are the Woodlands Cemetery in Philadelphia, and the graveyard of Christ Church in Bordentown, New Jersey. Records for wills and petitions can be found at the Mount Holly, New Jersey, Courthouse, Office of Probate.

Chapter 12

1. Charles Stewart to H. G. Otis, letter, 23 April 1829, Massachusetts Historical Society, Boston.

2. As told to Hopkinson on 14 February 1829. Burton Alva Konkle, *Joseph Hopkinson: 1770–1842* (Philadelphia: Univ. of Pennsylvania Press, 1931), 250.

3. John D. Hicks, George E. Mowry, and Robert E. Burke, *A History of American Democracy* (Boston: Houghton Mifflin, 1966), 154–55.

4. Hicks, *American Democracy*, 154.

5. Letters printed in their entirety in the *Bordentown Register*, 26 November 1869.

6. NARA, Naval Records Collection of the Office of Naval Records and Library, Journals of the Board of Navy Commissioners, April 1815–September 1842, vol. 10, PC30, entry 209, RG 45.

7. Naval Historical Foundation, *The Navy Department: A Brief History until 1945* Naval Historical Foundation Publication, series 2, no. 13 (Washington, D.C.: The Foundation, 1970), 2–3.

8. Naval Historical Foundation, *Navy Department*, 3.

9. Legal opinion on the construction of the act of Congress creating the Board of Navy Commissioners, 7 February 1815, Writings of Richard Rush, box 6, Rush Family Papers I, Princeton University Library.

10. Legal opinion, 7 February 1815, Rush Family Papers I.

11. Charles Oscar Paullin, *Paullin's History of Naval Administration, 1775–1911: A Collection of Articles from the U.S. Naval Institute Proceedings* (Annapolis, Md.: U.S. Naval Institute, 1968), 180.

12. NARA, Journals of the Board of Navy Commissioners, April 1815–September 1842.

13. NARA, Journals of the Board of Navy Commissioners, April 1815–September 1842.

14. NARA, Journals of the Board of Navy Commissioners, April 1815–September 1842.

15. NARA, Journals of the Board of Navy Commissioners, April 1815–September 1842.

16. Canney, *Sailing Ships*, 7.

17. Canney, *Sailing Ships*, 6.

18. Canney, *Sailing Ships*, 179.

19. Canney, *Sailing Ships*, 179.

20. Actually, this was not really the case at all. Many side-wheeled propelled warships were in action during the Civil War, and this means of propulsion was less vulnerable to enemy fire than was first thought. On this account, Donald Canney's excellent work on the old steam Navy should be explored further.

21. James Phinney Baxter, *Introduction of the Ironclad Warship* (Cambridge: Harvard Univ. Press, 1933), 337–38.

22. See also *American State Papers/U.S. Congress, Naval Affairs*, vol. 4 (New York: Arno Press, 1979), 704–707.

23. *American State Papers*, 215.

24. *American State Papers*, 216.

25. Paullin, *Paullin's History*, 181.

26. Paullin, *Paullin's History*, 185.

27. Paullin, *Paullin's History*, 177.

28. Canney, *Sailing Ships*, 110.

29. In *Sailing Ships of the U.S. Navy*, Mr. Canney provides an excellent summary of the rationale behind the maintenance of an American battle fleet of the "Old Navy." See pp. 110–11.

30. Dorwart, *Philadelphia Navy Yard*, 72 (see ch. 1, n. 1).

31. Paullin, *Commodore John Rodgers* (see ch. 6, n. 5).

32. Dorwart, *Philadelphia Navy Yard*, 72.

33. Chapelle, *History of the American Sailing*, 400 (see ch. 2, n. 8).

34. Canney, *Sailing Ships*, 402.

35. Pegram Harrison, "A Blind Eye toward the Slave Trade," *Naval History*, October 1996, 44.

36. Fred Schultz, "Not a Cruise Ship at All," *Naval History*, August 2003, 40.

37. Dorwart, *Philadelphia Navy Yard*, 71–72.

38. "History of Burlington County," unpublished local history, 498.

39. "History of Burlington County," 498.

40. Powell, *Richard Rush*.

41. Woodward, "Bordentown," 940.

42. Henry S. Patterson to Orestes A. Brownson, letter, 1839, Univ. of Notre Dame Archives.

43. Patterson to Brownson, letter, 1839.

44. Donald Chisholm, *Waiting for Dead Men's Shoes: Origins and Development of the U.S. Navy's Officer Personnel System, 1793–1941* (Stanford, Calif.: Stanford Univ. Press, 2001), 174.

45. Chisholm references Claude H. Hall's work, "Abel Parker Upshur: Conservative Virginian, 1790–1844," State Historical Society of Wisconsin, 1964. Hall mentions Charles Stewart provided advice to the new secretary, and he places Stewart with other reform-minded officers.

46. Chisholm, *Dead Men's Shoes*, 175.

47. Bernard D. Cummins, "The United States Navy in the Pacific: A History of the Pacific Station before the Mexican War, 1818–1846" (master's thesis, Wichita State Univ., 1975), 19.

48. Michael A. Palmer, "The Navy: The Continental Period, 1775–1890," Navy Department Library, www.history.navy.mil/history/history2.htm.

49. Canney, *Sailing Ships*, 90.

50. NARA, Naval Records Collection of the Office of the Naval Records and Library, Bainbridge to Navy Board of Commissioners, letter, 26 July 1815, M125, RG 45; NARA, Naval Records Collection of the Office of the Naval Records and Library, Bainbridge to Secretary of the Navy Crowninshield, letter, 14 September 1815, M125, RG 45.

51. NARA, Records of the Bureau of Naval Personnel, Logs of Ships and Stations, 1801–1846, Logs of U.S. Naval Ships, 1801–1915, *Independence*, 17 December 1841–31 December 1842, E118, vol. 9, RG 24.

52. A. B. Feuer, "A Question of Mutiny," *Naval History*, March/April 1994, 23.

53. Philip McFarland, *Sea Dangers: The Affair of the* Somers (New York: Schocken Books, 1985), 22.

54. McFarland, *Sea Dangers*, 173.

55. McFarland, *Sea Dangers*, 22.

56. McFarland, *Sea Dangers*, 121.

57. Harrison Hayford, ed., *The* Somers *Mutiny Affair* (Englewood Cliffs, N.J.: Prentice-Hall, 1959), 111.

58. A. B. Feuer, "A Question of Mutiny," 26.

59. Leonard F. Guttridge, *Mutiny: A History of Naval Insurrection* (Annapolis, Md.: U.S. Naval Institute Press, 1992), 113.

60. Hayford, Somers *Mutiny Affair*, 24.

61. Hayford, Somers *Mutiny Affair*, 156.

62. Craig L. Symonds, *Confederate Admiral: The Life and Wars of Franklin Buchanan* (Annapolis, Md.: U.S. Naval Institute Press, 1999), 70.

63. Symonds, *Confederate Admiral*, 22.

64. Benjamin Park, *The United States Naval Academy* (New York: G. P. Putnam's Sons, 1900), 119–20.

65. James Russell Soley, *History of the United States Naval Academy* (Washington, D.C.: U.S. Government Printing Office, 1876), 37.

66. Paullin, *Paullin's History*, 201.

67. Paullin, *Paullin's History*, 201.

68. Paullin, *Paullin's History*, 209–10.

Chapter 13

1. Robert Leckie, *From Sea to Shining Sea: From the War of 1812 to the Mexican War, The Saga of America's Expansion* (New York: HarperCollins, 1993), 500.

2. Leckie, *From Sea to Shining Sea*, 500.

3. Woodward, "Bordentown," 940–41.

4. Woodward, "Bordentown," 940–41.

5. Woodward, "Bordentown," 940–41.
6. Leckie, *From Sea to Shining Sea*, 501.
7. Chisholm, *Dead Men's Shoes*, 200.
8. Chisholm, *Dead Men's Shoes*, 202.
9. Chisholm, *Dead Men's Shoes*, 204.
10. Chisholm, *Dead Men's Shoes*, 204.
11. Chisholm, *Dead Men's Shoes*, 204.
12. Dorwart, *Philadelphia Navy Yard*, 75–76.
13. Dorwart, *Philadelphia Navy Yard*, 76.
14. Canney, *Sailing Warships*, 25.
15. Mason to David Conner, letter, 29 November 1846, Naval and Maritime Collection, Franklin Delano Roosevelt Presidential Library, Hyde Park, N.Y.
16. Dorwart, *Philadelphia Navy Yard*, 76.
17. Dorwart, *Philadelphia Navy Yard*, 77.
18. James E. Valle, *Rocks and Shoals: Naval Discipline in the Age of Fighting Sail* (Annapolis, Md.: U.S. Naval Institute Press, 1980), 4.
19. McKee, *A Gentlemanly and Honorable Profession*, 240–66 (see ch. 2, n. 2).
20. Valle, *Rocks and Shoals*, 248.
21. Valle, *Rocks and Shoals*, 251.
22. Paullin, *Paullin's History*, 239.
23. Paullin, *Paullin's History*, 240.
24. Paullin, *Paullin's History*, 240.
25. Woodward, "Bordentown," 240
26. Paullin, *Paullin's History*, 240.
27. Donovan Fitzpatrick and Saul Saphire, *Navy Maverick: Uriah Phillips Levy* (Garden City, N.Y.: Doubleday, 1963), 216.
28. Fitzpatrick and Saphire, *Navy Maverick*, 216.
29. Fitzpatrick and Saphire, *Navy Maverick*, 216.
30. National Archives and Records Administration, Captains' Letters to the Secretary of the Navy, 1805–61, 1866–85, roll 361, M125.
31. NARA, Captains' Letters to the Secretary of the Navy, 1805–61, 1866–85.

Chapter 14

1. Dorwart, *Philadelphia Navy Yard*, 81.
2. Chisholm, *Dead Men's Shoes*, 273.
3. Jeanette Gilder, *Scribner's Magazine*, November 1888, 45.
4. Dorwart, *Philadelphia Navy Yard*, 81.
5. Hicks, *American Democracy*, 312–13.
6. Chisholm, *Dead Men's Shoes*, 271.
7. Chisholm, *Dead Men's Shoes*, 272
8. "Disaster at Gosport," *Naval History*, April 1996, 21.
9. William Fowler Jr., *Under Two Flags: The American Navy in the Civil War* (New York: W. W. Norton, 1990), 80.
10. Chisholm, *Dead Men's Shoes*, 291–92.
11. Woodward, "Bordentown," 942–43.
12. Woodward, "Bordentown," 942–43.
13. Charles Stewart to Reverend Dr. Sprague, letter, 15 July 1863, Simon Gratz Collections (French Royalty/Napoleon III), case 9, box 26, Historical Society of Pennsylvania, Philadelphia.

14. Cote, *Fanny and Anna Parnell*, 17–18.

15. Woodward, "Bordentown," 943.

16. This may be one reason why the usually precise Stewart died intestate. See Probate Records at Mount Holly, New Jersey. Another reason may have been the issue of his second set of children by Margaret.

BIBLIOGRAPHY

Archival Sources

Franklin Delano Roosevelt Presidential Library, Hyde Park, N.Y.
  Logbook of the USS *Constitution*
  Naval Collection, Journals of Commodore Conner

Gardiner Public Library, Gardiner, Maine
  Yellow House Collection

Historical Society of Pennsylvania, Philadelphia
  Chares Jared Ingersoll Collection
  Meredith Papers
  Simon Gratz Collection

Independence Seaport Museum, Philadelphia
  Barry-Hayes Papers, John Barry Papers
  File 226 78.58 Ship *Canton*

Library of Congress, Washington, D.C.
  Edward Preble Papers
  Daniel Todd Paterson Papers
  Henry Clay Papers
  Horace Bucklin Sawyer Papers
  Louis Malesherbes Goldsborough Papers
  The Papers of David G. Farragut
  Papers of John Calhoun
  The Papers of the Rodgers Family, Stewart File
  The Peter Force Collection
  Thomas S. Hamersley Papers, 1821–24

Massachusetts Historical Society, Boston
  C.E. French Collection
  Otis Papers
  Tudor Family Papers

National Archives and Records Administration (NARA), Washington, D.C.
  Captains' Letters to the Secretary of the Navy, 1805–61, 1866–85, roll 361.
    M125

Census Records for 1840, 1850, and 1860

Naval Records Collection of the Office of Naval Records and Library, Area File (Atlantic and Mediterranean), 1775–1910, Record of the Court-Martial of Captain, The Honourable George Douglas, 28 June 1815, RG 45.

Naval Records Collection of the Office of Naval Records and Library. Board of Navy Commissioners, 1815–42. Journals of the Board of Navy Commissioners. RG 45

Naval Records Collection of the Office of Naval Records and Library. Naval Documents Related to the Quasi-War between the United States and France. Naval Operations, June 1800–November 1800. RG 45.

Naval Records Collection of the Office of Naval Records and Library. Records of Citizens of the United States, 1775–1908. Logs, Journals, and Diaries of Officers of the U.S. Navy at Sea, March 1777–June 1908. Journal of Midshipman F. Cornelius DeKraft. RG 45

Records of General Courts-Martial and Courts of Inquiry of the Navy Department, 1799–1867. M273 R19

Records of the Bureau of Naval Personnel. Decklog of USS *Dolphin*. E118. RG 24

Records of the Bureau of Naval Personnel. Logs of Ships and Stations, 1801–1946. Logs of U.S. Naval Ships, 1801–1915. *Franklin*. RG 24

Records of the Department of State. Dispatches from Special Agents to the Department of State, 1794–1906. RG 59

Records of the Department of State. Dispatches from U.S. Consuls in Havana, 1783– . RG 59.

Records of the Department of State. Dispatches from U.S. Consuls in Valparaiso, Chile, 1812–1906. RG 59.

Records of the Department of State. List of U.S. Consular Officers, 1789–1939, Toronto-Vlaardingen, NL. List of U.S. Consular Officers, 1780–1939, Lima-Maracaibo, Venezuela. RG 59.

Records of the Secretary of State. Dispatches from U.S. Consul in Havana, 1783– , 29 March 1833–8, December 1835. M899

Princeton University Library, Rare Books and Special Collection
"Memoir of Richard Rush," undated manuscript, Princeton Firestone Library
Rush Family Papers
Writings of Richard Rush

University of Notre Dame Archives
Henry S. Patterson to Orestes A. Brownson, letter, 1839

Books

Abbott, John S. C. *The History of the Civil War in America*. Springfield, Mass.: G. Bill, 1863–66.

Adams, John Quincy. *Memoirs of John Quincy Comprising Portions of His Diary from 1795 to 1848*. Edited by Charles Francis Adams. Philadelphia: J.B. Lippincott, 1878.

Allen, Gardner W. *Our Naval War with France*. Boston: Houghton Mifflin, 1909.

Baxter, James Phinney. *Introduction of the Ironclad Warship*. Cambridge: Harvard Univ. Press, 1933.

Bayard, Samuel. *A Sketch of the Life of Commodore Robert F. Stockton*. New York: Derby and Jackson, 1856.

Brady, Margery. *The Love Story of Charles Stewart Parnell and Katherine O'Shea*. Dublin: Mercier Press, 1991.

Brewington, Marion V. *Maritime Philadelphia, 1609–1837*. N.p., n.d.

Calcott, Lady Maria. *Journal of a Residence in Chile, during the Year 1822; and a Voyage from Chile to Brazil in 1823*. New York: Praeger, 1969.

Callahan, Edward, ed. *List of Officers of the United States Navy and the Marine Corps, 1775–1900*. New York: L. R. Hamersly, 1901.

Canney, Donald L. *Sailing Warships of the U.S. Navy*. London: Chatham Publishing, 2001.

Captain Barry of the United States. N.p., n.d.

Chandler, Charles Lyon, et. al. *Philadelphia, Port of History, 1609–1837*. Philadelphia: Philadelphia Maritime Museum, 1976.

Chappel, Howard I. *The History of the American Sailing Ships*. New York: W. W. Norton, 1935.

Chisholm, Donald. *Waiting for Dead Men's Shoes: Origins and Development of the U.S. Navy's Officer Personnel System, 1793–1941*. Stanford, Calif: Stanford University Press, 2001.

Cogar, William B. *Dictionary of Admirals of the U.S. Navy*. Annapolis, Md.: U.S. Naval Institute Press, 1989.

Cooper, James Fenimore. *The History of the Navy of the United States of America*. Annapolis, Md.: U.S. Naval Institute Press, 2001.

Cote, Jean. *Fanny and Anna Parnell: Ireland's Patriot Sisters*. New York: St. Martin's Press, 1991.

Dana, Richard Henry. *Two Years Before the Mast, A Personal Narrative*. New York: Signet Classics, 2000.

Davis, William C. *Duel Between the First Ironclads*. Garden City, N.Y.: Doubleday, 1975.

Doerflinger, Thomas F. *A Vigorous Spirit of Enterprise: Merchants and Economic Development in Revolutionary Philadelphia*. Chapel Hill: University of North Carolina Press, 1986.

Dorwart, Jeffery M. *The Philadelphia Navy Yard: From the Birth of the U.S. Navy to the Nuclear Age*. With Jean Wolf. Philadelphia: University of Pennsylvania Press, 2001.

Dudley, Wade G. *Splintering the Wooden Wall: The British Blockade of the United States, 1812–1815*. Annapolis, Md.: U.S. Naval Institute Press, 2003.

Dundonald, Thomas Cochrane. *Narrative of Services in the Liberation of Chili, Peru and Brazil from Spanish and Portuguese Domination*. London: J. Ridgway, 1859.

Elliott, Charles Winslow. *Winfield Scott: The Soldier and the Man*. New York: Arno Press, 1937.

Ellis, Joseph J. *American Sphinx: The Character of Thomas Jefferson*. New York: Vintage Books, 1995.

Fitzpatrick, Donovan and Saul Saphire. *Navy Maverick: Uriah Phillips Levy*. Garden City, N.Y.: Doubleday, 1963.

Footner, Geoffrey. USS *Constellation: From Frigate to Sloop of War*. Annapolis, Md.: U.S. Naval Institute Press, 2003.

Fowler, William. *Jack Tars and Commodores: The American Navy 1783–1815*. Boston: Houghton Mifflin, 1984.

————. *Under Two Flags: The American Navy in the Civil War.* New York: W. W. Norton, 1990.

Gardiner, Robert Hallowell. *Early Recollections of Robert Hallowell Gardiner, 1782–1864.* Hallowell, Maine: White and Horne, 1936.

Guttridge, Leonard F. *Mutiny: A History of Naval Insurrection.* Annapolis, Md.: U.S. Naval Institute Press, 1992.

Harding, J. *Biographical Sketch of Commodore Charles Stewart.* Philadelphia, 1838.

Harrison, Eliza Cope, ed. *Philadelphia Merchant: The Diary of Thomas P. Cope, 1800–1851.* South Bend, Ind.: Gateway Editions, 1978.

Harvey, Robert. *Cochrane: The Life and Exploits of a Fighting Captain.* New York: Carroll and Graf, 2000.

Hayford, Harrison, ed. *The* Somers *Mutiny Affair.* Englewood Cliffs, N.J.: Prentice-Hall, 1959.

Heffernan, Thomas Farel. *Mutiny on the Globe: The Fatal Voyage of Samuel Comstock.* New York: W. W. Norton, 2002.

Hicks, John D., George E. Mowry, and Robert E. Burke. *A History of American Democracy.* Boston: Houghton Mifflin, 1966.

Hoopes, Edna Miriam. *Richard Somers: Master Commandant of the United States Navy.* Atlantic City, N.J., 1933.

Irvin, Anthony. *Decatur.* New York: Charles Scribner's Sons, 1931.

Johnson, Robert Erwin. *Thence Round Cape Horn: The Story of the United States Naval Forces on Pacific Station, 1818–1923.* New York: Arno Press, 1930.

Johnson, Timothy D. *Winfield Scott: The Quest for Glory.* Lawrence: University Press of Kansas, 1998.

Jones, Charles C. *The Life and Service of Commodore Josiah Tattnall.* Savannah, Ga.: Morning News Steam Printing House, 1878.

Kilmarx, Robert A., ed. *America's Maritime Legacy: A History of U.S. Merchant Marine and Shipbuilding Industry Since Colonial Times.* Boulder, Colo.: Westview Press, 1979.

Koedel, Barbara E. *Glory at Last! A Narrative of the Naval Career of Master Commandant Richard Somers.* Somers Point, N.J.: Atlantic County Historical Society, 1993.

Leckie, Robert. *From Sea to Shining Sea: From the War of 1812 to the Mexican War, The Saga of America's Expansion.* New York: HarpersCollins, 1993.

Lewis, Charles Lee. *The Romantic Decatur.* Philadelphia: University of Pennsylvania Press, 1937.

Long, David. *Nothing Too Daring: A Biography of Commodore David Porter, 1780–1843.* Annapolis, Md.: U.S. Naval Institute, 1970.

Macdonough, Rodney. *Life of Commodore Thomas MacDonough.* Boston: Fort Hill Press, 1909.

Mackenzie, Alexander Slidell. *Life of Stephen Decatur: A Commodore in the Navy of the United States.* Boston: Little and Brown, 1846.

Maffeo, Steven E. *Most Secret and Confidential: Intelligence in the Age of Nelson.* Annapolis, Md.: U.S. Naval Institute Press, 2000.

Martin, Tyrone. *A Most Fortunate Ship.* Rev. ed. Annapolis, Md.: U.S. Naval Institute Press, 1997.

————. *The USS* Constitution's *Finest Fight, 1815: The Journal of Acting Chaplain Assheton Humphreys, U.S. Navy.* Mt. Pleasant, S.C.: Nautical and Aviation Publishing, 2000.

McAneny, Marguerite Loud. *Bicentennial Celebration of the Birthday of Commodore William Bainbridge.* Princeton, N.J.: Historical Society of Princeton, 1976.

284

McFarland, Philip. *Sea Dangers: The Affair of the* Somers. New York: Schocken Books, 1985.

McKee, Christopher. *A Gentlemanly and Honorable Profession: The Creation of the U.S. Naval Officer Corps, 1794–1815.* Annapolis, Md.: U.S. Naval Institute Press, 1991.

Park, Benjamin. *The United States Naval Academy.* New York: G. P. Putnam's Sons, 1900.

Parton, James. *Famous Americans of Recent Times.* Boston: Houghton, Mifflin, 1895.

Paullin, Charles Oscar. *Commodore John Rodgers, Captain, Commodore, and Senior Officer of the American Navy 1773–1838.* Annapolis, Md.: U.S. Naval Institute, 1909.

―――. *Paullin's History of Naval Administration, 1775–1911: A Collection of Articles from the U.S. Naval Institute Proceedings.* Annapolis, Md.: U.S. Naval Institute, 1968.

Philbrick, Nathaniel. *In the Heart of the Sea: The Tragedy of the Whaleship.* Essex. New York: Penguin Books, 2000.

Porter, David D. *Memoir of Commodore David Porter of the United States Navy.* Albany, N.Y.: J. Munsell, 1875.

Powell, John Harvey. *Richard Rush: Republican Diplomat, 1780–1859.* Philadelphia: University of Pennsylvania Press, 1942.

Pratt, Fletcher. *Preble's Boys: Commodore Preble and the Birth of American Sea Power.* New York: William Sloane Associates, 1950.

Richardson, Edgar P. *Philadelphia, 1800–1824.* N.p., n.d.

Rogers, Joseph Morgan. *Thomas H. Benton.* Philadelphia: G. W. Jacobs, 1905.

Roosevelt, Theodore. *The Naval War of 1812.* Annapolis, Md.: U.S. Naval Institute Press, 1987.

Salas, Eugenio Pereira. *Jeremias Robinson, Agente Norteamericano en Chile (1818–1823).* Santiago, Chile: Imprenta Universitaria Estado 63, 1939.

Schneller Jr., Robert J. *The Contentious Innovator: a Biography of Rear Admiral John A. Dahlgren U.S.N. (1809 – 1870).* Washington, D.C.: Brassey's, Inc., 1992.

―――. *Farragut: America's First Admiral.* Washington, D.C.: Brassey's, Inc., 2002.

Skaggs, David Curtis. *Thomas MacDonough: Master of Command in the Early U.S. Navy.* Annapolis, Md.: U.S. Naval Institute Press, 2003.

Smith, Gene A. *For the Purposes of Defense: The Politics of the Jeffersonian Gunboat Program.* Newark: University of Delaware Press, 1995.

―――. *Thomas ap Catesby Jones: Commodore of Manifest Destiny.* Annapolis, Md.: U.S. Naval Institute Press, 2000.

Soley, James Russell. *History of the United States Naval Academy.* Washington, D.C.: U.S. Government Printing Office, 1876.

Symonds, Craig L. *Confederate Admiral: The Life and Wars of Franklin Buchanan.* Annapolis, Md.: U.S. Naval Institute Press, 1999.

Tucker, Glenn. *Dawn Like Thunder: The Barbary Wars and the Birth of the U.S. Navy.* New York: Bobbs-Merrill, 1963.

Tucker, Spencer. *The Jeffersonian Gunboat Navy.* Columbia: University of South Carolina Press, 1993.

Tudor, John. *Diary of Deacon John Tudor.* Boston: Press of W. Spooner, 1896.

Tyng, Charles. *Before the Wind: The Memoir of an American Sea Captain.* Edited by Susan Fels. New York: Viking, 1999.

U.S. Congress. *Biographical Directory of the United States Congress, 1774–1989,* bicentennial edition. Washington, D.C.: U.S. Government Printing Office, 1989.

285

Valle, James E. *Rocks and Shoals: Naval Discipline in the Age of Fighting Sail*. Annapolis, Md.: U.S. Naval Institute Press, 1980.

Welles, Gideon. *Diary of Gideon Welles: Secretary of the Navy under Lincoln and Johnson*. 3 vols. Boston: Houghton Mifflin, 1911.

Wilkes, Charles. *Autobiography of Rear Admiral Charles Wilkes, U.S. Navy 1798–1877*. Edited by William Jarrett Morgan, et. al. Washington, D.C.: U.S. Government Printing Office, 1978.

Wilson, James Grant, and John Fiske. *Appleton's Encyclopedia of American Biography*. Vol. V. New York: Appleton, 1888.

Articles

Berube, Claude G., and John Rodgaard. "The Court-Martial of Charles Stewart." *Naval History*, October 2002.

Feuer, A. B. "A Question of Mutiny." *Naval History*, March/April 1994.

Gilder, Jeannette. *Scribner's Magazine*, November 1888.

Harrison, Pegram. "A Blind Eye Toward the Slave Trade." *Naval History*, October 1996.

Huskel, Earle W. "Montpelier: The Home of Commodore Charles Stewart." *Proceedings of the NJ Historical Society*, Vol. 69, No. 2 (April 1951).

Morgan, James Morris. *The Century Illustrated Monthly Magazine* 58 (1899).

Palmer, Michael A. "The Navy: The Continental Period, 1775–1890." Navy Department Library, www.history.navy.mil/history/history2.htm.

"Popular Portraits with Pen and Pencil: Charles Stewart, U.S. Navy." *The United States Magazine and Democratic Review* 28 (1851).

Schultz, Fred. "Not a Cruise Ship at All." *Naval History*, August 2003.

Silsbee, Nathanial. "The Chase of the Frigate Constitution." *Salem Register*, 28 July 1879.

Smith, H. D. "Rear-Admiral Charles Stewart, United States Navy." *The United Service: A Monthly Review of Military and Naval Affairs* 1 (1889).

Walsh, William S. "The American St. Helena, A Reminiscent Sketch of Old Bordentown." *Frank Leslie's Popular Monthly* 37, no. 2 (February 1894).

Miscellaneous

American State Papers/U.S. Congress, Naval Affairs. Vol. 4. New York: Arno Press, 1979.

Bordentown Register

Cummins, Bernard D. "The United States Navy in the Pacific: A History of the Pacific Station Before the Mexican War, 1818–1846." Master's thesis, Wichita State University, 1975.

"History of Burlington County." Unpublished local history.

Martin, Tyrone. Discussion with the authors, 21 April 2002.

Mount Holly, N.J., Office of Probate.

National Gallery, Washington, D.C.

Naval Historical Center, www.history.navy.mil

Naval Historical Foundation, *The Navy Department: A Brief History until 1945*. Naval Historical Foundation Publication, series 2, no. 13. Washington, D.C.: The Foundation, 1970.

U.S. Congress. The Debates and Proceedings in the Congress of the United States with an Appendix containing Important State Papers and Public Documents, Thirteenth Congress from May 24, 1813, to April 18, 1814. Printed by Gales and Seaton, 1854.

Von Vultee, William Augustus. Unpublished journal, Naval Historical Center, Washington, D.C.

Woodlands Cemetery, Philadelphia, Pa.

Woodward, E. M. "Bordentown and Its Environs." Unpublished manuscript, Bordentown Library Association, 1967.

INDEX

291

South America, 123
  revolutionary movements, 134, 135, 159
  See also Peru
South Carolina, 245, 247
South Carolina, USS, 122
Southard, Samuel L., 181, 183
Southwark Foundry, 217
Spain, 123, 134, 135–36
Spanish privateers, 174–75
Spanish Royalists, 136, 159–60, 162, 163, 168, 169
Spark, USS, 125
specie, 153–54, 179, 184, 186–87
Speedwell, 145
Spencer, John Canfield, 222
Spencer, Philip, 222–27
Spirit of the Times, 218–19
Spray, 1, 145
St. John's Episcopal Church, 201
State Department, 149
steam battery, 210–11
steam-powered warships, 210–13, 217–18n. 20, 236, 239
steamships, 153
Stedman, Edmund Clarence, 257
Stewart, Charles
  ability to command, 260–61
  as adviser during Civil War, 248
  on Board of Navy Commissioners, 208–15, 228
  as cabin boy, 7–10
  on *Chesapeake*, 21–23
  command of merchant ship, 12
  command of Tripoli blockading force, 39–54
  as commandant of Philadelphia Navy Yard, 215–18
  as commander of Home Squadron, 221, 224, 230
  as commander of Mediterranean Squadron, 110–32, 135, 136
  as commander of Pacific Squadron, 137–55
  as commander of Philadelphia Navy Yard, 234–39, 243
  commercial enterprises, 57
  commissioned as lieutenant, 11
  on *Constellation*, 23–27
  construction of gunboats and, 51, 55–56
  court of inquiry and, 82–83
  court-martials of others and, 128–30
  criteria for success, 12–13
  criticism of Board of Navy Commissioners, 229
  on Decatur, 39
  declared unfit for service, 239–41
  declines appointment to presidential cabinet, 110
  on Elliot court of inquiry, 227–28
  as farmer, 201–2
  funeral, 254–57
  gambling, 158
  health, 254, 259
  honorary degree from Princeton, 136–37
  injury to, 18
  innovations, 69–70, 73–74
  knowledge of international law, 170–73
  knowledge of naval strategy, 111
  lobbying efforts, 66–67
  loyalty to Union, 250–52
  marriage, 75–76
  personal characteristics, 95–96
  Peruvian government and, 169–70, 179–80, 184, 186
  Philadelphia crew and, 40–41
  as presidential candidate, 207, 209, 218–20, 231–33, 259
  on principles of blockade, 170–73
  promotion to captain, 54
  receives Sword of State of Pennsylvania, 113
  resignation, 246, 249
  second family, 203–4, 254, 261
  separation from Delia, 198–201
  ships commanded
    Argus, 60, 62–63
    Constellation, 60, 63–71
    Constitution, 73–93
    Essex, 52–54, 60
    Experiment, 14–21
    Franklin, 110, 112–32, 137–55
    Syren, 27–28, 29–52
  Somers Affair and, 222–27, 228
  steam-powered warships, view of, 211–13, 217–18
  U.S. Constitution and, 110–11, 128–29, 132, 206–7, 246
  See also court-martial of Stewart

ABOUT THE AUTHORS

CLAUDE BERUBE was a 2004 Brookings Institution LEGIS Fellow and a reserve officer in the U.S. Navy. His articles have appeared in *Maine History*, *Naval History*, and the U.S. Naval Institute *Proceedings*. He has worked in the U.S. Senate and for the Navy Department. He served on board the USS *Bunker Hill* in the Persian Gulf with Expeditionary Study Group Five.

JOHN RODGAARD has more than twenty years' experience as an intelligence analyst and is a captain and reserve intelligence officer in the U.S. Navy assigned to the Office of Naval Intelligence. He has contributed articles to the U.S. Naval Institute *Proceedings* and *Naval History* magazine.